Java Servlets™ Developer's Guide

About the Author

Karl Moss has been a software developer for over 17 years, working on various state-of-the-art technologies. He has worked on many mission-critical applications, such as Payroll and Accounts Receivable, as well as complex supporting applications, such as Bill of Materials and Work in Progress.

Karl is currently a Principal Software Engineer at Macromedia where he works on the JRun Application Server. His primary responsibilities include the servlet container and supporting application server framework. Karl is an old-timer when it comes to Java; he first started with JDK 1.0.2 in late 1995. At the time he was employed by Intersolv (now known as DataDirect Technologies) where he helped shape the first revisions of the JDBC specifications. While working on the JDBC specification Karl wrote the JDBC-ODBC Bridge, which is now a part of the JDK. Karl is the the co-author of *Java Database Programming with JDBC* (Coriolis).

Karl continues to participate in various expert groups, including the Servlet API Expert, of which he has been a member since its inception. Karl has provided technical advice for many publications and has written numerous online and printed articles, and has been invited to speak at many Java-related conferences.

Java Servlets™ Developer's Guide

Karl Moss

New York Chicago San Francisco
Lisbon London Madrid Mexico City Milan
New Delhi San Juan Seoul Singapore Sydney Toronto

McGraw-Hill/Osborne
2600 Tenth Street
Berkeley, California 94710
U.S.A.

To arrange bulk purchase discounts for sales promotions, premiums, or fund-raisers, please contact **McGraw-Hill**/Osborne at the above address. For information on translations or book distributors outside the U.S.A., please see the International Contact Information page immediately following the index of this book.

Java Servlets™ Developer's Guide

1234567890 FGR FGR 0198765432

ISBN 0-07-222262-X

Publisher	Brandon A. Nordin
Vice President & Associate Publisher	Scott Rogers
Editorial Director	Wendy Rinaldi
Associate Acquisitions Editor	Ben Walker
Project Editor	Katie Conley
Acquisitions Coordinator	Tim Madrid
Technical Editor	Phil Hanna
Copy Editor	Bill McManus
Proofreader	Pat Mannion
Indexer	Irv Hershman
Computer Designers	Kelly Stanton-Scott, Elizabeth Jang
Illustrators	Lyssa Wald, Michael Mueller
Series Designer	Roberta Steele
Cover Series Design	Greg Scott
Cover Illustration	Eliot Bergman

This book was composed with Corel VENTURA ™ Publisher.

Contents at a Glance

Contents

Acknowledgments

Writing a book is no small task, but fortunately I have been surrounded by a group of top-notch people throughout the process.

First I would like to thank all of the great folks at McGraw-Hill/Osborne for their support and encouragement. And to Phil Hanna, who served as my technical editor, I can't thank you enough for your insight and wisdom (beyond your years, of course).

I would also like to recognize my friends and co-workers at Macromedia on the JRun team. Not only are you some of the greatest software developers in the industry, but you are lots of fun to hang with. Dan, Edwin, Spike, Tom, Paul, Brian, Sean, Scott, Clement (and everyone else)—you guys rock!

And finally, I would like to thank Shanna, my wife, friend, and sanity provider—I couldn't have done it (yet again) without you. And to Vallory, Jillian, Austin, Joshua, and Nathaniel—thanks for not complaining too much, even though I've been spending much more time with Larry-Boy (my laptop) than with you.

Introduction

As the popularity of Java continues to soar, more and more people are taking a serious look at how to leverage this powerful language to perform useful tasks. The main focus of Java in the past has been on the client (or browser) side, specifically applets, which is only half of the picture. The server has traditionally been reserved for complex Common Gateway Interface (CGI) scripts written in C or perl; until now. JavaSoft has introduced the Java Servlet API which not only serves as a CGI replacement, but has all of the advantages of Java.

This book is designed to provide you with an in-depth understanding of the Servlet API and how to design and build real-world server applications. Throughout this book we'll be developing servlets (Java applications which utilize the Servlet API) and integrating other Java technologies such as JDBC, Java Mail, JNI, and J2ME.

Who Should Read This Book

This book is for developers and programmers interested in exploiting the power of Java on a web server. The focus of this book is on using the Servlet API and solving real-world problems using Java in a client/server environment.

This book assumes you are familiar with object-oriented programming and the Java programming language.

Examples Online

All of the applications developed for this book can also be downloaded online at http://www.servletguru.com. This site, hosted by Servlets.Net, also contains many running examples as well as links to other cool servlet sites. The example applications can also be found on http://www.osborne.com.

CHAPTER

1

Servlet Architecture and Environment

IN THIS CHAPTER:

What Are Servlets?

Why Use Servlets?

Servlet API Background

What Do You Need to Get Started?

What Is Apache Tomcat?

Licensing

Installation

Starting and Testing Tomcat

Configuration

Alternatives

Summary

The Internet has brought forth the invention of many new technologies in client/server computing, the most notable of which is Java. Java not only specifies a computer language, but also serves as a complete client/server solution in which programs are automatically downloaded to the client and executed. Much of the focus in the past has been on client-side development of applets and graphical user interface (GUI) components. Applets are an important part of client/server computing, but they are only half of the picture. This book takes an in-depth look at the other half of the picture: servlets.

What Are Servlets?

A servlet can be thought of as a server-side applet. Servlets are loaded and executed by a web server (which may be part of a larger application server), in the same manner that applets are loaded and executed by a web browser. As shown next, a servlet accepts requests from a client (via the web server), performs some task, and returns the results.

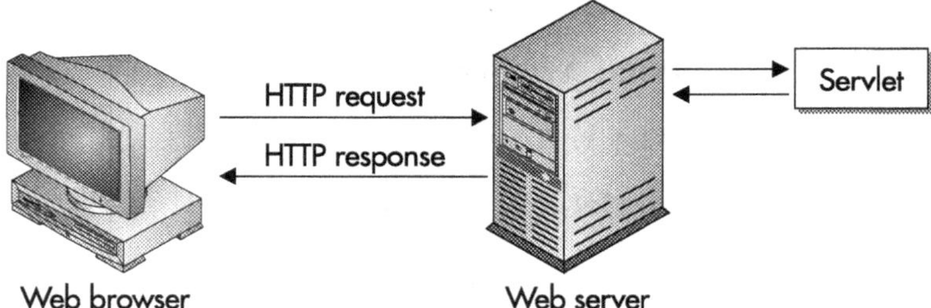

The following describes the basic flow when using servlets:

1. The client (most likely a web browser) makes a request via HTTP.
2. The web server receives the request and forwards it to the servlet. If the servlet has not yet been loaded, the web server loads it into the Java Virtual Machine (JVM) and executes it.
3. The servlet receives the HTTP request and performs some type of process.
4. The servlet returns a response to the web server.
5. The web server forwards the response to the client.

Because the servlet is executing on the server, the security issues usually associated with applets do not apply. This opens a tremendous number of opportunities that are not possible, or at least very difficult, when working with applets. Communicating with legacy systems via CORBA, RMI, sockets, and native calls are just a few examples. Also keep in mind that the web browser does not communicate directly with a servlet; the servlet is loaded and executed by the web server. This means that if your web server is secure behind a firewall, then your servlet is secure as well.

Why Use Servlets?

In their most basic form, servlets are a great replacement for Common Gateway Interface (CGI) scripts. CGI scripts are typically written in Perl or C, and are very much tied to a particular server platform. Since servlets are written in Java, they are immediately platform-independent. Java's promise of write once, run anywhere can now be realized on the server (this promise was never fully delivered on the client). Servlets have other distinct advantages over CGI scripts, as well:

- **Servlets are persistent.** Servlets are loaded only once by the web server and can maintain services (such as a database connection) between requests. CGI scripts, on the other hand, are transient. Each time a request is made to a CGI script, it must be loaded and executed by the web server. When the CGI script is complete, it is removed from memory and the results are returned to the client. All program initialization (such as connecting to a database) must be repeated each time a CGI script is used.
- **Servlets are fast.** Since servlets only need to be loaded once, they offer much better performance over their CGI counterparts.
- **Servlets are platform-independent.** As mentioned before, servlets are written in Java, which inherently brings platform independence to your development effort.
- **Servlets are extensible.** Being written in Java also brings all the other benefits of Java to your servlet. Java is a robust object-oriented programming language that can be easily extended to suit your needs.
- **Servlets are secure.** The only way to invoke a servlet from the outside world is through a web server. This brings a high level of security, especially if your web server is protected behind a firewall.

- **Servlets can be used with a variety of clients.** While servlets are written in Java, you'll see throughout this book that you can use them just as easily from Java applets as from a web browser. While Perl or CGI scripts can also be invoked from other clients using the HTTP protocol, communicating between a Java client and a servlet is made easy using standard Java serialization.

The number of ways to use servlets is limited only by your imagination. If you think about all the services available on the server that you have access to, such as database servers and legacy systems, the possibilities are virtually endless.

Servlet API Background

So who controls the Servlet API, and how are design decisions made? The Servlet API is formally known as JSR-053. A Java Specification Request (JSR) is part of the Java Community Process (JCP), which has a process in place to allow specifications to be proposed, reviewed, and finalized by a potentially large number of community experts. The expert list for JSR-053 is quite impressive and has enabled the Servlet API to benefit from years of industry experience. The lead specification engineer for a JSR controls many aspects of the specification in question (and interestingly is often a Sun Microsystems employee), but all changes to the specification are usually voted on and approved by the community experts. For more information about JSR-053, or to find out more about the JCP process, visit http://jcp.org/jsr/detail/53.jsp.

Before a JSR can be made public, it must also provide example code that not only validates the design, but also serves as a starting point for others who may wish to provide their own implementation. This example code, called the Reference Implementation (RI), is a very important aspect of a JSR—many times, the actual implementation of a specification illustrates weakness in the design. The RI for the Servlet API is known as Apache Tomcat, and is part of the Apache Jakarta Project (http://jakarta.apache.org). The Apache Jakarta Project charter is to "...provide commercial-quality server solutions based on the Java Platform that are developed in an open and cooperative fashion." We'll be examining Tomcat later in this chapter, but for now, realize that there is a free, open-source, production-quality web server that fully supports the latest servlet specification. Many of the experts working on JSR-053 also submit code to Apache Tomcat, and often proposed specification changes are put into code first to ensure their validity. This benefits you by ensuring a rock-solid specification and a high-quality reference implementation.

With the latest version of the servlet specification (version 2.3 as of the time of this writing), the API is quite mature. I foresee that future revisions will contain mostly errata and tightening of minor problem areas within the specification. For more in-depth information, as well as to download the servlet specification and API documentation, visit http://java.sun.com/products/servlets.

What Do You Need to Get Started?

Getting started with servlets is not difficult. All you need are the following components:

- **A JDK** The minimum requirement is JDK 1.2 (as dictated by the Servlet specification), but I would recommend using the latest official release for your operating system platform.
- **A web server** This may include Apache, Microsoft Internet Information Server (IIS), Netscape, or many others. Most servlet containers provide their own built-in web servers as well.
- **A servlet container** This is the part of the server that loads, initializes, and executes servlets. Tomcat is an excellent choice here, due to its status as the reference implementation, but others such as Resin, JRun, and ServletExec are also good choices (and all are free). Appendix C contains information on where to find these products.
- **An editor or integrated development environment (IDE)** You can certainly use a plain-text editor such as Notepad, vi, or emacs to perform servlet development, but an IDE (with built-in debugging capabilities) certainly makes the task of servlet writing much easier. Many, many IDE products are available on the market, and I will not even attempt to make a qualified judgment on the best one for your needs.
- **A client** Since servlets are part of the web server, you will need some type of client application that invokes the servlet. For most servlets, this will be a web browser (such as Internet Explorer or Netscape), but later in the book, we'll take a look at other ways to invoke servlets, such as from a Java application or applet.

What Is Apache Tomcat?

As previously mentioned, every JSR specification must provide a reference implementation. JSR-053, which specifies both Servlets and Java ServerPages, is no exception. The reference implementation is Apache Tomcat, part of the Apache Jakarta Project. The Jakarta Project encompasses more than just Tomcat; a whole host of interesting and innovative projects are going on under the Jakarta umbrella. I highly recommend visiting the Jakarta home page (http://jakarta.apache.org) and familiarizing yourself with these projects. They not only could prove to be quite useful in your own development project, but also all are open source, so you can use what you need.

Tomcat has indeed strived to attain a commercial-quality status. Tomcat has gone through many iterations, following the evolution of the servlet specification:

- **Tomcat 3.1** A now unsupported release, it is still available for legacy reasons.
- **Tomcat 3.2** Now in maintenance mode, this version supports the Servlet 2.2 and JSP 1.1 specifications. This is a highly stable, production-ready release.
- **Tomcat 3.3** This version focused on performance improvements and code refactoring on the 3.2 code base.
- **Tomcat 4.0** A new version from the ground up, this is the version that we will be examining. It supports the Servlet 2.3 and JSP 1.2 specifications, and is highly modular in design. It has lots of support not only for servlet developers, but also for developers who wish to get into the internals of the servlet container. You may read or hear the name "Catalina"; this was the code name for the Tomcat 4.0 servlet container (and "Jasper" is the JSP engine). Expect future releases of Tomcat to focus on performance improvements and management features.

Tomcat includes installers for many operating system platforms, documentation, sample applications, and limited management capabilities. The great thing about Tomcat is that if you find something missing, you can create your own implementation and contribute it back to the project—that is what open source is all about! I would certainly urge you to get involved; the more contributions that are made to the project, the better Tomcat is for the entire community.

Tomcat is also somewhat of an oddity insofar as it is a reference implementation that can be used in a production environment. I cannot think of any other reference implementation of a standard Java specification that openly competes in this manner. This has certainly raised some concern with other servlet container providers, because Sun in essence is paying for a portion of the development costs of Tomcat (dedicated Sun engineers are working on Tomcat) and then directly competing with sales of other products. As the quality of Tomcat continues to improve, it will be increasingly difficult for some vendors to justify the price tag of their products.

I believe that in the future we will see many application server products adopt Tomcat as their servlet container (throwing away their in-house implementation), by adding new features, management capabilities, and technical support.

An important aspect of the reference implementation is to "fill in the gaps" of a specification. It is very difficult to create a specification that answers every question; most specifications always seem to leave room for interpretation, meaning that, given a group of developers implementing the same specification, there will be many different solutions. The reference implementation is the place to go if you have any questions about interpretation. In other words, if you question how something in the servlet specification should behave, the answer will be the way that Tomcat has it implemented. For this reason alone, it is a good idea to develop your servlets using Tomcat.

Licensing

You may be asking yourself, "Gee, this all sounds great! Free commercial-quality software; but what's the catch?" Well, there really isn't a catch as long as you understand and follow the Apache Software License, under which Tomcat is released. You need to worry about this license only if you plan to redistribute Tomcat as part of your application. The following is the complete Apache Software License version 1.1 (found at http://www.apache.org/licenses):

```
The Apache Software License, Version 1.1

Copyright (c) 2000 The Apache Software Foundation. All rights
reserved.

Redistribution and use in source and binary forms, with or without
modification, are permitted provided that the following conditions
are met:

1. Redistributions of source code must retain the above copyright
notice, this list of conditions and the following disclaimer.

2. Redistributions in binary form must reproduce the above copyright
notice, this list of conditions and the following disclaimer in
the documentation and/or other materials provided with the
distribution.

3. The end-user documentation included with the redistribution,
if any, must include the following acknowledgment:
"This product includes software developed by the
```

```
Apache Software Foundation (http://www.apache.org/)."
Alternately, this acknowledgment may appear in the software itself,
if and wherever such third-party acknowledgments normally appear.

4. The names "Apache" and "Apache Software Foundation" must
not be used to endorse or promote products derived from this
software without prior written permission. For written
permission, please contact apache@apache.org.

5. Products derived from this software may not be called "Apache",
nor may "Apache" appear in their name, without prior written
permission of the Apache Software Foundation.

THIS SOFTWARE IS PROVIDED "AS IS" AND ANY EXPRESSED OR IMPLIED
WARRANTIES, INCLUDING, BUT NOT LIMITED TO, THE IMPLIED WARRANTIES
OF MERCHANTABILITY AND FITNESS FOR A PARTICULAR PURPOSE ARE
DISCLAIMED. IN NO EVENT SHALL THE APACHE SOFTWARE FOUNDATION OR
ITS CONTRIBUTORS BE LIABLE FOR ANY DIRECT, INDIRECT, INCIDENTAL,
SPECIAL, EXEMPLARY, OR CONSEQUENTIAL DAMAGES (INCLUDING, BUT NOT
LIMITED TO, PROCUREMENT OF SUBSTITUTE GOODS OR SERVICES; LOSS OF
USE, DATA, OR PROFITS; OR BUSINESS INTERRUPTION) HOWEVER CAUSED AND
ON ANY THEORY OF LIABILITY, WHETHER IN CONTRACT, STRICT LIABILITY,
OR TORT (INCLUDING NEGLIGENCE OR OTHERWISE) ARISING IN ANY WAY OUT
OF THE USE OF THIS SOFTWARE, EVEN IF ADVISED OF THE POSSIBILITY OF
SUCH DAMAGE.

This software consists of voluntary contributions made by many
individuals on behalf of the Apache Software Foundation. For more
information on the Apache Software Foundation, please see
http://www.apache.org.

Portions of this software are based upon public domain software
originally written at the National Center for Supercomputing
Applications, University of Illinois, Urbana-Champaign.
```

As you can see, the license is really not very stringent. In a nutshell, you basically need to give credit where credit is due by mentioning that you are using software from the Apache Software Foundation, and retain any copyright statements found in the source code. You do not owe Apache anything other than the respect that it deserves. Again, all of this becomes relevant only if you plan to redistribute Tomcat itself, not the servlets that run on Tomcat. The servlets that you develop are yours to do with what you will.

Installation

You can find a link to the latest "official" version of Tomcat from the Servlet API home page, http://java.sun.com/products/servlet. Since Tomcat is an open-source project and is being constantly updated by various committers, there are usually several versions to choose from. You can grab a nightly build version, which is a snapshot of the current development version (this is living on the edge), and you can even build Tomcat from the source code, but you will most likely want the "final" version, which has been "blessed" by the Tomcat developers as being stable and production-ready.

Once you have the appropriate installation package for your particular platform, simply follow the instructions found on the Tomcat home page. This may include unpacking the distribution package on UNIX platforms or executing an installer on Windows.

After installing Tomcat you may want to get familiar with the directory structure, as shown here:

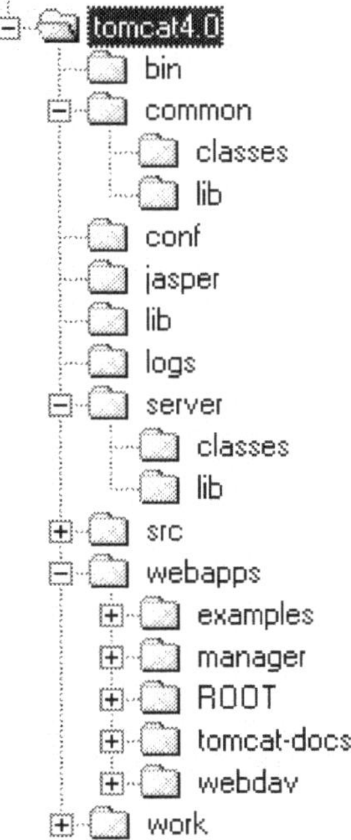

I have installed Tomcat in the tomcat4.0 directory (which will be referred to as CATALINA_HOME). Under CATALINA_HOME, you will find the following:

Subdirectory	Contents
bin	Contains scripts for starting and stopping Tomcat.
common	Contains classes and jar files that are common to all Tomcat servers.
conf	Contains general configuration information, such as the server definitions and user information.
jasper	Contains the Tomcat JSP engine, code named Jasper.
logs	Contains the runtime log files generated by Tomcat.
server	Contains classes and jar files that are common to all Web applications within a single server.
src	Contains the source code for the Tomcat server, including Catalina (the servlet engine), Jasper (the JSP engine), and example applications.
webapps	Contains Web applications that will automatically be loaded when Tomcat is started.
work	The temporary working directory used by Web applications.

Note that the logs and work directories are created the first time you start Tomcat. If you have simply installed Tomcat and have not started the server, these directories will not yet exist.

Starting and Testing Tomcat

Before starting Tomcat, you need to ensure that you have a JDK, version 1.2 or higher, installed and ready for use.

There are two ways to invoke Tomcat:

- Set an environment variable named CATALINA_HOME that references the installed root directory of Tomcat. In my case, this would be c:\tomcat4.0. After setting CATALINA_HOME, you can start Tomcat by executing the appropriate shell command. For Windows, the command is %CATALINA_HOME%\bin\startup. For UNIX, the command is $CATALINA_HOME/bin/startup.sh.

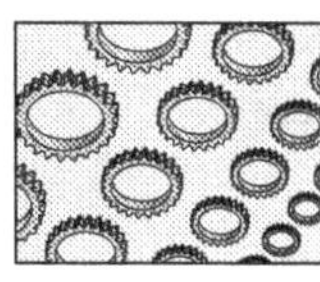

NOTE

The startup command is simply a thin wrapper around the "catalina start" command. You can also use the command "catalina run" to run Tomcat in the same window as the command shell, instead of creating a new window.

- Modify your current working directory and execute the appropriate shell command. For Windows (change the directory to your Tomcat bin directory), the command is startup. For UNIX (change the directory to your Tomcat bin directory), the command is ./startup.sh.

One other option available for Windows users is to start Tomcat from the Programs | Apache Tomcat 4.0 menu, which is created by Windows Installer.

After starting Tomcat, the default web application provided with Tomcat should be started. You can test the default web application by browsing http://localhost:8080, as shown next.

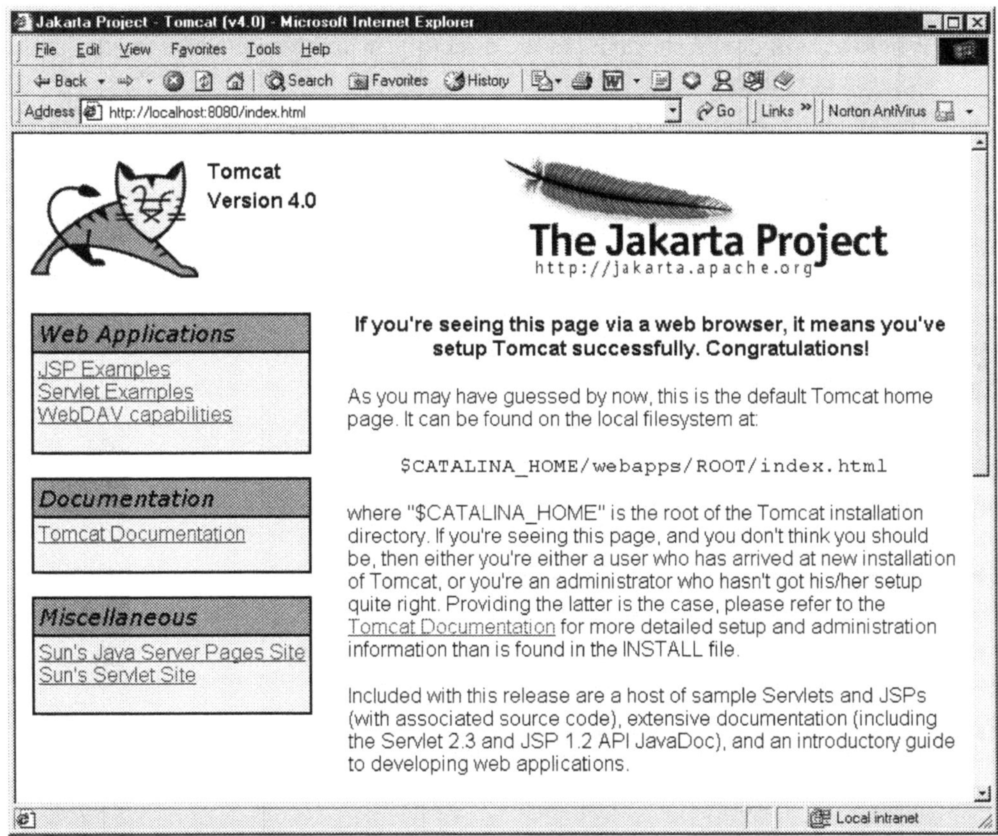

What if you don't see the Tomcat welcome page? There are a limited number of reasons why this could happen (this information comes straight from the Tomcat troubleshooting guide):

- The most common hiccup is when another web server (or any process for that matter) has laid claim to port 8080. This is the default HTTP port that Tomcat attempts to bind to at startup. To change this, open the file $CATALINA_HOME/conf/server.xml and search for 8080. Change it to a port that isn't in use, and is greater than 1024, because ports less than or equal to 1024 require superuser access to bind to. Restart Tomcat, and you're in business. Be sure that you replace 8080 in the URL you're using to access Tomcat. For example, if you change the port to 1977, you would request the URL http://localhost:1977/.
- An "out of environment space" error occurs when running the batch files in Windows 9x/Me-based operating systems. Right-click the Startup.bat and Shutdown.bat files. Click Properties and then select the Memory tab. For the Initial Environment field, enter something such as 4096. After you click Apply, Windows will create shortcuts in the directory, which you can use to start and stop the container.
- The localhost machine isn't found. This could happen if you're behind a proxy. If that's the case, make sure the proxy configuration for your browser knows that you shouldn't be going through the proxy to access the localhost machine. In Netscape, this is under Edit | Preferences | Advanced/Proxies, and in Internet Explorer, it is under Tools | Internet Options | Connections | LAN Settings.

Configuration

Tomcat 4.0 is highly configurable through the use of an XML file read during startup. This XML file, CATALINA_HOME/conf/server.xml, allows you to specify attributes of the Tomcat server, services, and connectors, described here:

- **Tomcat server** Represents a single JVM and consists of a collection of services.
- **Service** A collection of connectors that share a single context. In Tomcat terms, a service is a single engine.
- **Connector** Represents an endpoint by which requests are received and responses are returned. Within each connector, you can define any number

of "valves." Valves are very similar in concept to servlet filters, which were introduced with version 2.3 of the API (filters are covered in Chapter 6).

To gain a better understanding of the internal workings of Tomcat, let's take a look at some of the more important elements within the default configuration of the standalone Tomcat server. Once you understand how Tomcat is configured, you will be better able to customize the server to suit your particular needs, or even develop your own connectors or valves to add new functionality to the Tomcat server. For more in-depth information about server.xml, check out the Server Configuration Reference at http://jakarta.apache.org/tomcat/tomcat-4.0-doc/config/index.html, or just read through the server.xml file; it is very well documented and, being well-formed XML, is somewhat self-documenting.

The server element defines the characteristics of the servlet engine as a whole.

```
<Server port="8005" shutdown="SHUTDOWN">
```

The following attributes can be defined:

- **port** The TCP/IP port on which the server listens for a **shutdown** command. Note that the **shutdown** command must be initiated from the same system that is running the Tomcat server.
- **shutdown** The command string that must be on the listening port to shut down Tomcat. Modifying the **port** and/or **shutdown** values will prevent unscrupulous people from shutting down your server:

```
<Service name="Tomcat-Standalone">
```

The service element typically defines a servlet engine within the Tomcat server. In this case, the service is the standalone Tomcat service.

Within each service, you can define any number of connectors, which define request/response endpoints. The standalone service defines a non-Secure Sockets Layer (SSL) HTTP/1.1 connector residing on port 8080. Remember what port we used when we tested the Tomcat installation? That's right, 8080. This is the place you would change the port number if you didn't like the default value.

```
<Connector
className="org.apache.catalina.connector.http.HttpConnector"
          port="8080" minProcessors="5" maxProcessors="75"
          enableLookups="true" redirectPort="8443"
          acceptCount="10" debug="0" connectionTimeout="60000"/>
```

Some of the more interesting attributes, especially when attempting to performance-tune the server, are the following:

- **acceptCount** The maximum queue length for incoming connection requests when all possible request processing threads are in use. Any requests received when the queue is full will be refused.
- **maxProcessors** The maximum number of request processing threads to be created by this **connector**, which therefore determines the maximum number of simultaneous requests that can be handled.
- **minProcessors** The number of request processing threads that will be created when this **connector** is first started.
- **port** The TCP/IP port number on which this connector will create a server socket and await requests.

Within each Service, you then define a servlet engine (or Catalina entry point). All the requests coming from all the connectors will be routed through this engine entry point and be processed by all the valves defined within.

```
<Engine name="Standalone" defaultHost="localhost" debug="0">
```

Each engine can define global components that will be used by each valve within the engine, unless overridden by the valve. An example of a global component would be an engine-wide logger:

```
<Logger className="org.apache.catalina.logger.FileLogger"
        prefix="catalina_log." suffix=".txt"
        timestamp="true"/>
```

Note that other components can be defined on a global level as well, and thus be shared by all valves, but are typically defined at the valve level. These components include the following:

- **Context** Corresponds to the ServletContext object. When defining a Context, you can supply default attribute values as well as servlet context initialization parameters.
- **Loader** The Web application ClassLoader that will be used to load classes and resources.

- **Manager** The definition of a session manager used to create and maintain Hypertext Transfer Protocol (HTTP) sessions.
- **Realm** Represents a collection of user information, including user names, passwords, and roles. This may include information read from an XML file, JDBC database, or JNDI.

Any number of valves can be configured within an engine. Remember that a valve is inserted into the request/response flow and can add additional functionality during a request, or modify the request flow. A simple example is the AccessLogValve, which simply logs what resources are being requested:

```
<Valve className="org.apache.catalina.valves.AccessLogValve"
       directory="logs"  prefix="localhost_access_log." suffix=".txt"
       pattern="common"/>
```

Again, if you are interested in learning more about the internal workings of Tomcat 4.0, or want to start developing components for the Catalina engine, check out the online Tomcat documents. I encourage you to play around with the server.xml definitions or, better yet, use a debugger and step through the Tomcat code as it processes a request (this is made easy, because you have full access to the source code).

Alternatives

The servlet engine marketplace is indeed very large. A huge demand exists to add the capability to utilize the servlet technology on corporate web sites, and, not surprisingly, many alternatives are present. These alternatives range from free servlet engines (such as Tomcat, Caucho Resin, Macromedia JRun, and New Atlanta ServletExec) all the way to full-blown application servers (such as BEA WebLogic and IBM WebSphere). In fact, at the time of writing, in excess of 30 different servlet engine implementations are ready for use and/or purchase (see http://java.sun.com/products/servlet/industry.html for a somewhat complete list). Each of these implementations has its own strengths and weaknesses, as well as costs and benefits. The beautiful thing about the Servlet API is that it is standard across all of these implementations, meaning that you can develop an application using one engine (such as Tomcat) and deploy it using another (such as BEA WebLogic).

Summary

We've just taken a very quick look at Java servlets: what they are, why you should use them, and what you need to get started developing servlets. It is important to remember that despite the cute name of "servlet," servlets are extremely powerful and a core part of the J2EE (Java 2 Enterprise Edition) API family.

Tomcat 4.0 is a great way to get started with servlets. Not only is it the official reference implementation provided by Sun for the Servlet API, but it is open source and free for use. Tomcat is not a "toy"; I recommend its use for all servlet development, even if you will eventually deploy your servlets into a production environment that utilizes a different servlet engine.

Now that you understand how to install, configure, and test Tomcat, let's move on to how to develop servlets and how to get them running within Tomcat 4.0.

CHAPTER

2

Servlet Development

IN THIS CHAPTER:

Now that we've covered the basics of Tomcat 4.0, you are ready to actually see it in action. In this chapter, we will write a servlet that will receive an HTTP GET request, process parameters, and format the HTML that will be sent back to the client (or the web browser). If you've ever done this before with a CGI script, I'm sure you will agree that working with servlets is much easier.

The Basic Flow

Before looking at the basic flow of a servlet, let's review the Tomcat architecture and how an HTTP request winds up invoking a servlet.

The client (such as a web browser) will make a request to the server to fetch some resource. Tomcat will receive this request, either through its built-in web server on port 8080 or from what is called a *web server connector,* which is a piece of native code attached to the web server that will forward requests to the servlet engine and then figure out what type of resource has been requested. If a static resource, such as a file, is requested, the DefaultServlet will open the file, read it, and dump it back to the client. If a servlet is requested, the InvokerServlet will execute the servlet, which will return content back to the client (more on these special servlets a bit later in the chapter).

How exactly does the servlet engine know if a servlet should be invoked? On the client side, you need to specify a URL that names the specific resource that you want to fetch, as follows:

```
http://some.server.com/servlet/my_servlet?param=value
```

When Tomcat 4.0 starts, it reads a web application descriptor file, conf/web.xml, which sets the default values for all web applications (web applications are covered in Chapter 5). One of the things you can specify within a web application is a servlet mapping, which maps a request pattern to a servlet that will be invoked. The conf/web.xml file specifies several default mappings:

```
<!-- The mapping for the default servlet -->
<servlet-mapping>
  <servlet-name>default</servlet-name>
  <url-pattern>/</url-pattern>
</servlet-mapping>

<!-- The mapping for the invoker servlet -->
<servlet-mapping>
```

```
  <servlet-name>invoker</servlet-name>
  <url-pattern>/servlet/*</url-pattern>
</servlet-mapping>
```

The servlet-name elements refer to a servlet definition, which includes the class name of the servlet to invoke:

```
<servlet>
  <servlet-name>default</servlet-name>
  <servlet-class>org.apache.catalina.servlets.DefaultServlet</servlet-class>
</servlet>

<servlet>
  <servlet-name>invoker</servlet-name>
  <servlet-class>org.apache.catalina.servlets.InvokerServlet</servlet-class>
</servlet>
```

Thus, for our request URL containing /servlet/my_servlet?param=value, Tomcat will attempt to match the URL with the list of mappings (longest mapping first). The partial list is as follows:

```
/servlet/*
/
```

The /servlet/* pattern will match first, so its corresponding servlet will be invoked, which is the InvokerServlet; this servlet will simply ensure that the requested servlet is loaded and then pass control off. If we had requested a static resource, such as /index .html, the / pattern would match and the DefaultServlet would be invoked, causing the contents of the resource to be dumped to the client.

Now that we've established how the InvokerServlet gets control (and I encourage you to take a look at its source code), what happens next? The basic servlet lifecycle is as follows:

1. The servlet is loaded. If the servlet has not already been loaded, it will be resolved and loaded. The servlet is loaded only once; multiple threads of the same servlet will handle multiple client requests. The one exception is if the servlet implements the SingleThreadModel interface, in which case a pool of servlet instances will be created.
2. The servlet is initialized. The init() method on the servlet is called to allow for the servlet to perform some type of initialization (such as connecting to a database). The init() method is called only once, after a servlet is loaded and it

is guaranteed that the servlet engine will not send any requests to the servlet until the init() method completes (without throwing an exception).

3. The servlet service() method is invoked. The servlet performs some type of processing and returns a response.
4. If the servlet engine is terminated, or the servlet engine decides to unload the servlet for any reason, the destroy() method of the servlet will be invoked to allow for cleanup.

The Tomcat architecture has made it very easy to focus on writing just the servlet pieces that are needed to perform work; you don't need to be concerned about loading and unloading a servlet, handling the HTTP protocol, performing chaining, invoking filters, and so on. The Servlet API does a great job of compartmentalizing the areas of work that need to be done.

Servlet Example: Properties

To illustrate how easy it is to write a servlet, let's take a look at one that will simply return an HTML page to the client that contains information about the client, any parameters that were passed, and all the system properties of the server.

What Makes a Servlet a Servlet?

Before starting to write your first servlet, you first need to understand what makes a servlet a servlet. The Servlet API defines the javax.servlet.Servlet interface, which has the following methods (note that the full Servlet API can be found in Appendix A):

- **init()** Called by the servlet engine (also referred to as the servlet container) after the servlet is loaded. The init() method is passed a configuration object, which the servlet can use to read initialization parameters.
- **service()** Allows the servlet to process a request.
- **destroy()** Called when the servlet is being removed from the servlet engine.
- **getServletConfig()** Returns the javax.servlet.ServletConfig object, which holds initialization and startup information for the servlet.
- **getServletInfo()** Returns information about the servlet, such as the name, version, and author.

Every servlet must implement these methods. Although you could implement each of these methods every time you write a servlet, you can extend two handy abstract base classes instead, saving you time and providing you with additional functionality:

- **javax.servlet.GenericServlet** Extend this class if you want to write a protocol-independent servlet. We'll be writing these types of servlets when performing applet-to-servlet communication in Chapter 10. At a minimum, you must implement the abstract service() method; GenericServlet provides an empty implementation for the other Servlet interface methods.
- **javax.servlet.http.HttpServlet** Extend this class if you want to create a servlet that will be responding to HTTP requests. The HttpServlet class actually extends GenericServlet and adds additional methods for handling different types of HTTP requests (such as GET, POST, PUT, HEAD, and so forth). You should not override the service() method when using HttpServlet, which examines the HTTP method type and dispatches the request to a handler method, such as doGet() or doPost(), but instead implement the appropriate handler method.

One Servlet, One Instance

You should also be aware of a very easy pitfall, before getting started. When a servlet is loaded by the servlet container, only one instance of the servlet will be created. Big deal, right? Well, you really need to understand that the servlet container is heavily threaded. Each thread will handle a single request, and there may be multiple simultaneous requests to the server. This means that multiple threads may be calling the service() method of the same servlet instance at the same time. When developing a servlet and doing local testing, this may never cause a problem, but when put into production with hundreds or thousands of users, you could run into some serious issues.

The most common error is to declare a class field (or variable) and use it within the servlet service() method (or, when using HttpServlet, the doGet() or doPost() methods). Without synchronizing access to the class-level field, which will kill the performance of the servlet, you run the risk of multiple threads trying to use the same variable at the same time, causing big problems. In general, always avoid declaring class fields within servlets, unless they are to be used as read-only constants.

The Servlet API does provide a solution to the "one instance" problem, although I discourage you from using it. If your servlet implements the javax.servlet.SingleThreadModel interface, which is just a "marker" interface that contains no methods, the servlet container will create a pool of servlet instances and guarantee that only a single thread will be executing a servlet service() method at any given time. Understanding multithreaded programming concepts is much better than relying on the SingleThreadModel interface.

Writing the Servlet

Writing a servlet for use with an HTTP request requires only two basic steps:

1. Create a new servlet class that extends javax.servlet.http.HttpServlet.
2. Override one or both of the doGet() and doPost() methods. Remember that the HttpServlet base class calls these methods from its service() method depending upon the type of HTTP request.

A servlet can also optionally override the init() and destroy() methods to perform some type of initialization and destruction for the servlet. A good example of this would be to initialize a database connection in the init() method and close the connection in the destroy() method, which we'll be doing in Chapter 9.

Our Properties servlet is a good example of these steps. While the init() and destroy() methods do not perform any work, they illustrate how they are overridden. Remember that the source code for all the examples in this book can be found on www.servletguru.com. The following shows the complete code listing for the Properties servlet:

```
package com.omh;

import javax.servlet.*;
import javax.servlet.http.*;
import java.io.IOException;
import java.io.PrintWriter;

/**
 * First sample servlet. Returns any parameters and
 * lists server properties.
 */
public class Properties
        extends HttpServlet
{
    public void doGet(HttpServletRequest req,
```

```
                HttpServletResponse resp)
    throws ServletException, IOException
{
    // Get an output stream that takes into account
    // the proper character encoding
    PrintWriter out = resp.getWriter();
    // Print the HTML header to the output stream
    out.println("<html>");
    out.println("<head>");
    out.println("<title>My First Servlet</title>");
    out.println("</head>");
    out.println("<h2><center>");
    out.println("Information About You</center></h2>");
    out.println("<br>");

    // Create a table with information about the client
    out.println("<center><table border>");
    out.println("<tr>");
    out.println("<td>Method</td>");
    out.println("<td>" + req.getMethod() + "</td>");
    out.println("</tr>");

    out.println("<tr>");
    out.println("<td>User</td>");
    out.println("<td>" + req.getRemoteUser() + "</td>");
    out.println("</tr>");

    out.println("<tr>");
    out.println("<td>Client</td>");
    out.println("<td>" + req.getRemoteHost() + "</td>");
    out.println("</tr>");

    out.println("<tr>");
    out.println("<td>Protocol</td>");
    out.println("<td>" + req.getProtocol() + "</td>");
    out.println("</tr>");

    // Get and dump all of the request parameters
    java.util.Enumeration enum = req.getParameterNames();
    while (enum.hasMoreElements()) {
      String name = (String) enum.nextElement();
      out.println("<tr>");
      out.println("<td>Parameter '" + name + "'</td>");
      out.println("<td>" + req.getParameter(name) + "</td>");
      out.println("</tr>");
    }
```

```
        out.println("</table></center><br><hr><br>");

        // Create a table with information about the server
        out.println("<h2><center>");
        out.println("Server Properties</center></h2>");
        out.println("<br>");

        out.println("<center><table border width=80%>");

        java.util.Properties props = System.getProperties();
        enum = props.propertyNames();

        while (enum.hasMoreElements()) {
          String name = (String) enum.nextElement();
          out.println("<tr>");
          out.println("<td>" + name + "</td>");
          out.println("<td>" + props.getProperty(name) + "</td>");
          out.println("</tr>");
        }
        out.println("</table></center>");

        // Wrap up
        out.println("</html>");
        out.flush();
    }
    public void init() throws ServletException
    {
        // Initialize the servlet here. Use the
        // ServletConfig object to get initialization
        // parameters
        ServletConfig config = getServletConfig();
    }

    public void destroy()
    {
        // Clean up here
    }
}
```

You will most always need to import the following servlet API classes:

- **javax.servlet.*** This package contains the generic servlet interfaces and classes, as well as special servlet exceptions.

- **javax.servlet.http.*** This package contains the special interfaces and classes used when writing servlets responding to HTTP requests.

Since the Properties servlet will be responding to an HTTP GET request (we'll just request the servlet from our browser), the doGet() method has been implemented. We first grab the java.io.PrintWriter object from the response object, which allows us to send output back to the client. Then the servlet will gather information about the client and server and format the response using HTML tags so that the output is nicely formatted.

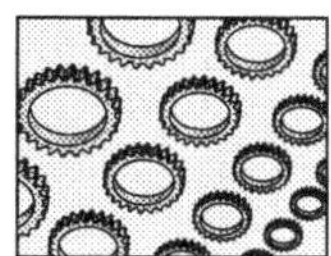

NOTE

To compile the servlet, you will need to have the Servlet API classes on your CLASSPATH. If you have installed Tomcat 4.0, these classes can be found in common/lib/servlet.jar off of the Tomcat root directory. Also keep in mind that the Properties servlet is part of the com.omh package.

Installing the Servlet

Before our new Properties servlet can be used, we need to install it within the server. The Servlet API defines the directory structure within the servlet engine, which we'll be covering in great detail in Chapter 5. For now, I'll assume that you are using Tomcat 4.0 and that we'll be installing the servlet as part of the root (or default) web application.

The root web application for Tomcat is located at webapps/ROOT. Under this directory is the standard Servlet API-defined directory structure. Servlets go under the WEB-INF/classes subdirectory (which may not exist for the root web application) and then must follow their package name. So, the location for our Properties servlet is as follows:

```
webapps/ROOT/WEB-INF/classes/com/omh/Properties.class
```

If you are not using Tomcat, the location will still be similar, but you will need to find out where web applications should be deployed.

See It in Action

Now that we have written, compiled, and installed out first servlet, let's see it in action. Be sure that Tomcat has been started and then request the following:

```
http://localhost:8080/servlet/com.omh.Properties
```

Remember that the /servlet in the URL will cause the InvokerServlet to be called from within Tomcat. The InvokerServlet will then determine which servlet to invoke (the rest of the URL, com.omh.Properties) and then call its service() method. Since the Properties servlet extended HttpServlet, the service() method will examine the HTTP request method (GET, in our case) and call the appropriate handler method (doGet). The doGet() method formats the response in HTML and returns it to the client. The following illustration shows the results of invoking the Properties servlet:

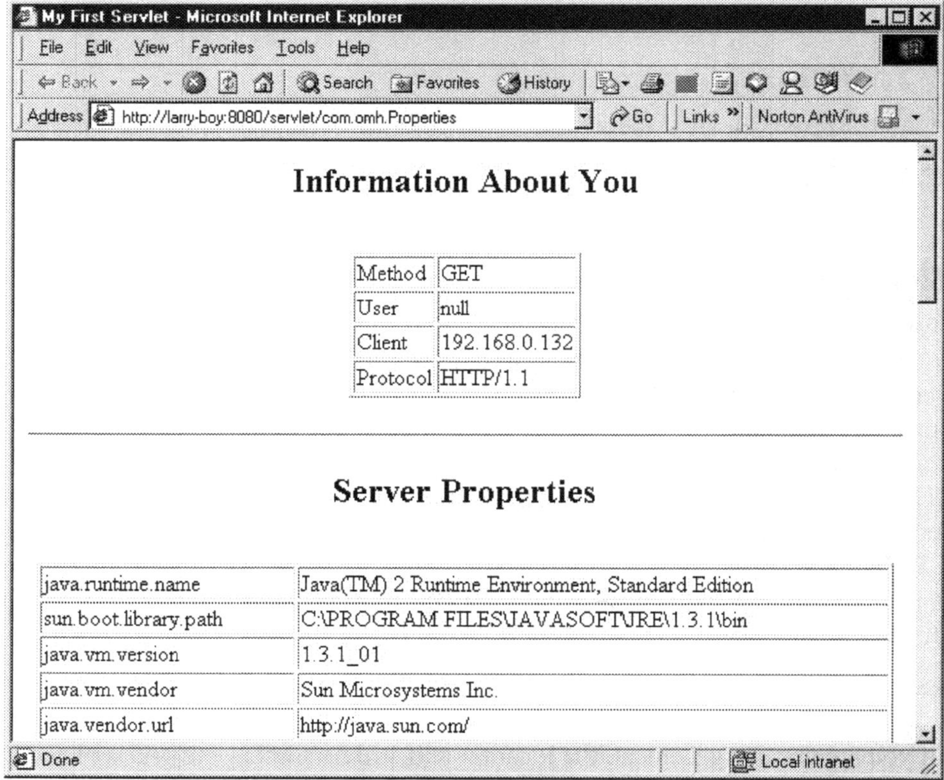

You can also request the servlet with request parameters, as shown next:

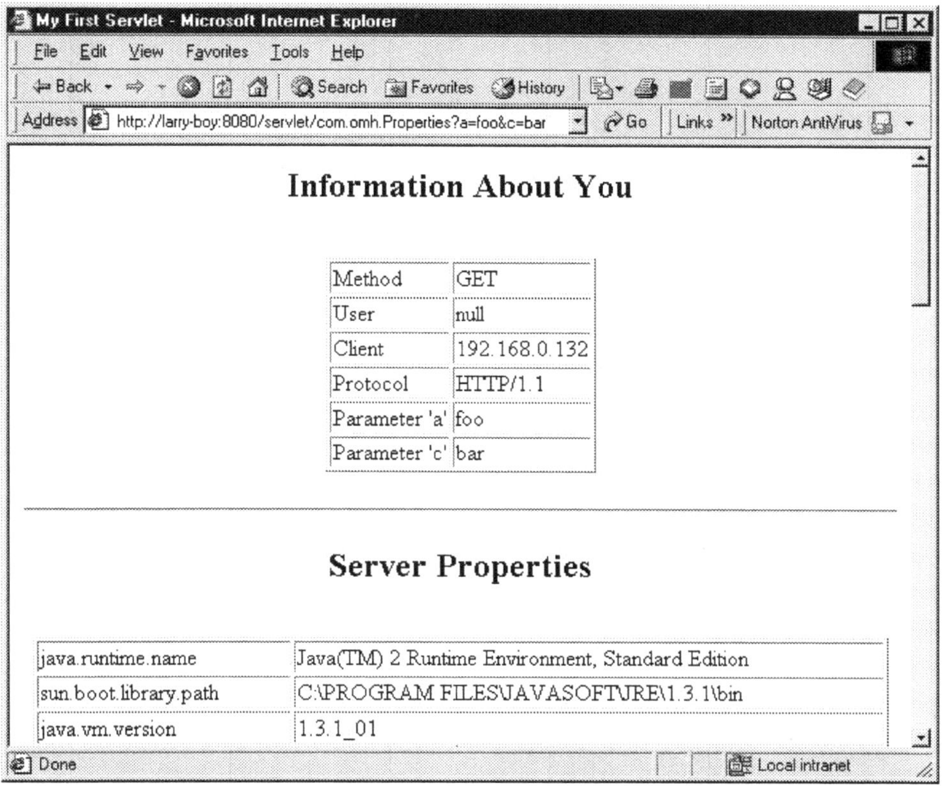

Summary

In this chapter, you saw how to write a simple servlet that accepted an HTML GET request and formatted the response as an HTML page. This chapter outlined the basic flow of a servlet, as well as the flow of an HTTP request through Tomcat, and examined some of the base servlet API classes and interfaces.

CHAPTER

3

Session Management

IN THIS CHAPTER:

In this chapter, we'll take a look at how you can use the Servlet API to manage data for an individual user across multiple HTTP requests. Remember that HTTP is a stateless protocol, unlike TCP which maintains a connection to the server for the duration of a session. The classic example of why maintaining a session is important is an Internet shopping system that must keep a list of items that are currently in each user's cart. To accomplish this, the server must be able to distinguish clients from one another and also provide a way to store data for each individual client between requests.

Session Tracking

The Servlet API provides a simple yet powerful model for keeping track of session information. A session from a web server's perspective consists of all the requests made during a single browser invocation. In other words, a session begins when you open the browser and ends when it is closed. The first obstacle in session tracking is uniquely identifying each client session. This can be done only by assigning some type of identifier to each client, storing that identifier with the client, and then having the client provide the identifier with each HTTP request to the server. Why not just use the IP address of the client machine for the identifier? Multiple clients may be running on an individual machine, or the requests may have been routed through a proxy server. In both cases, the IP address will not serve as a unique identifier. As we'll see later in this chapter, unique identifiers can be stored using cookies or by using a technique known as URL rewriting.

To best illustrate how to use the Servlet API to manage session information, let's just jump right in and take a look at a simple example. The following is a simple servlet that keeps track of the number of times a user has visited a site during the current browser session:

```
package com.omh.session;

import javax.servlet.*;
import javax.servlet.http.*;
import java.io.IOException;
import java.io.PrintWriter;

public class Counter
        extends HttpServlet
{
```

```
// Define our counter key into the session
static final String COUNTER_KEY = "Counter.count";

public void doGet(HttpServletRequest req,
                  HttpServletResponse resp)
    throws ServletException, IOException
{

    // Get the session object for this client session.
    // The parameter indicates to create a session
    // object if one does not exist
    HttpSession session = req.getSession(true);

    // Set the content type of the response
    resp.setContentType("text/html");

    // Get the PrintWriter to write the response
    PrintWriter out = resp.getWriter();

    // Is there a count yet?
    int count = 1;
    Integer i = (Integer) session.getAttribute(COUNTER_KEY);

    // If a previous count exists, set it
    if (i != null) {
        count = i.intValue() + 1;
    }

    // Put the count back into the session
    session.setAttribute(COUNTER_KEY, new Integer(count));

    // Print a standard header
    out.println("<html>");
    out.println("<head>");
    out.println("<title>Session Counter</title>");
    out.println("</head>");
    out.println("<body>");
    out.println("Your session ID is <b>" +
    session.getId());
    out.println("</b> and you have hit this page <b>" +
                count +
                "</b> time(s) during this browser session");
```

```
        out.println("<form method=GET action=\"" +
                    req.getRequestURI() + "\">");
                    out.println("<input type=submit " +
                    "value=\"Hit page again\">");
                    out.println("</form>");

        // Wrap up
        out.println("</body>");
        out.println("</html>");
        out.flush();
    }
}
```

The getSession() method of the HttpServletRequest object passed to the servlet is used to return the current session for the user. The single parameter to the method indicates whether a new session should be created if one does not yet exist (there is also a version of the method with no arguments that, by default, creates a new session). This will force a new session to be manufactured for you the first time a new user calls the servlet container. Note that the preceding statement refers to the *servlet container,* not just this particular servlet. All session data is maintained at the servlet container level and can be shared between servlets; this way, you can have a group of servlets working together to serve a single client session. Also, per the Servlet API specification, to ensure the session is properly maintained, the servlet developer must call the getSession() method before the response is committed. Why? After the response is committed, you can't send any additional HTTP headers, which means no cookies. This just means that, to be safe, you should get the session object before you start writing anything to the response output stream.

Once you have the session object, it works quite like a standard Java Hashtable or Collection. You can get and put any arbitrary object into the session by a unique key. Since the session data is stored at the web application level, you should be cautious in naming the keys, to maintain uniqueness. I suggest using the name of your servlet (even the full package name) as part of the key so that you don't accidentally overwrite the value set by another servlet.

In addition to storing application data, the session object contains many methods to access properties of the session, such as the session identifier (retrieved by the getId() method). The following shows the Counter servlet in action:

The first time a user visits the Counter servlet, a new session is created if one does not yet exist (remember that another servlet may have created a session object for the user). An Integer object is then retrieved from the session using a unique key. If no Integer object is found, an initial value of 1 is used; otherwise, the value is incremented by 1. The new value is then placed back into the session object. A simple HTML page is then returned for the browser to display that contains the session ID and the number of times that the user has visited the Counter page.

Managing Session Data

There are three aspects of managing session data that need to be kept in mind: session swapping, session relocation, and session persistence. How session data is managed is determined upon the implementation of the servlet container in use, since the specification does not dictate how it is to be done. Regardless of how (or even if) the underlying servlet container manages session data, you can be relatively certain that only data objects that implement java.io.Serializable can be swapped, relocated, or persisted. Serialization was added with JDK 1.1 and allows the state of an object to be written to an arbitrary output stream (such as a file). We'll be using serialization in Chapter 10 for applet-to-servlet communication.

Session Swapping

All servlet containers have a limited amount of resources available for storing session information (there's only so much memory on your server). In an effort to keep resource consumption under control, most servlet containers will place a limit on the number of sessions allowed to be resident in memory at any one time. An

LRU (Least Recently Used) algorithm can easily be implemented, because the last-accessed time is stored with the HttpSession object. If the maximum number of sessions is exceeded, the oldest sessions can be serialized to disk, freeing up memory for new sessions. This, of course, assumes that all the data objects stored in the session can be serialized (by implementing java.io.Serializable). If the session cannot be serialized, the servlet container has no choice but to keep it in memory. Once a session is requested that has been swapped to disk, it can be deserialized and placed back in memory.

Session Relocation

Nothing dictates that a servlet request must always be serviced by the same Java Virtual Machine (JVM), or even by the same physical server. Robust servlet containers and application servers have built-in load balancing to ensure that requests are processed as quickly and reliably as possible. In order for this to work properly with data that has been stored within a session, the session object must be relocatable. Once again, this relies on all the data stored in the session implementing java.io.Serializable. If the session object and all the stored data can be serialized, it is rather simple to move the object from one JVM to another. Note that the underlying engine has to worry about somehow synchronizing the session data.

Session Persistence

We've all heard the claims of web servers that remain up and running 24 hours a day, 7 days a week. But who are we kidding? Servers sometimes have to be shut down for maintenance (or, sadly, to clean up memory leaks). Once again, serialization can save the day. A servlet container can very easily serialize all the session objects and their data to disk during a shutdown and reload them when the server is brought back up. The user who has just added the last item to their shopping cart will thank you if all is not lost!

Session Lifetime

Nothing lasts forever, including session information. All servlet containers will eventually invalidate a session after the session has been idle for a certain length of time. This timeout value is part of the web application descriptor (web.xml) and is covered in greater detail in Chapter 5. What happens when a session is invalidated? The server will release all of the values bound to the session and then free the session object to be garbage-collected by the JVM (we'll see later that you can get notification of an object being unbound from the session). Note that you don't have to wait for the servlet container to time the session out; you can always call invalidate() to immediately end a session.

Exploring Other Sessions and Their Data

Just for a little historical viewpoint, the Servlet API used to allow you to gain access to other session objects and view the data bound to them. This is obviously a big security hole, because not only could a nasty servlet gather data from other sessions (such as credit card information), but sessions could also be destroyed. You may notice the HttpSessionContext object in the API; this class was deprecated as of version 2.1 of the servlet API.

Cookies

So far, we've seen how to track sessions using the Servlet API, but we really haven't seen how the unique session ID is maintained between the client and the server. One way is through the use of cookies, which were initially introduced by Netscape. A *cookie* is a piece of data that can be embedded in an HTTP request or response. In a typical scenario, the web server will embed a cookie value in a response header, and the browser will then return that same cookie value with each subsequent request. One of the pieces of information that can be stored is a unique session ID, which can then be used to bind a particular HTTP request to a session. Cookies also contain other properties, such as an optional comment, version number, and maximum lifetime. The following code shows the Cookies servlet, which displays some information about all the cookies present in the request header:

```
package com.omh.session;

import javax.servlet.*;
import javax.servlet.http.*;
import java.io.IOException;
import java.io.PrintWriter;

public class Cookies
        extends HttpServlet
{
    public void doGet(HttpServletRequest req,
                      HttpServletResponse resp)
        throws ServletException, IOException
```

```
    {

        // Set the content type of the response
        resp.setContentType("text/html");

        // Get the session. This will force a cookie
        // to be created
        req.getSession();

        // Get the PrintWriter to write the response
        PrintWriter out = resp.getWriter();

        // Get an array containing all of the cookies
        Cookie cookies[] = req.getCookies();

        // Write the page header
        out.println("<html>");
        out.println("<head>");
        out.println("<title>Servlet Cookie Information</title>");
        out.println("</head>");
        out.println("<body>");

        if ((cookies == null) || (cookies.length == 0)) {
            out.println("<center><h1>No Cookies found</h1>");
        }
        else {

            out.println("<center><h1>Cookies found</h1>");

            // Display a table with all of the info
            out.println("<table border>");
            out.println("<tr><th>Name</th><th>Value</th>" +
            "<th>Comment</th><th>Max Age</th></tr>");

            for (int i = 0; i < cookies.length; i++) {
                Cookie c = cookies[i];
                out.println("<tr><td>" + c.getName() +
                        "</td><td>" +
                        c.getValue() + "</td><td>" +
                        c.getComment() + "</td><td>" +
                        c.getMaxAge() + "</td></tr>");
            }
```

```
            out.println("</table></center>");
        }

        // Wrap up
        out.println("</body>");
        out.println("</html>");
        out.flush();
    }
}
```

Note that the HttpServletRequest object has a getCookies() method that returns an array of Cookie objects for the current request. I personally find it rather inconsistent with other Java objects (such as the Hashtable keys() method) that the getCookies() method returns an array rather than an enumeration. Perhaps this will be corrected in future revisions of the specification.

Back to the code. The Cookies servlet will first create a session, thus causing the servlet container to return a cookie back to the client that contains the session ID. The servlet specification dictates that the name of this cookie be JSESSIONID. The first time that the Cookies servlet is invoked, it will not find any cookies present:

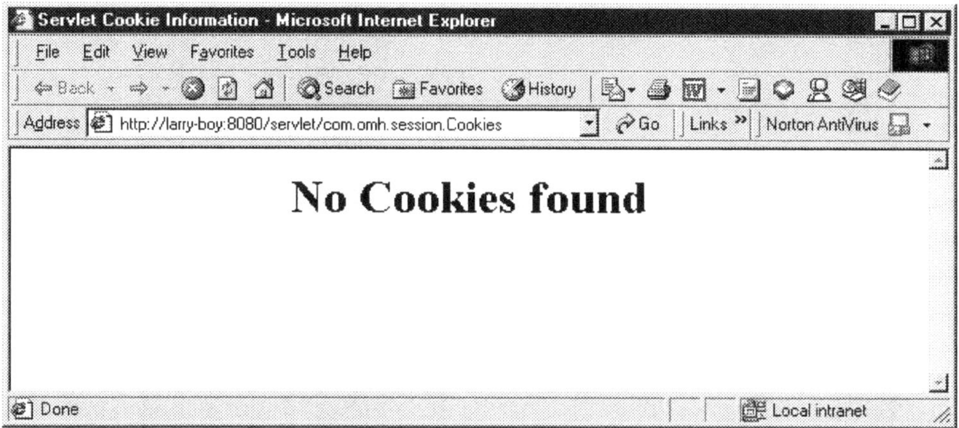

When the Cookies servlet returns the response from the first request, the JSESSIONID cookie is returned as well as part of the HTTP header. The cookie will be parsed by the browser and then sent to the server upon each new request, as shown next:

Allowing the use of cookies has caused a lot of confusion and concern, because some people believe that cookies are a violation of privacy (which is typically unfounded). Because of this, most browsers will allow users to disable cookies, thus making our job of session tracking a bit more difficult. So what if you can't rely on cookie support? You may have to fall back to URL rewriting, which has been in use with CGI for a long time.

URL Rewriting

So how do you handle the corporate users who must endure a paranoid IT department that turns off cookie support, or those stubborn Internet users who are surfing with really old browsers without cookie support? You'll have to use URL rewriting. All links and redirections that are created by a servlet must be encoded to include the session ID as part of the URL. Note that you cannot use URL rewriting with static HTML pages (all pages must be dynamic), because the URL must be encoded for each user to include the session ID. The way in which the URL is encoded is server-specific, but most likely will be in the form of an added parameter or additional path information.

To illustrate URL rewriting, let's make a few changes to our Counter servlet. The new servlet will be named CounterRewrite and will use URL rewriting to maintain session information between HTTP requests:

```
package com.omh.session;

import javax.servlet.*;
```

```
import javax.servlet.http.*;
import java.io.IOException;
import java.io.PrintWriter;

public class CounterRewrite
        extends HttpServlet
{

    // Define our counter key into the session
    static final String COUNTER_KEY = "Counter.count";

    public void doGet(HttpServletRequest req,
                      HttpServletResponse resp)
        throws ServletException, IOException
    {

        // Get the session object for this client session.
        // The parameter indicates to create a session
        // object if one does not exist
        HttpSession session = req.getSession(true);

        // Set the content type of the response
        resp.setContentType("text/html");

        // Get the PrintWriter to write the response
        PrintWriter out = resp.getWriter();

        // Is there a count yet?
        int count = 1;
        Integer i = (Integer) session.getAttribute(COUNTER_KEY);

        // If a previous count exists, set it
        if (i != null) {
            count = i.intValue() + 1;
        }

        // Put the count back into the session
        session.setAttribute(COUNTER_KEY, new Integer(count));

        // Print a standard header
        out.println("<html>");
```

```
        out.println("<head>");
        out.println("<title>Session Counter</title>");
        out.println("</head>");
        out.println("<body>");
        out.println("Your session ID is <b>" +
        session.getId());
        out.println("</b> and you have hit this page <b>" +
                    count +
                    "</b> time(s) during this browser session");

        String url = req.getRequestURI();
        out.println("<form method=GET action=\"" +
                    resp.encodeURL(url) + "\">");
                    out.println("<input type=submit " +
                    "value=\"Hit page again\">");
                    out.println("</form>");

        // Wrap up
        out.println("</body>");
        out.println("</html>");
        out.flush();
    }
}
```

Notice that the major change is the way in which we write the URL in the ACTION statement of the form. The encodeURL() method is used to modify the URL to include the session ID (the encodeRedirectURL should be used when sending a redirect page).

Want to see it work? Turn off cookie support in your browser and invoke the original Counter servlet. If you visit the page again, you will notice that a new session ID is generated and the hit count is always 1. This occurs because no way exists for the servlet container to bind the HTTP requests to the same client now that there are no cookies to store the session ID. If you now invoke the CounterRewrite servlet, you'll notice that the session ID is preserved and the counter increments with each visitation of the page, as shown next.

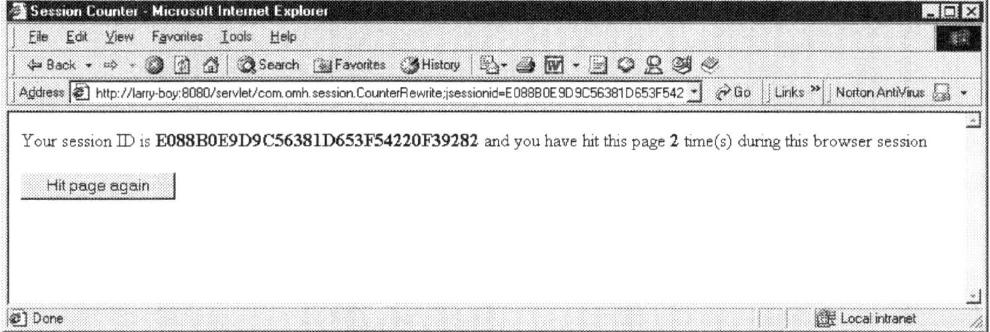

If you look at the URL in the Address area of the browser, you will notice the additional information that encodeURL added.

Session Tracking Without a Browser

Cookies and URL rewriting are great if you are running within a browser, but what if you want to write a stand-alone Java application that communicates directly with a servlet in which you need to manage session information? Or what if you are using the Java Plug-In, which, at the time of this writing, does not support the use of cookies? You will need to manually get the cookie containing the session ID from the first response and then set the session ID in each subsequent request header. To show how this is done, we'll create a simple application that requests a counter value from a servlet. Chapter 10 provides an in-depth look at applet-to-servlet communication, so we'll just focus on the particulars of getting and setting cookies from within Java. The following code shows the CounterServer servlet, which uses session tracking to keep a counter. The difference here is that we won't be formatting an HTML page to display within a browser; instead, the binary integer counter value is returned via a DataOutputStream.

```
package com.omh.session;

import javax.servlet.*;
import javax.servlet.http.*;
import java.io.IOException;
import java.io.ByteArrayOutputStream;
import java.io.DataInputStream;
import java.io.DataOutputStream;
```

```
public class CounterServer
        extends HttpServlet
{
    // Define our counter key into the session
    static final String COUNTER_KEY = "CounterServer.count";

    public void doPost(HttpServletRequest req,
                       HttpServletResponse resp)
        throws ServletException, IOException
    {
        // Get the session
        HttpSession session = req.getSession(true);

        // Is there a count yet?
        int count = 1;
        Integer i = (Integer) session.getAttribute(COUNTER_KEY);

        // If a previous count exists, set it
        if (i != null) {
            count = i.intValue() + 1;
        }

        // Put the count back into the session
        session.setAttribute(COUNTER_KEY, new Integer(count));

        // Get the input stream for reading data from the client
        DataInputStream in =
            new DataInputStream(req.getInputStream());

        // We'll be sending binary data back to the client so
        // set the content type appropriately
        resp.setContentType("application/octet-stream");

        // Data will always be written to a byte array buffer so
        // that we can tell the client the length of the data
        ByteArrayOutputStream byteOut = new ByteArrayOutputStream();

        // Create the output stream to be used to write the
        // data to our buffer
        DataOutputStream out = new DataOutputStream(byteOut);

        // If there is any data being sent from the client,
        // read it here
```

```
        // Write the data to our internal buffer.
        out.writeInt(count);

        // Flush the contents of the output stream to the
        // byte array
        out.flush();

        // Get the buffer that is holding our response
        byte[] buf = byteOut.toByteArray();

        // Notify the client how much data is being sent
        resp.setContentLength(buf.length);

        // Send the buffer to the client
        ServletOutputStream servletOut = resp.getOutputStream();

        // Wrap up
        servletOut.write(buf);
        servletOut.close();
    }
}
```

The basic session-management portion of the servlet should look quite familiar to you, since it is identical to our earlier counter servlets. But now, instead of formatting and returning HTML, the servlet creates a DataOutputStream and writes binary data back to the caller.

The real trick here is how the client, which is our Java application, manages the cookie information. The basic flow of our application is as follows:

1. Connect to the servlet using the java.net.URLConnection class.
2. Send a request to the servlet.
3. Read the response and, if the session ID has not yet been set, extract the value of the session ID.
4. Set the cookie value in any subsequent requests to the servlet.

The application is not very complicated, and the code can just as easily be used from within an applet, as well:

```
package com.omh.session;

import java.io.*;
```

```
public class CounterApp
{
    // The servlet url
    String servletURL;

    // The value of the session cookie
    String sessionCookie = null;

    /**
     * <p>Application entry point. This application requires
     * one parameter, which is the servlet URL
     */
    public static void main(String args[])
    {
        // Make sure we have an argument for the servlet URL
        if (args.length == 0)
        {
            System.out.println("\nServlet URL must be specified");
            return;
        }

        try {

            // Create a new object
            CounterApp app = new CounterApp(args[0]);

            // Get the count multiple times
            for (int i = 1; i <=5; i++)
            {
                int count = app.getCount();
                System.out.println("Pass " + i + " count=" + count);
            }
        }
        catch (Exception ex)
        {
            ex.printStackTrace();
        }

    }

    /**
     * Construct a new CounterApp object
     * @param url The servlet url
     */
    public CounterApp(String url)
```

```
{
    servletURL = url;
}

/**
 * Invokes a counter servlet and returns the hit count
 * that was returned by the servlet
 */
public int getCount() throws Exception
{
    // Get the server URL
    java.net.URL url = new java.net.URL(servletURL);

    // Attempt to connect to the host
    java.net.URLConnection con = url.openConnection();

    // Set the session ID if necessary
    if (sessionCookie != null)
    {
        con.setRequestProperty("cookie", sessionCookie);
    }

    // Initialize the connection
    con.setUseCaches(false);
    con.setDoOutput(true);
    con.setDoInput(true);

    // Data will always be written to a byte array buffer so
    // that we can tell the server the length of the data
    ByteArrayOutputStream byteOut =
            new ByteArrayOutputStream();

    // Create the output stream to be used to write the
    // data to our buffer
    DataOutputStream out = new DataOutputStream(byteOut);

    // Send any data to the servlet here

    // Flush the data to the buffer
    out.flush();

    // Get our buffer to be sent
    byte buf[] = byteOut.toByteArray();

    // Set the content that we are sending
    con.setRequestProperty("Content-type",
        "application/octet-stream");
```

```
        // Set the length of the data buffer we are sending
        con.setRequestProperty("Content-length",
            "" + buf.length);

        // Get the output stream to the server and send our
        // data buffer
        DataOutputStream dataOut =
            new DataOutputStream(con.getOutputStream());
        dataOut.write(buf);

        // Flush the output stream and close it
        dataOut.flush();
        dataOut.close();

        // Get the input stream we can use to read the response
        DataInputStream in =
            new DataInputStream(con.getInputStream());

        // Read the data from the server
        int count = in.readInt();

        // Close the input stream
        in.close();

        // Get the session cookie if we haven't already
        if (sessionCookie == null)
        {
            String cookie = con.getHeaderField("set-cookie");
            if (cookie != null)
            {
                sessionCookie = parseCookie(cookie);
                System.out.println("Setting session ID=" +
                        sessionCookie);
            }
        }

        return count;
    }

    /**
     * Parses the given cookie and returns the cookie key
     * and value. For simplicity the key/ value is assumed
     * to be before the first ';', as in:
     *
     * JSESSIONID=3509823408122; path=/
```

```
     *
     * @param rawCookie The raw cookie data
     * @return The key/value of the cookie
     */
    public String parseCookie(String raw)
    {
        String c = raw;

        if (raw != null)
        {
            // Find the first ';'
            int endIndex = raw.indexOf(";");

            // Found a ';', assume the key/value is prior
            if (endIndex >= 0) {
                c = raw.substring(0, endIndex);
            }
        }

        return c;
    }
}
```

Of interest here is the way in which the session ID is retrieved from the response "set-cookie" header, and how the cookie is set in the requests with the "cookie" request property. Invoking the application results in the proper count being returned from the servlet's session data:

```
java com.omh.session.CounterApp
    http://localhost:8080/servlet/com.omh.session.CounterServer
Setting session ID=JSESSIONID=0985C08279E3641455A816E363D3F235
Pass 1 count=1
Pass 2 count=2
Pass 3 count=3
Pass 4 count=4
Pass 5 count=5
```

Note that the command has been split over two lines to improve readability; it should be entered as a single line.

Session Events

In some cases, you will want notification of when an object is bound to or unbound from a session. When an object is bound to a session, it is the perfect time to perform some type of initialization, such as opening a file, starting a database transaction, or logging some statistics. Once the object is unbound (due to the client session terminating, the session timing out, or the servlet engine terminating), you may want to perform some type of cleanup, such as closing a file, committing or rolling back a database transaction, or logging some additional statistics. The Servlet API authors anticipated this need by providing the HttpSessionBindingListener interface, which contains two methods that must be implemented: valueBound() and valueUnbound() (the names are somewhat self-explanatory). To illustrate how to use the HttpSessionBindingListener interface, let's take a look at a simple servlet that will create a new instance of an object that will be bound to a session:

```
package com.omh.session;

import javax.servlet.*;
import javax.servlet.http.*;
import java.io.IOException;
import java.io.PrintWriter;

public class Binder
        extends HttpServlet
{
    public void doGet(HttpServletRequest req,
                      HttpServletResponse resp)
        throws ServletException, IOException
    {
        // Set the content type of the response
        resp.setContentType("text/html");

        // Get the PrintWriter to write the response
        PrintWriter out = resp.getWriter();

        // Get the session object for this client session.
        // The parameter indicates to create a session
        // object if one does not exist
        HttpSession session = req.getSession(true);

        // Create a new SessionObject
        SessionObject o = new SessionObject(getServletContext());

        // Put the new SessionObject into the session
        session.setAttribute("Binder.object", o);
```

```
        // Print a standard header
        out.println("<html>");
        out.println("<head>");
        out.println("<title>Session Binder</title>");
        out.println("</head>");
        out.println("<body>");
        out.println("Object bound to session " +
        session.getId());

        // Wrap up
        out.println("</body>");
        out.println("</html>");
        out.flush();
    }
}
```

Nothing new going on here. We've already seen how to get the session for a request and how to add objects to the session. What's different is the fact that the object being added to the session, SessionObject, implements the HttpSessionBindingListener interface:

```
package com.omh.session;.

import javax.servlet.*;.
import javax.servlet.http.*;.

public class SessionObject.
        implements HttpSessionBindingListener.
{.
    ServletContext context;.

    public SessionObject(ServletContext context).
    {.
        // Save the ServletContext so we can use the.
        // log method later.
        this.context = context;.
    }.

    public void valueBound(HttpSessionBindingEvent event).
    {.
        // Output the fact that we are being bound.
```

```
        context.log("" + (new java.util.Date()) +.
            " Binding " + event.getName() +.
            " to session " +.
            event.getSession().getId());.
    }.

    public void valueUnbound(HttpSessionBindingEvent event).
    {.
        // Output the fact that we are being bound.
        context.log("" + (new java.util.Date()) +.
            " Unbinding " + event.getName() +.
            " from session " +.
            event.getSession().getId());.
    }.

}
```

When the SessionObject is added to the session, the valueBound() method will be invoked by the servlet container. By the same token, the valueUnbound() method will be invoked when the SessionObject is removed from the session. The object can be removed from the session by using any of the following methods:

- Calling session.removeAttribute().
- Calling session.setAttribute() with the same attribute name. This will effectively remove the old value and replace it with a new value.
- Calling session.invalidate().
- Waiting for the session to be invalidated by the servlet container.

Invoking the Binder servlet will cause a SessionObject to be bound to the current session. Since the SessionObject implements the HttpSessionBindingListener interface, the valueBound() method will be called. Our implementation will simply print some information to the servlet log. Depending upon the servlet container, this output may go to a log file or to the console. Once the SessionObject is removed from the session, the valueUnbound() method will be called.

We have just looked at how a session object can be notified when it is being bound to and unbound from a session; you can also utilize application events to notify some external object that session objects are being added and removed, as well. Application events are covered in Chapter 7.

Summary

In this chapter, we've covered the basics of session management with the Servlet API. We've also seen how clients are identified using session identifiers, and two ways to persist the identifiers using Cookies and URL rewriting. Finally, we looked at session binding events and how the HttpSessionBindingListener interface can be used to track when objects are bound to and unbound from a session.

CHAPTER 4

Security

IN THIS CHAPTER:

Servlet Security Methodologies

HTTP Authentication

Custom HTTP Authentication

HTML Form Authentication

Applet Authentication

SSL

Summary

Now that you know how to write some basic servlets, how do you go about ensuring that the client is authorized to access the information that you are providing? In this chapter, we'll take a look at several different ways to authenticate users and discuss the pros and cons of each method. We'll also discuss Secure Sockets Layer (SSL) and how its use ensures the secure transmission of information.

Servlet Security Methodologies

Before getting too deep into security methods, let's take a high-level overview of the different ways that you can place constraints upon the access of your servlets:

- **Declarative security using the web application descriptor** This is covered in great detail in Chapter 5. For now, just be aware that you can rely upon the servlet container to prompt for user authentication, depending upon how you configure the server.
- **HTTP authentication** This utilizes the built-in authentication mechanisms found in the HTTP protocol.
- **Custom authentication** This is a do-it-yourself approach whereby you control every aspect of the security process. While you have the most flexibility with this method, it also requires the most work. Examples are gathering user credentials via an HTML form or Java applet and validating the user against some server repository.

So if the servlet container can handle user authentication and authorization for you, why bother even discussing other methodologies? First of all, you may be using a servlet container that either doesn't support declarative security (it was introduced with version 2.2 of the servlet API) or doesn't support it well. Second, and more important, the types of authentication we will be discussing, namely using HTTP and using HTML forms, are two of the ways that you can choose to configure a servlet container to challenge a user for their credentials. Understanding how these methods work will help you make good decisions when using servlet container security.

Before going too much further, let's define a couple of important security terms:

- **Authentication** The process of gathering user credentials (username and password) and validating them in the server. This typically requires checking the credentials against some user repository, such as a database or LDAP, and authenticating that the user is who he or she says he or she is.

- **Authorization** The process of making sure that the authenticated user is allowed to view or access a given resource. If a user is not authorized to view a resource, the server should not allow access.

HTTP Authentication

One of the most common ways to perform user authentication is to use the built-in authentication features of HTTP. When a client makes a request for a protected resource from the server, the server responds with a special request header and status code, which causes the browser to create a dialog box with which to gather the username and password. This is known as challenge-and-response; the server challenges the client (browser) to respond with authentication information. Once the client responds, the server can validate the user against its own database of users and either grant or deny access.

There are two options when using HTTP authentication: basic and digest. Basic authentication is, well, basic. It is widely supported by almost all browsers and, unfortunately, is also quite easy to reverse engineer. All the data sent from the client to the server (including the password) is encrypted using Base64 encoding. The word "encrypted" is used very lightly, because Base64 is not difficult to decode (as we'll see later in this chapter). It would not be a difficult task to create a program that emulates a web server and collects username and password information from unsuspecting users—in fact, this would be quite easy with a servlet! The bottom line is that basic authentication isn't a whole lot more secure than transmitting plain text, so don't use it in hopes of keeping your site 100 percent secure.

To see basic authentication in action, you need to configure your web server to protect resources with a basic authentication scheme. Of course, all web servers are not created equal, so you will have to read the manual to find out exactly how to do this within your environment. Once configured properly, attempting to access a protected resource will result in the web server challenging the client for authentication information (username and password). After the user enters the authentication information, it will be Base64-encoded and sent back to the web server for validation. After the username and password have been decoded, the web server will perform a validation against its own database of users. Once validated, the resource will be served (or perhaps a servlet will be invoked).

Custom HTTP Authentication

Using HTTP authentication is easy; the web browser takes care of prompting for the username and password while the web server manages the database of valid users. But what if you want to have more control over which users can access your site? Perhaps you already have user information stored in an external database or have an authentication scheme that the web server you are using can't manage. Or maybe you want to be able to control user authentication in a web server-independent way. In this case, you may want to consider using custom authentication. Custom authentication still uses the challenge-and-response scheme of HTTP authentication, but instead of the web server validating the user, that now becomes your responsibility. It is important to remember that custom authentication still uses Base64 encoding to transmit data, so it is no more secure that basic authentication (which, as we have already established, is not very secure).

Let's take a look at the CustomHttpLogin servlet, which will force the web browser to prompt for the username and password if the user has not yet logged in:

```
package com.omh.security;

import javax.servlet.*;
import javax.servlet.http.*;
import java.io.IOException;
import java.io.PrintWriter;

/**
 * This servlet uses HTTP Authentication to prompt for
 * a username and password and a custom authentication
 * routine to validate the user
 */
public class CustomHttpLogin
        extends HttpServlet
{
    // Define our counter key into the session
    static final String USER_KEY = "CustomLogin.user";

    public void doGet(HttpServletRequest req,
                      HttpServletResponse resp)
        throws ServletException, java.io.IOException
    {
        // Set the content type of the response
        resp.setContentType("text/html");
```

```
// Get the PrintWriter to write the response
PrintWriter out = resp.getWriter();

// Set the response header to force the browser to
// load the HTML page from the server instead of
// from a cache
resp.setHeader("Expires",
        "Tues, 01 Jan 1980 00:00:00 GMT");

// Get the user for the current session
HttpSession session = req.getSession();
String sessionUser = null;
if (session != null)
{
    sessionUser = (String) session.getAttribute(USER_KEY);
}

// If there is no user for the session, get the
// user and password from the authentication header
// in the request and validate
String user = null;
if (sessionUser == null)
{
    user = validUser(req);
}

// If there is no user for the session and the user was
// not authenticated from the request, force a login
if ((sessionUser == null) && (user == null))
{

    // The user is unauthorized to access this page.
    // Setting this status code will cause the browser
    // to prompt for a login
    resp.setStatus(HttpServletResponse.SC_UNAUTHORIZED);

    // Set the authentication realm
    resp.setHeader("WWW-Authenticate",
                   "BASIC realm=\"custom\"");

    // The following page will be displayed if the
    // user presses 'cancel'
    out.println("<html>");
```

```
            out.println("<head>");
            out.println("<title>Invalid User</title>");
            out.println("</head>");
            out.println("<body>");
            out.println("You are not currently logged in");
        }
        else
        {

            // If there is no user for the session, bind it now
            if ((sessionUser == null) && (session != null))
            {
                session.setAttribute(USER_KEY, user);
                sessionUser = user;
            }

            // Show the welcome page
            out.println("<html>");
            out.println("<head>");
            out.println("<title>Welcome</title>");
            out.println("</head>");
            out.println("<body>");
            out.println("<center><h2>Welcome " + sessionUser +
                    "!</h2></center>");
        }

        // Wrap up
        out.println("</body>");
        out.println("</html>");
        out.flush();
    }

    /**
     * Validate the user and password given in the authorization
     * header. This information is Base64 encoded and will
     * look something like:
     *
     *    Basic a2FybG1vc3M6YTFiMmMz
     *
     * @param req The request
     * @return The username if valid or null if invalid
     */
    protected String validUser(HttpServletRequest req)
```

```
{
    // Get the authorization header
    String encodedAuth = req.getHeader("Authorization");

    if (encodedAuth == null)
    {
        return null;
    }

    // The only authentication type we understand is BASIC
    if (!encodedAuth.toUpperCase().startsWith("BASIC"))
    {
        return null;
    }

    // Decode the rest of the string, which will be the
    // username and password
    String decoded = Decoder.base64(encodedAuth.substring(6));

    // We should now have a string with the username and
    // password separated by a colon, such as:
    //     karlmoss:a1b2c3
    int idx = decoded.indexOf(":");
    if (idx < 0)
    {
        return null;
    }
    String user = decoded.substring(0, idx);
    String password = decoded.substring(idx + 1);

    // Validate the username and password.
    if (!validateUser(user, password))
    {
        user = null;
    }

    return user;
}

/**
 * Validates the username and password
 * @param user The username
 * @param password The password
```

```
     * @return true if the username and password are valid
     */
    protected boolean validateUser(String user, String password)
    {
        boolean valid = false;

        if ((user != null) && (password != null))
        {

            // Just do a simple check now. A "real" check would
            // most likely use a database or LDAP server
            if (user.equals("karlmoss"))
            {
                valid = true;
            }
        }

        return valid;
    }
}
```

The CustomHttpLogin servlet uses an HTTP session (covered in Chapter 3) to store the current user and to determine if a user has been validated. If not, the WWW-Authenticate header will be added and the status code will be set to SC_UNAUTHORIZED, which will cause the browser to challenge the user for their credentials:

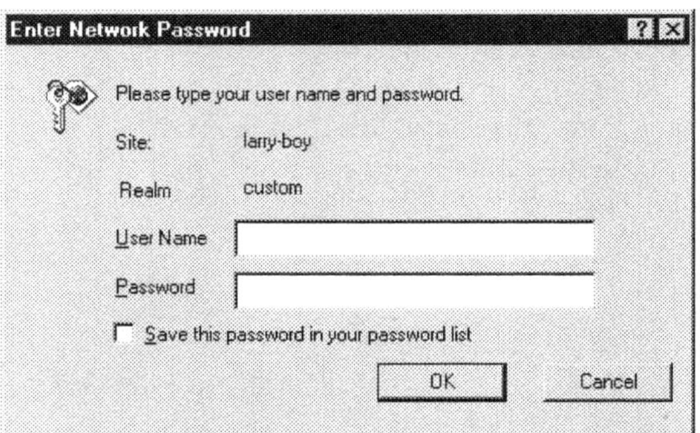

You may also notice that, in conjunction with setting the WWW-Authenticate header and status code, an HTML page has been formatted and returned as part of the response. This simple page will be displayed if the user clicks the Cancel button in the authentication dialog box, or if the maximum number of login tries is exceeded (the default is three times):

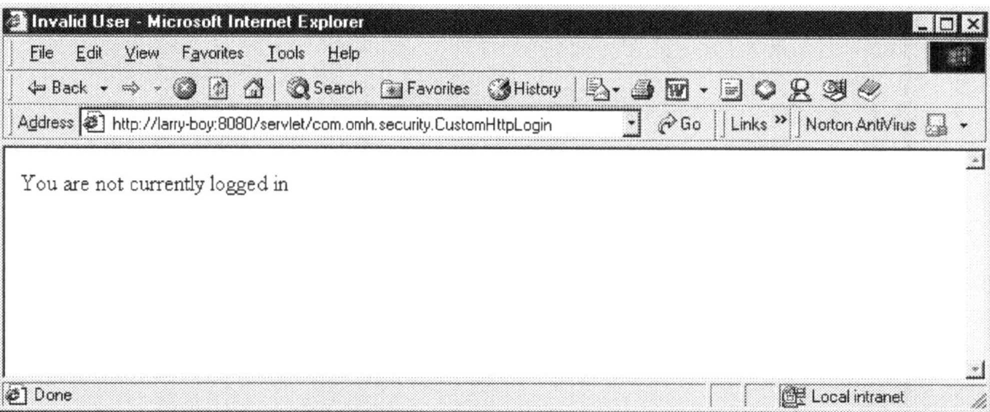

After the username and password are entered, the servlet gets control again. This time, we can get the Base64-encoded data stream from the request header. Decoding the stream is fairly simple using a well-known algorithm. The details of Base64 encoding can be found in RFC 1521, section 5.2. The Decoder class contains a static method to decode a Base64 string:

```
package com.omh.security;

public class Decoder
{

    /**
     * The base64 method was posted to the SERVLET-INTEREST
     * newsgroup (SERVLET-INTEREST@JAVA.SUN.COM). It is
     * assumed to be public domain.
     */
    static final char[] b2c=
    {
        'A','B','C','D','E','F','G','H','I','J','K','L','M','N','O','P',
        'Q','R','S','T','U','V','W','X','Y','Z','a','b','c','d','e','f',
        'g','h','i','j','k','l','m','n','o','p','q','r','s','t','u','v',
        'w','x','y','z','0','1','2','3','4','5','6','7','8','9','+','/'
    };

    static final char pad = '=';
    static byte[] c2b = null;

    /**
     * Decode a Base64 encoded string.
```

```
     * @param s The Base64 encoded string
     * @return The decoded string
     */
    public static String base64(String s)
    {
        if (c2b==null)
        {
            c2b = new byte[256];
            for (byte b=0;b<64;b++) c2b[(byte)b2c[b]]=b;
        }

        byte[] nibble = new byte[4];
        char[] decode = new char[s.length()];
        int d=0;
        int n=0;
        byte b;
        for (int i=0;i<s.length();i++)
        {
            char c = s.charAt(i);
            nibble[n] = c2b[(int)c];

            if (c==pad) break;

            switch(n)
            {
                case 0:
                    n++;
                    break;

                case 1:
                    b=(byte)(nibble[0]*4 + nibble[1]/16);
                    decode[d++]=(char)b;
                    n++;
                    break;

                case 2:
                    b=(byte)((nibble[1]&0xf)*16 + nibble[2]/4);
                    decode[d++]=(char)b;
                    n++;
                    break;

                default:
```

```
                    b=(byte)((nibble[2]&0x3)*64 + nibble[3]);
                    decode[d++]=(char)b;
                    n=0;
                    break;
            }
        }

        String decoded = new String(decode,0,d);
        return decoded;
    }
}
```

Picking out the username and password from the decoded stream couldn't be much easier. Can you see now why using basic authentication is not very secure? Of course, you'll want to add your own username/password validation routine, perhaps even using a JDBC data source (which is covered starting in Chapter 9). Once the user has been validated, access to the servlet is granted. Remember that session data is shared among servlets, so you can very easily create general-purpose routines that can be used by any number of servlets to perform user validation.

What if you wanted to take the authentication a bit further and provide some improved encoding of the username and password information? That's exactly what digest authentication attempts to do. No longer is the password transmitted over the network in Base64 for the unscrupulous to see. Instead, a digest of the password is created by using the username, password, URL, and a random nonce value that was generated by the server. The resulting encoded password is difficult (if not impossible) to decode by those with less than honorable intentions. While digest authentication seems like a major step in the right direction, currently, support is limited to only the most recent versions of web browsers.

HTML Form Authentication

Using custom authentication allows you to control how users are validated, but you still don't have any control over how the information is gathered within the web browser. The standard dialog box that is presented by the browser may not suit your needs. In this case, you may want to consider gathering information from the user with an HTML form. You not only can control the type of information that is gathered but also can customize the form's appearance (such as including graphics or additional instructions). HTML forms are covered in great detail in Chapter 8, but let's take a look at a simple example of how to gather user input with an HTML form and process the information with a servlet:

```
package com.omh.security;

import javax.servlet.*;
import javax.servlet.http.*;
import java.io.IOException;
import java.io.PrintWriter;

/**
 * This servlet creates an HTML form to gather a username and
 * password, validates the user, then allows the user to access
 * other pages.
 */
public class FormLogin
        extends HttpServlet
{
    public static String USER_KEY = "ServletLogin.user";
    public static String FIELD_USER = "username";
    public static String FIELD_PASSWORD = "password";

    public void doGet(HttpServletRequest req,
                      HttpServletResponse resp)
        throws ServletException, java.io.IOException
    {
        // Set the content type of the response
        resp.setContentType("text/html");

        // Get the PrintWriter to write the response
        java.io.PrintWriter out = resp.getWriter();

        // Set the response header to force the browser to
        // load the HTML page from the server instead of
        // from a cache
        resp.setHeader("Expires",
                       "Tues, 01 Jan 1980 00:00:00 GMT");

        // Get the URI of this request
        String uri = req.getRequestURI();

        // Get the current user. If one does not exist, create
        // a form to gather the user and password
```

```
    HttpSession session = req.getSession();
    String user = (String) session.getAttribute(USER_KEY);

    if (user == null)
    {
        // No user - create the form to prompt the user
        login(out, uri);
        return;
    }

    // Print a standard header
    out.println("<html>");
    out.println("<head>");
    out.println("<title>Welcome</title>");
    out.println("</head>");
    out.println("<body>");
    out.println("<center><h2>Welcome to our site!</h2>");
    out.println("</center><br><br>");
    out.println("<dir>Here are the Top Ten:");
    out.println("<dir>");
    out.println("<br>10 - Endangered Love (Barbara Manatee)");
    out.println("<br>9 - The Dance of the Cucumber");
    out.println("<br>8 - Larry's High Silk Hat");
    out.println("<br>7 - The Water Buffalo Song");
    out.println("<br>6 - The Yodeling Veterinarian of the Alps");
    out.println("<br>5 - The Song of the Cebu");
    out.println("<br>4 - His Cheeseburger");
    out.println("<br>3 - I Love My Lips");
    out.println("<br>2 - The Pirates Who Don't Do Anything");
    out.println("<br>1 - The Hairbrush Song");

    // Wrap up
    out.println("</body>");
    out.println("</html>");
    out.flush();
}

public void doPost(HttpServletRequest req,
                   HttpServletResponse resp)
    throws ServletException, java.io.IOException
{
    // Set the content type of the response
    resp.setContentType("text/html");
```

```
        // Get the PrintWriter to write the response
        java.io.PrintWriter out = resp.getWriter();

        // If the user is not yet logged in, validate
        HttpSession session = req.getSession(true);
        String user = (String) session.getAttribute(USER_KEY);

        if (user == null)
        {
            String username = req.getParameter(FIELD_USER);
            String password = req.getParameter(FIELD_PASSWORD);

            if (!validUser(username, password))
            {
                out.println("<html>");
                out.println("<title>Invalid User</title>");
                out.println("<body><center><h2>" +
                            "Invalid User!</h2><br>");
                out.println("Press the 'Back' button to try again");
                out.println("</center></body></html>");
                out.flush();
                return;
            }

            // We've got a valid user now, store the username in
            // the session
            session.setAttribute(USER_KEY, username);
        }

        // The current user has been validated.
        // Redirect to our main site
        resp.sendRedirect(req.getRequestURI());
    }

    /**
     * Formats the login page
     * @param out The output stream to write the response to
     * @param uri The requesting URI
     */
    protected void login(java.io.PrintWriter out, String uri)
```

```
        throws java.io.IOException
    {
        out.println("<html>");
        out.println("<head>");
        out.println("<title>Login</title>");
        out.println("<center><h2>Welcome! Please login</h2>");
        out.println("<br><form method=POST action=\"" +
                    uri + "\">");
        out.println("<table>");
        out.println("<tr><td>User ID:</td>");
        out.println("<td><input type=text name=" +
                    FIELD_USER + " size=30></td></tr>");
        out.println("<tr><td>Password:</td>");
        out.println("<td><input type=password name=" +
                    FIELD_PASSWORD + " size=10></td></tr>");
        out.println("</table><br>");
        out.println("<input type=submit value=\"Login\">");
        out.println("</form></center></body></html>");
    }

    /**
     * Validates the username and password
     * @param username The username
     * @param password The user password
     * @return true if the username/password is valid
     */
    protected boolean validUser(String username, String password)
    {
        boolean valid = false;

        // Perform a simple check to make sure the user is valid.
        if ((username != null) && (username.length() > 0))
        {
            valid = username.equals(password);
        }

        return valid;
    }
}
```

The FormLogin servlet will first check the session to see if the current user has been validated. If the user has not yet logged in, an HTML form will be created to gather the user information:

Once the user has entered the login information and clicked the Login button, the HTML form will POST the information back to the same FormLogin servlet in which the user is validated (in the doPost() method). If the user is valid, the browser will be redirected to the main page, as shown next:

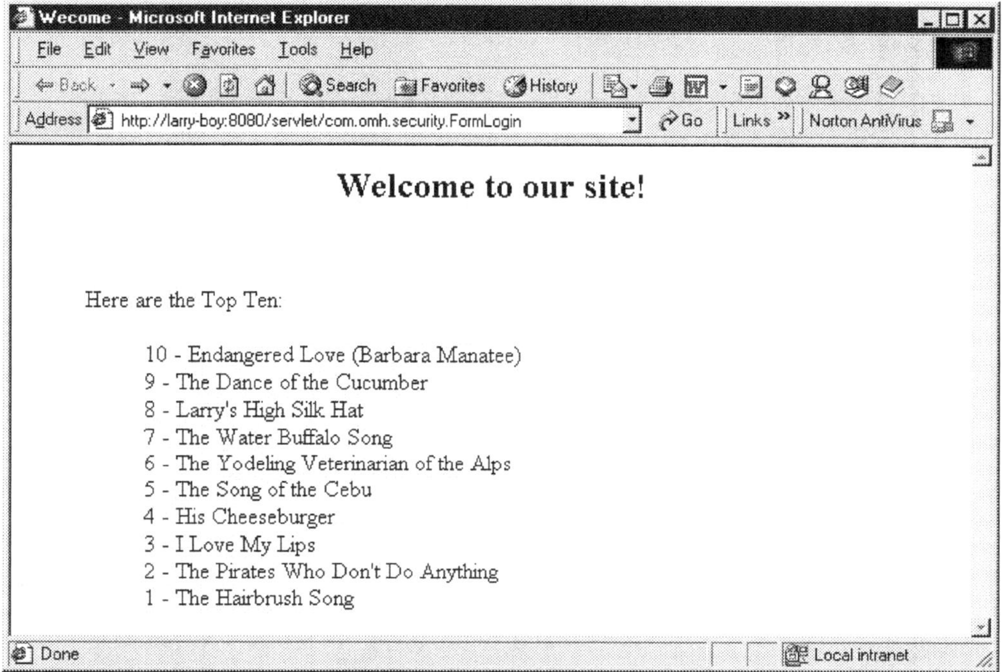

If you want to log off the current user, you can simply invalidate the session (via the HttpSession.invalidate() method) or wait for the session to automatically time out (refer to Chapter 3 for more details).

The HTML form that gathers the username and password is quite dull, so feel free to add a splash of color or graphics—you have complete control over the presentation.

So what's not to like? You have complete control over both the way the web browser prompts for information and how users are validated on the server. The major downside to using an HTML form is that the data is transmitted to the server in the request header of the POST in clear text. Once again, someone could peek in and capture this data without too much trouble.

Applet Authentication

The best we've been able to do so far is control the way the web browser prompts for user information, and how the user is validated on the server. Controlling the way in which the user information (including the password) is transmitted to the server has been out of our reach. For some applications, this might not be a severe limitation; lots of web pages out there use the techniques that we've already discussed. But what if you need to ensure that the user information you are transmitting is safe from eavesdropping? As we'll see in the next section, SSL solves this problem by encrypting all data that is exchanged between the client and the server (with a price, of course). Wouldn't it be nice if you could somehow encrypt the data yourself? By using an applet in the web browser that communicates with a servlet, you have the opportunity to control the format of the user data being transmitted.

We'll be taking a very detailed look at applet-to-servlet communication in Chapter 10. For now, we'll just cover the basics. In essence, the applet will open a URLConnection to a servlet, create a standard output stream, write data (possibly encrypted) to the stream, and wait for a response from the servlet. The servlet on the other side of the URLConnection will open an input stream to read the data sent from the applet (decrypting if necessary), validate the data, and return a response to the applet containing the results of the validation.

You may be concerned about using an applet due to the differing levels of Java support in the major browsers. The good news about this particular applet is that it was written using JDK 1.0.2. If your browser supports any level of Java, it should be able to run the LoginApplet (the code follows) without any problems.

```
package com.omh.security;

import java.applet.*;
import java.awt.*;
import java.io.*;
import java.net.*;

/**
 * This applet gathers a username and password and
 * then passes the information to a servlet to be
 * validated. If valid the servlet will send back the
 * location of the next page to be displayed. This
 * applet can be used with JDK 1.0.2 clients.
 */
public class LoginApplet
```

```
    extends Applet
{
    // Define the GUI widgets
    TextField username;
    TextField password;
    Label message;
    Button login;
    String codeBase;
    String servlet;
    String nextDoc;
    String sessionId;

    /**
     * Initialize the applet
     */
    public void init()
    {
        // Get the servlet name that will be validating
        // the username and password
        codeBase = "" + getCodeBase();
        servlet = getParameter("servlet");

        // Make sure we don't end up with a double '/'
        if (servlet != null)
        {
            if (servlet.startsWith("/") &&
                codeBase.endsWith("/"))
            {
                codeBase = codeBase.substring(0,
                            codeBase.length() - 1);
            }
        }

        // Get the session ID. This is a workaround for a
        // problem where the session ID of the original GET
        // is different than the session ID of our POST when
        // using URLConnection
        sessionId = getParameter("id");

        // Set our background color to blend in with a white
        // page
        setBackground(Color.white);
```

```
        // Set the layout to be a border layout. Place the message
        // area in the north, the login button in the south, and
        // the input areas in the center
        setLayout(new BorderLayout(0, 5));

        // Add the message area
        message = new Label();
        add("North", message);

        // Create the container for the input fields
        Panel p = new Panel();
        p.setLayout(new GridLayout(2, 2, 30, 20));

        // Add the username label and entry field
        p.add(new Label("Enter user name:"));
        username = new TextField(10);
        p.add(username);

        // Add the password label and entry field
        p.add(new Label("Enter password:"));
        password = new TextField(10);
        password.setEchoCharacter('*');
        p.add(password);

        add("Center", p);

        // Add the login button
        login = new Button("Login");
        add("South", login);

    }

    /**
     * Handle events
     */
    public boolean handleEvent(Event event)
    {
        if ((event != null) && (event.id == event.ACTION_EVENT))
        {
            if (event.target == login)
            {

                message.setText("");
```

```
        // Get the user and password
        String user = username.getText();
        String pw = password.getText();

        // May want to decrypt the user and/or password here

        // Validate the user. If the user is valid the
        // applet will show a new page; otherwise we'll
        // return back here
        boolean valid = false;
        try
        {
            valid = validate(user, pw);
        }
        catch (Exception ex)
        {
            ex.printStackTrace();
        }

        // Display a message for invalid users
        if (!valid)
        {
            message.setText("Invalid user - please try again");
        }
        else
        {

            // Show a new document
            try
            {
                URL url = new URL(nextDoc);
                System.out.println("showing " + url);
                getAppletContext().showDocument(url);
            }
            catch (Exception ex)
            {
                message.setText("Invalid document: " + nextDoc);
                ex.printStackTrace();
            }
        }
    }
}
return false;
```

```
    }

    /**
     * Validate the user and password. This routine will
     * communicate with a servlet that does the validation
     * @param user Username
     * @param pw Password
     * @return true if the user is valid
     */
    protected boolean validate(String user, String pw)
      throws Exception
    {
        boolean valid = false;

        // Get the server URL
        java.net.URL url = new java.net.URL(codeBase + servlet);

        // Attempt to connect to the host
        java.net.URLConnection con = url.openConnection();

        // Initialize the connection
        con.setUseCaches(false);
        con.setDoOutput(true);
        con.setDoInput(true);

        // Data will always be written to a byte array buffer so
        // that we can tell the server the length of the data
        ByteArrayOutputStream byteOut = new ByteArrayOutputStream();

        // Create the output stream to be used to write the
        // data to our buffer
        DataOutputStream out = new DataOutputStream(byteOut);

        // Send the proper session id
        out.writeUTF(sessionId);

        // Send the username and password
        out.writeUTF(user);
        out.writeUTF(pw);

        // Flush the data to the buffer
        out.flush();
```

```
        // Get our buffer to be sent
        byte buf[] = byteOut.toByteArray();

        // Set the content that we are sending
        con.setRequestProperty("Content-type",
            "application/octet-stream");

        // Set the length of the data buffer we are sending
        con.setRequestProperty("Content-length",
            "" + buf.length);

        // Get the output stream to the server and send our
        // data buffer
        DataOutputStream dataOut =
            new DataOutputStream(con.getOutputStream());
        dataOut.write(buf);

        // Flush the output stream and close it
        dataOut.flush();
        dataOut.close();

        // Get the input stream we can use to read the response
        DataInputStream in =
            new DataInputStream(con.getInputStream());

        // Read the response from the server
        valid = in.readBoolean();
        System.out.println("valid user=" + valid);

        // If the user is valid get the name of the next
        // document to display
        if (valid)
        {
            nextDoc = in.readUTF();
            System.out.println("next document=" + nextDoc);
        }

        // Close the input stream
        in.close();
        return valid;
    }
}
```

The init() method creates the input fields and formats the user interface:

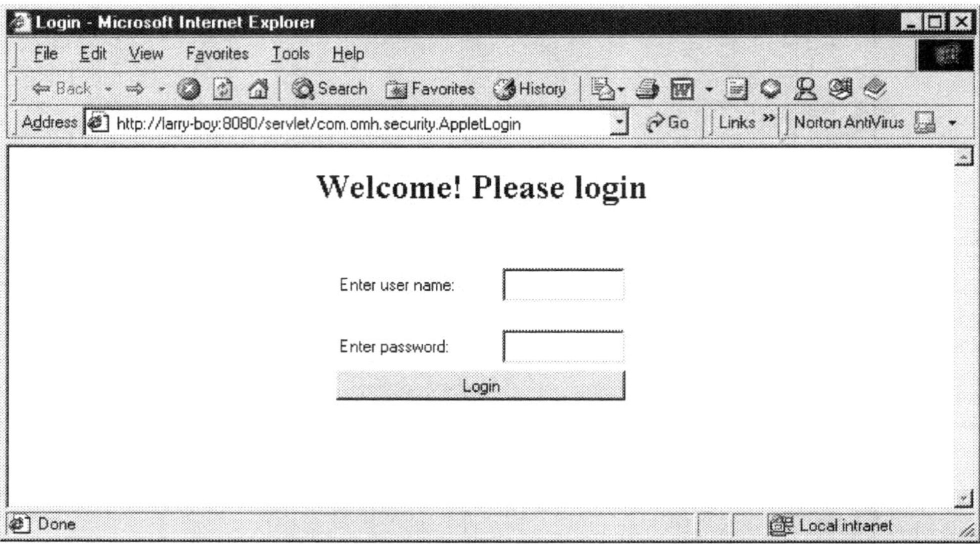

When the user clicks the Login button, the handleEvent() method will be invoked and the username and password will be retrieved from the input fields. You could very easily add some validation at this point to ensure that both input fields contain data. The validate() method transmits the username and password to our servlet and waits for a response. There is no data encryption being performed, but it would be quite easy to do so before writing the data to the output stream. The servlet will respond with a Boolean value to indicate whether the user is valid or not. If so, the URL of the next page to display is sent by the servlet, as well, and the next page will be shown in the browser (using the AppletContext.showDocument() method) as shown next:

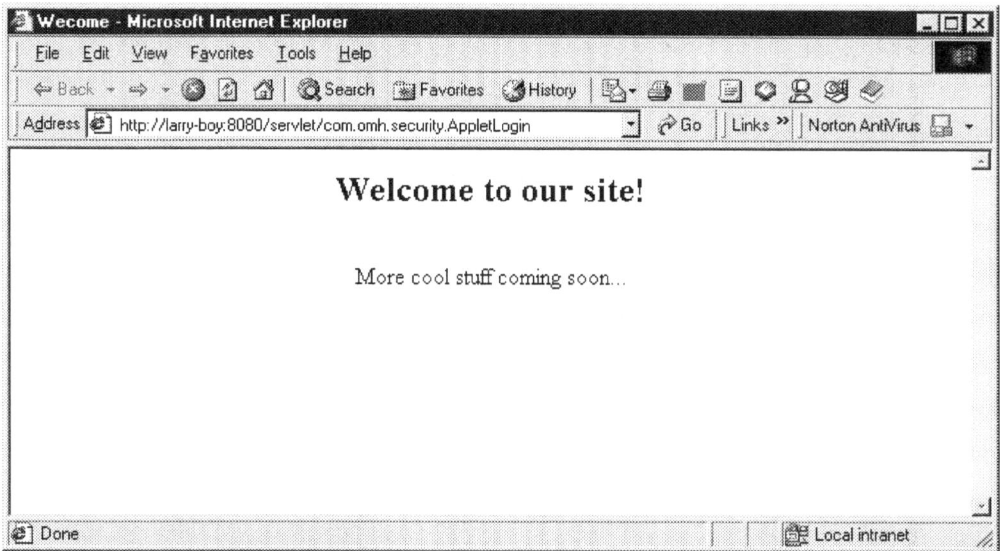

The following AppletLogin servlet contains code which reads the data sent by the applet in the doPost() method. An input stream is opened and the data is read in the same order that it was written by the applet (and decrypted if necessary). The username and password are retrieved and validated. If the user is valid, the location of the welcome page (which happens to be the AppletLogin servlet) is sent back to the applet.

```
package com.omh.security;

import javax.servlet.*;
import javax.servlet.http.*;
```

```
import java.io.ByteArrayOutputStream;
import java.io.DataInputStream;
import java.io.DataOutputStream;
import java.io.IOException;
import java.io.PrintWriter;
import java.util.Hashtable;

/**
 * This servlet creates an HTML page that will present an
 * applet that gathers the username and password. This servlet
 * will also validate the input and redirect the applet as
 * necessary.
 */
public class AppletLogin
        extends HttpServlet
{
    public static String USER_KEY = "ServletLogin.user";

    // Keep a cross reference of usernames to session id's
    static Hashtable crossRef = new Hashtable();

    public void doGet(HttpServletRequest req,
                      HttpServletResponse resp)
        throws ServletException, java.io.IOException
    {
        // Set the content type of the response
        resp.setContentType("text/html");

        // Get the PrintWriter to write the response
        PrintWriter out = resp.getWriter();

        // Set the response header to force the browser to
        // load the HTML page from the server instead of
        // from a cache
        resp.setHeader("Expires",
                       "Tues, 01 Jan 1980 00:00:00 GMT");

        // Get the current user. If one does not exist, create
        // a form to gather the user and password
        HttpSession session = req.getSession();
        String user = (String) session.getAttribute(USER_KEY);

        if (user == null)
```

```
    {
        // Check our cross-reference table
        user = (String) crossRef.get(session.getId());

        if (user != null)
        {
            // Found the user in the cross reference table.
            // Put the user in this session and remove from
            // the table
            session.setAttribute(USER_KEY, user);
            crossRef.remove(session.getId());
        }
    }

    if (user == null)
    {
        // No user - create the form to prompt the user
        login(out, req, resp);
        return;
    }

    // Print a standard header
    out.println("<html>");
    out.println("<head>");
    out.println("<title>Wecome</title>");
    out.println("</head>");
    out.println("<body>");
    out.println("<center><h2>Welcome to our site!</h2>");
    out.println("<br>");
    out.println("More cool stuff coming soon...");
    out.println("</center>");

    // Wrap up
    out.println("</body>");
    out.println("</html>");
    out.flush();
}

public void doPost(HttpServletRequest req,
                   HttpServletResponse resp)
    throws ServletException, java.io.IOException
{
    // Get the input stream for reading data from the client
```

```
DataInputStream in =
    new DataInputStream(req.getInputStream());

// We'll be sending binary data back to the client so
// set the content type appropriately
resp.setContentType("application/octet-stream");

// Data will always be written to a byte array buffer so
// that we can tell the client the length of the data
ByteArrayOutputStream byteOut =
    new ByteArrayOutputStream();

// Create the output stream to be used to write the
// data to our buffer
DataOutputStream out =
    new DataOutputStream(byteOut);

// Read the proper session id
String sessionId = in.readUTF();

// Read the username and password
String user = in.readUTF();
String password = in.readUTF();

// May want to decrypt the user and/or password here

// Validate the user
if (!validUser(user, password))
{
    // Send back a Boolean value indicating that the
    // user is invalid
    out.writeBoolean(false);
}
else
{
    // User valid. Set the user in our cross-reference table
    // and send back a Boolean valid indicating that the user
    // is valid
    crossRef.put(sessionId, user);
    out.writeBoolean(true);

    // Write the location of the next page
    String nextPage = req.getScheme() + "://" +
```

```
            req.getServerName() + ":" +
            req.getServerPort() +
            req.getRequestURI();

        // Use URL rewriting for session info
        out.writeUTF(nextPage);
    }

    // Flush the contents of the output stream to the
    // byte array
    out.flush();

    // Get the buffer that is holding our response
    byte[] buf = byteOut.toByteArray();

    // Notify the client how much data is being sent
    resp.setContentLength(buf.length);

    // Send the buffer to the client
    ServletOutputStream servletOut = resp.getOutputStream();

    // Wrap up
    servletOut.write(buf);
    servletOut.close();
}

/**
 * Formats the login page
 * @param out The output stream to write the response to
 * @param uri The request
 */
protected void login(PrintWriter out,
                     HttpServletRequest req,
                     HttpServletResponse resp)
    throws java.io.IOException
{
    // Get the session
    HttpSession session = req.getSession();

    out.println("<html>");
    out.println("<head>");
    out.println("<title>Login</title>");
    out.println("<center><h2>Welcome! Please login</h2>");
```

```
        out.println("<applet width=200 height=120");
        out.println("    name=\"LoginApplet\"");
        out.println("    codebase=\"/\"");
        out.println("    code=\"com.omh.security.LoginApplet\">");
        out.println("<param name=\"servlet\" value=\"" +
                    req.getRequestURI() + "\">");
        out.println("<param name=\"id\" value=\"" +
                    session.getId() + "\">");
        out.println("</applet>");
        out.println("</center></body></html>");
    }

    /**
     * Validates the username and password
     * @param username The username
     * @param password The user password
     * @return true if the username/password is valid
     */
    protected boolean validUser(String username, String password)
    {
        boolean valid = false;

        // Perform a simple check to make sure the user is valid.
        if ((username != null) && (username.length() > 0))
        {
            valid = username.equals(password);
        }

        return valid;
    }
}
```

When the servlet is first accessed by a web browser, the doGet() method is invoked and the session is checked for a username. The absence of a username indicates that a valid user has not yet been bound to the session. If this is the case, an HTML page is returned that contains an APPLET tag that will cause the browser to load the LoginApplet.

You may also notice that there are two PARAM tags that pass additional parameters to the applet. The servlet PARAM tag contains the name of the servlet that the applet will communicate with, which, in our case, is AppletLogin (the name of the current servlet can be retrieved using the getRequestURI() method). The id PARAM tag contains the session ID of the current session. The session ID will be sent back to the AppletLogin servlet so that we can identify the client. But why? Can't the servlet identify the browser by using the session ID provided in the HTTP request? Normally yes, but unfortunately the browser and the applet have two separate locations for storing cookies, so they will have two unique session IDs. When the data from the applet is validated, the session ID sent by the applet (which is the session ID of the browser) will be used to update a static Hashtable. The servlet can then check this Hashtable to see if the browser session ID has been validated.

Note that the LoginApplet applet must be installed in the document root of the web server so that it can be downloaded by the browser. Installing LoginApplet.class in the WEB-INF/classes directory of the default web application will not work, since that is where servlets go, not applets.

Now we have the best of all three worlds. We have control over how the user is prompted for authorization information, how that information is transmitted to the server, and how that information is validated on the server. But there is more to security than just user authentication. In some cases, you may want to encrypt the entire conversation between the web browser and the web server, which is exactly what SSL is designed to do.

SSL

A reliable way to ensure that the data being transmitted is secure is by using SSL. SSL sits on top of all socket communication and encrypts all data before being transmitted over the network, and decrypts the data once it reaches the target machine. This doesn't just happen by magic. You will have to purchase some type of digital certificate (available at www.verisign.com) and configure your web server to enable the use of SSL, assuming that the web server you are using supports SSL.

As a servlet developer, you don't need to be concerned about the details of SSL, or even if it is in use. The only way you will be able to tell that SSL is in use is by calling the getScheme() method on the request object. If SSL is being used, getScheme should return "https" (HTTP with SSL). SSL is widely used for e-commerce applications and is considered one of the best ways to ensure privacy when dealing with sensitive information (such as credit card numbers or financial data). The beauty of SSL is that, from the perspective of a servlet, it provides transparent encryption and decryption of data to ensure secure transactions.

Summary

In this chapter, we've just touched the tip of the security iceberg. We covered different ways to prompt for user authentication, as well as different ways to perform user validation on the server. Security is all about tradeoffs. How much risk are you willing to take with your data? How much effort are you willing to expend to protect your data? If you can live with a lightweight security scheme, then basic HTTP authentication may be sufficient. Want more control in the way that user information is validated? We saw how validation can be done using a custom HTTP authentication scheme. Need to gather more than just a username and password, or want to customize the look of the login page? Using HTML forms may be exactly what you need. Do you require control of the browser and the way in which users are validated, and want to implement your own encryption technique? We explored how to create a login applet that communicates with a servlet and allows you to have complete control over the entire authentication process.

User authentication is only the first step in securing your web site. Once a user has been validated, you may still need to keep private all the data exchanged between the client and the server. We briefly looked at SSL, which encrypts all the transmitted data to ensure privacy.

CHAPTER

5

Web Applications

IN THIS CHAPTER:

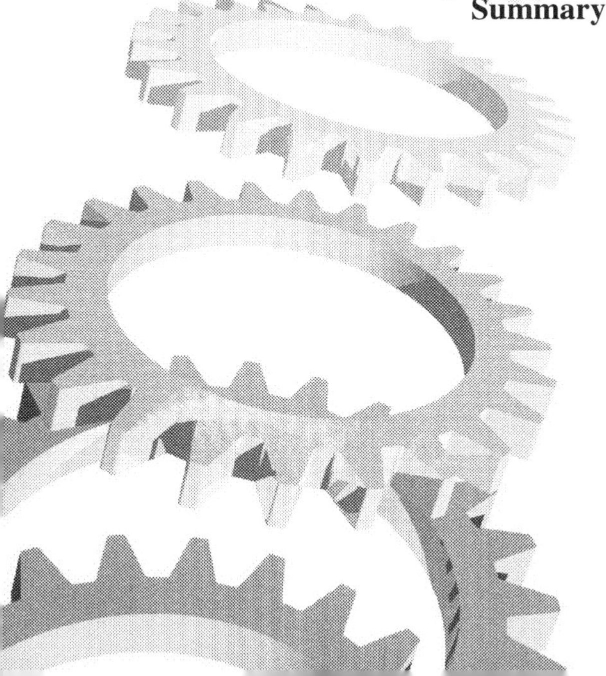

According to the Servlet specification: "A web application is a collection of servlets, HTML pages, classes, and other resources that make up a complete application on a web server. The web application can be bundled and run on multiple containers from multiple vendors."

Web applications are one of the more important concepts of the Servlet specification. Prior to version 2.2 (in which web applications were first introduced), the ability to develop a set of servlets and deploy them between servers (either using the same servlet container or containers from different vendors) was extremely difficult. You had to deal with issues such as the following:

- Where to place servlet classes
- How to supply initialization parameters for servlets
- Where to place other resources, such as HTML files and images
- How to configure the servlet container to route requests to the application
- How to physically copy files from one server to another
- How to install supporting libraries (JAR files)
- How to cleanly separate run-time environments (contexts) between applications

The notion of a web application has addressed all of these issues nicely, allowing you to achieve true application portability not only between servers, but also between servlet containers from different vendors.

Directory Structure

A web application contains a predefined directory structure that dictates where classes, libraries, and general resources are to reside. By dictating where different types of files are to reside, the servlet container can handle them appropriately. This enables servlet containers to find your classes by appending their location to the container ClassLoader so that classes can be resolved properly, for example.

The following table describes the general directory structure of a web application:

/	The web application root directory. General resources, such as HTML files, can be placed here. You are encouraged to create subdirectories beneath the root directory for better organization.
/WEB-INF	Contains the web application descriptor file named web.xml. This directory is not visible outside of the web application. In other words, a client cannot request to view the contents of the /WEB-INF directory (or any of its subdirectories).
/WEB-INF/classes	The location of any classes (including servlets) that are to be used by the web application. This is the root directory of any class packages.
/WEB-INF/lib	The location of any supporting libraries (JAR files). All JAR files found in this location will automatically be placed on the classpath. Servlets can be packaged in JAR files and placed here as well.

To further illustrate the directory structure of a web application, let's take a look at a simple example:

```
/index.html
/images/banner.gif
/images/logo.gif
/WEB-INF/web.xml
/WEB-INF/classes/com/omh/Properties.class
/WEB-INF/lib/jaxp.jar
/WEB-INF/lib/xalan.jar
```

This web application contains an HTML file at its root (index.html), which presumably references images in the /images directory. There is also a single class (most likely a servlet) in /WEB-INF/classes, as well as two supporting library JAR files in /WEB-INF/lib.

This entire directory structure would then be mapped within the servlet container to receive requests that begin with some prefix. For example, if the previous directory structure was found at /usr/home/sample-app, you might map any requests that contain the prefix of /sample-app to be routed to the web application rooted at /usr/home/sample-app. Servlet containers vary in how this is done. Tomcat 4.0 allows you to simply create a subdirectory under the /webapps directory from the Tomcat home. The web application would then take on the name of the directory name that you create. For example, the following directory structure under the Tomcat home would result in a web application named sample-app:

```
/webapps/sample-app/index.html
/webapps/sample-app/images/banner.gif
```

```
/webapps/sample-app/images/logo.gif
/webapps/sample-app/WEB-INF/web.xml
/webapps/sample-app/WEB-INF/classes/com/omh/Properties.class
/webapps/sample-app/WEB-INF/lib/jaxp.jar
/webapps/sample-app/WEB-INF/lib/xalan.jar
```

The sample-app web application would be started given its own context, meaning that its run-time environment would be separate from all other web applications. This does not mean that it would necessarily be running in its own Java Virtual Machine, but rather that the web application would not have direct knowledge or access to resources in other web applications. In the previous example, any HTTP request that started with the prefix /sample-app would be routed to the sample-app web application. Using Tomcat, you could access the index.html in the sample-app web application by requesting the URL:

```
http://localhost:8080/sample-app/index.html
```

Web Application Archive: WAR Files

Another great feature of web applications is the ability to bundle all the files together in a portable collection. This collection, known as a WAR file, is simply a JAR file that has its extension changed to .war.

It is great to be able to develop servlets within a web application directory, but when you are ready to deploy your application onto a production server, you certainly don't want to have to mess with all of those files. This is where the WAR file comes in. You can simply use the jar tool to create a new WAR file containing all of your resources and place the single WAR file directly into a running servlet container. The servlet container should recognize the new WAR file and automatically create a new mapping to handle incoming requests. Some servlet containers can run the web application directly out of the WAR file, while others may explode the WAR file on disk; it doesn't really matter. Note also that if you replace the WAR file with a newer version, the servlet container, according to the specification, is supposed to restart the web application with the new files contained within the WAR file. Not being forced to stop and restart the server just to deploy a new web application is a great thing!

For example, to create a new WAR file for our previous sample-app application, you can use the jar tool provided with the Java Development Kit:

```
jar -cf sample-app.war *
```

This will create a new archive file named sample-app.war that contains all the files from the current directory. The jar tool is recursive, so it would include any files contained within any subdirectories, as well. Note that you need to invoke the jar command from the root directory of the web application.

Deployment Descriptor

At the heart of every web application is its deployment descriptor. This descriptor, named web.xml, provides the configuration information necessary for a servlet container to properly load and initialize the web application. You can think of the deployment descriptor as the glue that holds all of the various components of the web application together.

As you can tell by its name, web.xml contains XML elements that describe the web application to the servlet container. All valid web.xml files must contain the following elements:

```
<!DOCTYPE web-app
    PUBLIC "-//Sun Microsystems, Inc.//DTD Web Application 2.3//EN"
    "http://java.sun.com/dtd/web-app_2_3.dtd">
<web-app>
</web-app>
```

The DOCTYPE element contains a reference to the DTD file that describes the XML grammar of the deployment descriptor. The full DTD is provided in Appendix B.

Within the <web-app> element, you will find other elements that describe various aspects of the web application. It is extremely important to note that you should place elements within web.xml in the same order as they are found in the DTD, to maintain portability between servlet containers; most validating parsers require that the order be preserved. In the following sections, I will present the various elements of the web application in their proper order. Since the web application descriptor is well-formed XML, most elements are self-describing and, in many cases, I will just be elaborating on the obvious.

Web Application Properties

The following elements describe general attributes of the web application (or context).

<icon>

This optional element defines a small and/or large icon that can be used by graphical tools that reference the web application:

```
<icon>
  <small-icon>/images/small.gif</small-icon>
  <large-icon>/images/large.gif</large-icon>
</icon>
```

The locations of the icon images are relative paths within the web application directory structure.

<display-name>

This optional element contains the name of the web application that will be used by management or deployment tools. The display-name element is also used by the ServletContext.getServletContextName() method, which follows.

```
<display-name>
  My sample web application
</display-name>
```

<description>

This optional element, shown next, is also used by tools to provide a more meaningful description of the web application.

```
<description>
  This sample web application illustrates web.xml
</description>
```

<distributable>

The presence of this optional element notifies the servlet container that this web application can be distributed between multiple nodes in a cluster.

```
<distributable/>
```

The ability to be distributed must be accounted for by the web application developer. Tomcat requires that any distributable web applications must place only serializable objects in the ServletContext, but doing so does not guarantee a well-behaved distributed application. You should also consider the following issues:

- Different instances of your servlet will be running on different JVMs. Avoid using instance or static variables to store servlet state.
- Different instances of your web application, and thus the ServletContext, will be running on different JVMs. Do not use the ServletContext to store application state. Consider using an external database.
- As mentioned, any session properties should be marked as serializable. Also remember that session property binding and unbinding can happen on different JVMs.
- Be careful about relying on synchronized blocks of code; synchronization only applies to the local JVM and not across multiple JVMs.

Context Initialization Parameters

Context initialization parameters can be specified in web.xml via the context-param element. These initialization parameters are available from the ServletContext object via the getInitParameter() method. Initialization parameters are available to any objects that have access to the ServletContext, such as servlets, filters, and application event listeners.

<context-param>

This optional element defines the name, value, and optional description of the context initialization parameter. Any number of context-param elements may be specified.

```
<context-param>
  <param-name>maxThings</param-name>
  <param-value>100</param-value>
  <description>The maximum number of things</description>
</context-param>

<context-param>
  <param-name>Author</param-name>
  <param-value>Karl Moss</param-value>
</context-param>
```

The following servlet will gather all the web application properties, including the servlet context initialization parameters, and create a web page:

```
package com.omh.webapps;

import javax.servlet.*;
import javax.servlet.http.*;
import java.io.*;
import java.util.*;

public class WebAppProperties
        extends HttpServlet
{
    public void doGet(HttpServletRequest req,
                      HttpServletResponse resp)
        throws ServletException, IOException
    {
        resp.setContentType("text/html");

        // Get an output stream that takes into account
        // the proper character encoding
        PrintWriter out = resp.getWriter();

        // Get the context
        ServletContext context = getServletContext();

        // Output the web application name
        String displayName = context.getServletContextName();
        if (displayName == null)
        {
            displayName = "(no display-name element defined)";
        }

        out.println("<html>");
        out.println("<head>");
        out.println("<title>Web Application Properties");
        out.println("</title>");
        out.println("</head><body>");
        out.println("<h1>Web Application Properties</h2>");
        out.println("<br>Name: " + displayName);
        out.println("<br>Context: " + req.getContextPath());

        // Create a table with all of the servlet context
        // initialization parameters
        out.println("<h2><center>");
        out.println("Initialization Parameters</center></h2>");
```

```
        out.println("<br>");

        out.println("<center><table border width=80%>");

        Enumeration enum = context.getInitParameterNames();

        while (enum.hasMoreElements()) {
          String name = (String) enum.nextElement();
          out.println("<tr>");
          out.println("<td>" + name + "</td>");
          out.println("<td>" +
                  context.getInitParameter(name) + "</td>");
          out.println("</tr>");
        }
        out.println("</table></center>");

        out.println("</body>");
        out.println("</html>");
        out.flush();
    }
}
```

The results of executing the servlet are as follows:

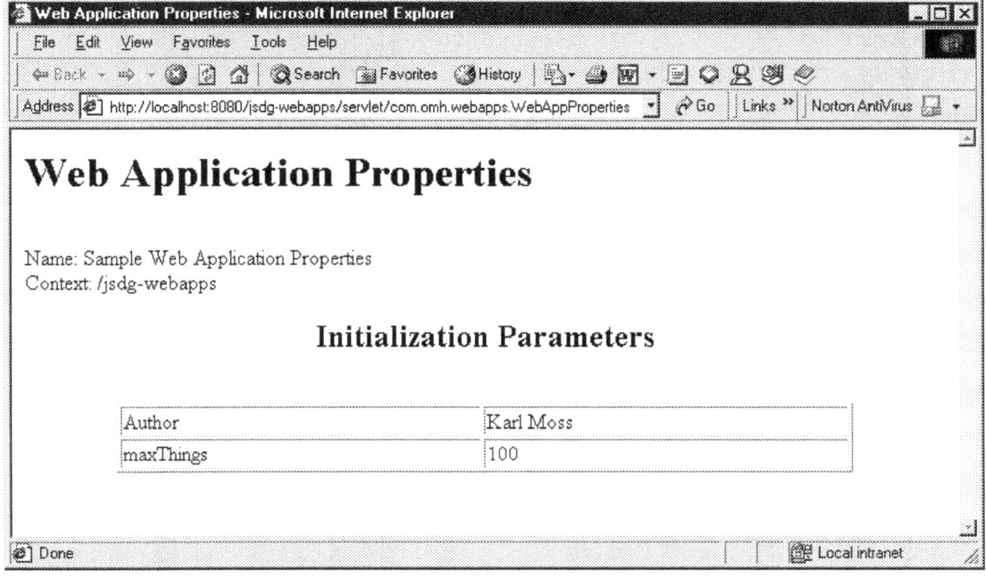

Filters

We'll be taking an in-depth look at filters in Chapter 6, but I'd like to provide an example of how filters are configured in web.xml so that you have a basic understanding of their use.

<filter>

The filter element contains elements that define a filter to the web application:

```
<filter>
  <icon>
    <small-icon>/images/small.gif</small-icon>
    <large-icon>/images/large.gif</large-icon>
  </icon>
  <filter-name>ucaseFilter</filter-name>
  <display-name>Uppercase Filter</display-name>
  <description>Converts all output to uppercase</description>
  <filter-class>com.omh.filters.UpperCaseFilter</filter-class>
  <init-param>
    <param-name>someParam</param-name>
    <param-value>someValue</param-value>
  </init-param>
</filter>
```

The icon, display-name, description, and init-param elements are all optional. You can specify any number of init-param elements.

<filter-mapping>

The filter-mapping element defines a mapping between either a URL or servlet name and an existing filter definition. The mapping is done by matching the filter-name elements:

```
<filter-mapping>
    <filter-name>ucaseFilter</filter-name>
    <url-pattern>/*</url-pattern>
  </filter-mapping>
```

The previous example will cause any requested URL that matches the url-pattern element to place the given filter on the invocation stack. Note that a wildcard of * can be used to match anything. You can also specify a single servlet that, when requested, will use the matching filter:

```
<filter-mapping>
<filter-name>ucaseFilter</filter-name>
  <servlet-name>Properties</servlet-name>
</filter-mapping>
```

Application Event Listeners

Application event listeners are the topic of Chapter 7, but I would like to provide an example of how listeners are configured in web.xml so that you have a grasp of their use.

<listener>

The listener element contains a mandatory listener-class element that defines the fully qualified class name of a class that implements one of the listener interfaces defined by the Servlet specification (starting with version 2.3). Any number of listener elements can be defined.

```
<listener>
  <listener-class>MyContextListener</listener-class>
</listener>
```

Servlets

Prior to the introduction of web applications, servlet configuration was done in a vendor-specific way. This meant that, to port servlets between containers, a tremendous amount of manual setup was required, which was very prone to error. The Servlet specification, by means of the web application, has solved this problem nicely by encapsulating the definition of a servlet within the deployment descriptor. The servlet definitions are carried along with the web application, which results in no additional work to port the servlet between vendor containers.

<servlet>

The minimum requirement for a servlet definition is the logical name of the servlet, given in the servlet-name element, as well as the fully qualified class name of the servlet (or, when using a JavaServer Page, a jsp-file element):

```
<servlet>
  <servlet-name>Properties</servlet-name>
  <servlet-class>com.omh.Properties</servlet-class>
</servlet>
```

After creating a servlet definition, you will still be required to define a servlet-mapping that will map a request URL with a particular servlet to invoke (we'll look at this later in this section). Some servlet containers, such as Tomcat, will allow servlets to be invoked by their logical servlet name by requesting the servlet invoker directly:

```
http://localhost:8080/servlet/Properties
```

It is important to note that the specification does not define this behavior, so if you are using some other servlet container, it may not function in this manner.

There are several other very important optional elements that you can use when defining a servlet. Along with the display-name and description elements that we have seen before, you can also define any number of servlet initialization parameters. These parameters can be accessed via the ServletConfig object that is provided during servlet initialization.

```
<servlet>
  <servlet-name>InitParams</servlet-name>
  <servlet-class>com.omh.webapps.ShowInitParams</servlet-class>
  <init-param>
    <param-name>Larry</param-name>
    <param-value>Cucumber</param-value>
  </init-param>
  <init-param>
    <param-name>Bob</param-name>
    <param-value>Tomato</param-value>
  </init-param>
</servlet>
```

The following servlet will gather all of the initialization parameters and format an HTML table to be viewed by the client:

```
package com.omh.webapps;

import javax.servlet.*;
import javax.servlet.http.*;
import java.io.*;
import java.util.*;

public class ShowInitParams
        extends HttpServlet
```

```
{
    public void doGet(HttpServletRequest req,
                      HttpServletResponse resp)
        throws ServletException, IOException
    {
        resp.setContentType("text/html");

        // Get an output stream that takes into account
        // the proper character encoding
        PrintWriter out = resp.getWriter();

        // Get the config object
        ServletConfig config = getServletConfig();

        out.println("<html>");
        out.println("<head>");
        out.println("<title>Servlet Initialization Parameters");
        out.println("</title>");
        out.println("</head><body>");

        // Create a table with all of the servlet
        // initialization parameters
        out.println("<h2><center>");
        out.println("Initialization Parameters</center></h2>");
        out.println("<br>");

        out.println("<center><table border width=80%>");

        Enumeration enum = config.getInitParameterNames();

        while (enum.hasMoreElements()) {
          String name = (String) enum.nextElement();
          out.println("<tr>");
          out.println("<td>" + name + "</td>");
          out.println("<td>" +
                  config.getInitParameter(name) + "</td>");
          out.println("</tr>");
        }
        out.println("</table></center>");

        out.println("</body>");
```

```
        out.println("</html>");
        out.flush();
    }
}
```

Executing the ShowInitParams servlet will result in the following:

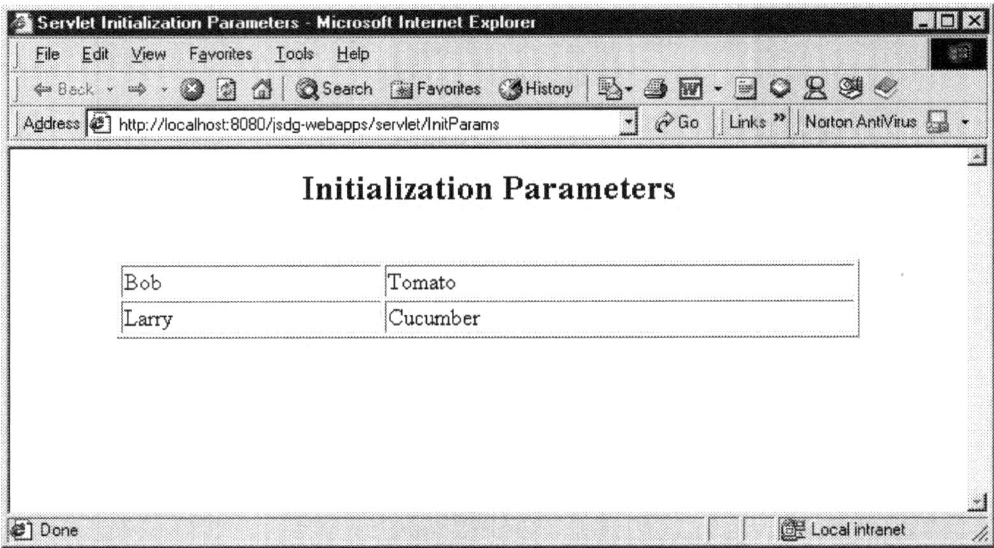

Another important optional element within the servlet definition is load-on-startup. If the load-on-startup element is present, the servlet container is supposed to load and initialize an instance of the servlet during the server startup sequence. The value of the load-on-startup element defines the load sequence; if the value is less than zero, then the servlet container can load the servlet whenever it chooses. If the value is greater than or equal to zero, the servlet container must load the servlet during startup. Servlets will be preloaded in order, with the servlet that has the lowest value loaded first, the next lowest value loaded second, and so on. If there are more than one load-on-startup elements with the same value, the servlet container is free to load them in any order.

```
<servlet>
  <servlet-name>Properties</servlet-name>
  <servlet-class>com.omh.Properties</servlet-class>
  <load-on-startup>5000</load-on-startup>
</servlet>
```

We'll be using the load-on-startup element later in Chapter 9 to start a JDBC Connection pool.

<servlet-mapping>

Once a servlet definition has been created, you then need to instruct the servlet container when the servlet should be invoked. This is done through defining a servlet-mapping, which links a request URL to the servlet that should be invoked.

In its simplest form, you can map a single URL to an individual servlet, such as the following:

```
<servlet-mapping>
  <servlet-name>InitParams</servlet-name>
  <url-pattern>/InitParams</url-pattern>
</servlet-mapping>
```

This mapping instructs the servlet container to invoke the servlet definition with a servlet-name of InitParams to be invoked whenever the URL /InitParams is requested:

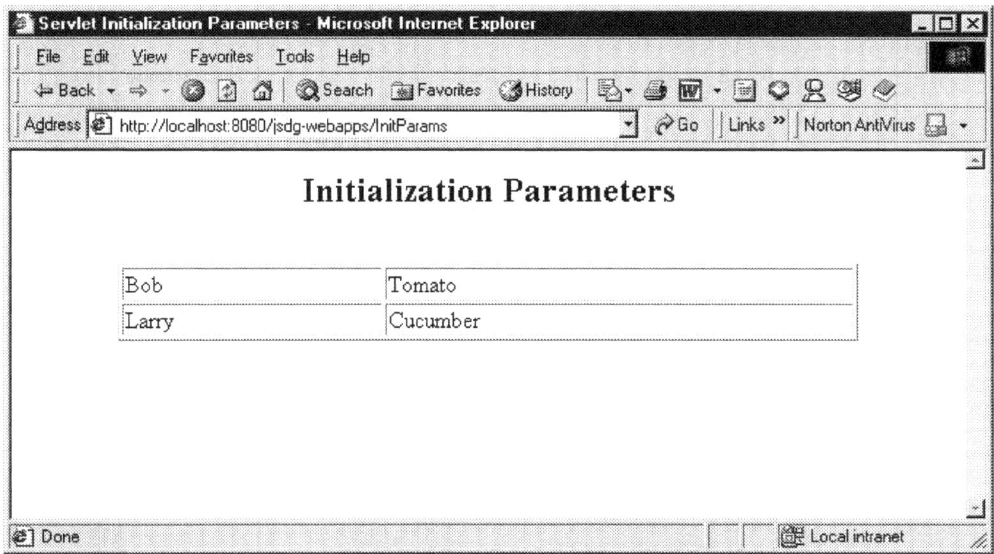

While this one-to-one relationship allows you to map logical URL names to servlets, the real power of using a url-pattern is in using a wildcard. The url-pattern allows you to use a trailing *, which indicates to match any request URL that starts with the url-pattern:

```
<servlet>
    <servlet-name>ProcessServlet</servlet-name>
    <servlet-class>com.omh.webapps.ProcessServlet</servlet-class>
  </servlet>

  <servlet-mapping>
    <servlet-name>ProcessServlet</servlet-name>
    <url-pattern>/process/*</url-pattern>
  </servlet-mapping>
```

Now, whenever the requested URL starts with /process/, the ProcessServlet will be invoked. The ProcessServlet simply outputs various elements of the requested URL, but it could be replaced with a servlet acting as a dispatcher that routes requests to other servlets by using the javax.servlet.RequestDispatcher.

```
package com.omh.webapps;

import javax.servlet.*;
import javax.servlet.http.*;
import java.io.*;
import java.util.*;

public class ProcessServlet
        extends HttpServlet
{
    public void doGet(HttpServletRequest req,
                      HttpServletResponse resp)
        throws ServletException, IOException
    {
        resp.setContentType("text/html");

        // Get an output stream that takes into account
        // the proper character encoding
        PrintWriter out = resp.getWriter();

        out.println("<html>");
        out.println("<head>");
```

```
        out.println("<title>Servlet Processor");
        out.println("</title>");
        out.println("</head><body>");

        out.println("<center><table border width=80%>");

        out.println("<tr><td>");
        out.println("Context Path</td><td>");
        out.println(req.getContextPath());
        out.println("</td></tr>");

        out.println("<tr><td>");
        out.println("Request URI</td><td>");
        out.println(req.getRequestURI());
        out.println("</td></tr>");

        out.println("<tr><td>");
        out.println("Servlet Path</td><td>");
        out.println(req.getServletPath());
        out.println("</td></tr>");

        out.println("<tr><td>");
        out.println("Path Info</td><td>");
        out.println(req.getPathInfo());
        out.println("</td></tr>");

        out.println("<tr><td>");
        out.println("Query String</td><td>");
        out.println(req.getQueryString());
        out.println("</td></tr>");

        out.println("</table></center>");

        out.println("</body>");
        out.println("</html>");
        out.flush();
    }
}
```

The two illustrations that follow show the ProcessServlet being requested with various URLs:

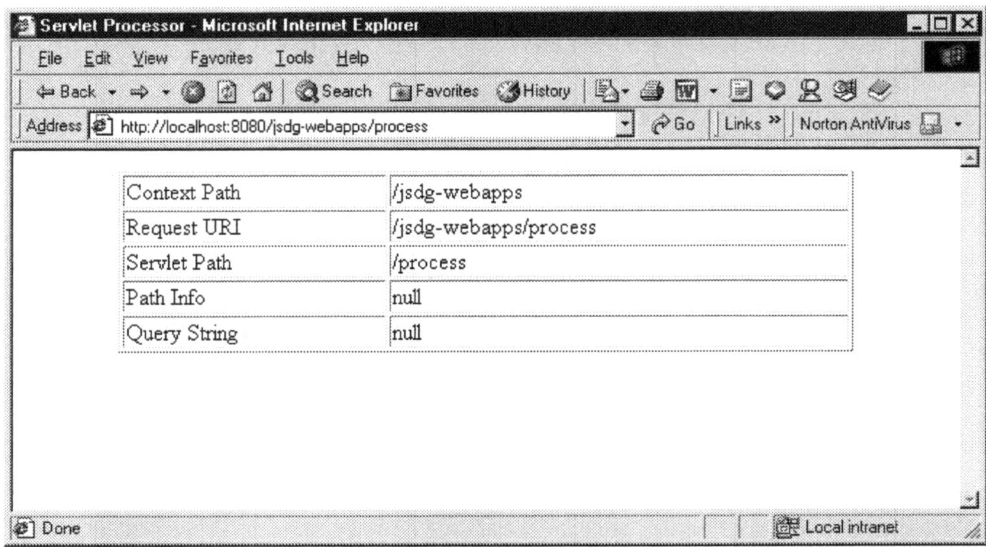

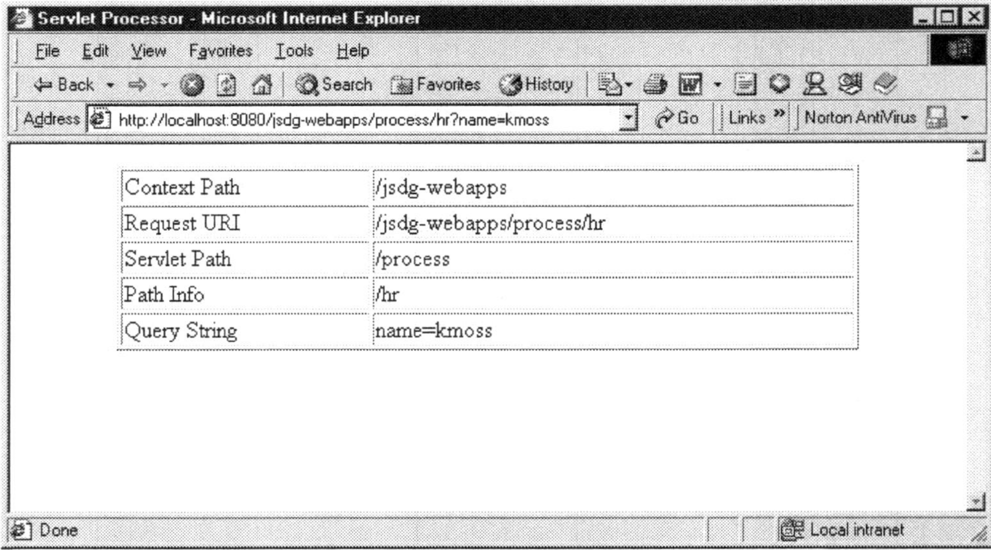

Session Properties

There is only one session attribute that can currently be defined in web.xml within the session-config element. The session-timeout specifies the number of minutes of inactivity before the servlet container invalidates a user session (remember that sessions were covered in Chapter 3). A negative value indicates that sessions should never be terminated by the servlet container due to a timeout.

```
<session-config>
  <session-timeout>30</session-timeout>
</session-config>
```

In future revisions of the specification, I can envision the session-config being expanded to include attributes for distributed applications.

MIME Mappings

The mime-mapping elements define a mapping between a file extension and its corresponding MIME type. These mappings are used by the ServletContext.getMimeType() method that returns the MIME type for a given filename. Remember that the MIME type is important to client browsers, so that they know what type of content is being returned by the server.

<mime-mapping>

Each mime-mapping element must contain an extension and mime-type element. You can specify any number of mime-mapping elements.

```
<mime-mapping>
  <extension>gif</extension>
  <mime-type>image/gif</mime-type>
</mime-mapping>
<mime-mapping>
  <extension>gz</extension>
  <mime-type>application/x-gzip</mime-type>
</mime-mapping>
<mime-mapping>
  <extension>htm</extension>
  <mime-type>text/html</mime-type>
</mime-mapping>
<mime-mapping>
  <extension>html</extension>
```

```
  <mime-type>text/html</mime-type>
</mime-mapping>
<mime-mapping>
  <extension>jar</extension>
  <mime-type>application/java-archive</mime-type>
</mime-mapping>
<mime-mapping>
  <extension>jpeg</extension>
  <mime-type>image/jpeg</mime-type>
</mime-mapping>
```

Welcome Files

As a web application developer, you can specify a list of filenames that will serve as a welcome file for requests made to a directory within your web application. The list of welcome files that you specify will apply to any directory request, not just the root directory.

<welcome-file-list>

The welcome-file-list element can contain any number of welcome-file elements that specify the resource that may be used as a welcome file in response to a directory request. For example:

```
<welcome-file-list>
  <welcome-file>
    index.html
  </welcome-file>
  <welcome-file>
    default.jsp
  </welcome-file>
</welcome-file-list>
```

This list specifies that either of the two files, index.html or default.jsp, can serve as a welcome file. The servlet container will check for index.html first and, if it exists, serve it to the client; otherwise, if default.jsp exists, it will be served. If no files in the welcome file list exist in the requested directory, the servlet container is free to return whatever it feels is appropriate. This may be a list of the files in the directory or a 404 (not found) response.

Consider the following web application structure:

```
/index.html
/images/header.gif
/images/footer.gif
/movies/default.jsp
/WEB-INF/web.xml
```

Assuming the welcome-file-list previously shown, with index.html and default.jsp, if a request is made to our web application (we'll assume it is called store) to view the root directory:

```
http://localhost:8080/store
```

the servlet container will check to see if the first welcome file in the list exists in the requested directory. In our case, it does, so index.html will be returned to the client (in actuality, you may be redirected to index.html, but you won't be able to tell the difference).

By the same token, if a request is made for the movies directory:

```
http://localhost:8080/store/movies
```

the servlet container will check for index.html, which does not exist. The container will move to the next welcome file in the list, default.jsp, and since it does exist, the JSP page will be invoked.

If a directory is requested that does not contain any of the welcome files defined in the welcome-file-list:

```
http://localhost:8080/store/images
```

the servlet container will either return a directory listing or simply return a status code of 404 (not found), effectively denying the client from browsing the directory.

Error Pages

Prior to the introduction of the web application, you, the servlet developer, had no control over the way error pages were returned to the client. Most web servers allow you to customize error pages depending upon the status code, but to do this in a generic way that worked with all web servers and servlet containers was impossible. Thanks to the Servlet specification, you now have very fine-grain control over the pages that are returned to the client in the event of an error.

<error-page>

The error-page element allows you to map either an exception type or error code to a URL that should be invoked. You can specify any number of error-page elements.

Let's first take a look at an error-page element that maps an error-code to a static HTML page:

```
<error-page>
  <error-code>404</error-code>xception-type>
  <location>
    /NotFound.html
  </location>
</error-page>
```

These elements will instruct the servlet container to return the page /NotFound.html, as specified in the location element, whenever an error-code of 404 is generated. All you need to do to test this is request a page that does not exist, and the servlet container will return your custom error page:

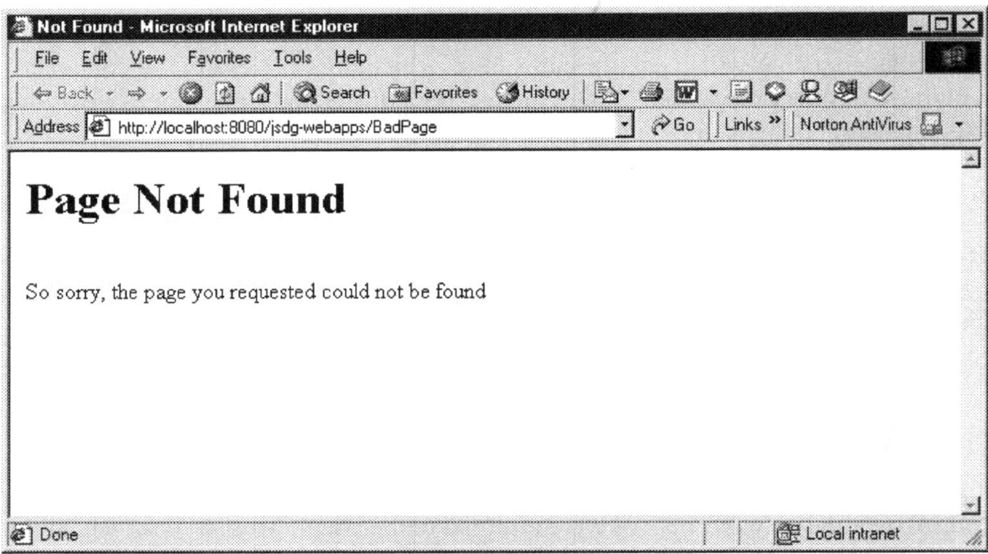

As previously mentioned, you could specify an exception-type element instead of an error-code. The exception-type defines the fully qualified package name of the exception type that you want to watch for and, if thrown, returns your own custom page:

```
<error-page>
  <exception-type>
    java.lang.NumberFormatException
  </exception-type>
  <location>
    /ServerError.html
  </location>
</error-page>
```

In this example, if a servlet throws a java.lang.NumberFormatException, the servlet container will check the list of error-page elements for a matching exception-type. If found, the page specified in the location element will be returned to the client. Let's invoke a servlet that simply throws a NumberFormatException:

```
package com.omh.webapps;

import javax.servlet.*;
import javax.servlet.http.*;
import java.io.*;
import java.util.*;

public class SendError
        extends HttpServlet
{
    public void doGet(HttpServletRequest req,
                      HttpServletResponse resp)
        throws ServletException, IOException
    {
        throw new NumberFormatException("Just kidding!");
    }
}
```

Requesting the SendError servlet will result in a NumberFormatException being thrown, which the servlet container will process using the error-page definitions, as follows:

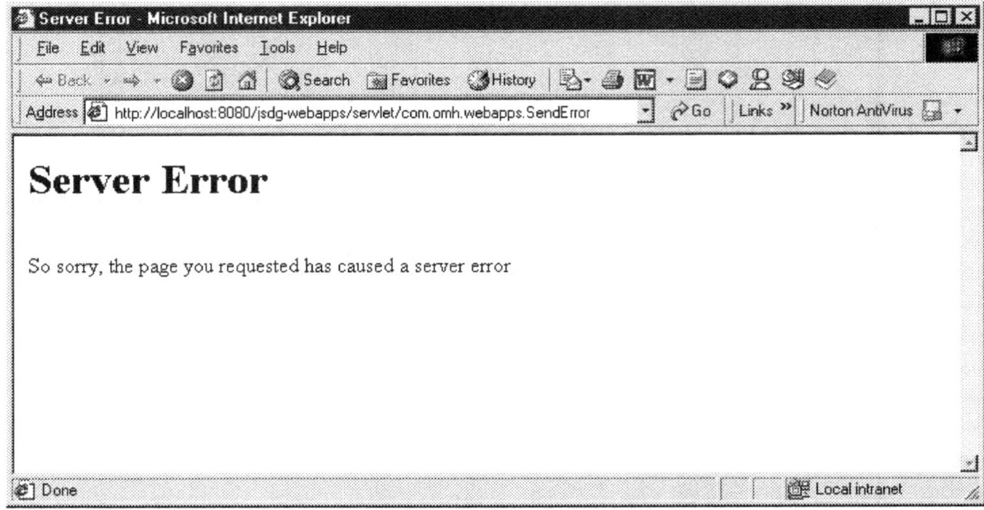

Providing the ability to return static error pages is great, but wouldn't it be nice to be able to customize the error pages on-the-fly with information about what caused the error? By specifying a servlet in the location element, you can generate the error page dynamically, and the Servlet specification provides some very useful request attributes that can be inspected for all of the pertinent information about what happened. The servlet container is required to add the following request attributes before invoking the page given in the location element:

Request Attribute Name	Object Type
javax.servlet.error.status_code	java.lang.Integer
javax.servlet.error.request_uri	java.lang.String
javax.servlet.error.servlet_name	java.lang.String
javax.servlet.error.message	java.lang.String
javax.servlet.error.exception_type	java.lang.Class
javax.servlet.error.exception	java.lang.Throwable

Let's take a look at a generic servlet that will format an error page and display all of the request attributes set by the servlet container:

```
package com.omh.webapps;

import javax.servlet.*;
import javax.servlet.http.*;
import java.io.*;
import java.util.*;

public class ErrorServlet
        extends HttpServlet
{
    public void doGet(HttpServletRequest req,
                      HttpServletResponse resp)
        throws ServletException, IOException
    {
        resp.setContentType("text/html");

        // Get an output stream that takes into account
        // the proper character encoding
        PrintWriter out = resp.getWriter();

        out.println("<html>");
        out.println("<head>");
        out.println("<title>Error Servlet");
        out.println("</title>");
        out.println("</head><body>");

        out.println("<center>The server has encountered an error!");
        out.println("<table border width=80%>");

        out.println("<tr><td>");
        out.println("Status code</td><td>");
        out.println(
                req.getAttribute("javax.servlet.error.status_code"));
        out.println("</td></tr>");

        out.println("<tr><td>");
        out.println("Request URI</td><td>");
        out.println(
                req.getAttribute("javax.servlet.error.request_uri"));
        out.println("</td></tr>");

        out.println("<tr><td>");
```

```
        out.println("Servlet name</td><td>");
        out.println(req.getAttribute("javax.servlet.error.servlet_name"));
        out.println("</td></tr>");

        out.println("<tr><td>");
        out.println("Message</td><td>");
        out.println(
                req.getAttribute("javax.servlet.error.message"));
        out.println("</td></tr>");

        out.println("<tr><td>");
        out.println("Exception type</td><td>");
        out.println(req.getAttribute("javax.servlet.error.exception_type"));
        out.println("</td></tr>");

        out.println("<tr><td>");
        out.println("</table></center>");

        // Output the stack trace if possible
        Throwable t =
             (Throwable) req.getAttribute("javax.servlet.error.exception");
        String trace = getStackTrace(t);
        if (trace != null)
        {
            out.println("<br><br><dir><pre>");
            out.println(trace);
            out.println("</pre></dir>");
        }

        out.println("</body>");
        out.println("</html>");
        out.flush();
    }

    /**
     * Captures an exception stack trace in a String
     */
    public static String getStackTrace(Throwable t)
    {
        String s = null;
        if (t != null)
        {
```

```
            // Create a writer to send the stack trace to
            CharArrayWriter w = new CharArrayWriter();
            PrintWriter out = new PrintWriter(w);
            t.printStackTrace(out);
            s = w.toString();
        }
        return s;
    }
}
```

This servlet will create a table that displays the request attribute values. Of note is the getStackTrace() method, which takes a Throwable object and converts the stack trace into a String that can then be printed to the output page.

Updating the error-page location elements to refer to the ErrorServlet gives us the ability to provide dynamic information about the cause of the error:

```
<servlet>
  <servlet-name>ErrorServlet</servlet-name>
  <servlet-class>com.omh.webapps.ErrorServlet</servlet-class>
</servlet>

<servlet-mapping>
  <servlet-name>ErrorServlet</servlet-name>
  <url-pattern>/ErrorServlet</url-pattern>
</servlet-mapping>

<error-page>
  <exception-type>
    java.lang.NumberFormatException
  </exception-type>
  <location>
    /ErrorServlet
  </location>
</error-page>

<error-page>
  <error-code>404</error-code>
  <location>
    /ErrorServlet
  </location>
</error-page>
```

The following illustrations show the custom error page in use. First we'll request a page that does not exist, resulting in a error code of 404:

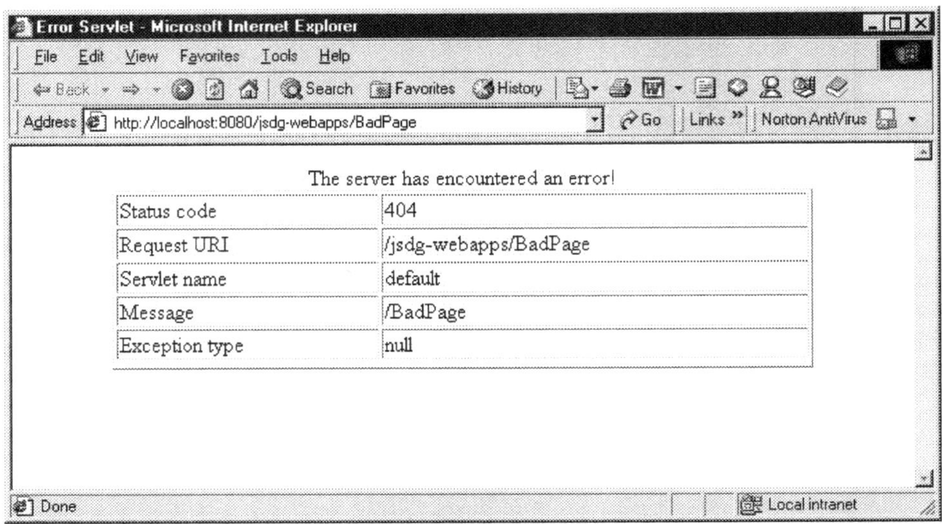

Next we'll request a servlet that purposefully throws a NumberFormatException, which will also invoke our custom error page:

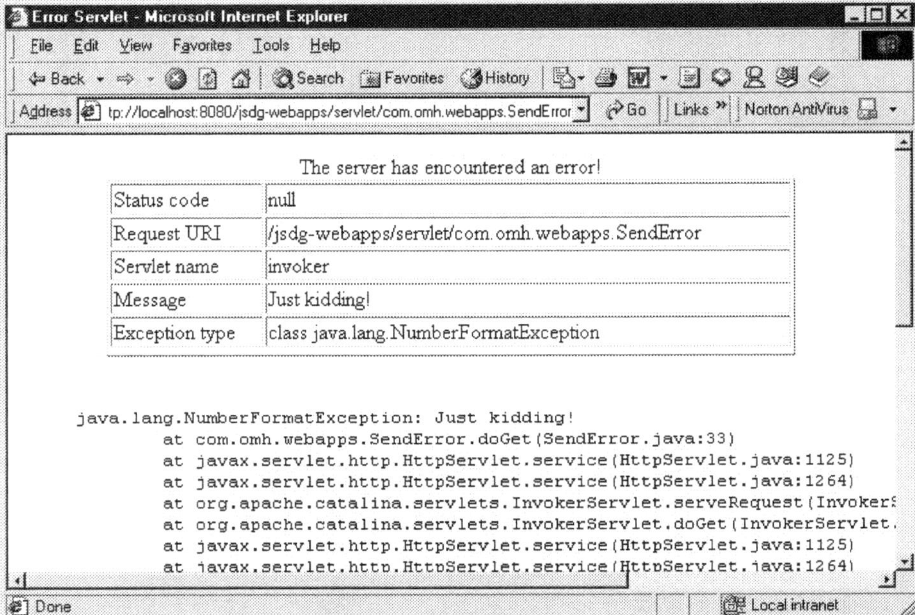

Declarative Security

Another big addition with the advent of web applications is servlet container-managed security. Back in Chapter 4 we looked at how to manage security for yourself. Now let's take a look at how simple it is to add security to your web applications, as well as some of the drawbacks to doing so.

<security-constraint>

In essence, servlet container-provided security is done by declaring what resources you would like to protect, and who has access to those resources:

```
<security-constraint>
  <web-resource-collection>
    <web-resource-name>
      Payroll Application
    </web-resource-name>
    <description>
      Protects the Payroll Application
    </description>
    <url-pattern>
      /payroll/*
    </url-pattern>
    <http-method>
      GET
    </http-method>
    <http-method>
      POST
    </http-method>
  </web-resource-collection>
  <auth-constraint>
    <role-name>
      payroll
    </role-name>
    <role-name>
      manager
    </role-name>
  </auth-constraint>
</security-constraint>
```

The security-constraint element contains nested elements that define what resources should be protected and who is allowed to access those resources. The web-resource-collection element defines the url-pattern to protect; this can be a single servlet or a group of resources within a particular directory. You can further clarify how the resources are to be protected by using http-method elements. Only a request that uses one of the provided HTTP methods will utilize the security-constraint. Omitting all http-methods implies that all HTTP methods will apply.

The security-constraint also defines which users are allowed access to the protected resources though the use of role-name elements. The security scheme defined by the Servlet specification is role-based, meaning that you assign users to act in certain roles (such as manager, user, administrator, and so on). Only users who belong to one of the roles listed in the role-name elements will be allowed access to the resources defined in the resource-collection.

Looking at the example security-constraint definition, the servlet container will do the following:

- Place a security constraint on all resources in the /payroll directory
- Only constrain the resources when the client uses an HTTP GET or POST method
- Only allow access to the resources to users who belong to either the manager or payroll role

<login-config>

The Servlet specification also gives you flexibility with regard to how user credentials (such as username and password) will be collected by the client. The specification defines four different authentication methods:

- HTTP basic authentication
- HTTP digest authentication
- HTTPS client authentication
- HTML form-based authentication

Depending upon the servlet container you are using, some, if not all, of these methods may be supported. All servlet containers, to my knowledge, provide HTTP basic and form-based authentication. Digest and HTTPS client authentication may be supported; if you are interested in using one of these techniques, consult the documentation provided by your servlet container vendor and ensure that your browser also supports it. We'll be looking at examples of HTTP basic and form-based authentication in detail.

In Chapter 4, we discussed the pros and cons of using HTTP basic authentication. HTTP basic authentication utilizes the built-in authentication mechanism defined by

HTTP to gather user credentials, namely the username and password. Once the credentials are gathered, the client transmits the data to the server in a Base64-encoded header, where it is decoded and validated by the server. How are the username and password validated? Well, this is where I think that the Servlet specification falls short. There is no generic way to define the user database; you must rely on the specific implementation of the servlet container you are using. Tomcat, for example, stores the username, password, and role information in an XML file named conf/tomcat-users.xml. Other servlet containers will utilize different files or perhaps provide a means to use a database or other operating system-specific authentication. Let's take a look at the default users file provided by Tomcat:

```
<!--
  NOTE:  By default, no user is included in the "manager" role required
  to operate the "/manager" web application.  If you wish to use this app,
  you must define such a user - the username and password are arbitrary.
-->
<tomcat-users>
  <user name="tomcat" password="tomcat" roles="tomcat" />
  <user name="role1"  password="tomcat" roles="role1"  />
  <user name="both"   password="tomcat" roles="tomcat,role1" />
</tomcat-users>
```

I added a new user for testing:

```
<user name="karlmoss"   password="jsdg" roles="manager" />
```

Now let's focus on the login-config element, which defines which type of authentication the servlet container should use when a user has requested a resource with a security constraint in place:

```
<login-config>
  <auth-method>
    BASIC
  </auth-method>
  <realm-name>
    Java Servlets Developer's Guide
  </realm-name>
</login-config>
```

Here, we are notifying the servlet container that we want to use HTTP basic authentication, which is defined by the auth-method element. The realm-name will be used when presenting the user with the dialog box to collect the username and password. If we were to request the following URL, which has a security-constraint placed upon it:

```
http://localhost:8080/jsdg-webapps/payroll/index.html
```

the servlet container will force the browser to collect the username and password for validation:

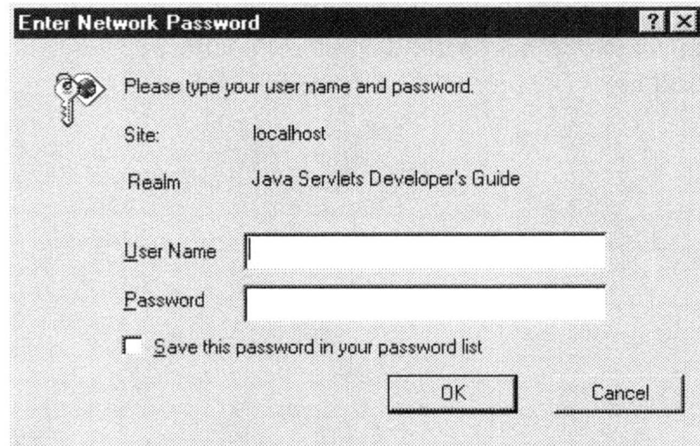

Entering an invalid username and password will result in the dialog box being displayed again. Once the username and password have been authenticated, the servlet container will check the role (or roles) that the user is in against the list of role-name elements defined for the security-constraint. If the user does not belong in a role that is defined, then access is denied, resulting in an "Unauthorized" message being returned. If you enter the username "karlmoss" and the password "jsdg" (as defined in tomcat-users.xml), you will be properly authenticated to the server. User "karlmoss" is also part of the "manager" role, which is one of the roles listed in the security-constraint. This will cause the server to authorize you to view the requested resource, and it will be displayed, as follows.

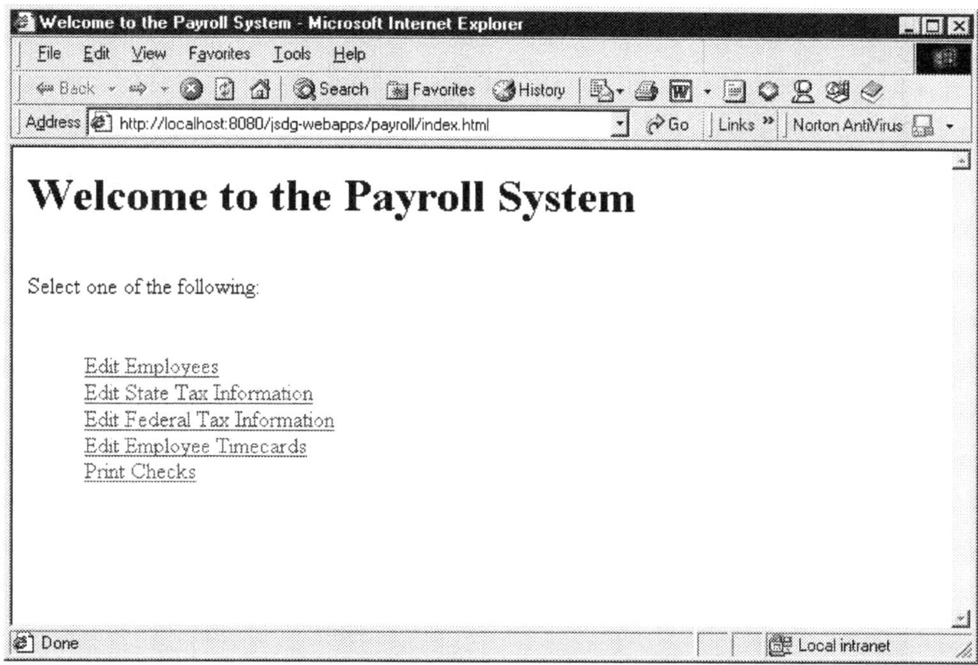

That's nice, but what if you want to customize the logon page to include a company logo or help information? This is what the HTTP form-based authentication method is for. Via web.xml, you can define the login page that will be sent to the user when attempting to access a constrained resource:

```
<login-config>
  <auth-method>
    FORM
  </auth-method>
  <form-login-config>
    <form-login-page>
      /Login.html
    </form-login-page>
    <form-error-page>
      /LoginError.html
    </form-error-page>
  </form-login-config>
</login-config>
```

The auth-method has now been changed to "FORM" and a new form-login-config element has been provided. The form-login-config defines the login page and, if the user enters an invalid password, the error page that will used. There are a few rules regarding the form-login-page:

- The username input field must be named "j_username"
- The password input field must be named "j_password"
- The form must use the POST method
- The form action must be "j_security_check"

These rules are in place so that the servlet container will be able to recognize a request for authentication, and how to get the data from the submitted form data. As long as you follow these rules, your form login page can be as creative as you like. Here's an example of a rather simple, and boring, login page:

```
<html>
<head>
<title>Login Form</title>
</head>
<body>
<center>
<h1>Please Login</h1>
<br>
<form method="POST" action="j_security_check">
Username: <input type="text" name="j_username"><br>
Password: <input type="password" name="j_password"><br>
<br>
<input type="submit" value="Login">
<input type="reset"  value="Reset">

</form>
</center>
</body>
</html>
```

If you were to request the same resource as before, with the new login-config definition in place, you would be prompted for your username and password via an HTML form, such as the example that follows:

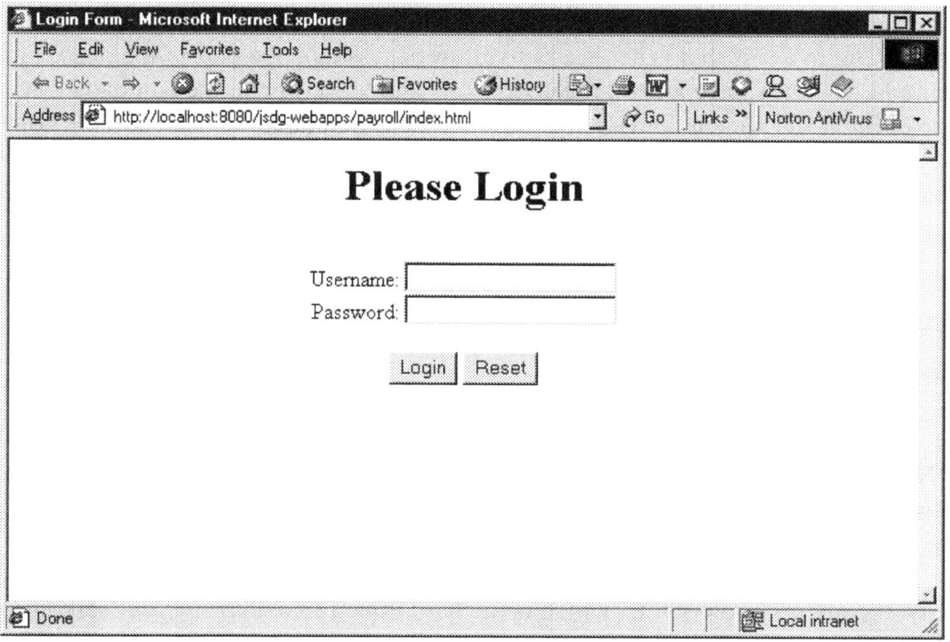

After entering a username and password, you will submit the form to the server for authentication and authorization. Just as was pointed out in Chapter 4, the huge drawback to using HTML forms is that the username and password will be transmitted in clear text (meaning not encoded) to the server. It would not be difficult for someone to capture the transmission and steal your username and password.

Before moving on, I would really encourage you to read the "Security" section of the Servlet specification. The specification does a good job of explaining key concepts and provides additional examples of how to secure your web application.

Programmatic Security

There is one last aspect of security that I would like to touch on, and that is the subject of programmatic security. So far, we have seen how to protect whole resources from being accessed, but what if you have a page that you want to customize depending upon the type of user that has requested it? This is where programmatic security comes in. The Servlet specification defines several methods as part of the javax.servlet.http.HttpServletRequest interface:

- getRemoteUser()
- isUserInRole()
- getUserPrincipal()

Using these methods, you can determine who is visiting your servlet, and whether they belong to a role that is necessary to allow access to some part of the page. For example, you may have an employee directory that everyone in the company can access, but if the person viewing the page is a manager, you may also add the home phone number of each employee to the list. In your servlet, you can simply place a condition to check for the authenticated user role:

```
if (request.isUserInRole("mgr"))
{
    // Do something extra
}
```

Note that there must be an authenticated user logged on to the web application before this will work, so you must have security constraints in place to force a logon.

Notice that I used the role "mgr" in the previous example. As part of the servlet definition, you can also create a cross-reference of role names. The reason for this is that if the servlet container uses a different role name than you have hard-coded in your servlet, you can easily create a mapping between the two. The security-role-ref element contains a role-name, which is the hard-coded role name in your servlet, and a role-link, which is the role name that the servlet container uses.

To illustrate programmatic security, let's take a look at a simple example. We'll create an EmployeeServlet that will generate a list of employees. We only want managers to be able to see the home phone number of the employees. To accomplish this, we'll use the isUserInRole() method.

```
package com.omh.webapps;

import javax.servlet.*;
import javax.servlet.http.*;
import java.util.*;
import java.io.*;

public class EmployeeServlet
        extends HttpServlet
{
    public void doGet(HttpServletRequest req,
                      HttpServletResponse resp)
        throws ServletException, IOException
    {
        resp.setContentType("text/html");

        // Get an output stream that takes into account
        // the proper character encoding
```

```
PrintWriter out = resp.getWriter();

// Create an array of employee info. This
// should be read out of a database
EmployeeInfo[] info = new EmployeeInfo[3];
info[0] = new EmployeeInfo("Bob", "498", "555-3029");
info[1] = new EmployeeInfo("Larry", "315", "555-5092");
info[2] = new EmployeeInfo("George", "982", "555-9286");

// Now check to see if we are being requested by
// a manager. If so, add the home phone number
// column in the employee table
boolean manager = req.isUserInRole("mgr");

out.println("<html>");
out.println("<head>");
out.println("<title>Employee List");
out.println("</title>");
out.println("</head><body>");

out.println("<center>");
out.println("Welcome, " + req.getRemoteUser());
out.println("<br><br>");
out.println("<table border width=80%>");

out.println("<tr><th>Name</th>" +
            "<th>Extension</th>");
if (manager)
{
    out.println("<th>Home Phone</th>");
}
out.println("</tr>");

for (int i = 0; i < info.length; i++)
{
    out.println("<tr>");
    out.println("<td>" + info[i].name + "</td>");
    out.println("<td>" + info[i].extension + "</td>");
    if (manager)
    {
        out.println("<td>" + info[i].homePhone + "</td>");
    }
    out.println("<tr>");
}
```

```
        out.println("</table></center>");

        out.println("</body>");
        out.println("</html>");
        out.flush();
    }
}
```

The list of employees is hard-coded in this example, but could very easily be read from a database (as we'll do in Chapter 9).

Before we can use this servlet, we need to set up the servlet alias and servlet-mapping entries in web.xml:

```
<servlet>
  <servlet-name>EmployeeListing</servlet-name>
  <servlet-class>com.omh.webapps.EmployeeServlet</servlet-class>
  <security-role-ref>
    <role-name>
      mgr
    </role-name>
    <role-link>
      manager
    </role-link>
  </security-role-ref>
</servlet>

<servlet-mapping>
  <servlet-name>EmployeeListing</servlet-name>
  <url-pattern>/hr/EmployeeListing</url-pattern>
</servlet-mapping>
```

Notice the security-role-ref element within the servlet alias. This cross-references the hard-coded "mgr" role name that the EmployeeServlet uses with the role name that the servlet container will use, which is "manager".

Now we need to protect our servlet so that the servlet container will authenticate a user. If you requested the servlet without first authenticating, isUserInRole() will always return false.

```
<security-constraint>
  <web-resource-collection>
    <web-resource-name>
```

```
      Human Resources Application
    </web-resource-name>
    <description>
      Protects the Human Resources Application
    </description>
    <url-pattern>
      /hr/*
    </url-pattern>
  </web-resource-collection>
  <auth-constraint>
    <role-name>
      user
    </role-name>
    <role-name>
      manager
    </role-name>
  </auth-constraint>
</security-constraint>
```

Let's first request our employee listing servlet using a normal "user". I've updated the tomcat-users.xml file so that the user "tomcat" is part of the "user" role. Requesting the servlet and logging on as "tomcat" results in the following:

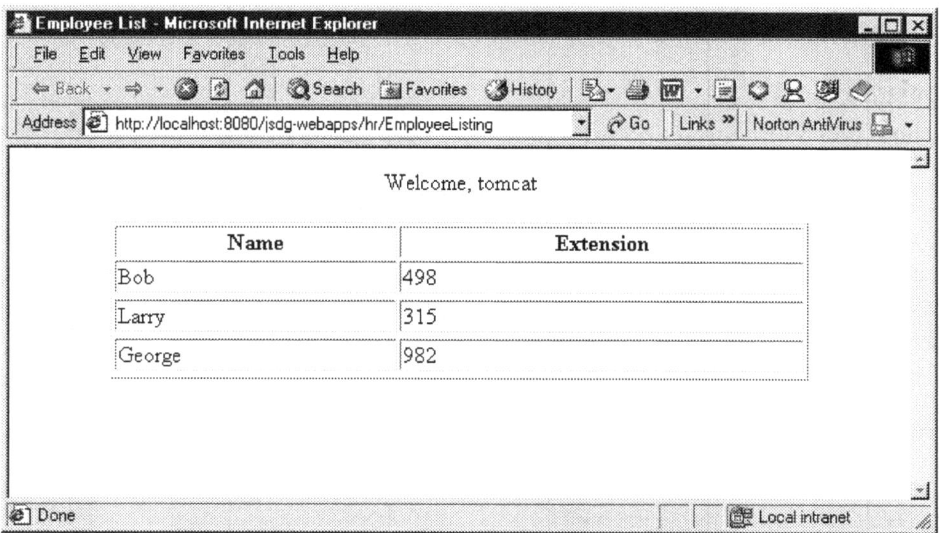

Just the employee name and extension are provided, not the home phone number. If we open another browser session and log on as "karlmoss", who is a manager, we'll get:

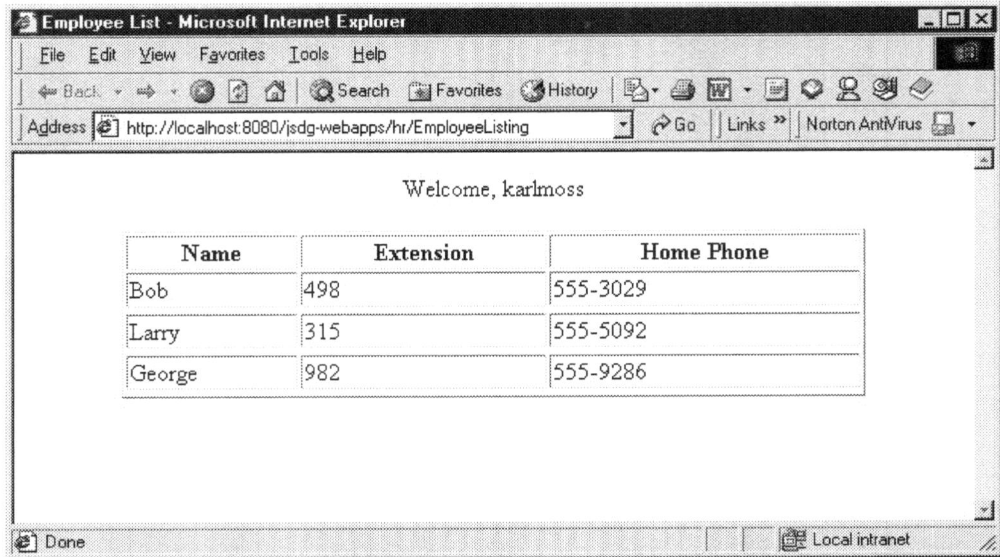

Same servlet, but this time the home phone number is included in the table.

Logging Off

So, how do you log off a user after they have been authenticated? Since user authentication data is stored as session attributes, you can simply invalidate the current session. This works well if you are using HTML form-based authentication, but unfortunately will not work when using HTTP basic authentication. The reason is that the authentication information is sent with each request (in the Authorization header), so even if you invalidate the session, the servlet container will reauthenticate the user when it sees the Authorization header.

Here's a simple servlet that logs off the current user:

```
package com.omh.webapps;

import javax.servlet.*;
import javax.servlet.http.*;
import java.util.*;
import java.io.*;
```

```
public class Logoff
        extends HttpServlet
{
    public void doGet(HttpServletRequest req,
                      HttpServletResponse resp)
        throws ServletException, IOException
    {
        resp.setContentType("text/html");

        // Get an output stream that takes into account
        // the proper character encoding
        PrintWriter out = resp.getWriter();

        HttpSession session = req.getSession();
        session.invalidate();

        out.println("Goodbye! You are now logged off");
    }
}
```

Summary

Web applications are one of the most powerful features of the Servlet specification. You can bundle all the files that are a part of your application into a web application archive (WAR), which enables you to easily port and deploy your servlets to other servers and servlet containers.

The heart of the web application is the descriptor file. This file, web.xml, allows you to describe your web application to the servlet container, including filters, listeners, servlets, servlet mappings, welcome files, and security constraints. Mastering the web application descriptor is crucial to developing successful web applications.

CHAPTER

6

Filters

IN THIS CHAPTER:

Your First Filter

Modifying the Response

Using XSLT to Transform Stock Quote Data

Summary

Filters are a powerful feature first introduced in version 2.3 of the Servlet API. Filters allow you to write a software component that can then be placed into the request and response flow of a servlet or group of servlets. A filter is not a servlet; filters do not typically create a response to a request but, rather, either modify or inspect the request to a servlet or response from a servlet. Note that you not only can configure filters to act upon servlet requests, but can also apply them to the access of any resource (such as static files).

Like servlets, filters have a specification-defined lifecycle:

- Filters are initialized by calling their init() method. The init() method is supplied with a FilterConfig object that allows the filter to access initialization parameters as well as reference to the ServletContext.
- The doFilter() method of the filter is invoked during the request processing of a resource. It is in the doFilter() method that you can inspect the request, modify request headers, modify the response, or skip the processing of the underlying resource altogether.
- The destroy() method is called when the filter is destroyed.

So what types of filters can you create? The servlet specification gives the following list of suggestions:

- **Authentication filters** If you think back to Chapter 4, you could very easily adapt the security examples to use a filter instead of a servlet.
- **Logging and auditing filters** The first filter you will create in this chapter will log the access of a servlet and supply the elapsed execution time.
- **Image conversion filters** Filters can very easily modify the output of a request, such as converting a JPEG image into GIF format.
- **Data compression filters** Tomcat supplies the code for a compression filter (named CompressionFilter).
- **Tokenizing filters** WML (Wireless Markup Language) is a perfect example of tokenizing; a tokenizing compiler converts tags into a single byte token in an effort to compress the response.
- **Filters that trigger resource access events** You may want to log the fact that certain resources are being requested.

- **XSLT filters** The last example in this chapter will illustrate the power of using filters to translate XML output into any number of target clients using XSL templates.

What makes a filter a filter? You must implement the javax.servlet.Filter interface, which includes the init(), doFilter(), and destroy() lifecycle events, and then configure the filter within a web application to place itself into the process chain of a resource request.

Your First Filter

Let's take a look at a very simple filter that will log the execution time of any requested resource:

```
package com.omh.filters;

import javax.servlet.*;
import javax.servlet.http.*;
import java.io.*;

/**
 * Simple filter for measuring servlet response times
 */
public class ResponseTimerFilter
        implements Filter
{
    protected FilterConfig config;

    public void init(FilterConfig config)
        throws ServletException
    {
        // Save the config object
        this.config = config;
    }

    public void destroy()
    {
    }

    public void doFilter(ServletRequest request,
```

```
                              ServletResponse response,
                              FilterChain chain)
            throws ServletException, IOException
        {
            // Save the start time
            long startTime = System.currentTimeMillis();

            // Invoke the next filter/servlet in the chain
            chain.doFilter(request, response);

            // Capture the elapsed time
            long elapsed = System.currentTimeMillis() - startTime;

            // Figure out what was requested. If we are not
            // processing an HTTP request just default the
            // name to servlet
            String name = "servlet";
            if (request instanceof HttpServletRequest)
            {
                name = ((HttpServletRequest) request).getRequestURI();
            }

            // Output the time
            config.getServletContext().log(name +
                    " took " + elapsed + " ms");
        }
    }
```

The init() method simply saves a reference to the FilterConfig object (since we'll use it later to access the ServletContext log() method). There is nothing to do in destroy(), since we don't have anything to gracefully tear down when the servlet container is done with the filter, but we must provide an empty implementation in order to fully implement the Filter interface.

The doFilter() method is where all the action is found. For our simple ResponseTimeFilter, all we do is save the current clock time, call the next filter in the chain (which will ultimately invoke the requested servlet or resource), and log the elapsed time of the request. After requesting any resource, the servlet container log file will contain something like the following:

```
2001-10-28 16:41:07 /jsdg-filters/Properties took 110 ms
```

In this case, I requested the Properties servlet using Tomcat 4.0. Note that we did nothing to modify the flow or content of the request or response, but this is certainly possible using filters (as we'll see next).

To notify the servlet container that you have a filter, you must add a filter definition and filter mapping to web.xml:

```
<filter>
  <filter-name>Timing Filter</filter-name>
  <filter-class>com.omh.filters.ResponseTimerFilter</filter-class>
</filter>

<filter-mapping>
  <filter-name>Timing Filter</filter-name>
  <url-pattern>/*</url-pattern>
</filter-mapping>
```

The <filter> element defines the name and fully qualified class name of the filter, while <filter-mapping> defines a URL pattern that, when matched, will have the corresponding filter placed in its execution stream. A single servlet name can be specified instead, which we'll use in the last example in the chapter. When using filters that overlap (meaning that more than one filter will be placed in the request chain), the filters will be applied in the same order in which they appear in web.xml.

Note that a complete web application can be found at www.servletguru.com, which contains all the filter source code as well as a complete web application descriptor (web.xml). The web application is named jsdg-filters.jar.

Modifying the Response

What if you want to modify the response of a servlet? The UpperCaseFilter does just this, changing the response of a servlet to all uppercase:

```
package com.omh.filters;

import javax.servlet.*;
import javax.servlet.http.*;
import java.io.*;

/**
 * Filter that uses a response wrapper to convert all
```

```
 * output to uppercase
 */
public class UpperCaseFilter
        implements Filter
{
    protected FilterConfig config;

    public void init(FilterConfig config)
        throws ServletException
    {
        // Save the config object
        this.config = config;
    }

    public void destroy()
    {
    }

    public void doFilter(ServletRequest request,
                         ServletResponse response,
                         FilterChain chain)
        throws ServletException, IOException
    {
        ServletResponse newResponse = response;

        // If this is an HttpRequest, wrap the response
        // with our CharArrayWriter so that we can get
        // the contents
        if (request instanceof HttpServletRequest)
        {
            newResponse = new CharResponseWrapper(
                    (HttpServletResponse) response);
        }

        // Invoke the next filter/servlet in the chain
        // using (perhaps) a wrapped response
        chain.doFilter(request, newResponse);

        if (newResponse instanceof CharResponseWrapper)
        {
            // Get the contents of the output. A String
```

```
            // is returned only if a Writer was used,
            // indicating text output. If getOutputStream
            // was used the output will go to the "real"
            // underlying output stream back to the client
            String text = newResponse.toString();
            if (text != null)
            {
                text = text.toUpperCase();

                // Now write the output to the real
                // output stream that goes back to
                // the client
                response.getWriter().write(text);
            }
        }
    }
}
```

The init() and destroy() methods are the same, but the doFilter() method now contains code to wrap the response object with a custom implementation. Left alone, all the response data from within a servlet will be routed back to the client via the response output stream. If we want to capture the output stream and modify it, we need to buffer the response locally before it is sent back to the client. That is the purpose of the CharResponseWrapper; it contains a java.io.CharArrayWriter, which will buffer all the output so that we can modify it after the servlet has executed:

```
import javax.servlet.*;
import javax.servlet.http.*;
import java.io.*;

/**
 * Simple response wrapper that utilizes a local CharArrayWriter
 * for output
 */
public class CharResponseWrapper
        extends HttpServletResponseWrapper
{
    protected CharArrayWriter charWriter;
    protected PrintWriter writer;
    protected boolean getOutputStreamCalled;
```

```
    protected boolean getWriterCalled;

    public CharResponseWrapper(HttpServletResponse response)
    {
        super(response);

        // Create the writer
        charWriter = new CharArrayWriter();
    }

    public ServletOutputStream getOutputStream()
        throws IOException
    {
        // Can't call getOutputStream if getWriter
        // has already been called
        if (getWriterCalled)
        {
            throw new IllegalStateException(
                    "getWriter already called");
        }

        getOutputStreamCalled = true;
        return super.getOutputStream();
    }

    public PrintWriter getWriter()
        throws IOException
    {
        if (writer != null)
        {
            return writer;
        }

        // Can't call getWriter if getOutputStream
        // has already been called
        if (getOutputStreamCalled)
        {
            throw new IllegalStateException(
                    "getOutputStream already called");
        }
        getWriterCalled = true;
```

```
        writer = new PrintWriter(charWriter);
        return writer;
    }

    public String toString()
    {
        String s = null;

        // Only return a String if the writer was
        // used.
        if (writer != null)
        {
            s = charWriter.toString();
        }
        return s;
    }
}
```

The CharResponseWrapper class extends javax.servlet.http.HttpServlet ResponseWrapper, which simply proxies each of the method calls made on the wrapper to the response object supplied in the constructor. Extending the HttpServletResponseWrapper allows you to easily add your own functionality to a response object without having to implement the entire interface. There is a corresponding request wrapper, as well.

Within the new response wrapper, we create a new CharArrayWriter when the response getWriter() method is called. Now, instead of the servlet response being written to the client, it will be buffered locally. We can grab a copy of the buffer by calling the toString() method on the response wrapper, which was overridden to return the String representation of the buffer. It is then an easy matter to call String.toUpperCase() and then dump the entire contents of the buffer to the "real" output stream of the original response object.

The filter is configured using the following entries in web.xml:

```
<filter>
  <filter-name>Upper Case Filter</filter-name>
  <filter-class>com.omh.filters.UpperCaseFilter</filter-class>
</filter>

<filter-mapping>
  <filter-name>Upper Case Filter</filter-name>
```

```
  <url-pattern>/*</url-pattern>
</filter-mapping>
```

Making a request to any servlet that uses getWriter() to create content will result in the response being returned in uppercase:

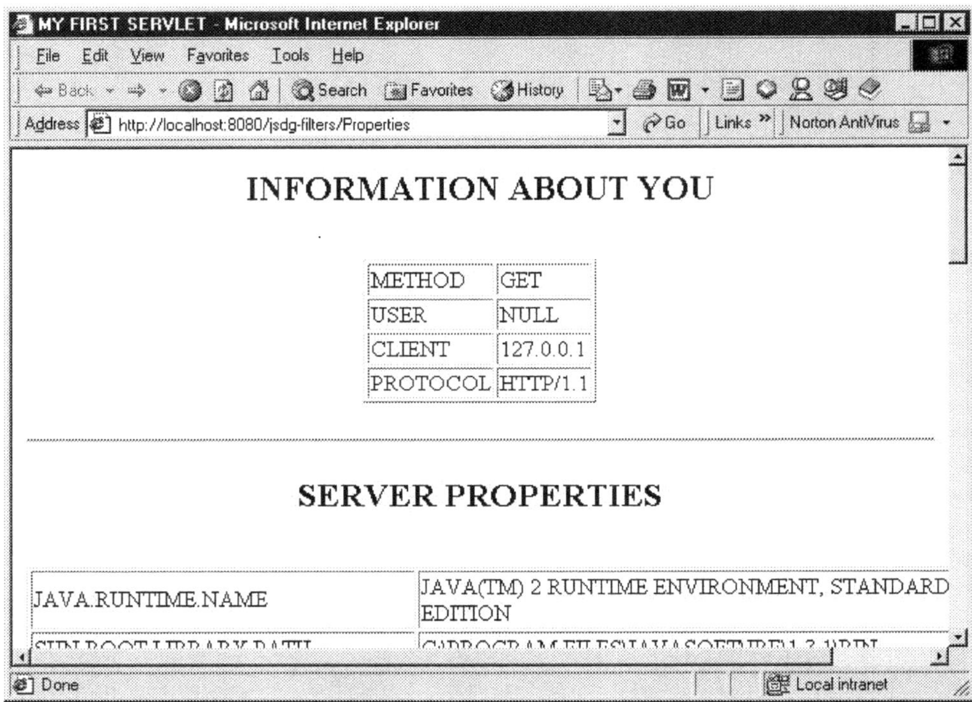

Using XSLT to Transform Stock Quote Data

Our final filter example is somewhat complex, but very powerful. We'll start with a servlet that gathers stock quote information and returns the data to the client in an XML representation. While the XML is nice, most end users would prefer to have the data formatted into a nice table for easy viewing. We'll be transforming the XML into an HTML document using an XSL template in a filter. By using a filter, we don't need to modify the servlet at all; all of the transformation takes place in the filter.

Let's first take a look at the StockServlet, which requests stock quotes and outputs the results in an XML document:

```
package com.omh.stocks;
import javax.servlet.*;
import javax.servlet.http.*;
import java.io.*;
import java.util.*;

public class StockServlet
        extends HttpServlet
{
    public void doGet(HttpServletRequest req,
                      HttpServletResponse resp)
        throws ServletException, java.io.IOException
    {
        PrintWriter out = resp.getWriter();

        // Get the symbols parameter. If missing, default
        // to the DOW and NASDAQ
        String symbols = req.getParameter("symbols");
        if (symbols == null)
        {
            symbols = "^DJI,^IXIC";
        }

        // Convert the comma-separated list of stock
        // symbols into a String[]
        StringTokenizer st = new StringTokenizer(symbols, ",");
        String[] symbolArray = new String[st.countTokens()];
        int i = 0;
        while (st.hasMoreElements())
        {
            String symbol = (String) st.nextElement();
            symbolArray[i++] = symbol;
        }

        // Get the info
        try
        {
            StockObject[] stocks =
                StockReader.getStockInfo(symbolArray);

            // Format the stock output as an XML document
            out.println("<?xml version=\"1.0\" ?>");
            out.println("<stock-quotes>");
            for (i = 0; i < stocks.length; i++)
            {
                StockObject o = stocks[i];
                outputStock(o, out);
```

```
            }
            out.println("</stock-quotes>");
        }
        catch (Exception ex)
        {
            throw new ServletException(ex.getMessage(), ex);
        }

    }

    public void doPost(HttpServletRequest req,
                       HttpServletResponse resp)
        throws ServletException, java.io.IOException
    {
        // POST is the same as GET
        doGet(req, resp);
    }

    /*
     * Outputs a single stock
     */
    protected void outputStock(StockObject so, PrintWriter out)
    {
        out.println(" <stock>");
        outputElement("symbol", so.getSymbol(), out);
        outputElement("company-name", so.getCompanyName(), out);
        outputElement("last-trade-date", so.getLastTradeDate(), out);
        outputElement("last-trade-time", so.getLastTradeTime(), out);
        outputElement("price", so.getPrice(), out);
        outputElement("change-amount", so.getChange(), out);
        outputElement("open-price", so.getOpenPrice(), out);
        outputElement("high-price", so.getHighPrice(), out);
        outputElement("low-price", so.getLowPrice(), out);
        outputElement("volume", so.getVolume(), out);
        out.println(" </stock>");
    }

    /*
     * Outputs a single stock element
     */
    protected void outputElement(String name, String data, PrintWriter out)
    {
        // Use a StringBuffer - much more efficient
        StringBuffer sb = new StringBuffer("  <");
        sb.append(name);
        sb.append(">");
        sb.append(data);
        sb.append("</");
```

```
            sb.append(name);
            sb.append(">");
            out.println(sb.toString());
        }
    }
```

Notice that the doPost() method simply calls doGet(). In this way, the servlet can be used by requesting it directly via a browser or calling it as part of a POST, such as from an HTML form.

The doGet() method first gets the "symbols" parameter. If it cannot find this parameter, the symbols will default to the Dow Jones industrial average and the Nasdaq composite index. The delayed stock data will then be gathered via the StockReader object using Yahoo!. The full source code is available at www .servletguru.com, so I will omit the listing here. Once the stock data has been gathered, an XML document is formatted and returned to the client:

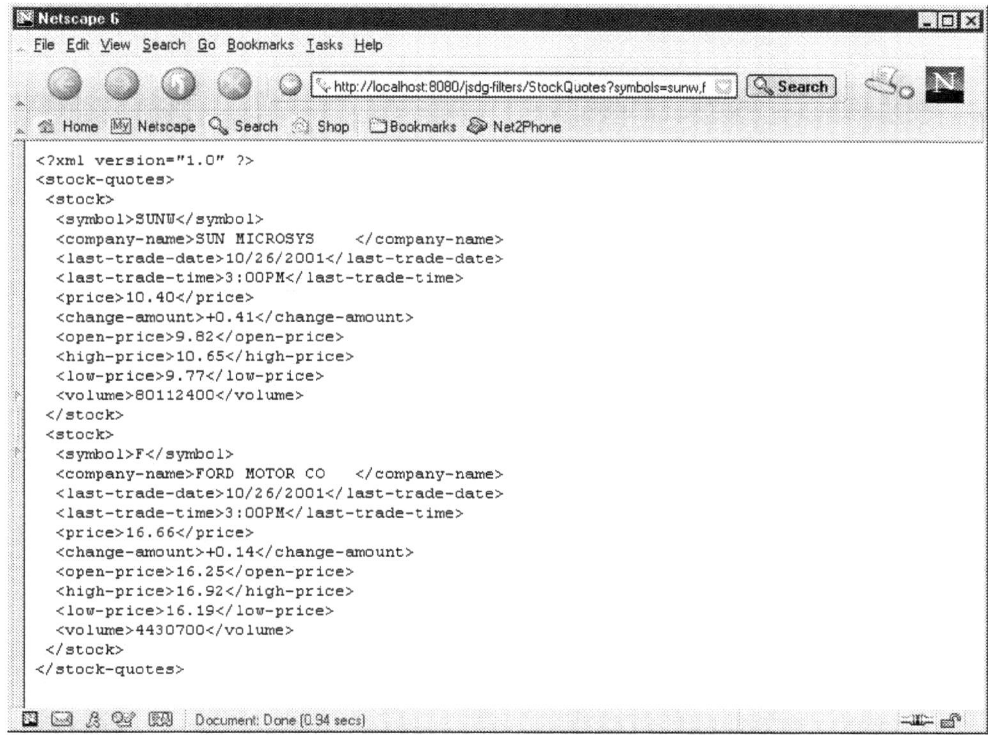

All the stock data is easily recognizable, especially since the XML describes them very well, but this type of result is not quickly digestible by most "normal" people that

I know. For that reason, we need to transform the XML into something that will be even easier to understand. Enter XML Stylesheet Language (XSL). XSL Transformations (also referred to as XSLT or XSL/T) define a markup language for converting one type of document into another. A very common case is to convert XML into HTML. XSL is a huge topic (with entire books devoted to it), so I will not even attempt to cover everything you need to know. For lots more information regarding XML and XSL for Java, check out http://java.sun.com/products/xml. Sun has developed a Java API for processing XML documents (called JAXP), and Apache provides an implementation for reading and writing XML documents, as well as applying XSL templates (the implementation is called xalan). Many examples and detailed tutorials are also available.

Let's take a look at the TransformationFilter, which, in many ways, is very similar to the UpperCaseFilter we looked at previously in that it enables us to capture the output from a servlet and modify it:

```
package com.omh.filters;

import javax.servlet.*;
import javax.servlet.http.HttpServletRequest;
import javax.servlet.http.HttpServletResponse;
import java.io.*;
import java.util.*;
import javax.xml.transform.TransformerFactory;
import javax.xml.transform.Transformer;
import javax.xml.transform.stream.StreamSource;
import javax.xml.transform.stream.StreamResult;

public class TransformationFilter
        implements Filter
{
    protected FilterConfig config;
    protected String agentMappingsFile;
    protected Map agentMappings;
    protected TransformerFactory factory;

    public void init(FilterConfig config)
        throws ServletException
    {
        // Save the config object
        this.config = config;
```

```
    // Get the name of the user agent to XSL template mapping
    // file
    agentMappingsFile =
            config.getInitParameter("agentMappings");
    if (agentMappingsFile == null)
    {
        throw new ServletException(
                "agentMappings parameter is required");
    }

    // Attempt to read and load the agent mapping file
    loadAgentMapping(agentMappingsFile);

    // Create a new transformer factory that we'll use to create
    // transformers
    factory = TransformerFactory.newInstance();
}

public void destroy()
{
}

public void doFilter(ServletRequest request,
                     ServletResponse response,
                     FilterChain chain)
    throws ServletException, IOException
{
    ServletResponse newResponse = response;

    // If this is an HttpRequest, wrap the response
    // with our CharArrayWriter so that we can get
    // the contents
    if (request instanceof HttpServletRequest)
    {
        newResponse = new CharResponseWrapper(
                (HttpServletResponse) response);
    }

    // Invoke the next filter/servlet in the chain
    // using (perhaps) a wrapped response
    chain.doFilter(request, newResponse);

    if (newResponse instanceof CharResponseWrapper)
```

```
        {
            // Get the contents of the output. A String
            // is returned only if a Writer was used,
            // indicating text output. If getOutputStream
            // was used the output will go to the "real"
            // underlying output stream back to the client
            String text = newResponse.toString();
            if (text != null)
            {
                HttpServletRequest hreq =
                        (HttpServletRequest) request;

                // Get the user agent and determine what
                // (if any) XSL template should be used
                // to transform the document
                String userAgent = hreq.getHeader("user-agent");

                // Find the XSL template for the user agent
                String xslFile = getTemplate(userAgent);

                if (xslFile != null)
                {
                    // Apply the template and send back to the
                    // client
                    applyTemplate(text, xslFile,
                                  response.getWriter());
                }
                else
                {
                    // Write the output to the real
                    // output stream that goes back to
                    // the client
                    response.getWriter().write(text);
                }
            }
        }
    }

    protected void loadAgentMapping(String name)
        throws ServletException
    {
        InputStream in = null;
```

```
// Get the resource
try
{
    in = config.getServletContext().getResourceAsStream(name);
    if (in == null)
    {
        // The resource was not found. Raise an exception
        throw new ServletException(name + " not found");
    }

    // Load the mappings into a Properties object
    Properties p = new Properties();
    p.load(in);

    // Calculate the path
    String path = "/";
    int pos = name.lastIndexOf("/");
    if (pos > 0)
    {
        path = name.substring(0, pos + 1);
    }

    // This SortedMap will be sorted with the longest
    // string first
    agentMappings =
            new TreeMap(new LongestFirstComparator());

    // Put the properties into a sorted map so that
    // the user agents are sorted
    Enumeration enum = p.keys();
    while (enum.hasMoreElements())
    {
        String key = (String) enum.nextElement();
        String value = (String) p.get(key);

        // Prepend the path if the resource doesn't start
        // with a slash
        if (!value.startsWith("/"))
        {
            value = path + value;
        }
        agentMappings.put(key, value);
```

```
            }
        }
        catch (IOException ex)
        {
            throw new ServletException(ex.getMessage(), ex);
        }
        finally
        {
            // Make sure the input stream gets closed
            if (in != null)
            {
                try
                {
                    in.close();
                }
                catch (Exception ex)
                {
                    // Ignore exceptions on close
                }
            }
        }
    }

    protected String getTemplate(String userAgent)
    {
        String file = null;

        // Rip through and find the first matching mapping
        // (the mappings are sorted longest first)
        Iterator i = agentMappings.keySet().iterator();
        while (i.hasNext())
        {
            String key = (String) i.next();
            if (userAgent.startsWith(key))
            {
                file = (String) agentMappings.get(key);
                break;
            }
        }

        // Find the default if one was given
        if (file == null)
        {
```

```
            file = (String) agentMappings.get("*");
        }
        return file;
    }

    protected void applyTemplate(String content,
                                 String name,
                                 PrintWriter writer)
        throws ServletException
    {
        InputStream in = null;

        try
        {
            in = config.getServletContext().getResourceAsStream(name);
            if (in == null)
            {
                // The resource was not found. Raise an exception
                throw new ServletException(name + " not found");
            }

            // Create a transformer to work with the given style
            // sheet
            StreamSource source = new StreamSource(in);
            Transformer transformer =
                    factory.newTransformer(source);

            // Transform it!
            StringReader reader = new StringReader(content);
            source = new StreamSource(reader);
            StreamResult result = new StreamResult(writer);
            transformer.transform(source, result);
        }
        catch (Exception ex)
        {
            throw new ServletException(ex.getMessage(), ex);
        }
        finally
        {
            // Make sure the input stream gets closed
            if (in != null)
            {
```

```
                try
                {
                    in.close();
                }
                catch (Exception ex)
                {
                    // Ignore exceptions on close
                }
            }
        }
4    }
}
```

The init() method now requires an initialization parameter, called "agentMappings", which is a path to a resource that contains a mapping of client types to XSL templates. In this way, we can configure the type of template to use depending upon the type of client, whether it be Internet Explorer, Netscape, or a Wireless Application Protocol (WAP) device (which we will explore in Chapter 13). Here's an example:

```
# agentMappings.properties
#
# Provides a mapping between an agent type and an XSL
# template that should be used in transforming a
# document that has the com.omg.filter.TransformationFilter
# filter applied
#
# User agents will match if the agent starts with the
# string given
#
# A special agent name of "*" is reserved to indicate that
# all agents should default to using the given xsl template
#
# The XSL template can either be an absolute path or relative
# path that will use the document base of this properties
# file.
#

Mozilla/4.0\ (compatible;\ MSIE=html_ie.xsl
```

Note that if the client type (this is the user-agent header in a servlet request) contains any white space, it must be escaped; thus, a blank " " becomes "\ ". The example given here is for an Internet Explorer browser. Client types are matched by checking if the user-agent from the client starts with the client type given in the mapping file; if a match is found, then the XSL template given will be used to transform the document. The following is a simple XSL template for transforming our stock quote data from XML to HTML:

```
<?xml version='1.0'?>
<xsl:stylesheet xmlns:xsl="http://www.w3.org/1999/XSL/Transform"
version="1.0">
 <xsl:output method="html"/>
 <xsl:template match="/">
  <HTML>
  <HEAD>
  <TITLE>Stock Quotes</TITLE>
  </HEAD>
  <BODY>
  <CENTER>
  <H2>Here Are Your Requested Stock Quotes</H2>
  <TABLE BORDER="1" CELLPADDING="2">
  <TR>
   <TH>Symbol</TH>
   <TH>Company Name</TH>
   <TH>Price</TH>
   <TH>Change</TH>
   <TH>Last Trade</TH>
  </TR>
  <xsl:for-each select="stock-quotes/stock">
   <TR>
    <TD><xsl:value-of select="symbol" /></TD>
    <TD><xsl:value-of select="company-name" /></TD>
    <TD ALIGN="RIGHT"><xsl:value-of select="price" /></TD>
    <TD ALIGN="RIGHT"><xsl:value-of select="change-amount" /></TD>
    <TD><xsl:value-of select="last-trade-date" />-
        <xsl:value-of select="last-trade-time" /></TD>
   </TR>
  </xsl:for-each>
  </TABLE></CENTER>
  </BODY>
  </HTML>
 </xsl:template>
</xsl:stylesheet>
```

In a nutshell, this template will match the first "/" found in the XML document and output the HTML header information, including the start of a table. Then, for each "stock-quotes/stock" element found in the XML document, a table row will be added picking out the data from the document. After all the elements have been processed, the closing HTML tags are added. Requesting stock quotes using an Internet Explorer browser will result in the following well-formatted document:

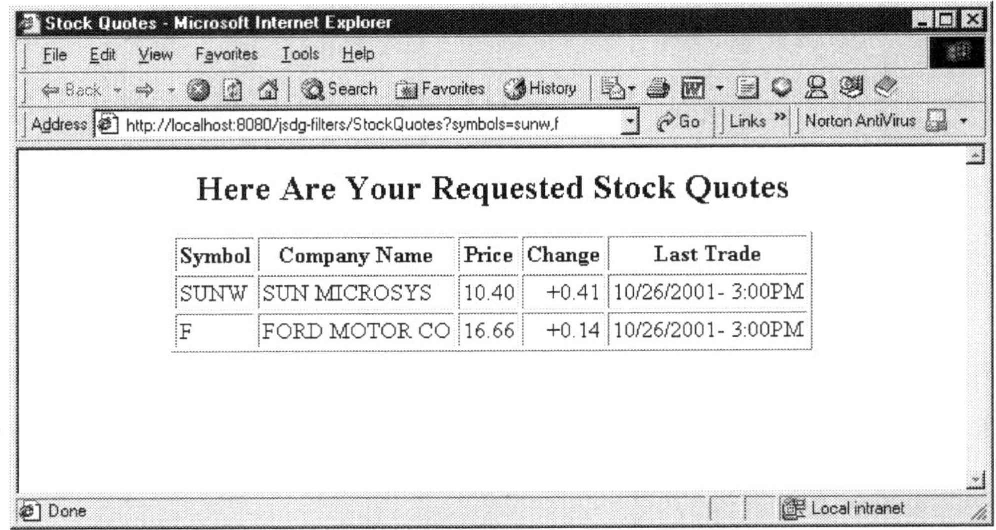

Note that to run this example, you will need to ensure that the JAXP implementation is available to the servlet container. The web application provided at www.servletguru.com includes the necessary JAR files in WEB-INF/lib, which is the location that the servlet specification defines for third-party libraries for use within the web application.

It is also very important to realize that our TransformationFilter is very generic; it does not contain anything specific to transforming stock quote information. All the XSL templates to use are specified in the user-agent mapping file, which is specified in web.xml:

```
<filter>
  <filter-name>StockServlet XSL Transformation Filter</filter-name>
  <filter-class>com.omh.filters.TransformationFilter</filter-class>
    <init-param>
      <param-name>agentMappings</param-name>
      <param-value>/stocks/agentMappings.properties</param-value>
    </init-param>
```

```
</filter>

<filter-mapping>
  <filter-name>StockServlet XSL Transformation Filter</filter-name>
  <servlet-name>StockQuotes</servlet-name>
</filter-mapping>
```

Note also that instead of specifying an <url-pattern> element for the filter mapping, a <servlet-name> is specified. In this way, we can very finely control which servlets will be processed using the filter. The TransformationFilter can be used in any number of applications; you simply need to create a new agent mapping file and XSL templates to transform your data. We'll be reusing this filter in Chapter 13 to transform an XML document into Wireless Markup Language (WML) for consumption by WAP devices.

Summary

In this chapter, we have examined one of the most powerful features of the Servlet specification. Filters enable us to investigate and modify the request to a servlet, and the response from a servlet.

We developed a simple filter for timing servlets, and then investigated how to modify the response of a servlet by converting documents to uppercase by using a response wrapper. Finally, we created a servlet that uses XSL templates to convert an XML document into HTML, showcasing one of the more exciting uses of filters.

CHAPTER

7

Application Event Listeners

IN THIS CHAPTER:

First introduced as part of version 2.3 of the Servlet specification, application event listeners allow you to receive notifications of certain web application events. The primary goal of providing application events is to allow you to better manage resources at either the context or HTTP session level. For example, you can be notified when a web application has been created and is ready to handle requests and create a pool of objects to be used by servlets. Conversely, when the web application is terminated, you can gracefully destroy the object pool.

Four different types of listeners are defined by the specification:

- **ServletContextListener** Allows notification of context lifecycle events (create and destroy)
- **ServletContextAttributesListener** Allows notification of context attribute changes (add, modify, and remove)
- **HttpSessionListener** Allows notification of HTTP session lifecycle events (create and destroy)
- **HttpSessionAttributesListeners** Allows notification of HTTP session attribute changes (add, modify, and remove)

Each of these listener interfaces can be implemented by a listener object. The object is registered with the web application via entries in the deployment descriptor (web.xml). Next, we'll take a look at simple examples of each type of listener as well as the corresponding configuration in web.xml.

ServletContextListener

Implementing the javax.servlet.ServletContextListener interface allows you to receive context lifecycle events. Note that there is a one-to-one relationship between a context and a web application, so it is safe to say that context lifecycle events can be viewed as web application lifecycle events as well.

The ServletContextListener is, in my opinion, the most powerful of the event listeners in that it allows you to manage resources that will be used by your web application, such as a JDBC connection pool (covered in Chapter 9). When you receive notification that the context has been created, you can create and initialize a pool of JDBC connections, and when the context is destroyed, you can properly tear it down.

Prior to the introduction of the ServletContextListener, many servlet developers would use a preloaded servlet to manage resources. The servlet would be preloaded when the web application started and its init() method would be called, which is where any resource initialization code would reside. When the web application was destroyed, the servlet destroy() method would be invoked and any resources would be destroyed as well. This is still a perfectly acceptable way to handle resources, but using the ServletContextListener is a much cleaner (and more elegant) way to handle context lifecycle events.

Let's take a look at a simple implementation that simply outputs messages to the servlet log file when context events take place:

```
package com.omh.listeners;

import javax.servlet.ServletContextListener;
import javax.servlet.ServletContextEvent;
import javax.servlet.ServletContext;

/**
 * Simple example of implementing the application lifecycle
 * event listener ServletContextListener
 */
public class MyContextListener
        implements ServletContextListener
{
    public void contextInitialized(ServletContextEvent event)
    {
        // Grab ahold of the ServletContext
        ServletContext context = event.getServletContext();

        context.log(context.getServletContextName() + " initialized");
    }

    public void contextDestroyed(ServletContextEvent event)
    {
        // Grab ahold of the ServletContext
        ServletContext context = event.getServletContext();

        context.log(context.getServletContextName() + " destroyed");
    }
}
```

When a web application is started, a ServletContext is created as well. Once the ServletContext has been initialized, the servlet container checks its internal list of listeners. If any listeners implement javax.servlet.ServletContextListener, the contextInitialized() method will be invoked on that listener. A similar process is followed when the web application is destroyed. The following shows how our event listener is configured within web.xml:

```
<web-app>

  <listener>
    <listener-class>
      com.omh.listeners.MyContextListener
    </listener-class>
  </listener>
</web-app>
```

Listeners are simply specified by adding a <listener> element with a corresponding <listener-class> entry that specifies the full package name of the class that implements one of the application event listeners. You can specify any number of listeners, and a single class can implement any number of the event listener interfaces. The order in which you specify event listeners in web.xml is important, because the servlet container will invoke the listeners in that same order when events occur. Note that when a context is destroyed, the listeners are invoked in reverse order. Remember that, in order to be fully portable, the <listener> elements in web.xml must appear in the same order as they appear in the XML grammar (refer to Chapter 5).

Using Tomcat 4.0, the servlet log file will contain the following messages after starting and then stopping the server:

```
Java Servlets Developer's Guide Listener Examples initialized

Java Servlets Developer's Guide Listener Examples destroyed
```

Note that you must specify a <display-name> element within web.xml in order to get the web application name from getServletContextName(). If you don't specify a <display-name>, you will get the message "null initialized" instead.

ServletContextAttributeListener

Implementing the javax.servlet.ServletContextAttributeListener interface allows you to receive notification when attributes are added, modified, or removed from the ServletContext for a web application. Perhaps you have a very complex web application that stores state information in the ServletContext and you require notification of certain changes in state. Maybe you allow a servlet to cache information in the context, and have a background thread automatically destroy the cache after a certain amount of time (the thread can be started when the attribute is added). Whatever the reason, implementing the ServletContextAttributeListener gives you fine-grain control over these events.

Again, let's take a look at an example that simply logs the context attribute events as they happen:

```
package com.omh.listeners;

import javax.servlet.ServletContextAttributeListener;
import javax.servlet.ServletContextAttributeEvent;
import javax.servlet.ServletContext;

/**
 * Simple example of implementing the application lifecycle
 * event listener ServletContextAttributeListener
 */
public class MyContextAttributeListener
        implements ServletContextAttributeListener
{
    public void attributeAdded(ServletContextAttributeEvent event)
    {
        // Grab ahold of the ServletContext
        ServletContext context = event.getServletContext();

        String attributeName = event.getName();
        Object attributeValue = event.getValue();

        context.log("Add context attribute " +
                    attributeName + "=" + attributeValue);
    }

    public void attributeRemoved(ServletContextAttributeEvent event)
    {
        // Grab ahold of the ServletContext
        ServletContext context = event.getServletContext();

        String attributeName = event.getName();
        Object attributeValue = event.getValue();

        context.log("Remove context attribute " +
                    attributeName + "=" + attributeValue);
    }
```

```
    public void attributeReplaced(ServletContextAttributeEvent event)
    {
        // Grab ahold of the ServletContext
        ServletContext context = event.getServletContext();

        String attributeName = event.getName();
        Object oldAttributeValue = event.getValue();
        Object attributeValue =
                context.getAttribute(attributeName);

        context.log("Replace context attribute " +
                    attributeName + "=" + attributeValue +
                    " old value=" + oldAttributeValue);
    }
}
```

To see the listener in action, you first need to configure it within web.xml

```
<listener>
  <listener-class>
    com.omh.listeners.MyContextAttributeListener
  </listener-class>
</listener>
```

and then create a simple servlet that uses context attributes:

```
package com.omh;

import javax.servlet.*;
import javax.servlet.http.*;
import java.io.IOException;
import java.io.PrintWriter;

/**
 * Simple servlet for testing a ServletContextAttributeListener
 */
public class TestContextAttributes
        extends HttpServlet
{
    public void doGet(HttpServletRequest req,
                      HttpServletResponse resp)
        throws ServletException, IOException
```

```
    {
        resp.setContentType("text/html");

        // Get an output stream that takes into account
        // the proper character encoding
        PrintWriter out = resp.getWriter();

        // Get the context
        ServletContext context = getServletContext();

        // Set, modify, and delete an attribute
        String name = "com.omh.name";

        out.println("Setting " + name + " to Bob<br>");
        context.setAttribute(name, "Bob");
        out.println("Setting " + name + " to Larry<br>");
        context.setAttribute(name, "Larry");
        out.println("Removing " + name);
        context.removeAttribute(name);
    }
}
```

Note that the context attribute name I'm using includes my class package name. This is a good idea for two reasons. First, using the package name will greatly reduce the chance that another application will use the same name. Second, it helps you debug problems, because the name will contain the package name of the code that put it there.

Requesting this servlet will cause something like the following to be logged to the servlet log file:

```
Add context attribute com.omh.name=Bob
Replace context attribute com.omh.name=Larry old value=Bob
Remove context attribute com.omh.name=Larry
```

HttpSessionListener

Implementing the javax.servlet.http.HttpSessionListener interface allows you to receive HTTP session lifecycle events. Much like the ContextListener interface, you can use these events to create and initialize resources, only this time the resources will be used by an individual session. Handling HTTP session lifecycle events is illustrated in MySessionListener, which follows:

```
package com.omh.listeners;

import javax.servlet.http.HttpSessionListener;
import javax.servlet.http.HttpSessionEvent;
import javax.servlet.http.HttpSession;
import javax.servlet.ServletContext;

/**
 * Simple example of implementing the application lifecycle
 * event listener HttpSessionListener
 */
public class MySessionListener
        implements HttpSessionListener
{
    public void sessionCreated(HttpSessionEvent event)
    {
        // Get the session that was created
        HttpSession session = event.getSession();

        // Get the ServletContext
        ServletContext context =
                session.getServletContext();

        String sessionId = session.getId();
        context.log("Session " + sessionId + " created");
    }

    public void sessionDestroyed(HttpSessionEvent event)
    {
        // Get the session that was destroyed
        HttpSession session = event.getSession();

        // Get the ServletContext
        ServletContext context =
                session.getServletContext();

        String sessionId = session.getId();
        context.log("Session " + sessionId + " destroyed");
    }
}
```

Again, to see the listener in action, you first need to configure it within web.xml as you did in the previous example:

```
<listener>
  <listener-class>
    com.omh.listeners.MySessionListener
  </listener-class>
</listener>
```

To test the listener, you simply need a servlet that creates a new session and immediately invalidates it:

```
package com.omh;

import javax.servlet.*;
import javax.servlet.http.*;
import java.io.IOException;
import java.io.PrintWriter;

public class TestSessionAttributes
        extends HttpServlet
{
    public void doGet(HttpServletRequest req,
                      HttpServletResponse resp)
        throws ServletException, IOException
    {
        resp.setContentType("text/html");

        // Get an output stream that takes into account
        // the proper character encoding
        PrintWriter out = resp.getWriter();

        // Get the session
        out.println("Creating new session<br>");
        HttpSession session = req.getSession();

        // Invalidate (or destroy) the session
        out.println("Destroying session");
        session.invalidate();
    }
}
```

Invoking the test servlet will yield the following log file entries:

```
Session C7E73556 created

Session C7E73556 destroyed
```

HttpSessionAttributeListener

Implementing the javax.servlet.http.HttpSessionAttributeListener interface allows you to receive notification of attributes being added to, modified within, or removed from an HTTP session. Note that this functionality already exists in the form of the HttpSessionBindingListener interface, but this interface must be implemented by the object that is being bound to the session; the HttpSessionAttributeListener interface allows you to receive events for all objects bound to the session. This can be very handy, for example, if you want to debug the use of attributes within a session.

Once again, let's look at a simple example that uses the servlet log file to trace the events as they happen:

```
package com.omh.listeners;

import javax.servlet.*;
import javax.servlet.http.*;

/**
 * Simple example of implementing the application lifecycle
 * event listener HttpSessionAttributeListener
 */
public class MySessionAttributeListener
        implements HttpSessionAttributeListener
{
    public void attributeAdded(HttpSessionBindingEvent event)
    {
        // Get the session
        HttpSession session = event.getSession();

        // Grab ahold of the ServletContext
        ServletContext context = session.getServletContext();

        String sessionId = session.getId();
        String attributeName = event.getName();
        Object attributeValue = event.getValue();
```

```
        context.log("Add session " + sessionId +
                    " attribute " +
                    attributeName + "=" + attributeValue);
    }

    public void attributeRemoved(HttpSessionBindingEvent event)
    {
        // Get the session
        HttpSession session = event.getSession();

        // Grab ahold of the ServletContext
        ServletContext context = session.getServletContext();

        String sessionId = session.getId();
        String attributeName = event.getName();
        Object attributeValue = event.getValue();

        context.log("Remove session " + sessionId +
                    " attribute " +
                    attributeName + "=" + attributeValue);
    }

    public void attributeReplaced(HttpSessionBindingEvent event)
    {
        // Get the session
        HttpSession session = event.getSession();

        // Grab ahold of the ServletContext
        ServletContext context = session.getServletContext();

        String sessionId = session.getId();
        String attributeName = event.getName();
        Object oldAttributeValue = event.getValue();
        Object attributeValue =
                session.getAttribute(attributeName);

        context.log("Replace session " + sessionId +
                    " attribute " +
                    attributeName + "=" + attributeValue +
                    " old value=" + oldAttributeValue);
    }
}
```

You should, by now, know how this listener is configured within web.xml:

```
<listener>
  <listener-class>
    com.omh.listeners.MySessionAttributeListener
  </listener-class>
</listener>
```

Now, any servlet that uses attributes within an HTTP session will cause entries in the servlet log file to be created. The following simple servlet will add an attribute, modify it, and then remove it from the current session:

```
package com.omh;

import javax.servlet.*;
import javax.servlet.http.*;
import java.io.IOException;
import java.io.PrintWriter;

public class TestSessionAttributes
        extends HttpServlet
{
    public void doGet(HttpServletRequest req,
                      HttpServletResponse resp)
        throws ServletException, IOException
    {
        resp.setContentType("text/html");

        // Get an output stream that takes into account
        // the proper character encoding
        PrintWriter out = resp.getWriter();

        // Get the session
        out.println("Creating new session<br>");
        HttpSession session = req.getSession();

        // Set, modify, and delete an attribute
        String name = "com.omh.session.name";

        out.println("Setting " + name + " to Junior<br>");
        session.setAttribute(name, "Junior");
        out.println("Setting " + name + " to Laura<br>");
        session.setAttribute(name, "Laura");
```

```
        out.println("Removing " + name + "<br>");
        session.removeAttribute(name);

        // Invalidate (or destroy) the session
        out.println("Destroying session");
        session.invalidate();
    }
}
```

Requesting this servlet will cause something like the following to be output to the current servlet log file:

```
Add session C7E73556 attribute com.omh.session.name=Junior
Replace session C7E73556 attribute com.omh.session.name=Laura
    old value=Junior
Remove session C7E73556 attribute com.omh.session.name=Laura
```

Summary

We've just taken a tour of the new application event listeners added to version 2.3 of the Servlet specification. Using these listeners gives you very fine-grained control over the processing of events within the servlet container. We looked at each of the four listener types (context, context attributes, session, and session attributes) as well as how to configure them within the web application via entries in the deployment descriptor.

CHAPTER

8

HTML Forms

IN THIS CHAPTER:

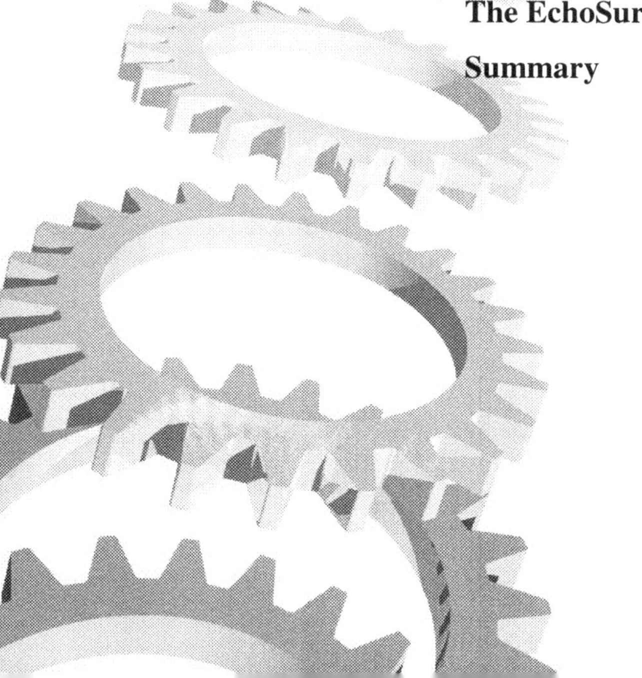

In the previous chapters, we've taken a look at some of the finer points of servlet writing; now it's time to put these basics to use and develop a "real world" example. This chapter is devoted to HTML forms, which are used to gather data from the user in many interactive web applications.

HTML Forms or Java Applets?

We all know that HTML is a great way to deliver information on the Web, but what is the best way to gather data and deliver it back to the server? As we'll see in later chapters, Java applets are one way to create an extremely powerful interactive web application. With this power comes some significant tradeoffs, one of which is the size of the applet, which can grow significantly as more and more functionality is added (just like any other type of program). Also, as you may well be aware, the behavior of applets may vary from browser to browser.

HTML forms, on the other hand, provide a very rich set of interactive elements and are supported by almost every browser. Most people find that HTML is very easy to write, and there are a number of HTML development environments available to make it even easier. HTML forms also have a much smaller footprint (the downloaded size of the application) than applets, which makes loading them over the Internet faster, thus reducing the amount of time that those impatient users have to wait. Forms, coupled with a server-side program (such as a servlet), are a great way to provide robust, interactive web applications.

Form Basics

Like every other HTML tag, forms have a start tag and an end tag. Within each form, you can include any number of input elements, such as text input fields, buttons, pull-down menus, check boxes, or clickable images. You can also place regular HTML content within the HTML tag, such as text and images. The text can be used to provide instructions for filling out the form, as well as form labels and prompts.

Once the user has filled out a form, they click a Submit button that will perform some action, which most likely will be to invoke a server-side process (such as a servlet) but can also include sending an e-mail. Once the Submit button has been clicked, the browser will package all of the input gathered from the user and send it off to a server process. The server will then route the package to the appropriate destination that will process the data, create a response (usually another HTML page), and send the response back to the browser.

A form can be placed anywhere inside the body of an HTML page, and more than one form can be placed in a single page (although they may not be nested). Browsers place the form elements into the formatted HTML page as if they were small images embedded into the text. There are no special layout rules for form elements; because of this, you'll need to use other HTML formatting elements (such as tables) or custom style sheets to control where the input elements are placed on the page.

Note that throughout this chapter, I'll be using all uppercase letters for tag names and attributes. This is to make these names stand out; if you prefer to use lowercase, then feel free to do so.

The <FORM> Tag

```
<FORM ACTION="url" METHOD="POST|GET">

</FORM>
```

You are required to define two form attributes: ACTION, which defines the URL of the server-side process to invoke, and METHOD, which defines how parameters are to be sent to the server. The following table provides a list of all the <FORM> tag attributes:

Attribute	Required	Description
ACTION	Yes	The URL of the server-side process that will receive the data when the form is submitted
ENCTYPE		Specifies how the data is to be encoded when transmitted to the server
METHOD	Yes	Controls the HTTP method to be used when sending data to the server; valid values are GET and POST

Note that there are a series of extended <FORM> tag attributes that are defined by Microsoft and/or Netscape, but we'll just be concentrating on those defined by the HTML specification.

The ACTION Attribute

The ACTION attribute, which is required, specifies the URL of the server-side process that is to receive the form data when it is submitted. In a traditional (nonservlet) environment, this would most likely point to a Common Gateway

Interface (CGI) script found in the cgi-bin directory. In our case, since we'll be using servlets, the URL will point to a servlet on a particular server.

An example ACTION attribute would look like this:

```
<FORM ACTION="http://www.servletguru.com/servlet/myServlet" …>
</FORM>
```

As an aside, you can also specify an e-mail address in place of the URL. Why would you want to do this? Some Internet providers may not allow you to place scripts on your web site, making it impossible to use a form to invoke a CGI script or servlet. However, you can use a mailto URL in the ACTION attribute that will cause all the form parameters and values to be mailed to the address given in the URL. The mail recipient can then process the form data as needed.

An example ACTION attribute with an e-mail URL would look like this:

```
<FORM ACTION="mailto:karlmoss@mindspring.com" …>
</FORM>
```

The body of the e-mail will contain the form parameter and value pairs, such as:

```
name=Junior
address=Bumblyburg
```

Note that if you are using an e-mail URL in the ACTION attribute, you need to consider the following:

- Your form will only work with browsers that support a mailto URL.
- After a form is submitted to an e-mail URL, the user will be left wondering if anything happened. Unlike submitting data to a script or servlet, which can respond with some type of confirmation HTML page, submitting data to an e-mail URL will simply leave the user staring at the form that was just completed. You can use JavaScript to solve this problem.
- You will want to set the ENCTYPE attribute (as described in the next section) to text/plain to ensure that the form parameters and values are in a human-readable format.
- You will have to process the form parameter values in the e-mail in some manner. This may include some type of batch process that reads each e-mail, parses the values of the parameters, and then takes some action.

The ENCTYPE Attribute

The web browser will encode the form data before it is passed to the server, which, in turn, may decode the parameters or simply pass them to the application. The default encoding format is the Internet Media Type named application/x-www-form-urlencoded. You can change the default encoding type with the ENCTYPE attribute in the <FORM> tag. The following table shows the valid ENCTYPE values

Value	Description
application/x-www-form-urlencoded	The default encoding format. Converts any spaces in the form parameter values to a plus sign (+), nonalphanumeric characters to a percent sign (%) followed by the two-digit hexadecimal ASCII value of the character, and line breaks within any multiline values into %0D%0A (carriage return/line feed).
multipart/form-data	Only used with forms that contain a file-selection field. The data is sent as a single document with multiple sections. The server must parse these sections to retrieve the data.
text/plain	Only used to send the form parameters and values via e-mail. Each element in the form is placed on a single line with the name and value separated by an equal (=) sign. Line breaks within any multiline values are converted into %0D%0A (carriage return/line feed).

You will most likely not have to change the default value of application/x-www-form-urlencoded and can omit the ENCTYPE attribute.

The METHOD Attribute

The METHOD attribute, which is required, specifies the method in which the web browser sends the form values to the server. There are two methods used to send the form values: POST and GET.

The POST method will cause the web browser to send the form values in two steps. The browser first contacts the server specified in the ACTION attribute and, once contact is made, sends the form values to the server as part of the message body. The server is expected to read and parse the parameters from the body of the message.

The GET method will cause the web browser to contact the server and send the form values in the message header. The browser will append the form values to the ACTION URL (as command-line arguments), separating the values by an ampersand (&).

Which should you use? Here are some guidelines:

- If the form has only a small number of fields, use the GET method.
- Since some servers limit the length of command-line arguments (which is how GET works), you will have to use POST for larger forms or forms that can contain long text values.
- If you are security conscious, use the POST method. Because the GET method passes the form values as command-line arguments after the URL, it is quite trivial to capture the data values with network sniffers or extract the data from server log files. The POST method, on the other hand, causes the data to be encrypted and sent in a separate transmission.

Passing Additional Parameters

You can very easily pass additional parameters to the ACTION URL by encoding them and adding them as command-line arguments. For example, if you have two parameters named a and b, you can encode them using the application/x-www-form-urlencoded style, like this:

```
a=3&b=24
```

An example URL that uses these additional parameters would look like this:

```
<FORM ACTION="http://myhost/servlet/myServlet?a=3&b=24" ...>
</FORM>
```

But wait, there is a catch (of course). The & character is a reserved character used by HTML to specify the character-entity insertion point. To get around this, you will need to replace any & character with its character-entity value, either & or &:

```
<FORM ACTION="http://myhost/servlet/myServlet?a=3&amp;b=24" ...>
</FORM>
```

Because of this confusion, some web servers allow you to separate parameter values with a semicolon (;) instead.

The <INPUT> Tag

The <INPUT> tag is used to define input fields for the form, such as text fields and buttons:

```
<INPUT TYPE="input type" NAME="parameter name"
    [additional attributes]>
```

The required TYPE attribute specifies the type of input field to use (as the following sections describe), and the required NAME attribute specifies the name that will be supplied to the server for the field. Note that you should take care in naming the fields; I would suggest that you shy away from using any special characters (except the underscore) and use only letters for the leading character. Specifically, don't use the +, &, or % characters, since they have special meaning when using application/x-www-form-urlencoding.

Note that there are attribute extensions that have been defined by Microsoft Internet Explorer and Netscape Navigator; I'll just focus on the standard attributes as defined by the HTML specification.

The Button Input Type

Using the button input type, you can create a button that can be clicked by the user of the form, but does not submit or reset the form. The following table shows the attributes for the button input type:

Attribute	Required	Description
NAME	Yes	The name of the button
VALUE	Yes	The button label

You might ask what the value of a button that does not submit or reset the form might be. Well, unless you are using JavaScript to perform some action, the answer is absolutely nothing. This is not a book about JavaScript; there are many books devoted solely to the subject of JavaScript. If you will be developing applications with HTML, I highly recommend that you investigate the use of JavaScript to make your web sites more dynamic. Regardless of that, the HTML code for presenting the user with multiple buttons follows:

```
<html>
<head>
<title>HTML Form Input - Buttons</title>
</head>
<body>
```

```
<form>
<input type=button name=action value="Next">
<input type=button name=action value="Previous">
</form>

</body>
</html>
```

The following shows the form being displayed in a browser:

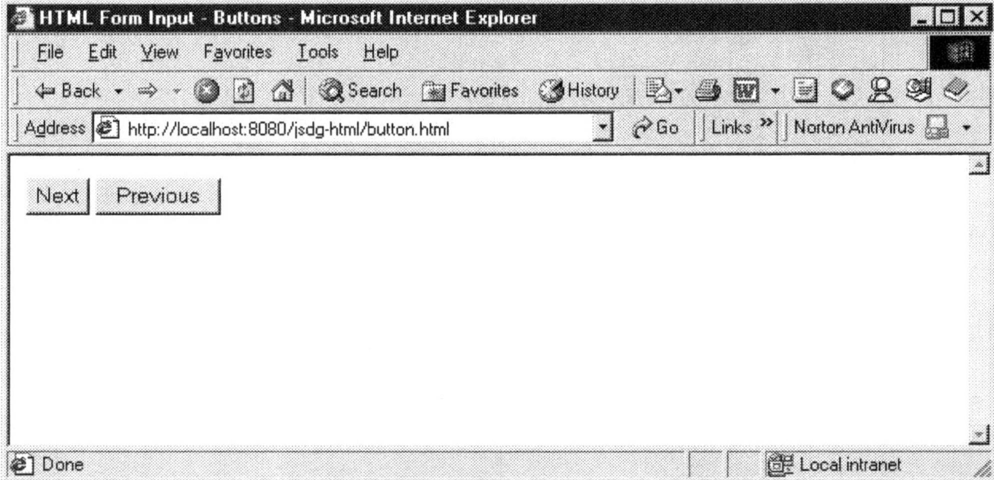

The Checkbox Input Type

The checkbox input type allows you to present the user of the form with a way to select and deselect a particular item. The following table shows the attributes for the checkbox input type:

Attribute	Required	Description
NAME	Yes	The name of the check box
VALUE	Yes	The value that will be sent to the server if the check box is selected
CHECKED		The presence of this attribute causes the check box to be selected by default

An example HTML file using check boxes follows. Note that you can (and will need to) embed HTML formatting instructions as well as other text with your input fields to make your forms come alive:

```
<html>
<head>
<title>HTML Form Input - Checkboxes</title>
</head>
<body>

<form>

Operating Systems:
<input type=checkbox name=os value="win32" checked>Win32
<input type=checkbox name=os value="unix">Unix
<input type=checkbox name=os value="solaris">Solaris

<br><br>
Browsers:
<br><dir>
<input type=checkbox name=browser value="ie">Internet Explorer
<br>
<input type=checkbox name=browser value="ns">Netscape Navigator
<br>
</dir>

</form>

</body>
</html>
```

The simple checkbox example is shown next running in a browser:

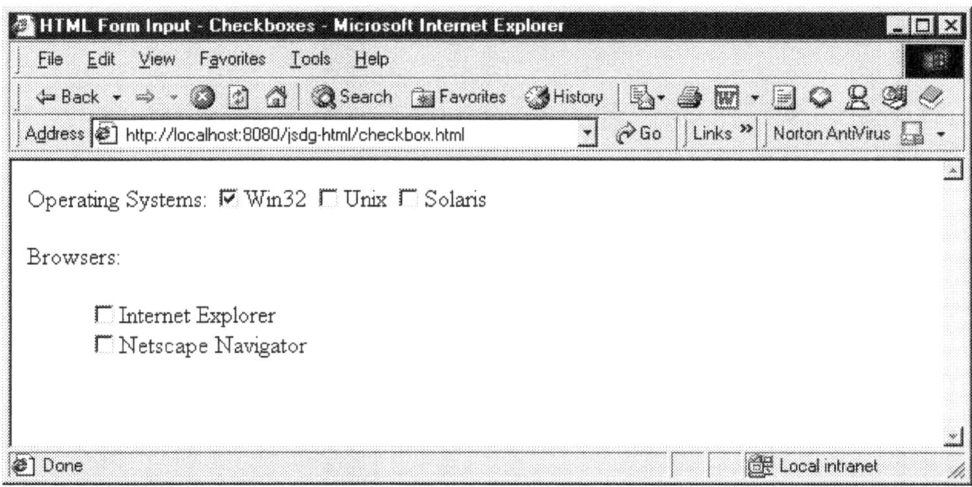

The File Input Type

The file input type allows the user to select a file that is stored on their local computer and send the contents of the file to the server when the Submit button is clicked. Note that the contents of the file are not automatically sent; by default, only the filename itself is sent. To get the contents sent, you need to specify METHOD="POST" and ENCTYPE="multipart/form-data". And since the Servlet API does not natively support multipart encoding (via getParameter), you need to do a lot of coding in your servlet. Also keep in mind that some servers will reject files over a certain length, to prevent denial of service attacks.

The web browser will create a text input field that will accept user input as well as a Browse button that will, when clicked, present the user with a platform-specific dialog box allowing a file to be selected. The following table shows the attributes for the file input type:

Attribute	Required	Description
ACCEPT		Sets the types of files that the user can select through a comma-separated list of MIME types, such as "image/" to select all images
MAXLENGTH		Maximum length (in characters) of the filename
NAME	Yes	The name of the file input field
SIZE		Size (in characters) of the input field
VALUE		The default filename

Following is an example HTML file that uses the file selection input type:

```
<html>
<head>
<title>HTML Form Input - File Selection</title>
</head>
<body>

<form>
My favorite file is:
<input type=file name=myfile size=25>
</form>

</body>
</html>
```

The following shows the file input box within a browser:

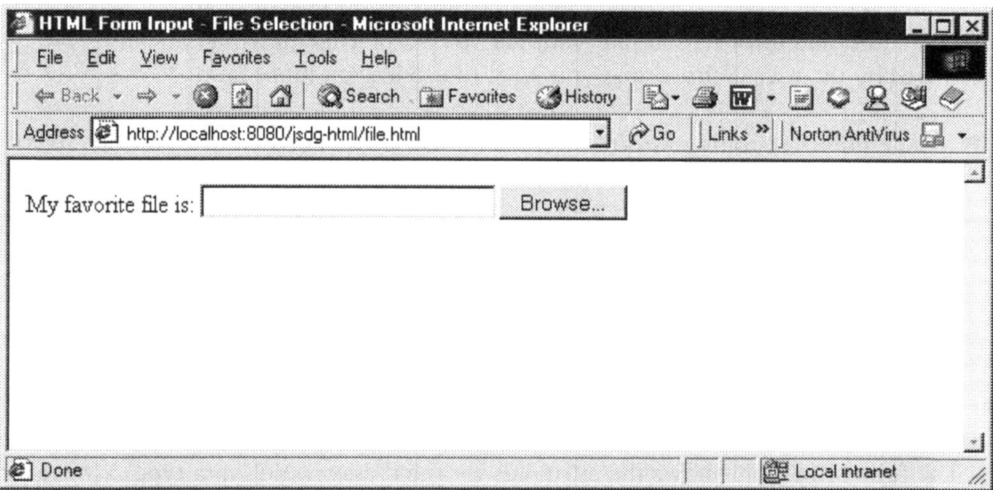

If the Browse button is clicked, a sample platform-specific dialog box is presented that allows the user to select a file.

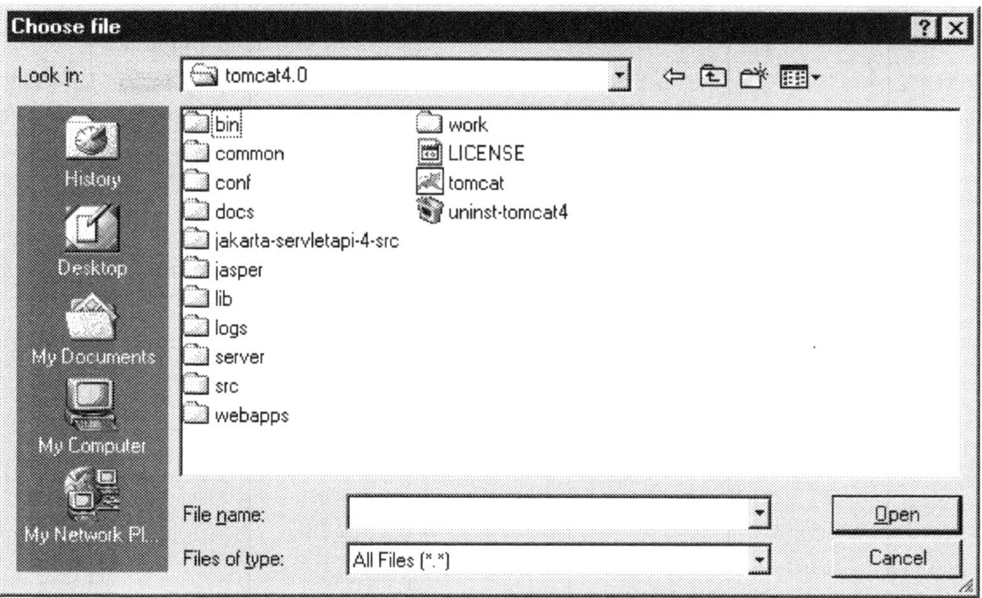

The Hidden Input Type

The hidden input type is one that is hidden from view of the user and is a way to embed additional information into your HTML form. This information cannot be modified by the user. Why would you want to use hidden input fields?

- To embed versioning information within the form. You can use a hidden form to send a version number of the HTML form to the server.
- To embed user identification within the form. You will typically be generating HTML forms on the server to be returned to the browser so you can embed information about the current user into the HTML form.
- To embed any additional information required by the server. You may be using a single servlet to serve multiple forms and need to embed some additional information in a form for the server to be able to process it properly.

The following table shows the attributes for the hidden field input type. Whenever a form is submitted to the server, the name and value of any hidden fields are sent to the server along with any other parameters.

Attribute	Required	Description
NAME	Yes	The name of the hidden field
VALUE	Yes	The value of the hidden field

Next is an example HTML page that uses a hidden field:

```
<html>
<head>
<title>HTML Form Input - Hidden Fields</title>
</head>
<body>

<form>
There is a hidden input field here (
<input type=hidden name=version value="1.0">
)
</form>

</body>
</html>
```

As expected when the hidden input field is processed by a browser it cannot be seen:

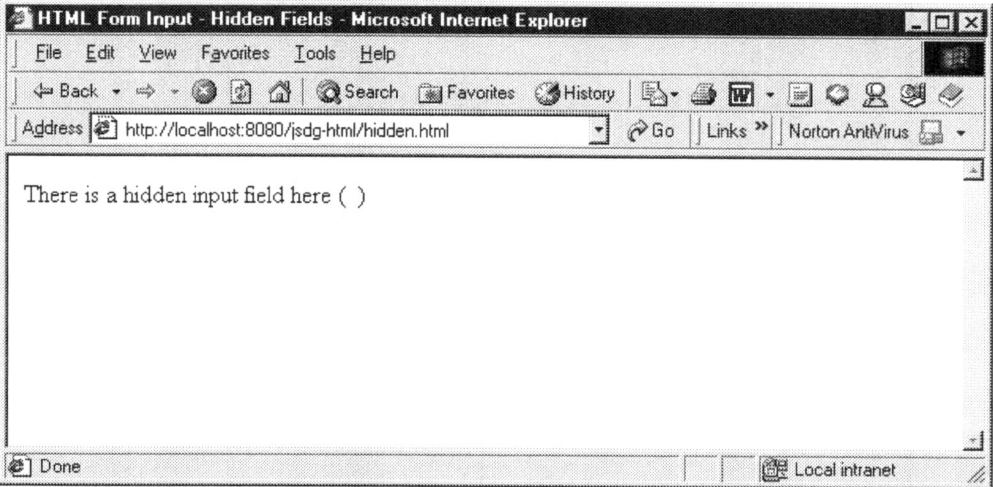

The Image Input Type

The image input attribute will create a custom button that has a clickable image. This custom button will be created using the image you specify and, when clicked by the user, submits the form and sends the X and Y coordinates of the mouse click within the image to the server. The values of the X and Y coordinates will be sent as <name>.x and <name>.y. Thus, if you create an image input named "map," the X and Y coordinates will be sent to the server as map.x and map.y.

The following table shows the attributes for the clickable image button:

Attribute	Required	Description
ALIGN		Image alignment with text: TOP, TEXTTOP, MIDDLE, ABSMIDDLE, CENTER, BOTTOM, BASELINE, ABSBOTTOM
BORDER		Specifies the thickness (in pixels) of the image border
NAME	Yes	The name of the image button
SRC	Yes	The URL of the image; this may be an absolute or relative path

The following form uses an image input type that allows the user to submit the form by clicking the image:

```
<html>
<head>
<title>HTML Form Input - Image Button</title>
</head>
<body>

<form>
Click here to submit the form
<input type=image name=submit src="images/submit.gif" align=middle>
</form>

</body>
</html>
```

The following shows the clickable image:

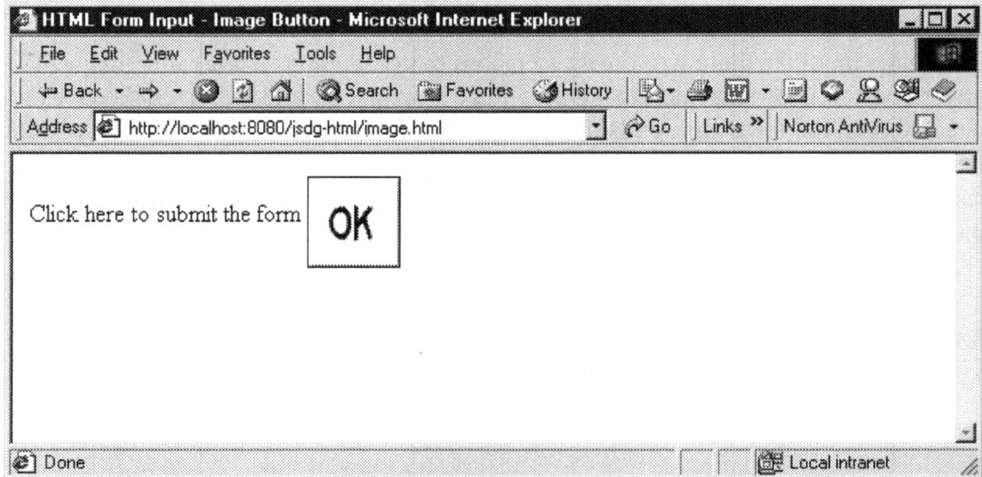

The Password Input Type

The password input type allows you to mask input from the user, as is typically done with password entry fields. Do not be mislead into thinking that the password will be encrypted or that any other type of security measures are taken with a password field; the password input type only hides the characters from view in the browser.

The following table shows the attributes for the password input field:

Attribute	Required	Description
MAXLENGTH		Maximum length (in characters) of the data
NAME	Yes	The name of the password field
SIZE		Size (in characters) of the field
VALUE		The default value of the field

Next is an example HTML file using a password input field:

```
<html>
<head>
<title>HTML Form Input - Password Input Field</title>
</head>
<body>

<form>
Enter your password:
<input type=password name=pwd size=10>
</form>

</body>
</html>
```

The following shows the password field within a browser. Note that all characters that are entered in the field are displayed as *:

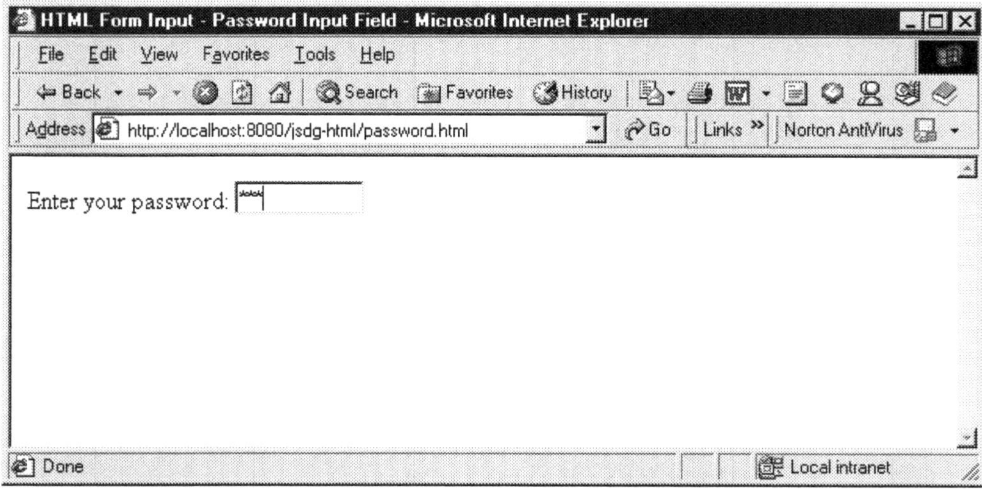

The Radio Input Type

The radio button input type enables you to present the user with a list of choices and allow them to choose exactly one. The following table lists the attributes for the radio button input type:

Attribute	Required	Description
CHECKED		The presence of this attribute causes this item to be the default selection
NAME	Yes	The name of the radio button field
VALUE	Yes	The value that will be sent to the server if this item is selected

Note that radio buttons with the same name will be considered part of the same group; only one item from a given group may be selected at any time. Also, if none of the radio button fields is selected, the browser will automatically select the first button in the group to be the default selection.

The following shows an example HTML file using a group of radio button fields:

```
<html>
<head>
<title>HTML Form Input - Radio Button</title>
</head>
<body>

<form>
How long have you been using Java?
<br><dir><dir>

<input type=radio name=time value="never">Never<br>
<input type=radio name=time value="lt6mo">Less than 6 months<br>
<input type=radio name=time value="6-12">6 - 12 months<br>
<input type=radio name=time value="12-24" checked>1 - 2 years<br>
<input type=radio name=time value="guru">I'm a Java guru<br>
</form>

</body>
</html>
```

The radio buttons are shown next within a browser:

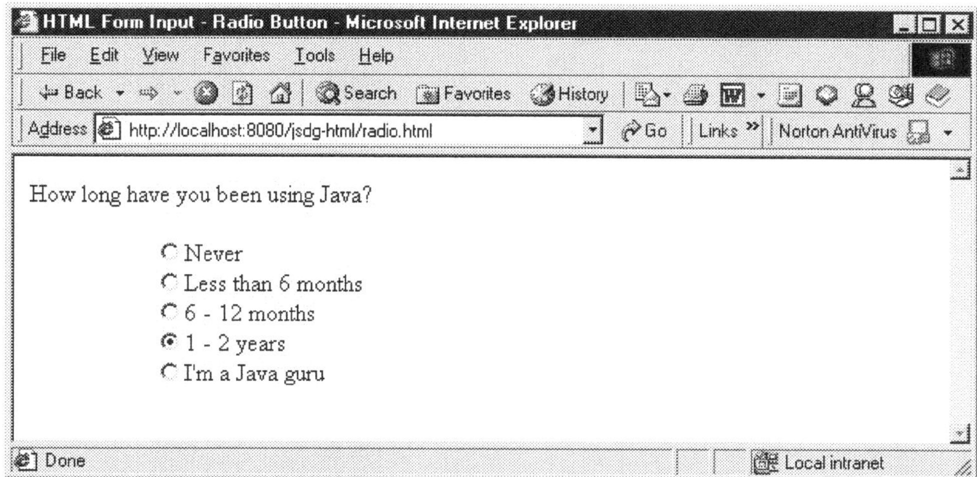

The Reset Input Type

The reset button input type allows you to place a "reset all input fields to their default values" button on the form. Unlike all other input types, the server is never aware of its presence; all of the processing performed when the reset button is clicked is done in the browser. There is one lone attribute for the reset button:

Attribute	Required	Description
VALUE		The reset button label; the default is "Reset"

The Submit Input Type

The submit button does exactly what you would imagine; when clicked by the user, it submits the form to the server for processing. The following are the attributes for the submit button:

Attribute	Required	Description
NAME		The optional name of the submit button
VALUE		The submit button label; the default is "Submit"

The following code show an example HTML file using several submit buttons. Note that the first submit button will have the default label of "Submit Query," the second submit button specifies its own label, while the third button specifies its own label and a button name. By supplying a button name, a parameter and value will be sent to the server when the button is clicked, which, in this case, will be action=add.

```
<html>
<head>
<title>HTML Form Input - Submit Buttons</title>
</head>
<body>

<form>
<input type=submit><br><br>
<input type=submit value="Process"><br><br>
<input type=submit value="Add" name=action>

</form>

</body>
</html>
```

The following shows the various submit buttons in action:

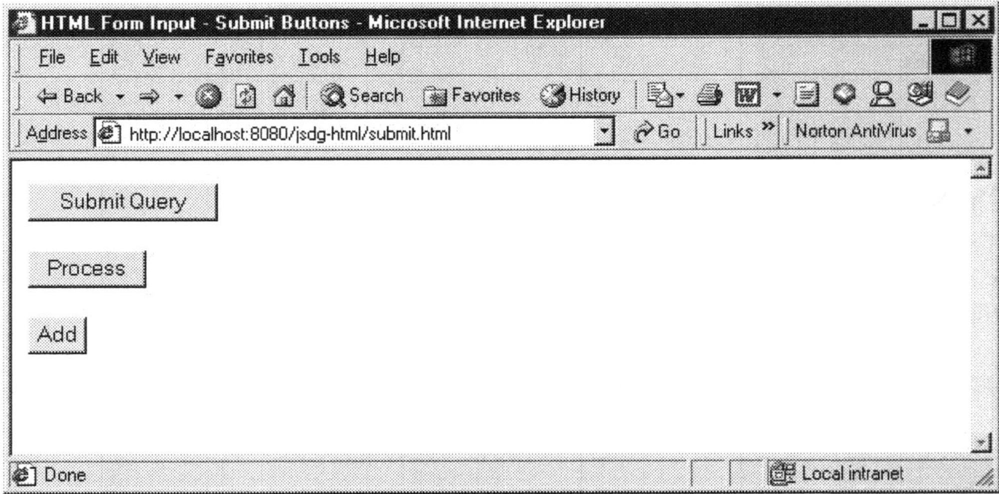

The Text Input Type

The most common input type that you will most likely use is a text input field. A text input field consists of a single input line where the user can enter up to a specified number of characters. The following table shows the attributes for the text input field:

Attribute	Required	Description
MAXLENGTH		Maximum length (in characters) of the data
NAME	Yes	The name of the input field
SIZE		Size (in characters) of the field
VALUE		The default value of the field

While you don't need to specify values for the size and maximum length of the input field, I would recommend that you do, because different browsers use different defaults. If the size is less than the maximum length, then the text can be scrolled within the input field.

The following shows an example HTML file using input fields:

```
<html>
<head>
<title>HTML Form Input - Text Input Field</title>
</head>
<body>

<form>

Name:
<input type=text name=name size=30 maxlength=30><br><br>

Address:
<input type=text name=address size=60 maxlength=60><br><br>

</form>

</body>
</html>
```

The following shows the text fields within a browser:

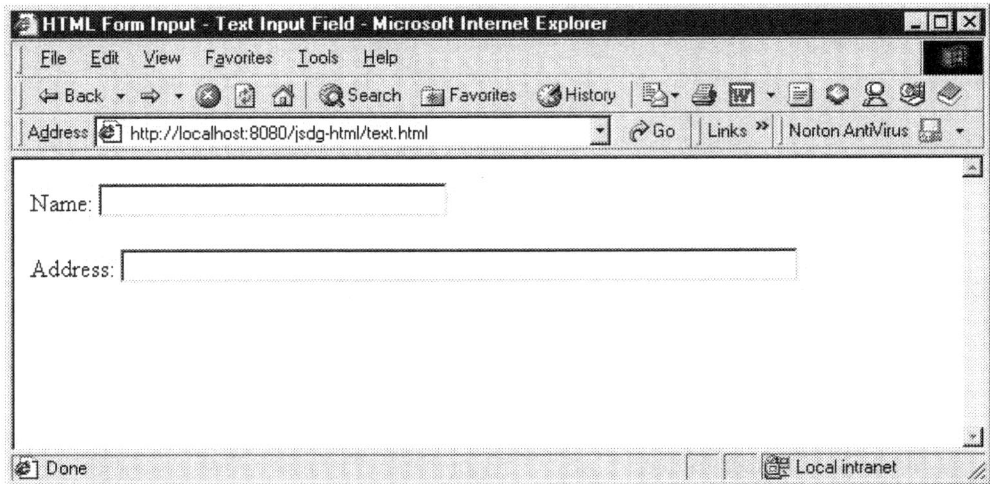

OK, so it doesn't look too pretty. We'll be taking a look at how to format the layout of the input fields later using HTML tables.

The <SELECT> Tag

Check boxes and radio buttons are great, but what about pull-down menus and list boxes? That's where the <SELECT> tag comes in. With the <SELECT> tag, you can very easily create pull-down menus and list boxes where the user can make selections depending upon the choices you present. The basic structure of the tag is as follows:

```
<SELECT NAME=name SIZE=size MULTIPLE>
<OPTION>tags...
</SELECT>
```

As with other input types, the NAME attribute is required and is the name of the parameter that is sent to the server when the form is submitted. The MULTIPLE attribute directs the browser to allow multiple selections by the user; this would be used in a list box that allows the user to choose more than one item. The SIZE attribute specifies the maximum number of options visible to the user; if the SIZE attribute is less than the number of options given, then the user can scroll through the options.

Note that there are attribute extensions that have been defined by Microsoft Internet Explorer and Netscape Navigator; I'll just focus on the standard attributes as defined by the HTML specification.

To best illustrate this, let's take a look at an HTML example. The first <SELECT> tag sets up a pull-down menu, and the second tag sets up a list box that allows multiple selections. Each option is specified by an <OPTION> tag that specifies the value that will be sent to the server if the option is selected. The <OPTION> tag also has one optional attribute, which is SELECTED. If this attribute is present (it has no value), then the option will be selected by default. Note that to create a pull-down menu, the SIZE attribute should be set to 1.

```
<html>
<head>
<title>HTML Form Input - Select Tag</title>
</head>
<body>

<form>
How long have you been using Java?
<select name=time size=1>
 <option value="never">Never
 <option value="lt6">   Less than 6 months
 <option value="6-12"> 6 - 12 months
 <option value="12-24">1 - 2 years
 <option value="guru"> I'm a Java guru
</select>

<br><br>
Operating Systems:
<select name=os size=4 multiple>
 <option value="win32">Windows
 <option value="solaris">Solaris
 <option value="hp">HP-UX
 <option value="linux">Linux
</select>
</form>
</body>
</html>
```

The following illustration shows what the pull-down menu and list box look like in a browser. Note that if multiple selections are made in the list box, multiple parameter values will be sent to the server.

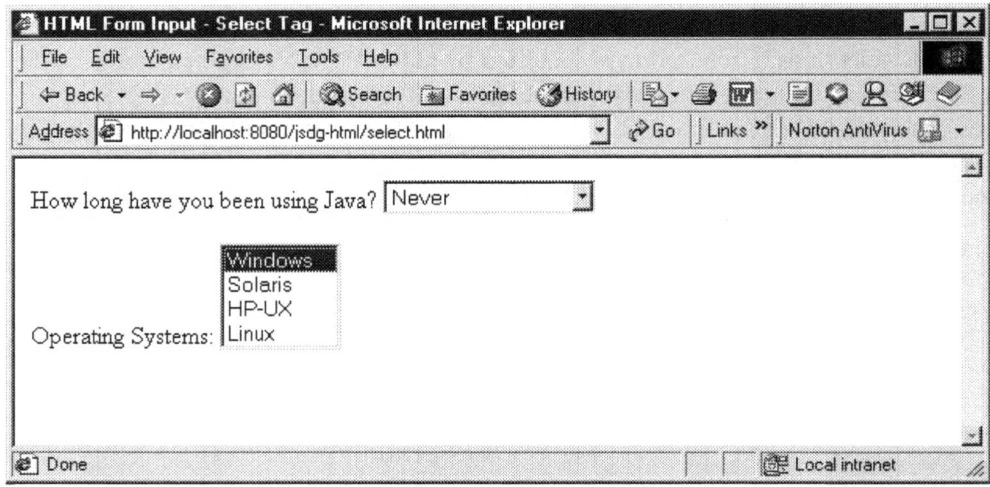

The <TEXTAREA> Tag

The <TEXTAREA> tag will create a multiline text entry area. This is quite useful for gathering comments or address information. The following is the basic structure of the <TEXTAREA> tag:

```
<TEXTAREA NAME=name COLS=n ROWS=m>
default value
</TEXTAREA>
```

Again, there are attribute extensions that have been defined by Microsoft Internet Explorer and Netscape Navigator; I'll just focus on the standard attributes as defined by the HTML specification.

Any plain text found between the <TEXTAREA> tag and the end tag will be considered the initial default value of the text area—no special HTML tags are allowed; it must be plain text.

I highly recommend that you provide values for the COLS and ROWS attributes to ensure a consistent look and feel between various browsers. You may not like the defaults that are chosen for you.

The following shows an example HTML file that uses a <TEXTAREA> tag:

```
<html>
<head>
<title>HTML Form Input - Text Area</title>
</head>
<body>

<form>
Comments?<br>
<textarea name=comments cols=60 rows=5>
</textarea>

</form>
</body>
</html>
```

The following shows the textarea field within a browser:

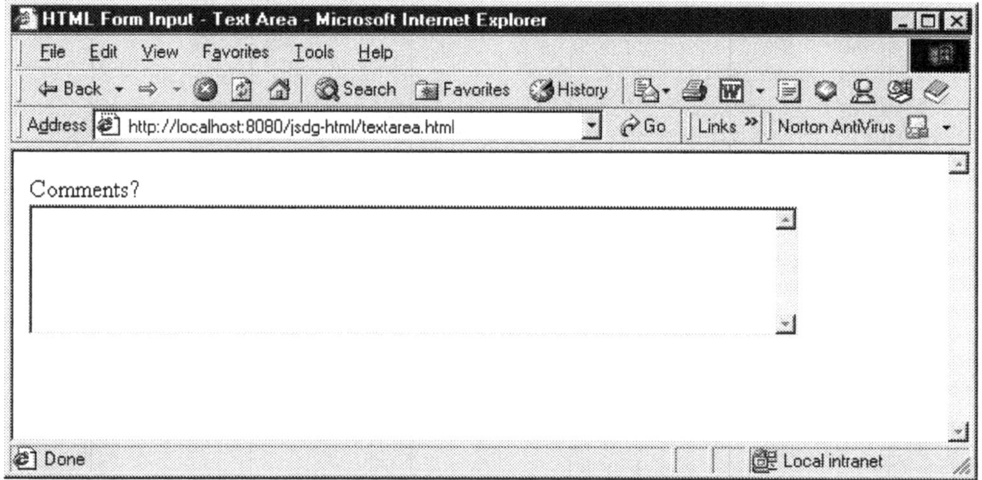

Putting It All Together: A Survey Form

Now that we have covered all the basic form input types, let's put it all together by creating a user survey form. Remember that the input fields by themselves do not give us any power over controlling where the fields will be placed; we'll have to rely on other HTML capabilities to properly lay out the form. In this case, I'm going to use an HTML table to ensure that everything lines up nicely.

```
<html>
<head>
<title>Customer Survey</title>
</head>
<body>
<h1><center>Customer Survey</center></h1>
<hr><br>

<form method=POST action="EchoSurvey">
<table border=0>
 <tr>
  <td align=right>Name:</td>
  <td colspan=2 align=left><input type=text name=name size=40></td>
 </tr>
 <tr>
  <td align=right>Email Address:</td>
  <td colspan=2 align=left><input type=text name=email size=40></td>
 </tr>
 <tr valign=top>
  <td align=right>Age:</td>
  <td align=left>
   <input type=radio name=age value="<18">Less than 18<br>
   <input type=radio name=age value="18-25">18 - 25
   </td>
  <td align=left>
   <input type=radio name=age value="26-40">26-40<br>
   <input type=radio name=age value=">40">Over 40
   </td>
 </tr>
 <tr valign=top>
  <td align=right>Operating Systems:</td>
  <td align=left>
   <select name=os size=5 multiple>
    <option>Win/95
    <option>NT
    <option>Solaris
    <option>HP-UX
    <option>Other
   </select>
   </td>
```

```
  </tr>
  <tr>
   <td></td>
   <td><input type=checkbox name=more value="yes">
       Send me more information
   </td>
  </tr>
  <tr>
   <td align=right>Comments:</td>
   <td colspan=2 align=left>
    <textarea name=comments cols=40 rows=4>
    </textarea>
    </td>
  </tr>
  <tr>
   <td></td>
   <td>
    <input type=reset value="Clear Form">
    <input type=submit value="Submit">
    </td>
  </tr>
</table>

</form>

</body>
</html>
```

A few things to note about the HTML:

- When the form is submitted (by clicking the Submit button), the form data will be sent to the URL specified in the <FORM> tag—in this case, the EchoSurvey servlet.
- By placing the labels and input fields into a table cell, the rows are automatically aligned so that the form flows well. In some cases, the input fields span multiple columns in order to keep the width of the overall table smaller.
- The list box allows multiple operating systems to be selected. The servlet will have to handle multiple values for the same parameter name.

Now let's take a look at our survey running in a browser:

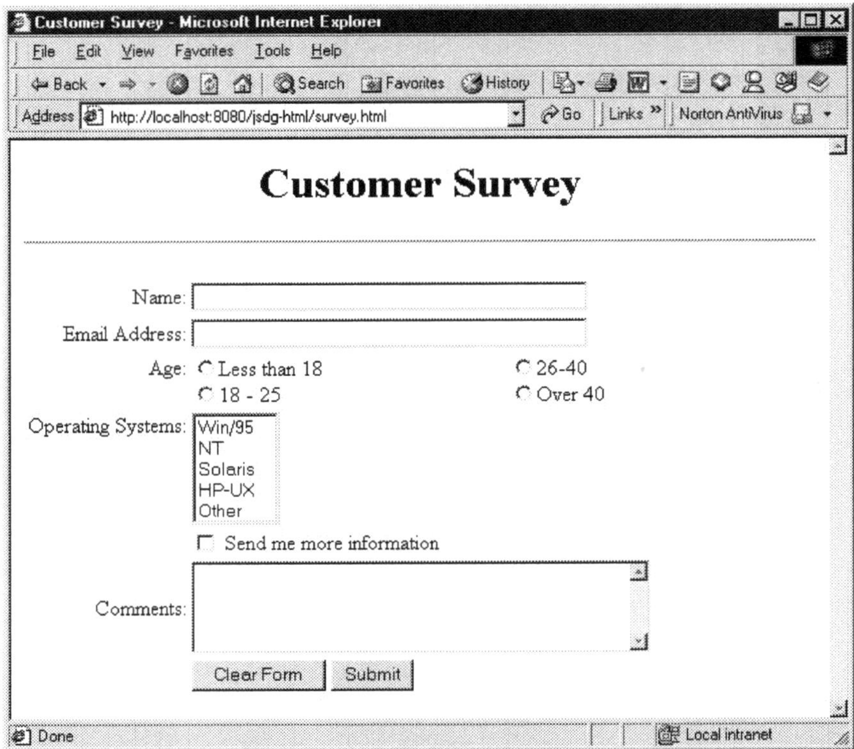

Once the user fills out all the information and clicks the Submit button, all the values will be sent to the server. It is important to note that HTML does not provide a mechanism for performing client-side validation of the data that is entered by the user (although you can use JavaScript); you'll have to validate the information on the server and return error information via an HTML page if necessary.

Let's go ahead and try the survey page out. The following illustrations show a completed survey page and the response from the server once the Submit button is clicked.

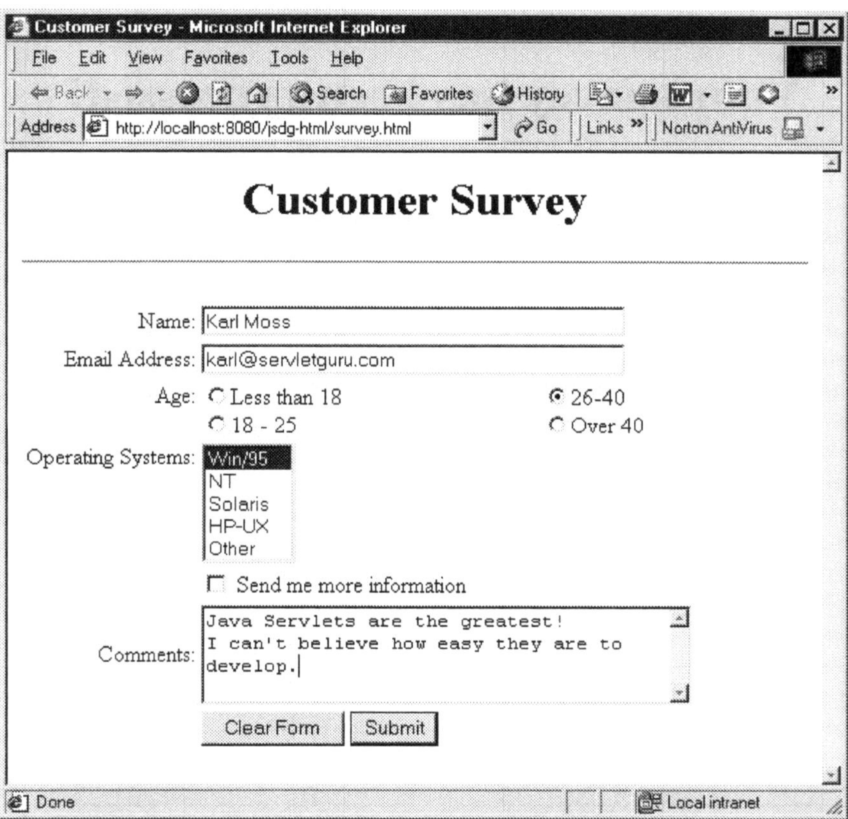

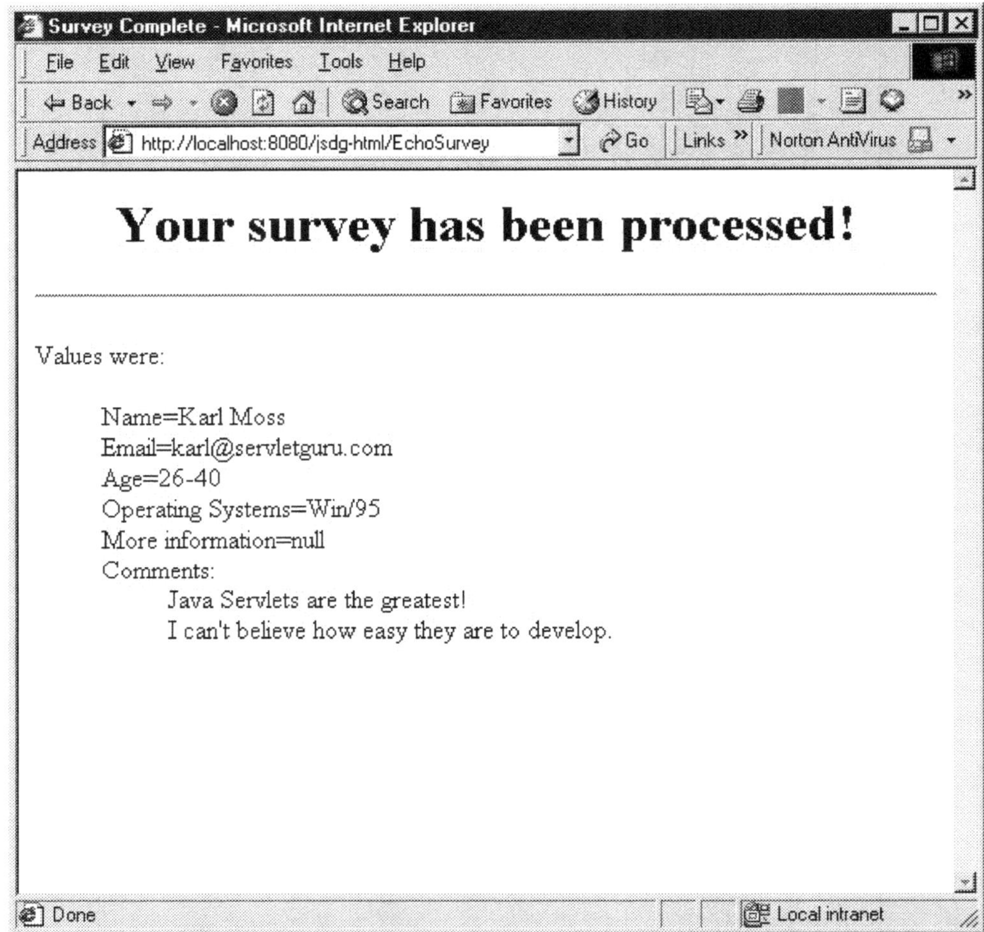

Clicking the Survey button invoked the EchoSurvey servlet, which simply retrieved all the values entered by the user on the HTML form and echoed them back to the user. Let's take a closer look at what the servlet had to do to get the data.

The EchoSurvey Servlet

The EchoSurvey servlet is a great example of how to retrieve parameter values that are sent to the servlet via a form submission. The servlet API makes it quite easy; the data is just one method call away. This method, getParameterValue(), takes a String argument, which is the parameter name. Remember that all the input types in the HTML form require a name—this is, the parameter name that is sent to the server. The getParameterValue() method returns either a String value for the given parameter or null if the parameter name is not found. Remember the list box input type that allows multiple selections? It can send multiple values to the server for a single parameter name. To process a parameter that may contain multiple values, the getParameterValues() method can be used, which returns an array of String values. Parameters with a single value will be returned in the first element (element 0) of the array.

Let's take a look at the servlet code:

```
package com.omh;

import javax.servlet.*;
import javax.servlet.http.*;
import java.io.*;
import java.util.*;

public class EchoSurvey
        extends HttpServlet
{
    public void doPost(HttpServletRequest req,
                       HttpServletResponse resp)
        throws ServletException, java.io.IOException
    {
        // Set the content type of the response
        resp.setContentType("text/html");

        // Create a PrintWriter to write the response
        PrintWriter out =
            new PrintWriter(resp.getOutputStream());

        // Print a standard header
        out.println("<html>");
        out.println("<head>");
        out.println("<title>Survey Complete</title>");
        out.println("</head>");
        out.println("<body>");
        out.println("<h1><center>Your survey has been processed!");
        out.println("</center></h1><hr><br>");
        out.println("Values were:");
        out.println("<dir>");
```

```
// Get the name
String name = req.getParameter("name");
out.println("Name=" + name + "<br>");

// Get the email address
String email = req.getParameter("email");
out.println("Email=" + email + "<br>");

// Get the age
String age = req.getParameter("age");
out.println("Age=" + age + "<br>");

// Get the operating system. There could be more than one
// value
String values[] = req.getParameterValues("os");
out.print("Operating Systems=");
if (values != null)
{
    for (int i = 0; i < values.length; i++)
    {
        if (i > 0) out.print(", ");
        out.print(values[i]);
    }
}
out.println("<br>");

// Get the 'more information' flag
String more = req.getParameter("more");
out.println("More information=" + more + "<br>");

// Get the comments
String comments = req.getParameter("comments");
out.println("Comments:<br>");
out.println("<dir>");

// Comment lines are separated by a carriage return/line feed
// pair - convert them to an HTML line break <br>
out.println(toHTML(comments));
out.println("</dir>");

out.println("</dir>");

// Wrap up
out.println("</body>");
```

```
        out.println("</html>");
        out.flush();
    }

    /**
     * <p>Convert any carriage return/line feed pairs into
     * an HTML line break command (<br>)
     *
     * @param line Line to convert
     * @return line converted line
     */
    private String toHTML(String line)
    {
        if (line == null)
        {
            return null;
        }

        StringBuffer sb = new StringBuffer();

        // Loop through and find the carriage return. Assume that
        // the following character is a line feed
        int begin = 0;
        while (true)
        {
            int pos = line.indexOf(0x0D, begin);
            if (pos < 0)
            {
                break;
            }

            sb.append(line.substring(begin, pos));
            sb.append("<br>");

            // Skip the line feed
            begin = pos + 1;
        }

        // Append whatever is left
        sb.append(line.substring(begin));

        return sb.toString();
    }
}
```

Note that the EchoSurvey servlet extends the HttpServlet class and implements the doPost() method. This method is invoked by the web server when an HTTP POST operation is done, which occurs when the user clicks the Submit button on our survey form. Inside the doPost() method, we get the output stream from the HTTP response object that is used to print the HTML page that will be sent back to the user. Once we have the output stream, it's a simple matter to retrieve all the form data and echo the values in HTML.

One thing to remember when working with a multiline text input field: the lines are separated by a carriage return/line feed pair (0x0D 0x0A). In our example, we've converted these ASCII control characters into an HTML line-break command (<br>).

Don't forget that you'll have to map the servlet to match the action command in the HTML form:

```
<servlet>
  <servlet-name>EchoSurvey</servlet-name>
  <servlet-class>com.omh.EchoSurvey</servlet-class>
</servlet>

<servlet-mapping>
  <servlet-name>EchoSurvey</servlet-name>
  <url-pattern>/EchoSurvey</url-pattern>
</servlet-mapping>
```

Summary

In this chapter, we've taken an in-depth look at HTML forms and all the different types of input possible, including various types of buttons, check boxes, radio buttons, list boxes, and text input fields. All of these various types of input were explained in detail, and a working example of each was provided. We then put together a customer survey form that used many types of HTML input and formatted the form using an HTML table so that the columns of the form would be aligned properly. A simple servlet, EchoSurvey, was used to illustrate how to process the data that is sent to the server when the Submit button is clicked.

Now that we have the basics of writing HTML forms, we're going to concentrate on how to use a database on the server from within a servlet. The next chapter will focus on how to use JDBC to retrieve and update database information as well as how to manage database connections.

CHAPTER

9

Using JDBC in Servlets

IN THIS CHAPTER:

One of the most common uses of servlets is to access corporate information residing in a database; some studies suggest that up to 80 percent of all applications utilize some type of data stored in a relational database. In this chapter, we'll explore JDBC, the Java API specification for connecting to databases and manipulating data, and how to use database information from within servlets.

JDBC Overview

What is JDBC? In a nutshell, JDBC (which used to stand for Java Database Connectivity but now is apparently no longer an acronym) is an API specification that defines the following:

- How to interact with corporate data sources from Java applets, applications, and servlets
- How to use JDBC drivers
- How to write JDBC drivers

Complete books have been written on JDBC drivers (in fact, I have written one such book), but I'll attempt to cover the basics in a single chapter. With this brief overview, you should have enough information to start developing data-aware Java applications.

The JDBC project was begun late in 1995 and was headed by Rick Cattel and Graham Hamilton at JavaSoft. The JDBC API is based on the X/OPEN Call Level Interface (CLI) that defines how clients and servers interact with one another when using database systems. Interestingly enough, Microsoft's Open Database Connectivity (ODBC) is also based on the X/OPEN CLI, so you should consider it a (distant) cousin. JavaSoft wisely sought the advice and input of leading database vendors to help shape and mold the JDBC specification. Because of the API review process (see the Java Community Process web site, www.jcp.org, for information regarding how specifications are created and approved), there was already significant vendor participation and endorsement when the API was made public.

Interoperability: The Key to JDBC

The major selling point of JDBC is database interoperability. What exactly does that mean? It means that by using the JDBC API for database access, you can change the underlying database driver (or engine) without having to modify your application.

Taking this one step further, you do not need to be aware of the quirks (also known as features) of a particular database system when you are developing your application; you write to the standard JDBC API specification and plug in the appropriate JDBC driver for the database that you want to use (see Figure 9-1). All of the nasty database implementation details of interfacing to a particular database system are left to the JDBC driver vendors.

Remember that the JDBC API specification is a "two-way street"; it defines not only how you as the application developer will interact with a database, but also how a JDBC driver must be written to preserve interoperability. To this end, Sun has developed a JDBC driver certification suite that verifies that a JDBC adheres to the specification and behaves in a predictable manner.

The JDBC-ODBC Bridge

As previously mentioned, Microsoft's ODBC specification shares the same heritage as JDBC: the X/OPEN CLI. Both APIs also share the language they use, which is SQL. SQL (commonly pronounced "sequel") used to be an acronym for Structured Query Language, but has since grown out of this acronym and is just a three-letter word with no vowels. SQL defines both the way that databases are defined and maintained, with a data definition language (DDL), and how data is read and updated, with a data manipulation language (DML).

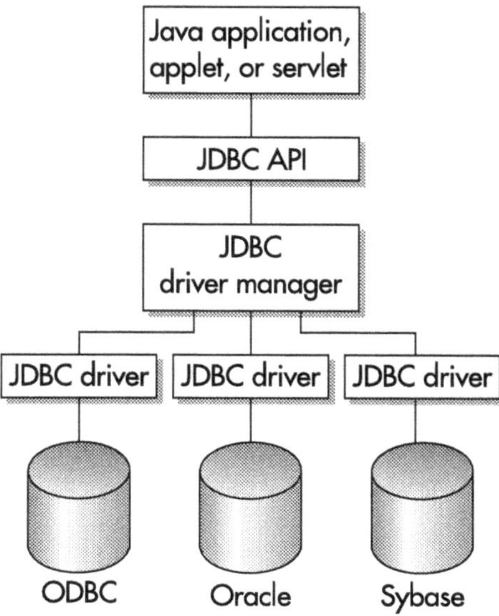

Figure 9-1 *JDBC interoperability*

One thing that ODBC had in 1996 that JDBC didn't was industry acceptance. ODBC, at that time, was the de facto standard for database access and held widespread popularity throughout the industry. Not only did every Microsoft database product come with an ODBC driver, but all major database vendors (such as Oracle, Sybase, Informix, and so on) had ODBC drivers for their products as well. How could Sun leverage the existing investment that companies had in ODBC and transfer some of its popularity into the realm of JDBC? The answer was the JDBC-ODBC Bridge.

The JDBC-ODBC Bridge is a JDBC driver that uses native (C language) libraries that make calls to an existing ODBC driver to access a database engine. As the author of the JDBC-ODBC Bridge, I have frequently been asked about the "inside story" of how and why the Bridge was developed.

The Inside Edition

Early on in the vendor review stage (late 1995), the JDBC specification was sent to INTERSOLV (then Merant, now DataDirect Technologies), which was (and still is) the leading ODBC driver vendor. I was part of the ODBC team at that time and had just finished developing an ODBC driver for FoxPro. Luckily, I had already begun to follow Java and was writing applications in my spare time just like everyone else (Java was still young, and very few companies had resources dedicated to Java programming). I was approached by my manager and was asked (okay, I begged) to review this new database access specification called JDBC. I think that this first draft was version 0.20 and vaguely resembled what we call JDBC today.

INTERSOLV was very interested in making a name for itself in the Java world and thus forged an agreement (with a signed contract) to implement a JDBC driver that would use existing ODBC drivers. In exchange for this development effort (plus one year of support), Sun would make a press release announcing this new partnership between Sun and INTERSOLV; no money ever changed hands. Sounds like Sun got a good deal, doesn't it? Since I had already been reviewing the specification, I was chosen (OK, I begged again) to develop this JDBC-ODBC Bridge. I started work in March of 1996 and the Bridge was completed in May in spite of continuous API changes and revisions.

Sun's main motivation for the Bridge, which it planned to give away for free, was to provide JDBC developers with an immediate way to start writing JDBC applications and, in their words, to "set the hook" so that JDBC would be widely accepted. Time has proven that these plans have certainly paid off.

Limitations

There are many limitations surrounding the use of the JDBC-ODBC Bridge, as well as many things that you should keep in mind:

- The Bridge was never intended to be a production piece of software, nor is it officially supported by Sun; it was developed as a prototyping and marketing tool. While I do know of many corporations using the Bridge for mission-critical applications, if another JDBC driver is available for the database that you are using, you should evaluate using it.
- The Bridge uses native (C language) code, which has severe implications. The Bridge cannot be used in untrusted applets, and all of the native libraries must be installed and configured on each machine. This includes not only the native library that comes with the Bridge (JdbcOdbc.dll or JdbcOdbc.so, depending upon the operating system) but also all the ODBC libraries, all the ODBC drivers, and all the libraries that the ODBC driver requires to function. Once all of this software is properly installed, you must also configure ODBC and create a new data source. This type of setup is a far cry from Java's "zero-install" model.
- Since the Bridge uses existing ODBC drivers, any bugs that exist in the ODBC driver will be encountered when using the Bridge.
- If your ODBC driver can't do it, neither will the Bridge when using that ODBC driver. Many people think that using the Bridge and their favorite ODBC driver will "web-enable" the ODBC driver and magically allow the database to be accessed over the Internet; this is certainly not true. Remember that the ODBC driver is running on the client machine and the way that it accesses its data has not changed.

Having said all of that, the Bridge will continue to be the only way to access some database products (such as Microsoft Access). There are many databases that come with an ODBC driver but do not, and will not, ship with a corresponding JDBC driver. In this case, the Bridge will be the only way to get to the data, unless you are willing to write a JDBC driver of your own.

JDBC Driver Types

The JDBC specification defines four basic types of JDBC drivers. It is important to understand the qualities of each type so that you can choose the right JDBC driver to suit your needs. One of the first questions that you will be asked if you go shopping for JDBC drivers is, "What type do you need?" The following sections describe the four basic types of JDBC drivers.

Type 1: The JDBC-ODBC Bridge

As previously explained, the JDBC-ODBC Bridge is provided by Sun as part of its JDK (starting with 1.1). The Bridge is part of the sun.jdbc.odbc package and is not required to be ported by vendors that provide a Java Virtual Machine (JVM). Remember that the Bridge uses native ODBC methods and has limitations in its use (see Figure 9-2).

You might consider using the Bridge in the following situations:

- For quick system prototyping.
- For three-tier database systems.
- For database systems that provide an ODBC driver but no JDBC driver.
- As a low-cost database solution where you already have an ODBC driver.

Type 2: Java to Native API

The Java to native API driver makes use of local native libraries provided by a vendor to communicate directly to the database (see Figure 9-3). This type of driver has many of the same restrictions as the JDBC-ODBC Bridge, because it uses native libraries. The most severe restriction is that it can't be used in untrusted applets. Also note that since the JDBC driver uses native libraries, those libraries must be installed and configured on each machine that will be using the driver. Most major database vendors provide a type 2 JDBC driver with their products.

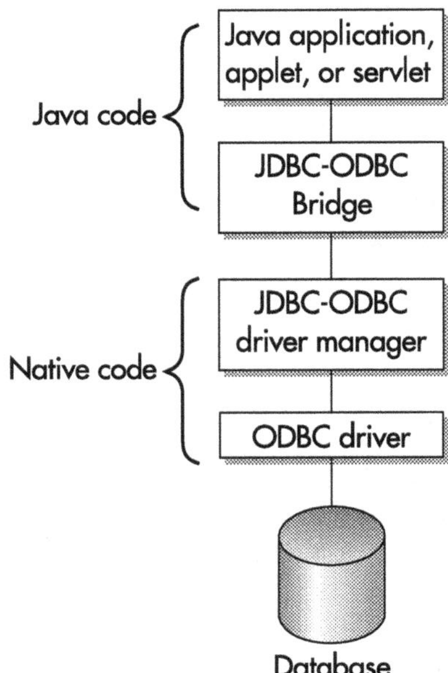

Figure 9-2 *The JDBC-ODBC Bridge (type 1 driver)*

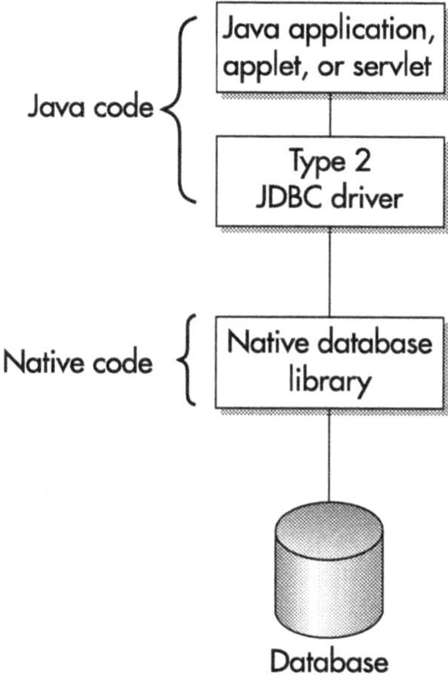

Figure 9-3 *Java to native API (type 2 driver)*

You might consider using Java to native API drivers in the following situations:

- As an alternative to using the JDBC-ODBC Bridge. Type 2 drivers will perform better than the Bridge, because they interface directly with the database.
- As a low-cost database solution where you are already using a major database system that provides a type 2 driver (such as Oracle, Informix, Sybase, and so on). Many vendors bundle their type 2 drivers with the database product.

Type 3: Java to Proprietary Network Protocol

This type of JDBC driver is by far the most flexible. It is typically used in a three-tier solution and can be deployed over the Internet. Type 3 drivers are pure Java and communicate with some type of middle tier via a proprietary network protocol that the driver vendor usually creates (see Figure 9-4). This middle tier most likely resides on a web or database server and, in turn, communicates with the database product via the type 1, type 2, or type 4 driver. Type 3 drivers are usually developed by companies not associated with a particular database product and may prove to be costly because of the benefits that they provide.

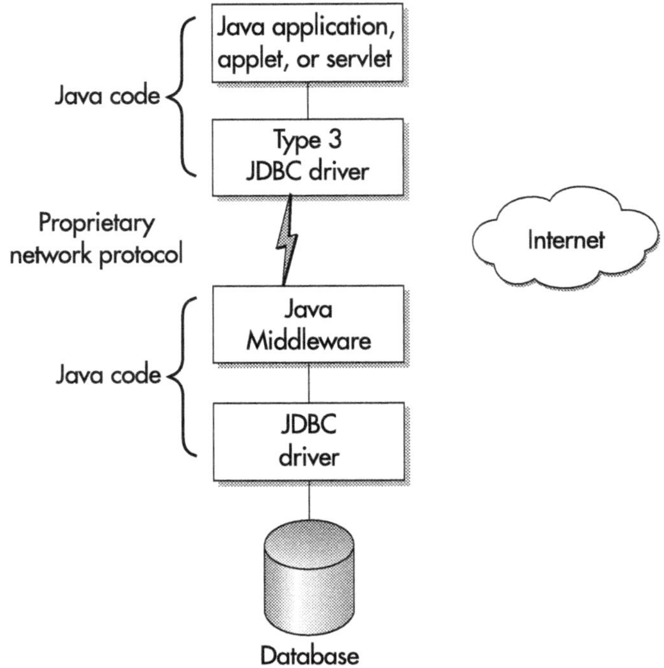

Figure 9-4 *Java to proprietary network protocol (type 3 driver)*

You might consider using a Java proprietary network protocol driver in the following situations:

- For web-deployed applets that do not require any preinstallation or configuration of software.
- For secure systems where the database product will be protected behind a middle tier.
- As a flexible solution where many different database products are in use. The middle-tier software can usually interface to any database product that can be accessed via JDBC.
- For a client that requires a small "footprint." The size of a type 3 driver is usually much smaller than all other types.

Type 4: Java to Native Database Protocol

Type 4 JDBC drivers are pure Java drivers that communicate directly with the database engine via its native protocol (see Figure 9-5). These types of drivers may be deployable over the Internet, depending upon the native communication protocol. The advantage that type 4 drivers have over all the other drivers is performance; there are no layers of native code or middle-tier software between the client and the database engine.

You might consider using a Java to native database protocol driver in the following situations:

- When high-performance is critical.
- For environments where only one database product is in use. If you do not have to worry about supporting multiple database systems, then a type 4 driver may be all that you need.
- For web-deployed applets, depending upon the capabilities of the driver.

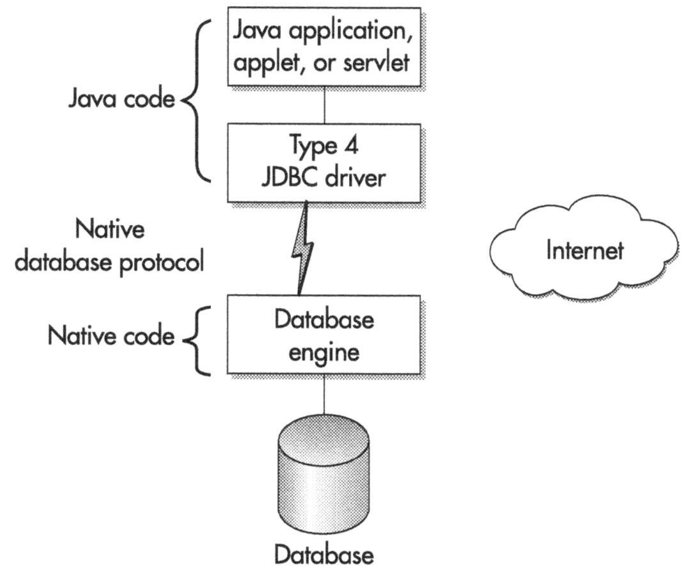

Figure 9-5 *Java to native database protocol (type 4 driver)*

And the Winner Is...

If you've skipped ahead to find out which type of driver will solve the world's problems, then you will be greatly disappointed; the answer is, "It depends." There are four types of JDBC drivers because there are a great variety of database needs. You will just have to weigh each of your requirements with the capabilities of each driver type to find the one that best suits your needs.

There does seem to be some confusion, however, over the preference of the different driver types. Just because type 4 is the highest driver type number, it does not imply that it is better than type 3, 2, or 1. Only your particular requirements will be able to point you to the right JDBC driver.

The Basic JDBC Flow

All JDBC applications follow the same basic flow:

1. Establish a connection to the database.
2. Execute a SQL statement.
3. Process the results.
4. Disconnect from the database.

Let's take a closer look at each one of these steps.

Establishing a Connection

The first step in using a database product via JDBC is to establish a connection. JDBC connections are specified by a URL, which has the following general format:

```
jdbc:subprotocol:subname
```

where *subprotocol* is the kind of database connectivity being requested (such as odbc, oracle, informix, and so on) and *subname* provides additional information required to establish a connection. When a connection URL is requested from the JDBC DriverManager, each of the known JDBC drivers is asked if it can service the given URL. The following is an example of requesting a connection to an ODBC data source named "MyData" via the JDBC-ODBC Bridge:

```
Connection con = DriverManager.getConnection("jdbc:odbc:MyData");
```

That's all fine and dandy, but how does the JDBC DriverManager know what JDBC drivers are available on the system? Good question! There are two mechanisms for notifying the DriverManager that a JDBC driver is available: the jdbc.drivers property and JDBC driver registration.

The jdbc.drivers system property is referenced by the DriverManager to get a list of JDBC drivers available on the system. It contains a colon-separated list of JDBC driver class names that the DriverManager can use in an attempt to satisfy a connection request.

Driver registration is much more common and gives you greater control over what JDBC driver you will use. All JDBC drivers are required to register themselves with the DriverManager when they are instantiated, which can be accomplished in either of two ways:

```
Class.forName("foo.Driver").newInstance();
```

or

```
new foo.Driver();
```

I personally prefer to use the Class.forName() method, but they both have the same effect; the JDBC driver will register itself with the DriverManager so that it can be used to service a connection request. Note that many drivers will register themselves in their static initializer, which gets invoked when the driver class is first referenced.

Executing a SQL Statement

Once a connection to the database has been established, you are ready to execute SQL statements that will perform some type of work. Before executing a SQL statement, you first need to create a statement object that provides an interface to the underlying database SQL engine. There are three different types of statement objects:

- **Statement** The base statement object that provides methods to execute SQL statements directly against the database. The Statement object is great for executing one-time queries and DDL statements such as CREATE TABLE, DROP TABLE, and so forth.
- **PreparedStatement** This statement object is created using a SQL statement that will be used multiple times, replacing only the data values to be used. Methods exist to specify the input parameters used by the statement.
- **CallableStatement** This statement object is used to access stored procedures in the database. Methods exist to specify the input and output parameters used by the statement.

The following is an example of using the Statement class to execute a SQL SELECT statement:

```
Statement stmt = con.createStatement();
ResultSet rs = stmt.executeQuery("SELECT * FROM MyTable");
```

Processing Results

After executing a SQL statement, you must process the results. Some statements will only return an integer value containing the number of rows affected (such as an UPDATE or DELETE statement). SQL queries (SELECT statements) will return a ResultSet that contains the results of the query. The ResultSet is made up of columns and rows; column values are retrieved by a series of *get* methods for each database type (such as getString(), getInt(), getDate(), and so on). Once you have retrieved all of the values you need from a row, you can call the next() method to move to the next row in the ResultSet. Older versions of the JDBC specification allow forward-only cursors; JDBC 2.0 has a more robust cursor control, with which you can move backward and position to absolute rows as well.

Disconnecting

Once you are done with a ResultSet, Statement, or Connection object, you should close them properly. The Connection object, ResultSet object, and all of the various Statement objects contain a close() method that should be called to ensure that the underlying database system frees all of the associated resources properly.

Some developers prefer to leave references hanging around and let the garbage collector take care of cleaning up the object properly. I strongly advise that when you are finished with a JDBC object, you call the close() method. Doing so should minimize any memory leaks caused by dangling objects left in the underlying database system.

JDBC Example: SimpleQuery

To illustrate all of the basic steps necessary when using JDBC, let's take a look at a very simple Java application that will connect to a Microsoft Access database using the JDBC-ODBC Bridge, execute a query against an employee database, display the results of the query, and perform all of the necessary cleanup.

Since we will be using the JDBC-ODBC Bridge (part of the JDK) and Microsoft Access (if you are using Microsoft Office, then you have it installed), we first need to configure an ODBC data source. For Windows, there is an ODBC administration tool that makes it easy to set up data sources; if you are using a UNIX platform, you'll have to edit the odbc.ini configuration file by hand (note that there is no Microsoft Access ODBC driver for UNIX). To start the ODBC administration program, select ODBC from the Control Panel (Start | Settings). Note that some versions of Windows will not show the ODBC data sources option by default; you must first click View All Control Panel Options. The following is an example of the administration screen:

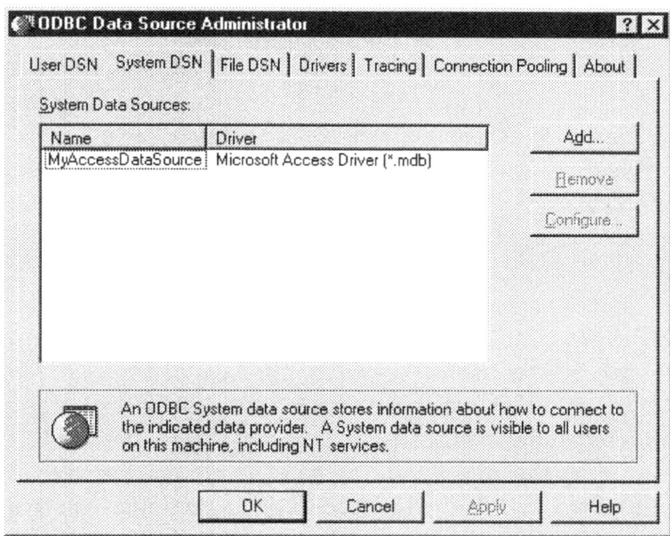

Click the Add button to add a new data source (make sure you first select the System DSN tab). You will then be presented with a list of all of the installed ODBC drivers on your system (from the odbcinst.ini configuration file).

When you select an installed ODBC driver (such as Microsoft Access, in our case), a configuration program is invoked that is specific to that particular driver. This is the configuration screen for Microsoft Access:

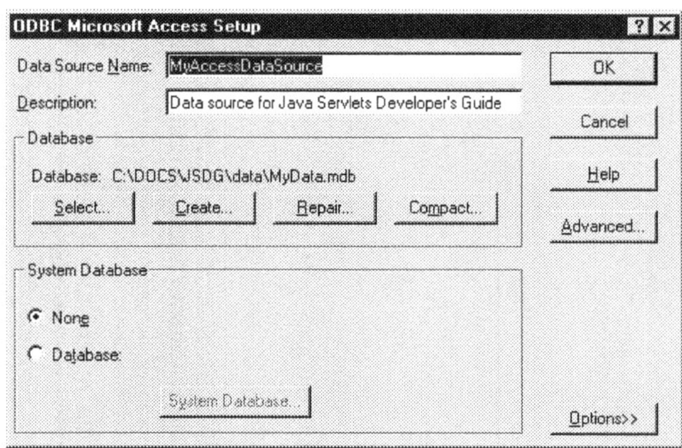

You'll need to enter the data source name (DSN) and any other pertinent information required for the particular database in use. For this example, use "MyAccessDataSource" as the DSN and MyData.mdb for the database file. MyData.mdb contains a prebuilt employee table and can be found on the book's web site. You can also find a Java application named com.omh.db.BuildEmployee that was used to build this particular database. The BuildEmployee application is a great example of generic JDBC programming; it makes no assumptions about the type of database being used and uses introspection (via DatabaseMetaData) to gain information about the database in use. I highly recommend browsing the source code.

There is one potential "gotcha" when using the JDBC-ODBC Bridge from a servlet container on some versions of Windows (such as NT). ODBC uses the concept of a "User" DSN and a System DSN. A System DSN can be used by an application that is installed as an NT Service, while a User DSN is available only to applications for the current user. Some servlet containers will be installed as an NT Service and thus only have access to System DSN information; be sure you configure your ODBC data source properly. If you want to see what you have configured, feel free to jump ahead to Chapter 15, in which we'll be writing a servlet that lists all of the ODBC DSNs that the servlet engine can access.

The following shows the code for the SimpleQuery application that will dump the contents of the Employee table from the Access database to the standard output device:

```
package com.omh.db;

import java.sql.*;

/**
 * This simple application will connect to a Microsoft Access
 * database using the JDBC-ODBC Bridge, execute a query against
 * an employee database, display the results, and then perform
 * all of the necessary cleanup
 */

public class SimpleQuery
{
    /**
    * Main entry point for the application
    */
    public static void main(String args[])
    {
        try
        {
```

```
            // Perform the simple query and display the results
            performQuery();
        }
        catch (Exception ex)
        {
            ex.printStackTrace();
        }
    }

    public static void performQuery() throws Exception
    {
        // The name of the JDBC driver to use
        String driverName = "sun.jdbc.odbc.JdbcOdbcDriver";

        // The JDBC connection URL
        String connectionURL = "jdbc:odbc:MyAccessDataSource";

        // The JDBC Connection object
        Connection con = null;

        // The JDBC Statement object
        Statement stmt = null;

        // The SQL statement to execute
        String sqlStatement =
            "SELECT Empno, Name, Position FROM Employee";

        // The JDBC ResultSet object
        ResultSet rs = null;

        try
        {

            System.out.println("Registering " + driverName);

            // Create an instance of the JDBC driver so that it has
            // a chance to register itself
            Class.forName(driverName).newInstance();

            System.out.println("Connecting to " + connectionURL);

            // Create a new database connection. We're assuming that
            // additional properties (such as username and password)
```

```
// are not necessary
con = DriverManager.getConnection(connectionURL);

// Create a statement object that we can execute queries
// with
stmt = con.createStatement();

// Execute the query
rs = stmt.executeQuery(sqlStatement);

// Process the results. First dump out the column
// headers as found in the ResultSetMetaData
ResultSetMetaData rsmd = rs.getMetaData();

int columnCount = rsmd.getColumnCount();

System.out.println("");
String line = "";
for (int i = 0; i < columnCount; i++)
{
    if (i > 0)
    {
        line += ", ";
    }

    // Note that the column index is 1-based
    line += rsmd.getColumnLabel(i + 1);
}
System.out.println(line);

// Count the number of rows
int rowCount = 0;

// Now walk through the entire ResultSet and get each
// row
while (rs.next())
{
    rowCount++;

    // Dump out the values of each row
    line = "";
    for (int i = 0; i < columnCount; i++)
    {
```

```
                    if (i > 0)
                    {
                        line += ", ";
                    }

                    // Note that the column index is 1-based
                    line += rs.getString(i + 1);
                }
                System.out.println(line);
            }

            System.out.println("" + rowCount + " rows, " +
            columnCount + " columns");
        }
        finally
        {

            // Always clean up properly!
            if (rs != null)
            {
                rs.close();
            }
            if (stmt != null)
            {
                stmt.close();
            }
            if (con != null)
            {
                con.close();
            }
        }
    }
}
```

As you can see, the four basic steps (establish a connection, execute a SQL statement, process the results, and disconnect from the database) are shown. The output from the application is as follows:

```
Registering sun.jdbc.odbc.JdbcOdbcDriver
Connecting to jdbc:odbc:MyAccessDataSource

Empno, Name, Position
1, Nebby K. Nezzer, President
```

```
2, Mr. Lunt, Foreman
3, Rack, Jr. Executive
4, Shack, Jr. Executive
5, Benny, Jr. Executive
6, George, Security Guard
7, Laura, Delivery Driver
7 rows, 3 columns
```

JDBC Servlet: EmployeeList

Now that you've had a whirlwind tour of JDBC, let's create a simple servlet that puts your newfound knowledge to use. Writing a servlet to use JDBC is really no different than writing the SimpleQuery application that we just saw; we'll still use the same basic steps to connect, execute, process, and close. The real difference is in how we process the results. Instead of printing the information to the standard output device (the screen), we'll need to format the HTML that will be sent back to the client.

The following shows the source code for a simple servlet (EmployeeList) that will use JDBC to get all of the employee information for our mythical company Nezzer's Chocolate Factory. The results of our query will be formatted into an HTML table and returned to the client.

```
package com.omh.db;

import javax.servlet.*;
import javax.servlet.http.*;
import java.util.*;
import java.io.*;
import java.sql.*;

/**
 * This is a simple servlet that will use JDBC to gather all
 * of the employee information from a database and format it
 * into an HTML table.
 */

public class EmployeeList
        extends HttpServlet
{
    public void doGet(HttpServletRequest req,
                      HttpServletResponse resp)
```

```
        throws ServletException, IOException
    {
        // Set the content type of the response
        resp.setContentType("text/html");

        PrintWriter out = resp.getWriter();

        // Print the HTML header
        out.println("<html>");
        out.println("<head>");
        out.println("<title>Employee List</title>");
        out.println("</head>");
        out.println("<h2><center>");
        out.println("Employees for Nezzer's Chocolate Factory");
        out.println("</center></h2>");
        out.println("<br>");

        // Create any addition properties necessary for connecting
        // to the database, such as user and password
        Properties props = new Properties();
        props.put("user", "karlmoss");
        props.put("password", "servlets");

        query("sun.jdbc.odbc.JdbcOdbcDriver",
              "jdbc:odbc:MyAccessDataSource",
              props,
              "SELECT Empno, Name, Position FROM Employee",
              out);

        // Wrap up
        out.println("</html>");
        out.flush();
        out.close();
    }

    /**
     * Given the JDBC driver name, URL, and query string,
     * execute the query and format the results into an
     * HTML table
     *
     * @param driverName JDBC driver name
     * @param connectionURL JDBC connection URL
```

```
     * @param props Addition connection properties, such as user
     * and password
     * @param query SQL query to execute
     * @param out PrintWriter to use to output the query results
     * @return true if the query was successful
     */
    private boolean query(String driverName, String connectionURL,
                          Properties props, String query,
                          PrintWriter out)
    {
        boolean rc = true;

        // The JDBC Connection object
        Connection con = null;

        // The JDBC Statement object
        Statement stmt = null;

        // The JDBC ResultSet object
        ResultSet rs = null;

        // Keep stats for how long it takes to execute
        // the query
        long startMS = System.currentTimeMillis();

        // Keep the number of rows in the ResultSet
        int rowCount = 0;

        try
        {

            // Create an instance of the JDBC driver so that it has
            // a chance to register itself
            Class.forName(driverName).newInstance();

            // Create a new database connection.
            con = DriverManager.getConnection(connectionURL, props);

            // Create a statement object that we can execute queries
            // with
            stmt = con.createStatement();

            // Execute the query
```

```
        rs = stmt.executeQuery(query);

        // Format the results into an HTML table
        rowCount = formatTable(rs, out);

    }
    catch (Exception ex)
    {
        // Send the error back to the client
        out.println("Exception!");
        ex.printStackTrace(out);
        rc = false;
    }
    finally
    {
        try
        {
            // Always close properly
            if (rs != null)
            {
                rs.close();
            }
            if (stmt != null)
            {
                stmt.close();
            }
            if (con != null)
            {
                con.close();
            }
        }
        catch (Exception ex)
        {
            // Ignore any errors here
        }
    }

    // If we queried the table successfully, output some
    // statistics
    if (rc)
    {
        long elapsed = System.currentTimeMillis() - startMS;
        out.println("<br><i>" + rowCount + " rows in " +
```

```
            elapsed + "ms</i>");
        }

        return rc;
    }

    /**
     * Given a JDBC ResultSet, format the results into
     * an HTML table
     *
     * @param rs JDBC ResultSet
     * @param out PrintWriter to use to output the table
     * @return The number of rows in the ResultSet
     */
    private int formatTable(ResultSet rs, PrintWriter out)
            throws Exception
    {
        int rowCount = 0;

        // Create the table
        out.println("<center><table border>");

        // Process the results. First dump out the column
        // headers as found in the ResultSetMetaData
        ResultSetMetaData rsmd = rs.getMetaData();

        int columnCount = rsmd.getColumnCount();

        // Start the table row
        StringBuffer sb = new StringBuffer("<tr>");

        for (int i = 0; i < columnCount; i++)
        {

            // Create each table header. Note that the column index
            // is 1-based
            sb.append("<th>");
            sb.append(rsmd.getColumnLabel(i + 1));
            sb.append("</th>");
        }
```

```
        // End the table row
        sb.append("</tr>");
        out.println(sb.toString());

        // Now walk through the entire ResultSet and get each
        // row
        while (rs.next())
        {
            rowCount++;

            // Start a table row
            sb = new StringBuffer("<tr>");

            // Dump out the values of each row
            for (int i = 0; i < columnCount; i++)
            {

                // Create the table data. Note that the column index
                // is 1-based
                sb.append("<td>");
                sb.append(rs.getString(i + 1));
                sb.append("</td>");
            }

            // End the table row
            sb.append("</tr>");
            out.println(sb.toString());
        }

        // End the table
        out.println("</table></center>");

        return rowCount;
    }
}
```

Note that EmployeeList contains two very generic methods for processing JDBC information: query() and formatTable(). The parameters for the query() method specify everything that JDBC needs in order to instantiate the JDBC driver, establish a connection, and execute a query. The formatTable() method will then take the results of a query (a ResultSet object) and create an HTML table that contains all of the data.

You might also notice that the total amount of time to process the HTML request is included in the HTML output. We'll be using this time as a baseline later when we start improving performance through connection pooling.

The following illustration shows the results of the EmployeeList servlet. Don't forget to configure the servlet appropriately in the web descriptor.

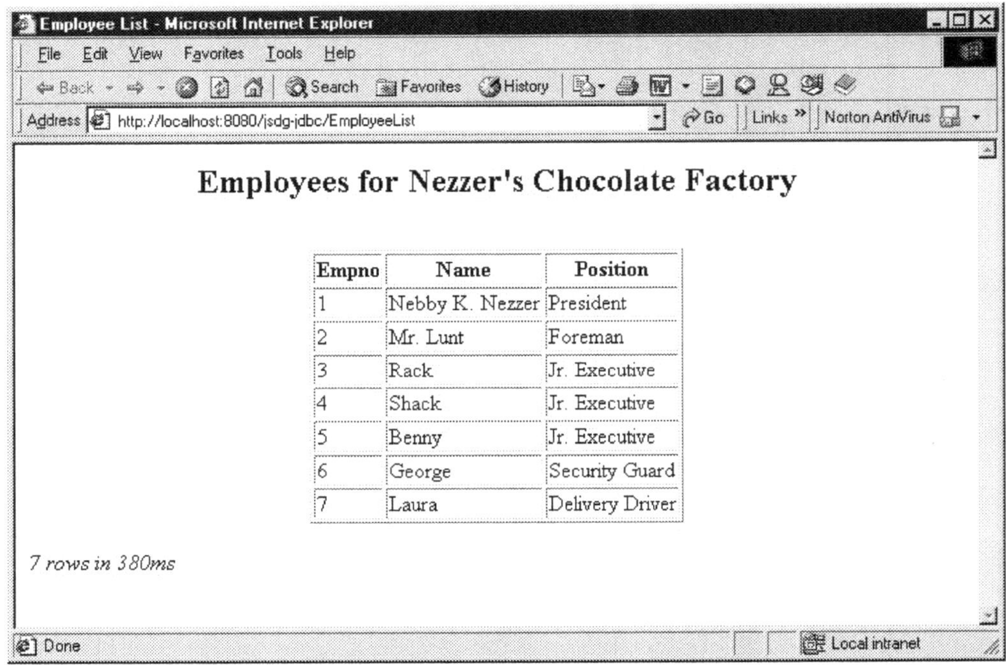

Limitations

The following are just a few things to keep in mind about our EmployeeList servlet:

- It works well for small amounts of data. If you are working with tables that have a large number of rows (hundreds or thousands), then it would be inefficient to dump the entire contents in a single HTML table. Not only would this take a while to complete, but from a user's perspective, it would not be very useful.
- All of the columns in the table are converted into a String when placed into the HTML table. This will not be appropriate for binary data such as images.

- The servlet establishes a new connection to the database with every GET request. Performing a database connection is a very expensive operation and not very efficient. In fact, creating a new connection for every new request will kill a high-traffic web server very quickly.

Let's take a look at ways we can solve these limitations.

Splitting the Output into Separate Pages

If you have a large amount of data to return to the user, you certainly don't want to put it all on one page. Not only would it be difficult for the user to maneuver through the data, but it also would take a long time to generate and download the HTML page. One way to solve this problem is to split data over many pages and let the user click a Next button to view the next portion of data. If you've ever used a search engine on the Web (which I know you have), you are familiar with how this works.

Here's our plan of attack for implementing a servlet that can break up the output over multiple pages:

1. Connect to the database and submit a query.
2. Process the results of the query, only outputting up to the maximum number of rows allowed on a single page.
3. If the maximum number of rows is exceeded, place a Next button at the bottom of the page and embed information within the HTML document that can be used to reposition the ResultSet cursor if the Next button is clicked.
4. If the Next button is clicked, a new query will be executed and the ResultSet cursor will be repositioned to where we left off. The results are processed as before.

Let's look at the IndyList servlet, which will list all of the past winners of the Indianapolis 500. The basic code is identical to that of the EmployeeList servlet, so I'll just point out the major differences.

First, we need to limit the number of rows that are shown when processing the ResultSet:

```
/**
 * Given a JDBC ResultSet, format the results into
```

```
 * an HTML table
 *
 * @param rs JDBC ResultSet
 * @param out PrintWriter to use to output the table
 * @param uri Requesting URI
 * @return The number of rows in the ResultSet
 */
private int formatTable(ResultSet rs, PrintWriter out,
                        String uri)
        throws Exception
{
    int rowsPerPage = 10;
    int rowCount = 0;

    // Keep track of the last year found
    String lastYear = "";

    // This will be true if there is still more data in the
    // table
    boolean more = false;

    // Create the table
    out.println("<center><table border>");

    // Process the results. First dump out the column
    // headers as found in the ResultSetMetaData
    ResultSetMetaData rsmd = rs.getMetaData();

    int columnCount = rsmd.getColumnCount();

    // Start the table row
    StringBuffer sb = new StringBuffer("<tr>");

    for (int i = 0; i < columnCount; i++)
    {

       // Create each table header. Note that the column index
       // is 1-based
       sb.append("<th>");
       sb.append(rsmd.getColumnLabel(i + 1));
       sb.append("</th>");
    }
```

```
// End the table row
sb.append("</tr>");
out.println(sb.toString());

// Now walk through the entire ResultSet and get each
// row
while (rs.next())
{
    rowCount++;

    // Start a table row
    sb = new StringBuffer("<tr>");

    // Dump out the values of each row
    for (int i = 0; i < columnCount; i++)
    {

        // Create the table data. Note that the column index
        // is 1-based
        String data = rs.getString(i + 1);
        sb.append("<td>");
        sb.append(data);
        sb.append("</td>");

        // If this is the year column, cache it
        if (i == 0)
        {
            lastYear = data;
        }
    }

    // End the table row
    sb.append("</tr>");
    out.println(sb.toString());

    // If we are keeping track of the maximum number of
    // rows per page and we have exceeded that count
    // break out of the loop
    if ((rowsPerPage > 0) &&
        (rowCount >= rowsPerPage))
    {
        // Find out if there are any more rows after this one
```

```
                more = rs.next();
                break;
            }
        }

        // End the table
        out.println("</table></center>");

        if (more)
        {

            // Create a 'Next' button
            out.println("<form method=POST action=\"" +
                        uri + "\">");
            out.println("<center>");
            out.println("<input type=submit value=\"Next " +
                        rowsPerPage + " rows\">");
            out.println("</center>");
            // Page was filled. Put in the last year that we saw
            out.println("<input type=hidden name=lastYear value=" +
                        lastYear + ">");
            out.println("</form>");
        }

        return rowCount;
    }
```

Note that if we did have to limit the number of rows returned to the client that a submit button will be generated in the HTML that, when clicked, will cause the servlet to be invoked again. A hidden field is added that maintains the last year shown on the page. The year is a unique key in this particular table, which we can use as a starting point when called again. If we are on the last page of data for the table, the Next button is not generated.

The Uniform Resource Identifier (URI) of the servlet was retrieved from the HttpRequest object given when the servlet was invoked.

When the Next button is clicked, we need to be able to start where we left off. Using the value of the hidden field that was generated when the ResultSet was processed, we can create a new SQL statement with a WHERE clause that will return the proper data. The value of the hidden field is easy to retrieve:

```
// Get the last year shown on the page that
// called us. Remember that we are sorting
// the years in descending order.
String lastYear = req.getParameter("lastYear");
if (lastYear == null)
{
    lastYear = "9999";
}
```

I'm using the value of the hidden field to generate the SQL statement:

```
SELECT * from IndyWinners where year<lastYear order by Year desc
```

The default value of lastYear is 9999, so if the parameter is not set (like the first time the servlet is invoked), all of the years will be selected. Otherwise, the search will be limited to those years that are less than the last year. Note that I'm sorting the years in descending order so that the most current winners are shown first. This type of searching is not really very efficient and has the possibility of being inaccurate. Each time the Next button is clicked, a new query is executed; this may be expensive if the database engine does not cache previous queries. Also, if another user happens to modify the table by adding, deleting, or updating a row, the new query will reflect those changes. Ideally, we should have a single ResultSet that we can persist and move forward and backward through as the user requests data. Unfortunately, JDBC 1.x does not allow for any cursor movement other than forward. JDBC 2.0 does allow drivers to expose expanded cursor support that makes this task possible.

Also note that the only way that this can work is with tables that have a unique key (the year, in our case). We have to be able to uniquely identify the last row that was displayed so that we can pick up where we left off. The absolute best way to do this is with a unique row identifier, such as Oracle's ROWID. This ROWID is present in all tables, and you can use it to uniquely reference rows. You can query the underlying database about the presence of some type of unique identifier with DatabaseMetaData.getBestRowIdentifier(). If a row identifier does not exist, you will have to design your table so that a unique key is present instead. Since I'm using Microsoft Access, which does not supply a unique row identifier, I am using the unique year column instead.

The first page of the query is shown next. The illustration that follows it shows the results after the Next button is clicked.

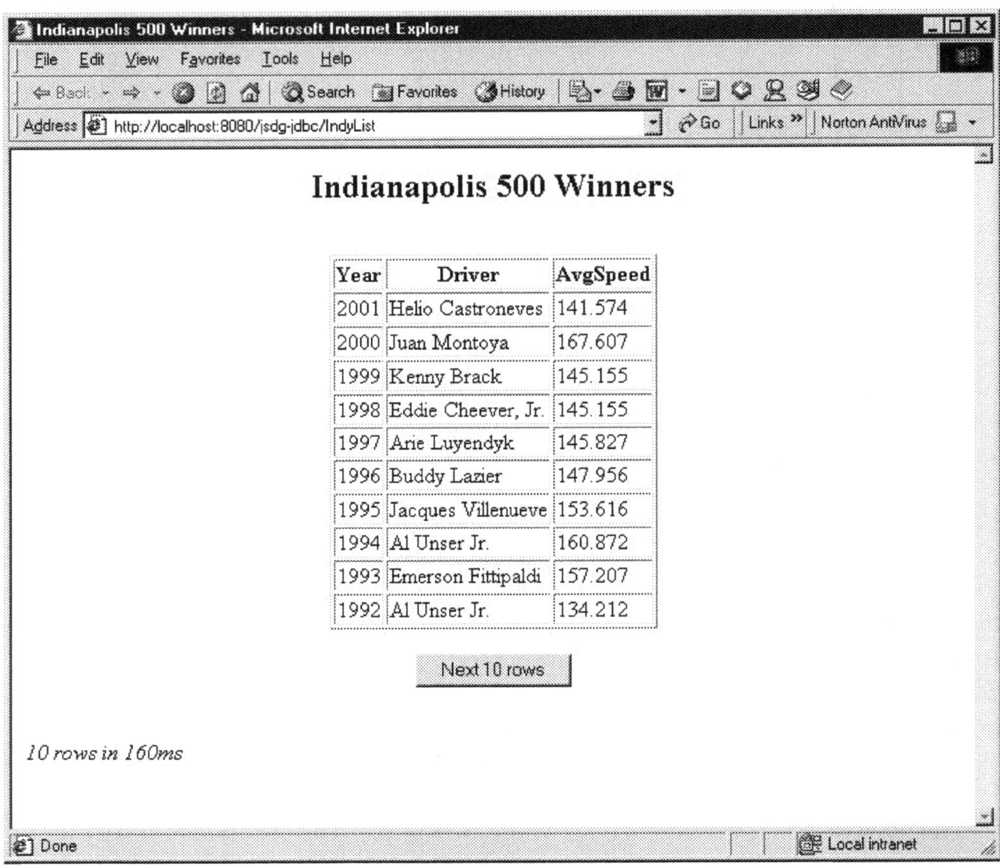

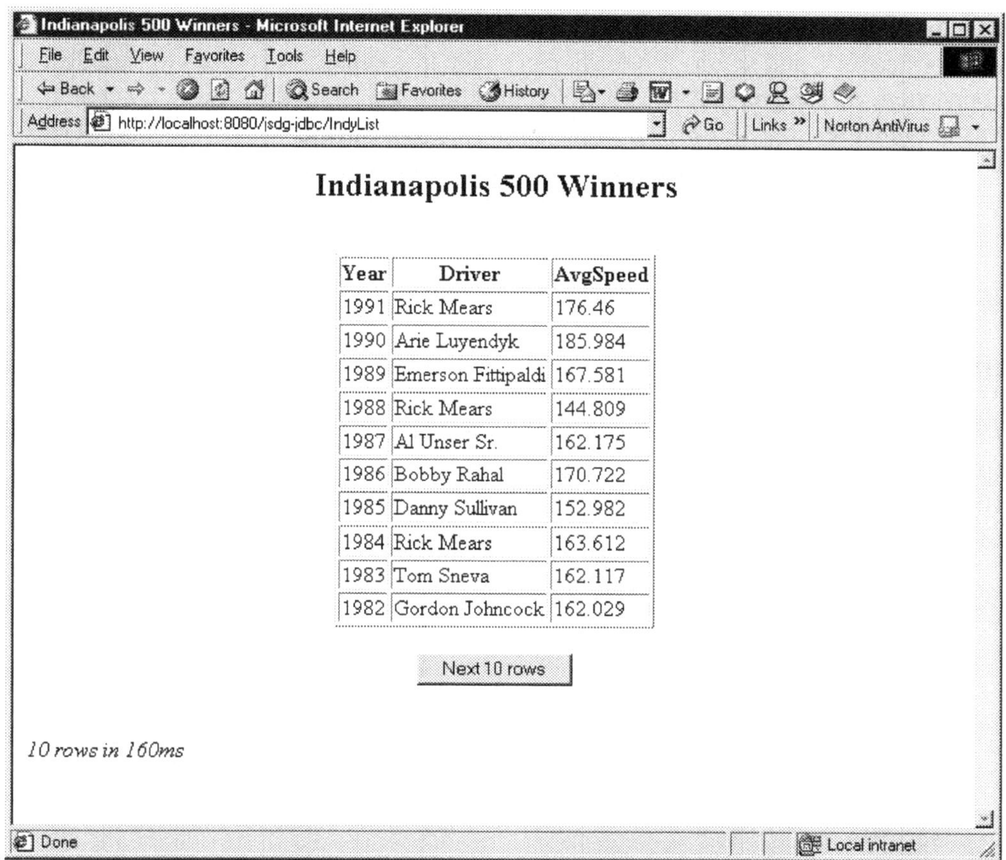

Indianapolis 500 Winners

Year	Driver	AvgSpeed
1991	Rick Mears	176.46
1990	Arie Luyendyk	185.984
1989	Emerson Fittipaldi	167.581
1988	Rick Mears	144.809
1987	Al Unser Sr.	162.175
1986	Bobby Rahal	170.722
1985	Danny Sullivan	152.982
1984	Rick Mears	163.612
1983	Tom Sneva	162.117
1982	Gordon Johncock	162.029

Connection Pooling

As previously mentioned, one of the most expensive database operations is establishing a connection. Depending upon the database engine you are using, a connection might have to perform protocol handshaking, verify user information, open disk files, create memory caches, and so on. While we can't take away the time it takes to establish a connection, we can preallocate a pool of connections that are ready for use. By creating this pool in a separate thread, we can let another process take the performance hit and let the main application (a servlet) grab the next connection that is ready without having to wait.

There are many side benefits to having a connection pool, as well. You can monitor connection usage, limit the maximum number of connections allowed, establish timeout parameters for badly behaved connections, and so on.

Writing the ConnectionPool Object

Let's take a look at a connection pool implementation that I have named ConnectionPool (pretty clever, huh?). The connection pool attributes are determined by a configuration file that, by default, is named ConnectionPool.cfg. The following is an example configuration file:

```
# ConnectionPool.cfg
#
# Defines connection pool parameters
#

JDBCDriver=sun.jdbc.odbc.JdbcOdbcDriver
JDBCConnectionURL=jdbc:odbc:MyAccessDataSource
ConnectionPoolSize=5
ConnectionPoolMax=100
ConnectionUseCount=5
ConnectionTimeout = 2
User=karl
Password=servlets
```

- **JDBCDriver** The class name of the JDBC driver to use for the connection pool. The example is using the JDBC-ODBC Bridge.
- **JDBCConnectionURL** The URL of the connection to establish. The example is specifying to create an ODBC connection through the Bridge for the data source MyAccessDataSource.
- **ConnectionPoolSize** The minimum size of the connection pool. The ConnectionPool object will ensure that there are always at least this number of connections in the pool.

- **ConnectionPoolMax** The maximum size of the connection pool. Note that the actual size of the connection pool may be limited by the underlying JDBC driver as well.
- **ConnectionUseCount** If non-zero, this is the maximum number of times the connection may be used before it is closed and a new connection is created in its place. Some JDBC drivers may have problems reusing connections for an indefinite amount of time; this parameter is available to work around this type of problem.
- **ConnectionTimeout** If non-zero, this is the number of minutes a connection may be idle (with no users) before it is terminated and a new connection is created in its place. This can prevent "stale" connections.
- **Other properties** Any other properties found in the configuration file (user and password, in our case) are considered properties that must be passed on to the JDBC driver when establishing a connection.

The following code is used to create the initial pool (the complete source code can be found at www.servletguru.com):

```
/**
 * Creates the initial connection pool. A timer thread
 * is also created so that connection timeouts can be
 * handled.
 *
 * @return true if the pool was created
 */
private void createPool() throws Exception
{
    // Sanity check our properties
    if (driverName == null)
    {
        throw new Exception("JDBCDriver property not found");
    }
    if (connectionURL == null)
    {
        throw new Exception("JDBCConnectionURL property not found");
    }
    if (connectionPoolSize < 0)
    {
        throw new Exception("ConnectionPoolSize property not found");
    }
    if (connectionPoolSize == 0)
```

```
{
    throw new Exception("ConnectionPoolSize invalid");
}
if (connectionPoolMax < connectionPoolSize)
{
    trace("WARNING - ConnectionPoolMax is invalid and will " +
          "be ignored");
    connectionPoolMax = -1;
}
if (connectionTimeout < 0)
{
    // Set the default to 30 minutes
    connectionTimeout = 30;
}

// Dump the parameters we are going to use for the pool.
// We don't know what type of servlet environment we will
// be running in - this may go to the console or it
// may be redirected to a log file
trace("JDBCDriver = " + driverName);
trace("JDBCConnectionURL = " + connectionURL);
trace("ConnectionPoolSize = " + connectionPoolSize);
trace("ConnectionPoolMax = " + connectionPoolMax);
trace("ConnectionUseCount = " + connectionUseCount);
trace("ConnectionTimeout = " + connectionTimeout +
      " seconds");

// Also dump any additional JDBC properties
Enumeration enum = JDBCProperties.keys();
while (enum.hasMoreElements())
{
    String key = (String) enum.nextElement();
    String value = JDBCProperties.getProperty(key);
    trace("(JDBC Property) " + key + " = " + value);
}

// Attempt to create a new instance of the specified
// JDBC driver. Well behaved drivers will register
// themselves with the JDBC DriverManager when they
// are instantiated
trace("Registering " + driverName);
Driver d = (Driver) Class.forName(driverName).newInstance();

// Create the vector for the pool
pool = new Vector();

// Bring the pool to the minimum size
```

```
        fillPool(connectionPoolSize);
    }

    /**
     * Adds a new connection to the pool
     *
     * @return Index of the new pool entry, or -1 if an
     * error has occurred
     */
    private int addConnection()
    {
        int index = -1;

        try
        {
            // Calculate the new size of the pool
            int size = pool.size() + 1;

            // Create a new entry
            fillPool(size);

            // Set the index pointer to the new connection if one
            // was created
            if (size == pool.size())
            {
                index = size - 1;
            }
        }
        catch (Exception ex)
        {
            ex.printStackTrace();
        }
        return index;
    }

    /**
     * Brings the pool to the given size
     */
    private synchronized void fillPool(int size) throws Exception
    {
        boolean useProperties = true;
        String userID = null;
        String password = null;

        // If the only properties present are the user id and
        // password, get the connection using them instead of
        // the properties object
```

```
if (JDBCProperties != null)
{
    // Make sure there are only 2 properties, and they are
    // the user id and password
    if (JDBCProperties.size() == 2)
    {
        userID =
        getPropertyIgnoreCase(JDBCProperties, "user");
        password =
        getPropertyIgnoreCase(JDBCProperties, "password");

        // If all we've got is a user id and password then
        // don't use the properties
        if ((userID != null) && (password != null))
        {
            useProperties = false;
        }
    }
}

// Loop while we need to create more connections
while (pool.size() < size)
{
    ConnectionObject co = new ConnectionObject();

    // Create the connection
    if (useProperties)
    {
        co.con = DriverManager.getConnection(connectionURL,
                          JDBCProperties);
    }
    else
    {
        co.con = DriverManager.getConnection(connectionURL,
                          userID, password);
    }

    // Do some sanity checking on the first connection in
    // the pool
    if (pool.size() == 0)
    {
        // Get the maximum number of simultaneous connections
        // as reported by the JDBC driver
        DatabaseMetaData md = co.con.getMetaData();
        maxConnections = md.getMaxConnections();
    }
```

```
        // Give a warning if the size of the pool will exceed
        // the maximum number of connections allowed by the
        // JDBC driver
        if ((maxConnections > 0) &&
            (size > maxConnections))
        {
            trace("WARNING: Size of pool will exceed safe maximum of " +
                  maxConnections);
        }

        // Clear the in use flag
        co.inUse = false;

        // Set the last access time
        touch(co);

        pool.addElement(co);
    }
}
```

As you can see, the connections are kept in a small wrapper object (called ConnectionObject) that contains the JDBC connection as well as the use count and last access time. The ConnectionObjects are kept in a global Vector. Note how the DatabaseMetaData is used to query the JDBC driver for the maximum number of concurrent connections allowed. Note also that a timer thread was created that will call back into the ConnectionPool object so that connection timeouts and general housekeeping can be performed. One of the most vital housekeeping operations is to check for connections that were closed outside of the connection pool; an application could have inadvertently closed a Connection. With each timer tick (every 20 seconds), all of the connections are checked to make sure they are still open; if a connection is no longer open, it is removed from the pool and a new one is created in its place.

The getConnection() method will find an available connection in the pool (or create one if necessary) and return it to the caller:

```
/**
 * Gets an available JDBC Connection. Connections will be
 * created if necessary, up to the maximum number of connections
 * as specified in the configuration file.
 *
 * @return JDBC Connection, or null if the maximum
 * number of connections has been exceeded
 */
public synchronized Connection getConnection()
```

```
{
    // If there is no pool it must have been destroyed
    if (pool == null)
    {
        return null;
    }

    Connection con = null;
    ConnectionObject connectionObject = null;
    int poolSize = pool.size();

    // Get the next available connection
    for (int i = 0; i < poolSize; i++)
    {

        // Get the ConnectionObject from the pool
        ConnectionObject co = (ConnectionObject)
        pool.elementAt(i);

        // If this is a valid connection and it is not in use,
        // grab it
        if (co.isAvailable())
        {
            connectionObject = co;
            break;
        }
    }

    // No more available connections. If we aren't at the
    // maximum number of connections, create a new entry
    // in the pool
    if (connectionObject == null)
    {
        if ((connectionPoolMax < 0) ||
            ((connectionPoolMax > 0) &&
             (poolSize < connectionPoolMax)))
        {
            // Add a new connection.
            int i = addConnection();

            // If a new connection was created, use it
            if (i >= 0)
            {
```

```
                connectionObject = (ConnectionObject)
                pool.elementAt(i);
            }
        }
        else
        {
            trace("Maximum number of connections exceeded");
        }
    }

    // If we have a connection, set the last time accessed,
    // the use count, and the in use flag
    if (connectionObject != null)
    {
        connectionObject.inUse = true;
        connectionObject.useCount++;
        touch(connectionObject);
        con = connectionObject.con;
    }

    return con;
}
```

Closing a connection with the ConnectionPool close() method does not necessarily close the connection; it may just be placed back into the connection pool ready for another use:

```
/**
 * Places the connection back into the connection pool,
 * or closes the connection if the maximum use count has
 * been reached
 *
 * @param Connection object to close
 */
public synchronized void close(Connection con)
{
    // Find the connection in the pool
    int index = find(con);

    if (index != -1)
    {
        ConnectionObject co = (ConnectionObject)
        pool.elementAt(index);
```

```
            // If the use count exceeds the max, remove it from
            // the pool.
            if ((connectionUseCount > 0) &&
                (co.useCount >= connectionUseCount))
            {
                trace("Connection use count exceeded");
                removeFromPool(index);
            }
            else
            {
                // Clear the use count and reset the time last used
                touch(co);
                co.inUse = false;
           }
       }
   }
```

ConnectionPool Example: A Local Pool

One usage for our new ConnectionPool object is to embed it within a servlet. Let's rewrite the EmployeeList servlet that we saw earlier in this chapter to use the ConnectionPool—we'll call it FastEmployeeList1. First, we need to define a ConnectionPool instance variable to hold our local copy of the connection pool:

```
package com.omh.db;

import com.omh.jdbc.ConnectionPool;

import javax.servlet.*;
import javax.servlet.http.*;
import java.util.*;
import java.io.*;
import java.sql.*;

/**
 * This is a simple servlet that will use JDBC to gather all
 * of the employee information from a database and format it
 * into an HTML table. This servlet uses a local connection
 * pool.
 */
```

```
public class FastEmployeeList1
        extends HttpServlet
{
    // Our connection pool. Note that instance variables are
    // actually global to all clients since there is only
    // one instance of the servlet that has multiple threads
    // of execution
    ConnectionPool connectionPool;
```

Even though it is spelled out in the comment block above the instance variable, it's worth repeating: you should consider instance variables as global in nature to all invocations of the servlet. The reason is that there are multiple threads executing using only one instance of the servlet.

Now we can override the init() and destroy() methods of the servlet to create the connection pool and destroy it, respectively:

```
/**
 * Initialize the servlet. This is called once when the
 * servlet is loaded. It is guaranteed to complete before any
 * requests are made to the servlet
 *
 * @param cfg Servlet configuration information
 */
public void init(ServletConfig cfg)
        throws ServletException
{
    super.init(cfg);

    // Create our connection pool
    connectionPool = new ConnectionPool();

    // Initialize the connection pool. This will start all
    // of the connections as specified in the connection
    // pool configuration file
    try
    {
        connectionPool.initialize();
    }
    catch (Exception ex)
    {
```

```
            // Convert the exception
            ex.printStackTrace();
            String msg = "Unable to initialize connection pool";
            throw new ServletException(msg, ex);
        }
    }

    /**
     * Destroy the servlet. This is called once when the servlet
     * is unloaded.
     */
    public void destroy()
    {
        // Tear down our connection pool if it was created
        if (connectionPool != null)
        {
            connectionPool.destroy();
        }
        super.destroy();
    }
```

Next, we can simply modify the original code to use the ConnectionPool object to get a connection, instead of requesting one from the JDBC DriverManager. When we are finished with the query, we also need to call the close() method on the ConnectionPool object to release it back into the pool:

```
    /**
     * Given the SQL query string, execute the query and
     * format the results into an HTML table
     *
     * @param query SQL query to execute
     * @param out PrintWriter to use to output the query results
     * @return true if the query was successful
     */
    private boolean query(String query, PrintWriter out)
    {
        boolean rc = true;

        // The JDBC Connection object
        Connection con = null;
```

```
// The JDBC Statement object
Statement stmt = null;

// The JDBC ResultSet object
ResultSet rs = null;

// Keep stats for how long it takes to execute
// the query
long startMS = System.currentTimeMillis();

// Keep the number of rows in the ResultSet
int rowCount = 0;

try
{

    // Get an available connection from our connection pool
    con = connectionPool.getConnection();

    // Create a statement object that we can execute queries
    // with
    stmt = con.createStatement();

    // Execute the query
    rs = stmt.executeQuery(query);

    // Format the results into an HTML table
    rowCount = formatTable(rs, out);

}
catch (Exception ex)
{
    // Send the error back to the client
    out.println("Exception!");
    ex.printStackTrace(out);
    rc = false;
}
finally
{
    try
    {
```

```
                // Always close properly
                if (rs != null)
                {
                    rs.close();
                }
                if (stmt != null)
                {
                    stmt.close();
                }
                if (con != null)
                {
                    // Put the connection back into the pool
                    connectionPool.close(con);
                }
            }
            catch (Exception ex)
            {
                // Ignore any errors here
            }
        }

        // If we queried the table successfully, output some
        // statistics
        if (rc)
        {
            long elapsed = System.currentTimeMillis() - startMS;
            out.println("<br><i>" + rowCount + " rows in " +
                        elapsed + "ms</i>");
        }

        return rc;
    }
```

After the servlet has been compiled and configured in web.xml, you should see a dramatic improvement in performance over the original EmployeeList servlet, as shown next:

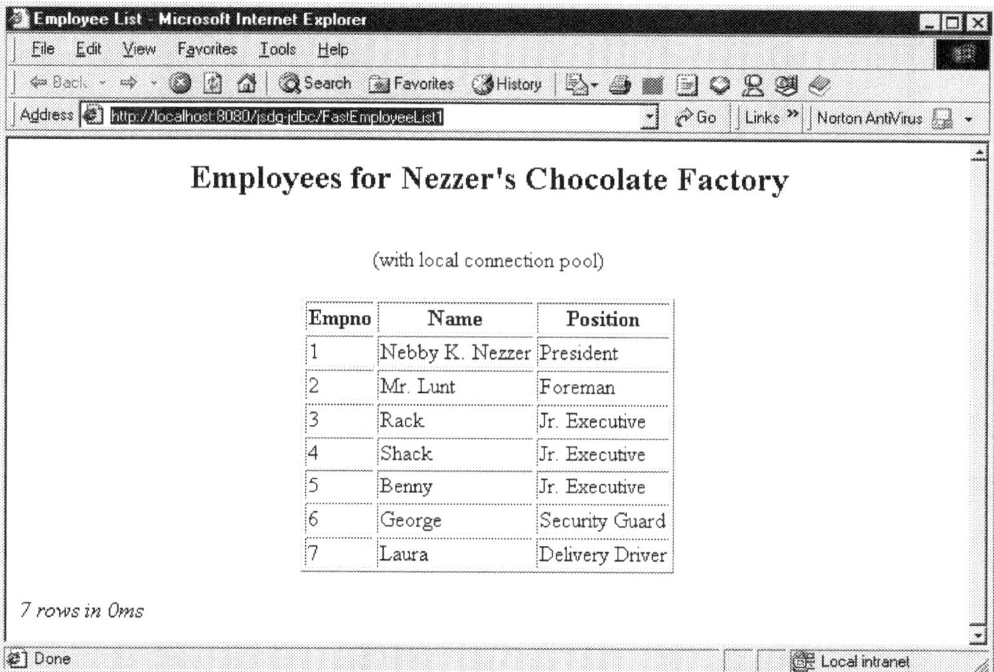

Note the time it took to execute the query. All I can say is "Wow!"

All of the time necessary to create the connection pool is taken in the init() method of the servlet. Remember that the init() method is called once when the servlet is first loaded; you may want to configure your web server to preload the servlet when the system is started so that the first user doesn't have to wait for the pool to be created.

ConnectionPool Example: A Global Pool

How could things possibly get any better? The previous example used a connection pool that was local to the servlet; in reality, you aren't going to want to have a pool for each of your servlets. Let's look at a way we can make the connection pool global to any servlet. We can do this by writing a simple servlet that owns the connection pool and is loaded when the system is started. Once the pool has been initialized, we can store a reference to the pool in the web application context.

```
package com.omh.db;

import com.omh.jdbc.ConnectionPool;
import com.omh.jdbc.ConnectionObject;

import javax.servlet.*;
import javax.servlet.http.*;
import java.util.*;
import java.io.*;
import java.sql.*;
import java.text.SimpleDateFormat;

/**
 * This is a simple servlet that holds a global connection
 * pool. The Servlet context is used to store a named attribute
 * so that other servlets have access to the connection pool
 */

public class ConnectionServlet
        extends HttpServlet
{
    // Our connection pool.
    ConnectionPool connectionPool;

    // Context attribute key
    public static String CONNECTION_POOL_KEY =
                    "com.omh.db.ConnectionServlet";

    // Used to format dates
    SimpleDateFormat formatter =
            new SimpleDateFormat("yyyy.MM.dd hh:mm:ss.SSS");

    /**
     * Initialize the servlet. This is called once when the
     * servlet is loaded. It is guaranteed to complete before any
     * requests are made to the servlet
     *
     * @param cfg Servlet configuration information
     */
    public void init(ServletConfig cfg)
            throws ServletException
    {
        super.init(cfg);

        // Create our connection pool
        connectionPool = new ConnectionPool();
```

```
    // Initialize the connection pool. This will start all
    // of the connections as specified in the connection
    // pool configuration file
    try
    {
        connectionPool.initialize();
    }
    catch (Exception ex)
    {
        // Convert the exception
        ex.printStackTrace();
        throw new ServletException
            ("Unable to initialize connection pool", ex);
    }

    // Add the connection pool to the context so that other servlets
    // can find us
    ServletContext context = getServletContext();
    context.setAttribute(CONNECTION_POOL_KEY, connectionPool);
}

/**
 * Destroy the servlet. This is called once when the servlet
 * is unloaded.
 */
public void destroy()
{
    // Remove the attribute from the context
    getServletContext().removeAttribute(CONNECTION_POOL_KEY);

    // Tear down our connection pool if it was created
    if (connectionPool != null)
    {
        connectionPool.destroy();
    }
    super.destroy();
}

public void doGet(HttpServletRequest req,
                  HttpServletResponse resp)
        throws ServletException, IOException
{
    // Set the content type of the response
    resp.setContentType("text/html");

    PrintWriter out = resp.getWriter();

    // Print the HTML header
```

```
        out.println("<html>");
        out.println("<head>");
        out.println("<title>Connection Pool Status</title>");
        out.println("</head>");
        out.println("<h2><center>");
        out.println("Connection Pool Status");
        out.println("</center></h2>");
        out.println("<br><center>");

        if (connectionPool == null)
        {
            out.println("No pool active");
        }
        else
        {
            out.println("<table>");
            out.println("<tr><th>Connection #</th>");
            out.println("<th>In Use</th>");
            out.println("<th>Use Count</th>");
            out.println("<th>Last Accessed</th></tr>");

            Enumeration enum =
                    connectionPool.getConnectionPoolObjects();

            int i = 0;
            while (enum.hasMoreElements())
            {
                ConnectionObject co =
                        (ConnectionObject) enum.nextElement();

                // Output the stats
                out.println("<tr><td>" + i + "</td>");
                out.println("<td>" + co.isInUse() + "</td>");
                out.println("<td>" + co.getUseCount() + "</td>");
                out.println("<td>" + format(co.getLastAccess()) +
                            "</td></tr>");
                i++;
            }
            out.println("</table>");
        }
        out.println("</center>");

        // Wrap up
        out.println("</html>");
        out.flush();
        out.close();
    }
```

```
    /**
     * Formats the last accessed time into a human-readable
     * string. This method is synchronized because
     * the SimpleDateFormat object is not thread-safe.
     */
    protected synchronized String format(long ms)
    {
        String s = formatter.format(new java.util.Date(ms));
        return s;
    }
}
```

Again, we have created the connection pool in the init() method and destroyed it in the destroy() method. Note that once the connection pool has been initialized, we add it as an attribute to the web application context. This allows other servlets within the web application to gain access to the pool and share its connections. Also notice that by using a servlet to hold the connection pool, it is very easy to provide a status of the pool by invoking the servlet. The ConnectionPool servlet has implemented doGet() and formats a quick status that can be viewed by a browser:

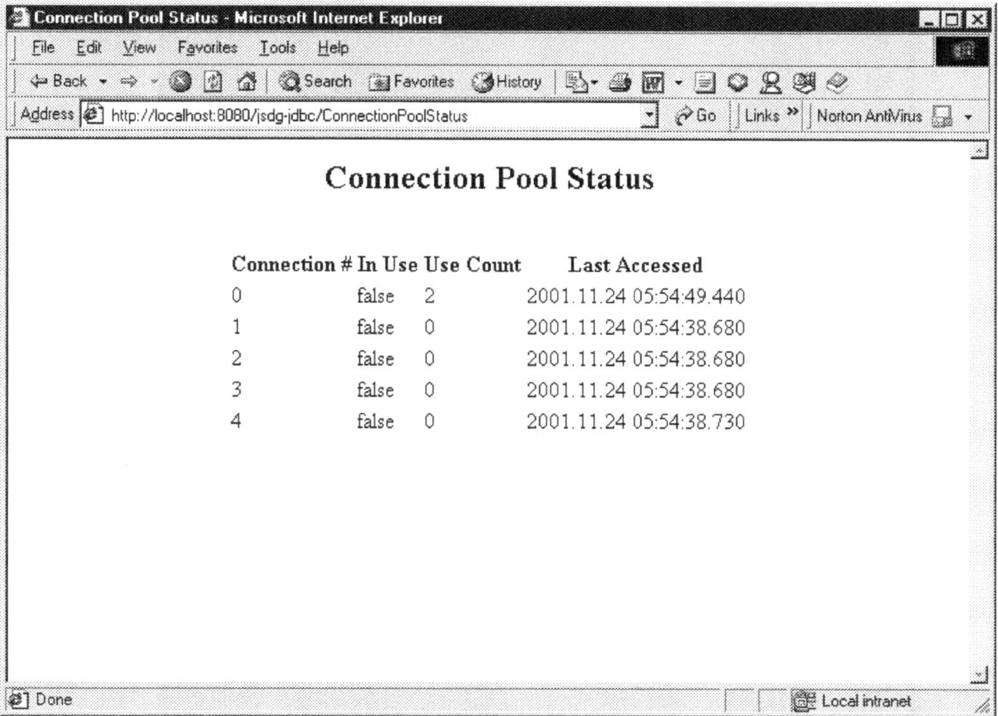

Using this new ConnectionServlet servlet is quite easy. All we need to do is configure the servlet to load when the servlet container starts:

```
<servlet>
  <servlet-name>ConnectionServlet</servlet-name>
  <servlet-class>com.omh.db.ConnectionServlet</servlet-class>
  <load-on-startup>1</load-on-startup>
</servlet>

<servlet-mapping>
  <servlet-name>ConnectionServlet</servlet-name>
  <url-pattern>/ConnectionPoolStatus</url-pattern>
</servlet-mapping>
```

Now we can modify the FastEmployeeList1 servlet to look up the global pool instead of using a local pool:

```
/**
 * Given the SQL query string, execute the query and
 * format the results into an HTML table
 *
 * @param query SQL query to execute
 * @param out PrintWriter to use to output the query results
 * @return true if the query was successful
 */
private boolean query(String query, PrintWriter out)
{
    boolean rc = true;

    // Our connection pool
    ConnectionPool pool = null;

    // The JDBC Connection object
    Connection con = null;

    // The JDBC Statement object
    Statement stmt = null;

    // The JDBC ResultSet object
    ResultSet rs = null;
```

```
// Keep stats for how long it takes to execute
// the query
long startMS = System.currentTimeMillis();

// Keep the number of rows in the ResultSet
int rowCount = 0;

try
{
    // Get an available connection from our connection pool
    ServletContext context = getServletContext();
    String key = ConnectionServlet.CONNECTION_POOL_KEY;
    Object o = context.getAttribute(key);

    // Found?
    if (o == null)
    {
        out.println("No connection pool!");
    }
    else if (!(o instanceof ConnectionPool))
    {
        out.println("Invalid connection pool!");
    }
    else
    {
        pool = (ConnectionPool) o;
        con = pool.getConnection();

        // Create a statement object that we can execute queries
        // with
        stmt = con.createStatement();

        // Execute the query
        rs = stmt.executeQuery(query);

        // Format the results into an HTML table
        rowCount = formatTable(rs, out);
    }
}
catch (Exception ex)
{
```

```
            // Send the error back to the client
            out.println("Exception!");
            ex.printStackTrace(out);
            rc = false;
        }
        finally
        {
            try
            {
                // Always close properly
                if (rs != null)
                {
                    rs.close();
                }
                if (stmt != null)
                {
                    stmt.close();
                }
                if (con != null)
                {
                    // Put the connection back into the pool
                    pool.close(con);
                }
            }
            catch (Exception ex)
            {
                // Ignore any errors here
            }
        }

        // If we queried the table successfully, output some
        // statistics
        if (rc)
        {
            long elapsed = System.currentTimeMillis() - startMS;
            out.println("<br><i>" + rowCount + " rows in " +
                        elapsed + "ms</i>");
        }

        return rc;
    }
```

The rest of the servlet (named FastEmployeeList2) is basically the same as FastEmployeeList1, as shown next:

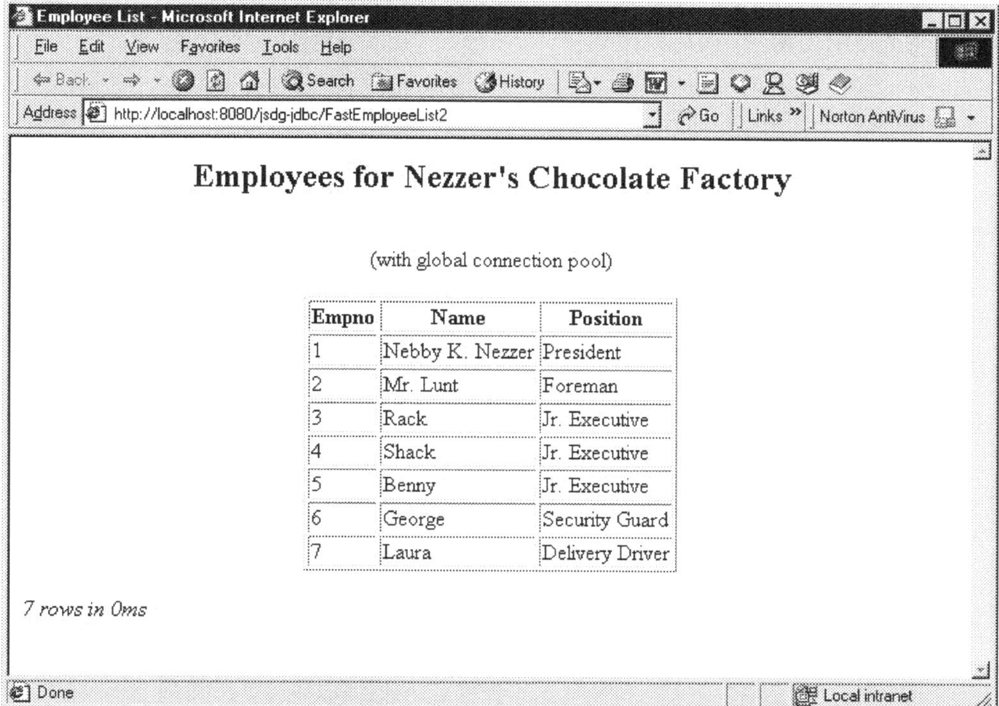

There is another way to hold a connection pool for your web application, which is by using a javax.servlet.ServletContextListener (application event listeners are covered in Chapter 7). Instead of using the servlet init() and destroy() methods, you can implement the ServletContextListener and use the contextInitialized() and contextDestroyed() methods.

Working with Images

A very important aspect of any web page is the visual content, including images. The Employee table that we have been working with contains a column that stores the image of each employee. Moving the image over the Web is as easy as reading the picture with JDBC, setting the HTTP response header, and dumping the raw data back to the client. The client will be responsible for rendering the image properly within the browser.

Image Example: ImageServer

To process image data from a database, let's take a look at a generic servlet, named ImageServer, that will accept parameters that specify the location of the image and return the image back to the client. We've already seen how to use connection pooling, which will be used to ensure adequate performance. The main logic in the servlet consists of executing the query, reading the binary data, and writing to the output stream that eventually winds up back at the client:

```
package com.omh.db;

import com.omh.jdbc.ConnectionPool;

import javax.servlet.*;
import javax.servlet.http.*;
import java.io.*;
import java.sql.*;

/**
 * This servlet will query the database for a stored binary
 * image, read it, and return it to the client.
 */

public class ImageServer
        extends HttpServlet
{
    public void doGet(HttpServletRequest req,
                      HttpServletResponse resp)
          throws ServletException, IOException
    {
        // Get the table to query
        String tableName = req.getParameter("table");

        // Get the column to query
        String columnName = req.getParameter("column");

        // Get the 'where' clause for the query
        String whereClause = req.getParameter("where");

        // Attempt to get the image
        getImage(resp, tableName, columnName, whereClause);
    }
```

```
/**
 * Reads the database for an image and outputs that image
 * to the client
 *
 * @param resp The response from the servlet
 * @param table The name of the table containing the data
 * @param column The column name of the stored image
 * @param where The SQL where clause to uniquely identify
 * the row
 */
private void getImage(HttpServletResponse resp,
                      String table, String column,
                      String where)
        throws IOException
{
    // Our connection pool
    ConnectionPool pool = null;

    // Format the SQL string
    String sql = "select " + column + " from " + table +
                 " where " + where;

    // The JDBC Connection object
    Connection con = null;

    // The JDBC Statement object
    Statement stmt = null;

    // The JDBC ResultSet object
    ResultSet rs = null;

    try
    {

        // Get an available connection from our connection pool
        ServletContext context = getServletContext();
        String key = ConnectionServlet.CONNECTION_POOL_KEY;
        Object o = context.getAttribute(key);

        // Should sanity-check here to ensure the pool is
        // not null and is the correct type of object
        pool = (ConnectionPool) o;
```

```
// Get an available connection from our connection pool
con = pool.getConnection();

// Create a statement object that we can execute queries
// with
stmt = con.createStatement();

// Execute the query
rs = stmt.executeQuery(sql);

// If this is an empty result set, send back a nice
// error message
if (!rs.next())
{
    resp.setContentType("text/html");

    PrintWriter pout = resp.getWriter();

    pout.println("No matching record found");
    pout.flush();
    pout.close();
}

// We have results! Read the image and write it to
// our output stream
resp.setContentType("image/gif");

// Get the output stream
ServletOutputStream out = resp.getOutputStream();

// Get an input stream to the stored image
InputStream in = rs.getBinaryStream(1);

// Some database systems may not be able to tell us
// how big the data actually is. Let's read all of it
// into a buffer.
ByteArrayOutputStream baos = new ByteArrayOutputStream();

byte b[] = new byte[1024];
while (true)
{
    int bytes = in.read(b);
```

```
            // If there was nothing read, get out of loop
            if (bytes == -1)
            {
                break;
            }

            // Write the buffer to our byte array
            baos.write(b, 0, bytes);
        }

        // Now we have the entire image in the buffer. Get
        // the length and write it to the output stream
        b = baos.toByteArray();

        resp.setContentLength(b.length);
        out.write(b, 0, b.length);
        out.flush();
        out.close();
    }
    catch (Exception ex)
    {
        // Set the content type of the response
        resp.setContentType("text/html");

        PrintWriter pout = resp.getWriter();

        pout.println("Exception!");
        ex.printStackTrace(pout);
        pout.flush();
        pout.close();
    }
    finally
    {
        try
        {
            // Always close properly
            if (rs != null)
            {
                rs.close();
            }
            if (stmt != null)
            {
```

```
                    stmt.close();
                }
                if (con != null)
                {
                    // Put the connection back into the pool
                    pool.close(con);
                }
            }
            catch (Exception ex)
            {
                // Ignore any errors here
            }
        }
    }
}
```

Notice how the content header is set for the response. If an exception or error occurs, the content type is set to "text/html" so that we can send back a human-readable message. If the image is read properly, the content type is set to "image/gif", which notifies the client that image data will follow. We also have to set the length of the raw image data. The most reliable way to determine this from JDBC is to read the entire contents of the binary column into a ByteArrayOutputStream, which will cache all of the data in a byte array. Once all of the data has been read, we can set the content length and then dump the cache to the output stream.

The ImageServer servlet takes three parameters:

- **table** The name of the database table to query.
- **column** The name of the column that holds the image.
- **where** The SQL where clause that will cause the required row to be selected.

For example:

```
ImageServer?table=Employee&column=Picture&where=Empno=1
```

The previous query has a problem, though. To specify the where clause, which contains an equal sign, we need to encode it before it is sent to the server. The hexadecimal value of = is 3d:

```
ImageServer?table=Employee&column=Picture&where=Empno%3d1
```

The following shows an image retrieved from the database:

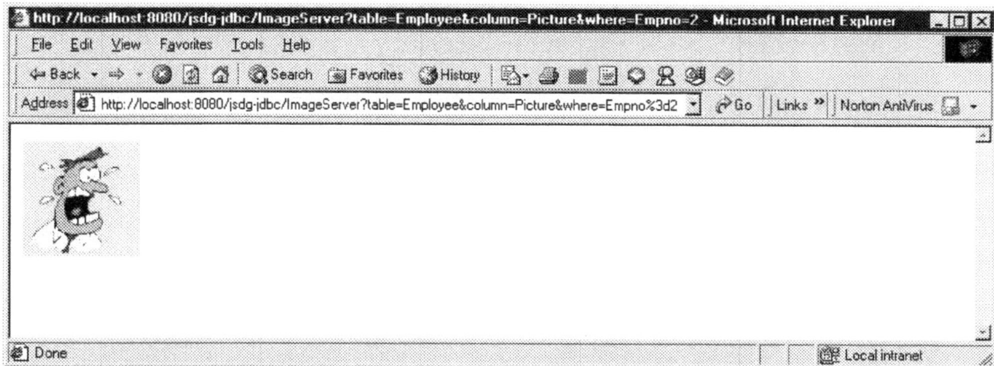

Adding Images to EmployeeList

Now that we have a servlet that will return image data, let's update the EmployeeList servlet to include a link to an image of the employee. The following shows the Java code that will insert a new column into the HTML table that, when clicked, will invoke the ImageServer servlet that will return the image:

```
/**
 * Given a JDBC ResultSet, format the results into
 * an HTML table
 *
 * @param rs JDBC ResultSet
 * @param out PrintWriter to use to output the table
 * @return The number of rows in the ResultSet
 */
private int formatTable(ResultSet rs, PrintWriter out)
        throws Exception
{
    int rowCount = 0;

    // Create the table
    out.println("<center><table border>");

    // Process the results. First dump out the column
    // headers as found in the ResultSetMetaData
    ResultSetMetaData rsmd = rs.getMetaData();
```

```
int columnCount = rsmd.getColumnCount();

// Start the table row
StringBuffer sb = new StringBuffer("<tr>");

for (int i = 0; i < columnCount; i++)
{

    // Create each table header. Note that the column index
    // is 1-based
    sb.append("<th>");
    sb.append(rsmd.getColumnLabel(i + 1));
    sb.append("</th>");
}

// Add a column for the employee picture
sb.append("<th>Picture</th>");

// End the table row
sb.append("</tr>");
out.println(sb.toString());

// Now walk through the entire ResultSet and get each
// row
while (rs.next())
{
    String empNo = null;
    rowCount++;

    // Start a table row
    sb = new StringBuffer("<tr>");

    // Dump out the values of each row
    for (int i = 0; i < columnCount; i++)
    {
        // Save the data since we need to reference it
        // later. Some JDBC drivers do not allow the
        // same column value to be fetched more than
```

```
                // once
                String data = rs.getString(i + 1);

                // Save the employee number - it's the first
                // column
                if (i == 0)
                {
                    empNo = data;
                }

                // Create the table data. Note that the column index
                // is 1-based
                sb.append("<td>");
                sb.append(data);
                sb.append("</td>");
            }

            // Add a special column in the table for the picture
            sb.append("<td>Click ");
            sb.append("<a href=ImageServer");
            sb.append("?table=Employee");
            sb.append("&column=Picture");
            sb.append("&where=Empno%3d");
            sb.append(empNo);
            sb.append(">here</a>");
            sb.append("</td>");

            // End the table row
            sb.append("</tr>");
            out.println(sb.toString());
        }

        // End the table
        out.println("</table></center>");

        return rowCount;
    }
```

After configuring your web application for the ImageServer and EmployeeList2 servlets, invoking the EmployeeList2 servlet will produce the following:

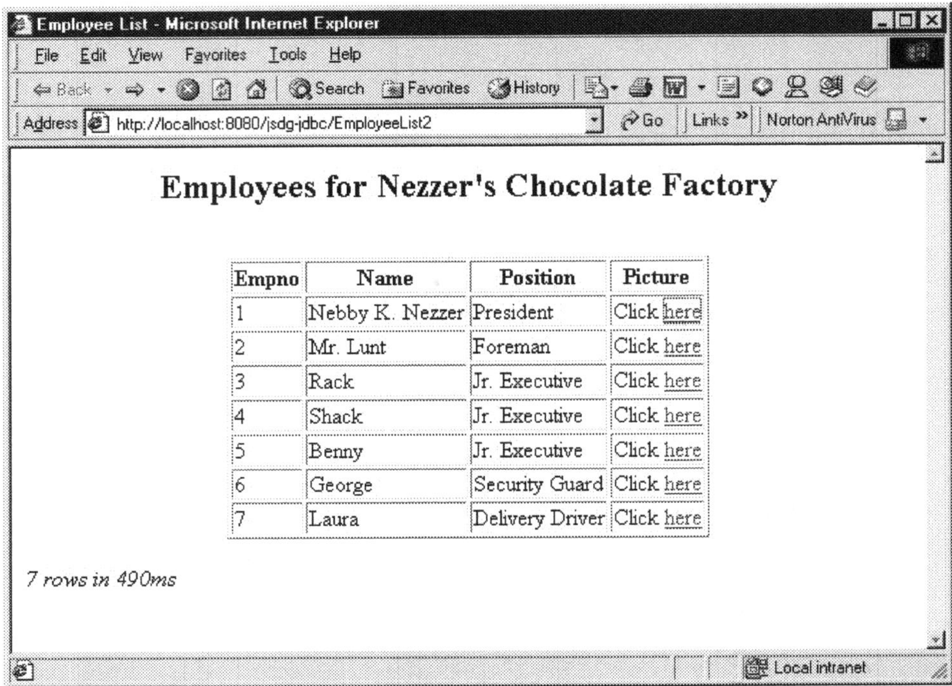

Notice the new column in the table that contains a link to the image of the employee. Clicking one of the new picture columns will result in the ImageServer being invoked with the appropriate parameters:

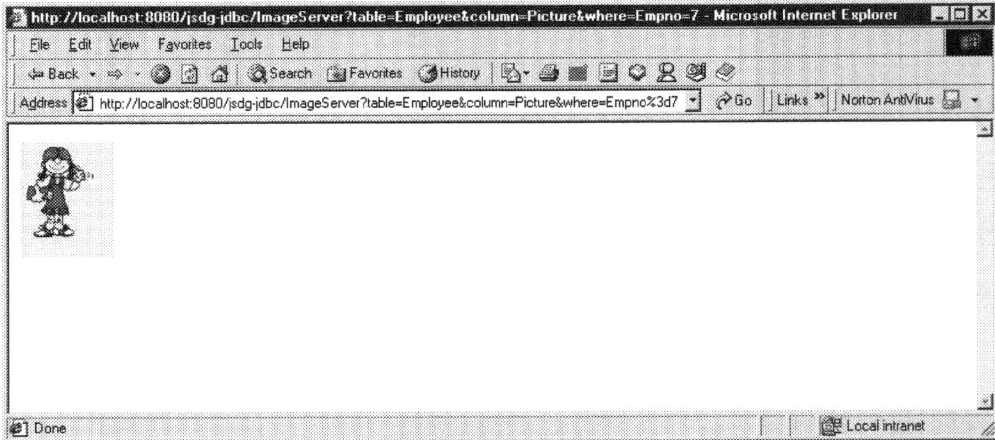

Summary

We've really covered a lot of ground in this chapter. JDBC is no small topic, but I hope that you now have a firm grasp of what it is, what types of JDBC drivers are available, and the basic steps in writing a JDBC application. I hope that you have also realized how easy it is to publish database information on the Web by using servlets. This is exciting stuff!

We also covered ways to improve usability and performance by splitting output between multiple pages and using connection pooling. Both of these techniques are important building blocks when creating an industrial-strength JDBC solution for the Web.

In Chapter 10, we will move away from the static world of HTML pages and into the dynamic world of Java applets. We'll start taking a look at how to invoke servlet methods from an applet by using HTTP tunneling.

CHAPTER

10

Applet-to-Servlet Communication

IN THIS CHAPTER:

HTTP

What Is Tunneling

The Basic Flow

Tunneling for Java 1.0.2

Using Serialization

Summary

In this chapter, we're going to take a look at how to use server-side objects from Java applets. Java's Remote Method Invocation (RMI) specification defines how to do this using TCP/IP over a secure network, but we'll be using a process known as *HTTP tunneling* that will allow us to make remote method calls over an unsecure network such as the Internet.

HTTP

Hypertext Transfer Protocol (HTTP) is an Internet client/server protocol designed for the delivery of hypertext materials such as HTML, images, and sounds. All HTTP communication uses 8-bit characters, which ensures the safe transmission of all forms of data; this will become an important point later when we discuss the topic of sending and receiving binary data. Let's take a look at the basic steps in servicing an HTTP service request:

1. **Open the connection.** It is very important to remember that HTTP is a *stateless* protocol, meaning that each request is treated as an independent entity. Because of this, you must make a new connection for each request. This is quite unlike TCP/IP, for example, where a connection can be maintained for the life of a given client session. As you'll see a little later, using servlet session tracking solves the stateless server problem.
2. **Send a request.** The client will send a message to the Web server requesting some type of service. The request contains HTTP request headers that define the type and length of the request packet followed by the request data.
3. **Service the request.** The Web server will service the request. In our case, we'll be writing a new servlet to process the request.
4. **Send the response.** The server will send (or forward) a response to the client. The response contains a set of response headers that define the type and length of the response packet followed by the response data.
5. **Close the connection.** Remember that HTTP is stateless; connections cannot be preserved between requests.

You might think that HTTP is used just for requesting and downloading documents from a secure server over the Internet. This is certainly the most common use of HTTP; however, we can use it to serve other purposes, as well, such as method call tunneling.

What Is Tunneling

I like to think of tunneling as a way to to create within an existing road of communication (HTTP) a subprotocol to perform specific tasks. The subprotocol that we'll be creating will contain all the information necessary to create an object on the Web server, invoke methods on that object, and return results back to the client. The great thing about using HTTP tunneling is that you can concentrate on the specifics of the subprotocol without having to be concerned about transporting the data packets between the client and server—HTTP was designed for this very purpose and does it quite well.

The Basic Flow

To further illustrate the notion of tunneling, let's expand upon the basic HTTP flow provided earlier:

1. **Open the HTTP connection.** Again, HTTP is a stateless protocol, so you have to open a new connection for each request.
2. **Format the method request.** This will include some type of method indicator that describes which method to invoke and any parameters that are required by the method.
3. **Set the HTTP request headers.** This includes the type of data being sent (binary) and the total length of the data.
4. **Send the request.** Write the binary stream to the server.
5. **Read the request.** The target servlet will be invoked and given the HTTP request data. The servlet can then extract the method to invoke and any necessary parameters. Note that if this is the first request for a given client, a new instance of the server object will be created.
6. **Invoke the method.** The method will be called on the server object.
7. **Format the method response.** If the method that was invoked throws an exception, the error message will be sent to the client; otherwise, the return type (if any) will be sent.
8. **Set the HTTP response headers.** Just like the request headers, the type and length of the data being sent must be set.

9. **Send the request.** The binary data stream will be sent to the Web server, which in turn will be returned back to the client.
10. **Close the connection.**

There's a lot of work going on just to send a single request. For performance reasons, you should always try to pass as much information as possible with each request/response; the weak link in the HTTP tunneling chain is creating a new connection for each request.

Tunneling for Java 1.0.2

A lot of focus has been placed on the current versions of the Java Developer's Kit (JDK), whether it be JDK 1.2 or JDK 1.3 (or later). Don't forget about the first official release of the JDK: version 1.0.2. You might not think that it is important to use this version for much of anything, but I have found that later versions of the JDK are not totally supported in some browsers or that the behavior is (at best) unpredictable. Applets created with JDK 1.0.2, on the other hand, seem quite well behaved in all of the Java-enabled browsers that I have tried. Sure, there's a lot of new functionality in the later versions of the JDK, but if you have some somewhat basic applet requirements that can be satisfied using version 1.0.2, you may want to consider using it, especially if you will be distributing your applet over the Internet (as opposed to an intranet), where you do not have control over the type or version of browser being used.

Marshaling Parameters and Return Values

Marshaling quite simply is the process of packaging a piece of data for transmission and unpackaging it after it has been received. Later in this chapter, you will discover that, starting with JDK 1.1, this is made very easy with serialization; not so with JDK 1.0.2. Java 1.0.2 provides us with a mechanism to read and write all the basic scalar data types (boolean, char, byte, short, int, long, float, double, and String); all other types of data must be marshaled as a combination of these types. Also, when you write a particular type of data, the reader must know what type of data to expect. You can get around this by preceding each piece of data with some type of indicator, but there is no generic way to determine what type of data is present.

Using DataOutputStream and DataInputStream

To illustrate how to marshal data with any version of the JDK, let's take a look at a simple client application that uses java.io.DataOutputStream for writing the request data and java.io.DataInputStream for reading the response data. The flow of our client application is as follows:

1. Open an HTTP connection.
2. Format the request data.
3. Send the request to the server.
4. Read the response data.
5. Close the HTTP connection.

The server (which we'll look at a bit later) will simply read the request data and echo it back to the client.

To invoke the test application, you must supply the URL of the server process that will echo the data (a servlet, of course!):

```
java com.omh.tunnel.TestDataStream
    http://localhost:8080/jsdg-tunnel/DataStreamEcho
```

Note that the command has been split over multiple lines to improve readability; it should be entered as a single line.

The following code shows the TestDataStream application source code:

```
package com.omh.tunnel;

import java.io.*;

/**
  * This application shows how to read data from and write data
  * to a servlet using data input/output streams.
  */
public class TestDataStream
{
    /**
     * Application entry point. This application requires
     * one parameter, which is the servlet URL
     */
    public static void main(String args[])
    {
        // Make sure we have an argument for the servlet URL
        if (args.length == 0)
        {
            System.out.println("\nServlet URL must be specified");
            return;
```

```
}

try
{

    System.out.println("Attempting to connect to " + args[0]);

    // Get the server URL
    java.net.URL url = new java.net.URL(args[0]);

    // Attempt to connect to the host
    java.net.URLConnection con = url.openConnection();

    // Initialize the connection
    con.setUseCaches(false);
    con.setDoOutput(true);
    con.setDoInput(true);

    // Data will always be written to a byte array buffer so
    // that we can tell the server the length of the data
    ByteArrayOutputStream byteOut = new ByteArrayOutputStream();

    // Create the output stream to be used to write the
    // data to our buffer
    DataOutputStream out = new DataOutputStream(byteOut);

    System.out.println("Writing test data");

    // Write the test data
    out.writeBoolean(true);
    out.writeByte(1);
    out.writeChar(2);
    out.writeShort(3);
    out.writeInt(4);
    out.writeFloat(5);
    out.writeDouble(6);
    out.writeUTF("Hello, Karl");

    // Flush the data to the buffer
    out.flush();

    // Get our buffer to be sent
    byte buf[] = byteOut.toByteArray();

    // Set the content that we are sending
    con.setRequestProperty("Content-type",
            "application/octet-stream");

    // Set the length of the data buffer we are sending
```

```
            con.setRequestProperty("Content-length",
                    "" + buf.length);

            // Get the output stream to the server and send our
            // data buffer
            DataOutputStream dataOut =
                    new DataOutputStream(con.getOutputStream());
            //out.write(buf, 0, buf.length);
            dataOut.write(buf);

            // Flush the output stream and close it
            dataOut.flush();
            dataOut.close();

            System.out.println("Reading response");

            // Get the input stream we can use to read the response
            DataInputStream in =
                    new DataInputStream(con.getInputStream());

            // Read the data from the server
            boolean booleanValue = in.readBoolean();
            byte byteValue = in.readByte();
            char charValue = in.readChar();
            short shortValue = in.readShort();
            int intValue = in.readInt();
            float floatValue = in.readFloat();
            double doubleValue = in.readDouble();
            String stringValue = in.readUTF();

            // Close the input stream
            in.close();

            System.out.println("Data read: " +
                    booleanValue + " " +
                    byteValue + " " +
                    ((int) charValue) + " " +
                    shortValue + " " +
                    intValue + " " +
                    floatValue + " " +
                    doubleValue + " " +
                    stringValue);
        }
        catch (Exception ex)
        {
            ex.printStackTrace();
        }
    }
}
```

Notice how the request data is actually being written to an in-memory buffer (java.io.ByteArrayOutputStream). We could have written the data directly to the HTTP output stream, but then you could not set the request length in the request header properly. To be able to do this, we write all the data to a buffer and then retrieve the raw byte array, from which we can then get the length. After the request headers are set, we can get the HTTP output stream from the URLConnection object and write out the entire contents of the internal buffer. Once the data has been sent, we can request an input stream from the URLConnection object, which will be used to read the response. Note that requesting the input stream will block execution on the thread until the response is received. Once we have the input stream, we can simply read the data and display what was echoed by the servlet, as shown in the following illustration:

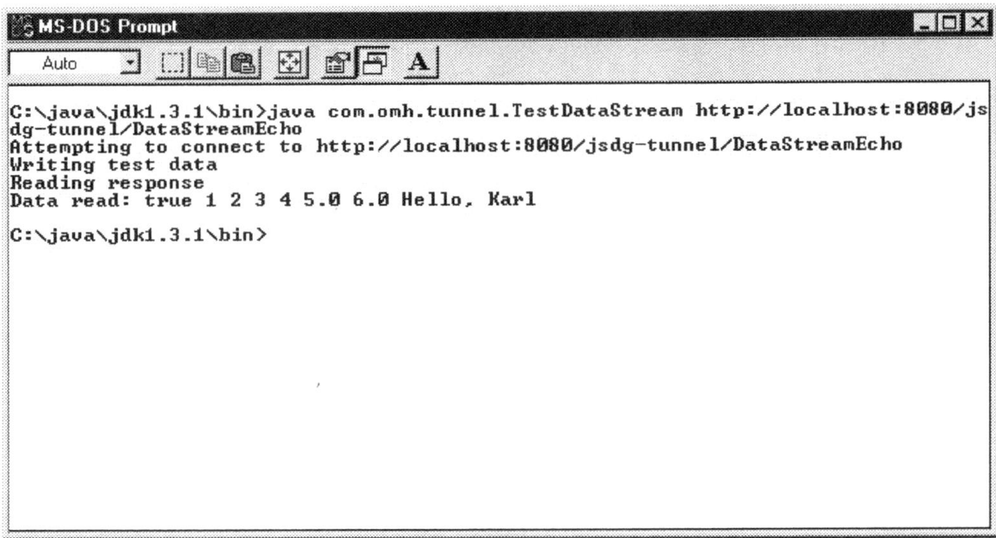

What about the servlet? From looking at the client, you should be able to write the servlet quite easily, since the process is very similar:

1. Wait for a service request from a client.
2. Read the request data. It is very important to remember to read the data in the same order that it was written by the client.
3. Write the response using the data read from the request.

The following shows the code for the DataStreamEcho servlet:

```
package com.omh.tunnel;

import javax.servlet.*;
import javax.servlet.http.*;
import java.io.*;

/**
  * This servlet shows how to read data from and write data
  * to a client using data input/output streams.
  */
public class DataStreamEcho
        extends HttpServlet
{
    public void service(HttpServletRequest req,
                        HttpServletResponse resp)
            throws ServletException, IOException
    {
        // Get the input stream for reading data from the client
        DataInputStream in =
            new DataInputStream(req.getInputStream());

        // We'll be sending binary data back to the client so
        // set the content type appropriately
        resp.setContentType("application/octet-stream");

        // Data will always be written to a byte array buffer so
        // that we can tell the client the length of the data
        ByteArrayOutputStream byteOut = new ByteArrayOutputStream();

        // Create the output stream to be used to write the
        // data to our buffer
        DataOutputStream out = new DataOutputStream(byteOut);

        // Read the data from the client.
        boolean booleanValue = in.readBoolean();
        byte byteValue = in.readByte();
        char charValue = in.readChar();
        short shortValue = in.readShort();
        int intValue = in.readInt();
        float floatValue = in.readFloat();
        double doubleValue = in.readDouble();
        String stringValue = in.readUTF();

        // Write the data to our internal buffer.
        out.writeBoolean(booleanValue);
        out.writeByte(byteValue);
        out.writeChar(charValue);
        out.writeShort(shortValue);
        out.writeInt(intValue);
        out.writeFloat(floatValue);
        out.writeDouble(doubleValue);
        out.writeUTF(stringValue);
```

```
        // Flush the contents of the output stream to the
        // byte array
        out.flush();

        // Get the buffer that is holding our response
        byte[] buf = byteOut.toByteArray();

        // Notify the client how much data is being sent
        resp.setContentLength(buf.length);

        // Send the buffer to the client
        ServletOutputStream servletOut = resp.getOutputStream();

        // Wrap up
        servletOut.write(buf);
        servletOut.close();
    }
}
```

Remember to configure the DataStreamEcho servlet in web.xml so that it is mapped properly to the URL we used when invoking the TestDataStream application:

```
<servlet>
  <servlet-name>DataStreamEcho</servlet-name>
  <servlet-class>com.omh.tunnel.DataStreamEcho</servlet-class>
</servlet>

<servlet-mapping>
  <servlet-name>DataStreamEcho</servlet-name>
  <url-pattern>/DataStreamEcho</url-pattern>
</servlet-mapping>
```

The Base Tunnel Client Class

Now that you know how to get data back and forth between the client and server, let's get started on some supporting classes to make method tunneling much easier. Since I had the distinct advantage of looking ahead in this chapter, I know that we are going to write two types of clients: a lite version (for marshaling scalar types only) and a full version (using Java serialization). Because of this, I think it would be an excellent idea to implement an abstract base class that these two types of clients can extend.

What types of methods will the client need? All clients will definitely need to initialize themselves. Since we are invoking methods on the server, part of this initialization step should be to instantiate the server-side object. The following code shows the initialization method from the base client class. Note that since these methods are part of a base class that will be extended, I am adding an underscore to each method name to reduce the likelihood of a naming collision.

```
/**
 * Initializes the client. Also makes a server request
 * to initialize the server as well.
 */
public void _initialize() throws TunnelException
{
    try
    {
        // Create a new buffer that will hold our data
        ByteArrayOutputStream buffer = new ByteArrayOutputStream();

        // Create a method header. An ordinal value of -1 is
        // reserved for initializing the server
        _createHeader(buffer, -1);

        // Invoke the method. This will send the initialization
        // header to the server
        DataInput in = _invokeMethod(buffer.toByteArray());

        // Get the handle to the object that was just
        // created
        objectHandle = in.readInt();

        // Close properly
        _close(in);
    }
    catch (IOException ex)
    {
        // Re-throw as a tunnel exception
        ex.printStackTrace();
        throw new TunnelException(ex.getMessage());
    }
}
```

All this method does is send a message packet to the server instructing it to instantiate a new server-side object (we'll get to that later). It's important to note the basic steps involved in sending our packet of data to the server:

1. Create a new in-memory buffer to hold the contents of the data stream.
2. Invoke a helper method to create the packet header. We're going to invoke remote methods by assigning each method an ordinal (a number) that will uniquely identify a particular method. The ordinal -1 is reserved to indicate that the request is not to invoke a method but rather to initialize the server.

3. Invoke a helper method to send the request packet to the server. This method will return an input stream that we can then use to read any return values from the server.

If you think back to the TestDataOutput sample application presented earlier, this should all sound quite familiar.

The following shows the code necessary to create the packet header that will be used on every tunneled method request:

```
/**
 * Starts a method by creating the method header.
 * The header consists of the method ordinal to invoke.
 *
 * @param buffer Buffer to hold the header data
 * @param ordinal Method ordinal to invoke on the server
 * @return Output stream to be used to send parameters
 */
public DataOutput _createHeader(ByteArrayOutputStream buffer,
         int ordinal)
    throws TunnelException
{
    try
    {
        // Get an output stream to use to write data to the buffer
        DataOutput out = _getOutputStream(buffer);

        // Write the method ordinal
        out.writeInt(ordinal);

        // If we are not initializing the object we need to send
        // the object handle along with the header
        if (ordinal != -1)
        {
            out.writeInt(objectHandle);
        }

        _flush(out);
        return out;
    }
    catch (IOException ex)
    {
        // Re-throw as a tunnel exception
        ex.printStackTrace();
        throw new TunnelException(ex.getMessage());
    }
}
```

Not a lot of magic going on here; this code is just opening an output stream, writing the method ordinal, and flushing the data to the output stream. But wait!

What are these _getOutputStream() and _flush() methods? Each client that extends the base client will have to implement these abstract methods to create the proper type of output stream and to flush the data if necessary. By defining these methods as abstract, we can write a very generic base class that can be reused for different types of tunnel clients.

The last method we need to look at from the base class is the one that actually sends the packet to the server:

```
/**
 * Sends the given buffer that will cause a remote
 * method to be invoked.
 *
 * @param buffer Buffer containing data to send to the server
 * @return Input stream to be used to read the response from
 * the server
 */
public DataInput _invokeMethod(byte buf[])
    throws TunnelException
{
    DataInput in = null;

    try
    {
        // Get the server URL
        URL url = _getURL();
        if (url == null)
        {
            throw new IOException("Server URL has not been set");
        }

        // Attempt to connect to the host
        URLConnection con = url.openConnection();

        // Initialize the connection
        con.setUseCaches(false);
        con.setDoOutput(true);
        con.setDoInput(true);

        // Set the content that we are sending
        con.setRequestProperty("Content-type",
                "application/octet-stream");

        // Set the length of the data buffer we are sending
        con.setRequestProperty("Content-length",
                "" + buf.length);

        // Get the output stream to the server and send our
        // data buffer
        DataOutputStream out =
                new DataOutputStream(con.getOutputStream());
```

```
            out.write(buf);

            // Flush the output stream and close it
            out.flush();
                out.close();
            // Get the input stream we can use to read the response
            in = _getInputStream(con.getInputStream());

            // The server will always respond with an int value
            // that will either be the method ordinal that was
            // invoked, or a -2 indicating an exception was thrown
            // from the server
            int ordinal = in.readInt();

            // Check for an exception on the server.
            if (ordinal == -2)
            {
                // Read the exception message and throw it
                String msg = in.readUTF();
                throw new TunnelException(msg);
            }
        }
        catch (IOException ex)
        {
            // Re-throw as a tunnel exception
            ex.printStackTrace();
            throw new TunnelException(ex.getMessage());
        }

        // Return the input stream to be used to read the rest
        // of the response from the server
        return in;
    }
```

The first thing that is done is to connect to a given URL. The URL is set when the tunnel client is instantiated (which we'll see how to do later). Part of connecting to a particular URL is initializing the connection settings. Of note here is the setUseCaches() method, which tells the browser whether to use internal caching for information or to always read directly from the connection itself. In our case, we will turn off all browser caching capabilities. Next, we'll set the request headers (the data type and data length) and write the data buffer to the server. After the request is sent, we will block until a response is available. Notice the _getInputStream() method, which will return the type of input stream being used by the client; it is an abstract method that must be implemented by each tunnel client. Once the response has arrived, we can read the response header, which will always be prefixed with the same method ordinal that was sent in the request header. A returning ordinal value of -2 indicates that an exception was encountered during the execution of the remote method. If this is the case, we can read the exception message from the input stream and throw a new exception to the client. If all goes well, we can return the input stream back to the caller so that it can read any additional data that was sent by the server.

The Tunnel "Lite" Client

Writing the client implementation for our "lite" tunnel client is very straightforward. Remember that our definition of a lite client is one that uses DataInputStream and DataOutputStream to marshal data. This type of client can be used with any version of the JDK.

```
package com.omh.tunnel.client;

import java.io.*;

/**
 * This class implements the necessary TunnelClientInterface
 * methods for 'tunnel lite' which is intended for use by
 * JDK 1.0.2 clients. The marshaling of data is done with
 * simple output streams and writing basic scalar data types.
 */
public abstract class TunnelLiteClient
        extends BaseTunnelClient
{

    /**
     * Gets an input stream to be used for reading data
     * from the connection. The lite version uses a standard
     * data input stream for reading data.
     *
     * @param in Input stream from the connection URL
     * @return Input stream to read data from the connection
     */
    public DataInput _getInputStream(InputStream in)
        throws IOException
    {
        // Create a new DataInputStream for reading data from
        // the connection.
        return new DataInputStream(in);
    }
```

```
    /**
     * Gets an output stream to be used for writing data to
     * an internal buffer. The buffer will be written to the
     * connection. The lite version uses a standard data
     * output stream for writing data.
     *
     * @param buffer Buffer to hold the output data
     * @return Output stream to write data to the buffer
     */
    public DataOutput _getOutputStream(ByteArrayOutputStream buffer)
        throws IOException
    {
        // Create a new DataOutputStream for writing data to
        // the buffer.
        return new DataOutputStream(buffer);
    }

    /**
     * Flushes any buffered data to the output stream
     *
     * @param out Output stream to flush
     */
    public void _flush(DataOutput out) throws IOException
    {
        // Flush the data to the buffer
        ((DataOutputStream) out).flush();
    }
}
```

The Base Tunnel Servlet Class

In the same manner that we created an abstract base client class, we need to create a base servlet class as well. Just like the client, it will contain abstract methods to create input and output streams specific to the type of marshaling being used. The base servlet class follows:

```
package com.omh.tunnel.server;

import javax.servlet.*;
import javax.servlet.http.*;
import java.io.*;
import java.util.Hashtable;
```

```
/**
 * This is the base server class used for HTTP tunneling.
 */

public abstract class BaseTunnelServlet
        extends HttpServlet
{
    // Constant key value for getting/setting the server object
    // table into the session object
    static final String OBJECT_TABLE = "ObjectTable";

    /**
     * Services the HTTP request
     *
     * @param req The request from the client
     * @param resp The response from the servlet
     */
    public void service(HttpServletRequest req,
                        HttpServletResponse resp)
        throws ServletException, IOException
    {
        // Get the input stream for reading data from the client
        DataInput in = _getInputStream(req.getInputStream());

        // Get the session object or create one if it does not
        // exist. A session will persist as long as the client
        // browser maintains a connection to the server.
        HttpSession session = req.getSession(true);

        // Get the server object table bound to the session. This may
        // be null if this is the first request. If so create a
        // new object table for the session
        Hashtable objectTable =
            (Hashtable) session.getAttribute(OBJECT_TABLE);

        if (objectTable == null)
        {
            objectTable = new java.util.Hashtable();

            // Add the server object to the HTTP session
            session.setAttribute(OBJECT_TABLE, objectTable);
        }

        // We'll be sending binary data back to the client so
        // set the content type appropriately
        resp.setContentType("application/octet-stream");
```

```
// Data will always be written to a byte array buffer so
// that we can tell the client the length of the data
ByteArrayOutputStream byteOut = new ByteArrayOutputStream();

// Create the output stream to be used to write the
// data to our buffer
DataOutput out = _getOutputStream(byteOut);

// Read the method ordinal from the input stream. All
// request headers contain a method ordinal
int ordinal = in.readInt();

// The server object
Object serverObject;

// The object handle
int objectHandle;

// Evaluate the ordinal. -1 is reserved for initializing
// the server
switch (ordinal)
{

case -1:

    // Create a new instance of the server object
    serverObject = _getNewInstance();

    // Send the response back to the client indicating
    // that the server object is ready for method
    // calls.
    out.writeInt(ordinal);

    // Get the object handle
    objectHandle = serverObject.hashCode();

    // Put the object in the object table for the session
    objectTable.put(new Integer(objectHandle), serverObject);

    // Part of the initial object response is the object
    // handle
    out.writeInt(objectHandle);
    break;

default:

    // Read the object handle from the request header
```

```
        objectHandle = in.readInt();

        // Attempt to find the object in the object table for
        // the session
        serverObject = objectTable.get(new Integer(objectHandle));

        // We have to have a server object in order to invoke
        if (serverObject == null)
        {
            throwException(out, "Invalid server object");
        }
        else
        {
            try
            {
                // The response needs to always include the ordinal
                // that was invoked.
                out.writeInt(ordinal);
                _flush(out);

                // Invoke the method for the given ordinal
                _invokeMethod(serverObject, ordinal, in, out);
            }
            catch (Exception ex)
            {

                // Any exceptions thrown by invoking the server
                // method should be sent back to the client. Make
                // sure we are working with a 'pure' output stream
                // that does not contain any other data
                byteOut = new ByteArrayOutputStream();
                out = _getOutputStream(byteOut);
                throwException(out, ex.getMessage());
            }
        }
    }

    // Flush the contents of the output stream to the
    // byte array
    _flush(out);

    // Get the buffer that is holding our response
    byte[] buf = byteOut.toByteArray();

    // Notify the client how much data is being sent
    resp.setContentLength(buf.length);
```

```
        // Send the buffer to the client
        ServletOutputStream servletOut = resp.getOutputStream();

        // Wrap up
        servletOut.write(buf);
        servletOut.close();
    }

    /**
     * Sends a packet to the client that will cause
     * an exception to be thrown
     *
     * @param out Output stream
     * @param message Exception message
     */
    public void throwException(DataOutput out, String message)
        throws IOException
    {
        // -2 is reserved for exceptions
        out.writeInt(-2);
        out.writeUTF(message);
    }

    /**
     * Creates a new instance of the server object. This
     * method must be implemented by the server.
     *
     * @return Instance of the server object
     */
    public abstract Object _getNewInstance()
        throws ServletException;

    /**
     * Invokes the method for the ordinal given. If the method
     * throws an exception it will be sent to the client. This
     * method must be implemented by the server.
     *
     * @param Object Server object
     * @param ordinal Method ordinal
     * @param in Input stream to read additional parameters
     * @param out Output stream to write return values
     */
    public abstract void _invokeMethod(Object serverObject, int ordinal,
                                       DataInput in, DataOutput out)
        throws Exception;

    /**
```

```
     * Creates an input stream to be used to read data
     * sent from the client. This method must be implemented
     * by the server
     *
     * @param servletInput Servlet input stream from the servlet
     * request header
     * @return Input stream to read data from the client
     */
    public abstract DataInput _getInputStream(
            ServletInputStream servletInput)
        throws IOException;

    /**
     * Closes the input stream. The default implementation does
     * nothing.
     *
     * @param in Input stream to close
     */
    public void _close(DataInput in) throws IOException
    {
    }

    /**
     * Gets an output stream to be used for writing data to
     * an internal buffer. The buffer will be written to the
     * client. This method must be implemented by the server.
     *
     * @param buffer Buffer to hold the output data
     * @return Output stream to write data to the buffer
     */
    public abstract DataOutput _getOutputStream(
            ByteArrayOutputStream buffer)
        throws IOException;

    /**
     * Flushes any buffered data to the output stream. The
     * default implementation does nothing.
     *
     * @param out Output stream to flush
     */
    public void _flush(DataOutput out) throws IOException
    {
    }
}
```

The basic flow of the service method is as follows:

1. Create an input stream to read the request from the client. The server implementation that extends the base servlet will create the proper type of input stream.
2. Get the instance of the server-side object from the session.
3. Set up the response header.
4. Create an in-memory buffer to hold the raw data of the response. We need to set the length of the response in the response header, so we'll cache the response data in an internal buffer and then get the length.
5. Read the method ordinal indicating which method to invoke on the server object. An ordinal of -1 directs us to initialize the server by instantiating a new server object and placing it in the session object.
6. Invoke the method. The server implementation will evaluate the method ordinal, read any parameters, and invoke the proper method. Once the method has been invoked, the server implementation will write any return value to the output stream so that it can be forwarded to the client.
7. Send the response buffer to the client.

The Tunnel "Lite" Server

Writing the server implementation for our "lite" tunnel server is very similar to the "lite" client:

```
package com.omh.tunnel.server;

import javax.servlet.*;
import javax.servlet.http.*;
import java.io.*;

/**
 * This is the base class to be extended by server objects
 * that are using HTTP lite tunneling.
 */
public abstract class TunnelLiteServer
        extends BaseTunnelServlet
{
    /**
     * Creates an input stream to be used to read data
```

```
     * sent from the client.
     *
     * @param servletInput Servlet input stream from the servlet
     * request header
     * @return Input stream to read data from the client
     */
    public DataInput _getInputStream(ServletInputStream servletInput)
        throws IOException
    {
        // Create a new DataInputStream for reading data from
        // the client.
        return new DataInputStream(servletInput);
    }

    /**
     * Gets an output stream to be used for writing data to
     * an internal buffer. The buffer will be written to the
     * client
     *
     * @param buffer Buffer to hold the output data
     * @return Output stream to write data to the buffer
     */
    public DataOutput _getOutputStream(ByteArrayOutputStream buffer)
        throws IOException
    {
        // Create a new DataOutputStream for writing data to
        // the buffer.
        return new DataOutputStream(buffer);
    }

    /**
     * Flushes any buffered data to the output stream
     *
     * @param out Output stream to flush
     */
    public void _flush(DataOutput out) throws IOException
    {
        // Flush the data to the buffer
        ((DataOutputStream) out).flush();
    }
}
```

Note that we are using DataInputStream and DataOutputStream just like the client.

Tunneling Example: RemoteMathLite

To bring all of these pieces together, let's write a very simple applet that will perform some simple math operations (add, subtract, and multiply). Big deal, right? The exciting aspect of this applet is that all the calculations will be performed on the server via HTTP tunneling.

Writing the Server Interface

I always like to begin by defining an interface that describes the methods available on a particular server object. While this is not necessary for what we are doing now, it will be critically important in Chapter 11 when we start automating the creation of remote objects. If you have worked with CORBA, you are already used to writing the Interface Definition Language (IDL) necessary to generate CORBA proxies and stubs; in essence, we will be doing the same thing.

The following shows the interface definition for our Math object:

```
package com.omh.tunnel;

/**
 * This interface defines the methods available for
 * performing math
 */
public interface MathInterface
{
    /**
     * Adds two numbers
     */
    double add(double a, double b);

    /**
     * Subtracts two numbers
     */
    double subtract(double a, double b);

    /**
     * Multiplies two numbers
     */
    double multiply(double a, double b);

}
```

As you can see, we have three methods: add(), subtract(), and multiply().

Writing the Server Object

Implementing the three math methods is, as you would expect, no difficult task. Note that there is nothing special about implementing the server object even though we will be using it via HTTP tunneling.

```
package com.omh.tunnel;

/**
 * This class performs simple math functions in order to
 * illustrate remote method tunneling.
 */
public class Math implements MathInterface
{
    public double add(double a, double b)
    {
        return (a + b);
    }

    public double subtract(double a, double b)
    {
        return (a - b);
    }

    public double multiply(double a, double b)
    {
        return (a * b);
    }

}
```

Writing the Client Proxy

We now have to implement the client proxy. A proxy is defined by *The Random House College Dictionary, Revised Edition* as "…the agency, function, or power of a person authorized to act as the deputy or substitute for another." We are interested in creating a proxy to take the place of the real Math object and instead tunnel any method calls to the server where they will be processed. Our client Math proxy (RemoteMathLiteClient) will extend our "lite" client class and implement the Math interface that we defined earlier. We then have to implement each method in the interface and, using methods in the base class, write any parameters to the output stream that will be sent to the server. After invoking the remote method, an input stream will be returned that we can use to read any return values from the method call.

```
package com.omh.tunnel;

import com.omh.tunnel.client.TunnelLiteClient;
import com.omh.tunnel.client.TunnelException;

import java.io.*;

/**
 * This class implements the 'lite' client for tunneling
 * calls to the Math object.
 */
public class RemoteMathLiteClient
    extends TunnelLiteClient
    implements MathInterface
{

    /**
     * Constructs a new RemoteMathLiteClient for the
     * given URL. The URL should contain the root location of
     * the servlet that will be invoked (i.e. http://larryboy/).
     */
    public RemoteMathLiteClient(String url)
        throws TunnelException, IOException
    {
        // Append the remote 'lite' server name
        url += "RemoteMathLiteServer";

        // Set the URL
        _setURL(new java.net.URL(url));

        // Initialize the client and server
        _initialize();
    }

    /**
```

```
     * Adds two numbers
     */
    public double add(double a, double b)
    {
        double n = 0;
        try
        {
            // Create an internal buffer
            ByteArrayOutputStream baos = new ByteArrayOutputStream();

            // Create an output stream to write the request
            DataOutputStream out =
                (DataOutputStream) _createHeader(baos, 0);

            // Output the parameters
            out.writeDouble(a);
            out.writeDouble(b);

            // Invoke the method and read the response
            DataInputStream in =
                (DataInputStream) _invokeMethod(baos.toByteArray());

            // Read the return value
            n = in.readDouble();

            // Wrap up
            out.close();
            in.close();
        }
        catch (Exception ex)
        {
            ex.printStackTrace();
        }
        return n;
    }

}
```

Note that the initialize routine specifies the name of the servlet to invoke; we'll be creating this next. Also, I've only shown the code for the add() method; subtract() and multiply() are identical other than the method ordinal that is used.

Writing the Server Stub

The server stub will extend the base lite server and implement the _getNewInstance() and _invokeMethod() routines. Though it may not look like it, the stub is actually the servlet that will be invoked; all of the servlet details have already been implemented in the base class that the stub extends. The _getNewInstance() method will return an instance of the server object that will be persisted with the HTTP session object in the web server. In our case, this is the Math object with the implementation for all of the math routines (add, subtract, and multiply).

The _invokeMethod() method will be given an instance of the server object (retrieved from the HTTP session), the method ordinal of the method to invoke on the server object, an input stream to read parameters from, and an output stream that will be used to write return values. The complete code follows:

```
package com.omh.tunnel;

import com.omh.tunnel.server.TunnelLiteServer;
import javax.servlet.*;
import javax.servlet.http.*;
import java.io.*;

/**
 * This class implements the 'lite' server for tunneling
 * remote Math method calls
 */
public class RemoteMathLiteServer
    extends TunnelLiteServer
{
    /**
     * Creates a new instance of the server object.
     *
     * @return Instance of the server object
     */
    public Object _getNewInstance()
        throws ServletException
    {
        return new Math();
    }

    /**
     * Invokes the method for the ordinal given. If the method
     * throws an exception it will be sent to the client.
     *
     * @param Object Server object
     * @param ordinal Method ordinal
     * @param in Input stream to read additional parameters
     * @param out Output stream to write return values
     */
    public void _invokeMethod(Object serverObject, int ordinal,
```

```
                              DataInput in, DataOutput out)
        throws Exception
    {
        // Cast the server object
        Math math = (Math) serverObject;

        // Cast the input/output streams
        DataInputStream dataIn = (DataInputStream) in;
        DataOutputStream dataOut = (DataOutputStream) out;

        // Evaluate the ordinal
        switch (ordinal)
        {

        case 0: // add
            double a0 = dataIn.readDouble();
            double b0 = dataIn.readDouble();
            double n0 = math.add(a0, b0);
            out.writeDouble(n0);
            break;

        case 1: // subtract
            double a1 = dataIn.readDouble();
            double b1 = dataIn.readDouble();
            double n1 = math.subtract(a1, b1);
            out.writeDouble(n1);
            break;

        case 2: // multiply
            double a2 = dataIn.readDouble();
            double b2 = dataIn.readDouble();
            double n2 = math.multiply(a2, b2);
            out.writeDouble(n2);
            break;

        default:
            throw new Exception("Invalid ordinal: " + ordinal);
        }
    }
}
```

Writing the Applet

To test this lite remote object, I'll be using JDK 1.0.2 to prove that it works as described. Because of this, our MathLiteApplet will use the handleEvent() applet method instead of the JDK 1.1 event model. Don't worry, we'll be writing an applet using the event model later in this chapter. Since this is not a book on applet programming (there are plenty of those around), I won't spend too much time diving into the particulars of applet development. The critical piece of this applet is how to create our remote object. In essence, all we need to do is create an instance of our client proxy and cast it to the Math interface that we have defined. This is another great benefit of using interfaces: you can invoke the remote object by making calls on the interface without having to know (or care) that it is indeed a remote object. This makes remote object programming much easier, because there is no special syntax to learn; just make method calls on an object—the client proxy is hiding all of the work.

The following shows the complete code for the applet. Again, note how the client proxy is instantiated and how making remote method calls is done with a simple call on the interface.

```
package com.omh.tunnel;

import java.applet.*;
import java.awt.*;

/**
 * This calculator applet demonstrates how to use the
 * tunnel clients to perform remote method calls using
 * JDK 1.0.2 style events.
 */

public class MathLiteApplet
        extends Applet
{
    // Define the GUI widgets
    TextField output;
    Button b0;
    Button b1;
    Button b2;
    Button b3;
    Button b4;
    Button b5;
    Button b6;
    Button b7;
    Button b8;
    Button b9;
    Button dot;
    Button mult;
    Button add;
    Button sub;
    Button div;
    Button equals;
```

```
Button clear;

// Our memory area
double mem;
int opType;
boolean newOp = false;

// Operation types
public static final int NONE = 0;
public static final int MULTIPLY = 1;
public static final int ADD = 2;
public static final int SUBTRACT = 3;

// Interface to our remote object
MathInterface math;

/**
 * Initialize the applet
 */
public void init()
{
    setLayout(new BorderLayout(0, 5));

    // Create the output text area for the amount
    output = new TextField("0");
    output.disable();
    add("North", output);

    // Create the container for the buttons
    Panel p = new Panel();
    p.setLayout(new GridLayout(4, 4, 3, 3));

    b0 = new Button("0");
    b1 = new Button("1");
    b2 = new Button("2");
    b3 = new Button("3");
    b4 = new Button("4");
    b5 = new Button("5");
    b6 = new Button("6");
    b7 = new Button("7");
    b8 = new Button("8");
    b9 = new Button("9");
    dot = new Button(".");
```

```
        mult = new Button("X");
        add = new Button("+");
        sub = new Button("-");
        div = new Button("/");
        equals = new Button("=");
        clear = new Button("C");

        // First row   7 8 9 +
        p.add(b7);
        p.add(b8);
        p.add(b9);
        p.add(add);

        // Second row  4 5 6 -
        p.add(b4);
        p.add(b5);
        p.add(b6);
        p.add(sub);

        // Third row   3 2 1 X
        p.add(b1);
        p.add(b2);
        p.add(b3);
        p.add(mult);

        // Fourth row  0 . C =
        p.add(b0);
        p.add(dot);
        p.add(clear);
        p.add(equals);

        add("Center", p);

        // Create an instance of our remote object
        try
        {
            math = new RemoteMathLiteClient(getCodeBase() + "/");
        }
        catch (Exception ex)
        {
            ex.printStackTrace();
        }
    }
```

```
/**
 * Handle events
 */
public boolean handleEvent(Event event)
{
    if ((event != null) && (event.id == event.ACTION_EVENT))
    {
        if (event.target == b0)
        {
            append("0");
        }
        else if (event.target == b1)
        {
            append("1");
        }
        else if (event.target == b2)
        {
            append("2");
        }
        else if (event.target == b3)
        {
            append("3");
        }
        else if (event.target == b4)
        {
            append("4");
        }
        else if (event.target == b5)
        {
            append("5");
        }
        else if (event.target == b6)
        {
            append("6");
        }
        else if (event.target == b7)
        {
            append("7");
        }
        else if (event.target == b8)
        {
            append("8");
```

```
            }
            else if (event.target == b9)
            {
                append("9");
            }
            else if (event.target == dot)
            {
                append(".");
            }
            else if (event.target == mult)
            {
                compute(MULTIPLY);
            }
            else if (event.target == add)
            {
                compute(ADD);
            }
            else if (event.target == sub)
            {
                compute(SUBTRACT);
            }
            else if (event.target == equals)
            {
                compute();
            }
            else if (event.target == clear)
            {
                output.setText("0");
                mem = 0;
                opType = NONE;
            }
        }
        return false;
    }

    /**
     * Append the given number to the output text
     */
    protected void append(String s)
    {
        // If this is the first value after an operation, clear
        // the old value
        if (newOp)
```

```
    {
        newOp = false;
        output.setText("");
    }

    String o = output.getText();

    // Make sure it can fit
    if (o.length() >= 12)
    {
        return;
    }

    // First check if there is a decimal. If so, just tack
    // the string on the end
    if (o.indexOf(".") >= 0)
    {
        o += s;
    }
    else
    {
        // Otherwise check to see if the number is zero. If
        // it is, set the text to the given string
        if (o.equals("0"))
        {
            o = s;
        }
        else
        {
            o += s;
        }
    }

    output.setText(o);
}

/**
 * Compute the result
 */
protected void compute()
{
    double current =
        Double.valueOf(output.getText()).doubleValue();
```

```
        switch (opType)
        {

        case MULTIPLY:
            if (math != null)
            {
                mem = math.multiply(mem, current);
            }
            break;

        case ADD:
            if (math != null)
            {
                mem = math.add(mem, current);
            }
            break;

        case SUBTRACT:
            if (math != null)
            {
            mem = math.subtract(mem, current);
            }
            break;

        default:
            mem = current;
            break;
        }

        opType = NONE;

        String s = "" + mem;

        // Truncate if a whole number
        if (s.endsWith(".0"))
        {
            s = s.substring(0, s.length() - 2);
        }
        output.setText(s);
    }

    protected void compute(int type)
```

```
    {
        // If there is a current operation, execute it
        if (opType != NONE)
        {
            compute();
        }
        else
        {
            mem = Double.valueOf(output.getText()).doubleValue();
        }

        opType = type;
        newOp = true;
    }
}
```

See It in Action

After adding the RemoteMathLiteServer servlet to web.xml and writing a simple HTML page to load our applet, it's time to give it a test drive:

```
<html>
<head>
<title>Simple Calculator</title>
</head>
<body>
<h2>Simple calculator applet that makes remote method
calls using applet to servlet communication</h2>
<center>
<hr>
<applet width=300
        height=200
        name="MathLiteApplet"
        code="com.omh.tunnel.MathLiteApplet"
        archive="client/MathLite.jar">
</applet>
</center>
</body>
</html>
```

I've placed all of the supporting classes in a JAR file named MathLite.jar, which is specified in the archive attribute of the applet tag.

After entering values and selecting an operator type, clicking the Calculate button will contact the remote servlet, which will then invoke the proper method on the server-side object. The return value is then read from the server and placed in the result field.

The following shows the applet in action:

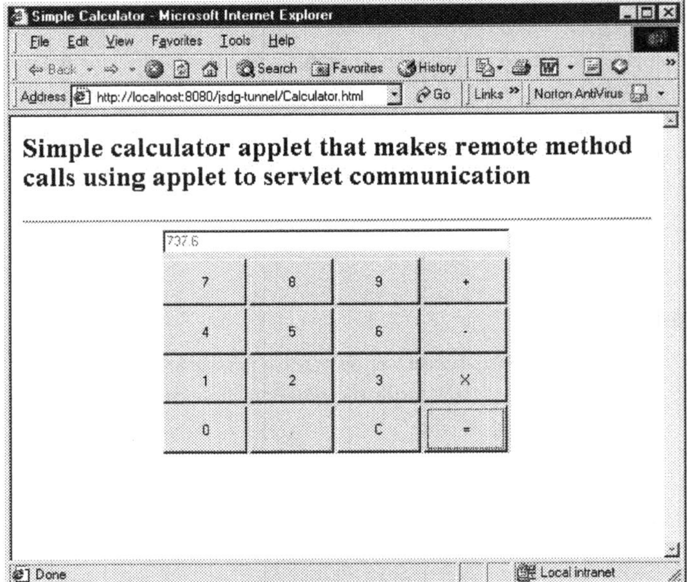

Using Serialization

Starting with JDK 1.1, we have a new option for marshaling data between a client and server: serialization. Serialization is the process of storing (serializing) and retrieving (deserializing) the internal state of an object without having to be aware of the internal structure of that object. In other words, the JVM handles writing all the properties of an object and can, given this stored information, re-create the object at a later time and place. Sun added serialization to the JDK to enable RMI to pass objects between a client and server; we'll take this built-in functionality and put it to use in a new version of our tunneling client and server.

Before going too far, there are a few pitfalls when using serialization:

- Not all objects are serializable. An object must implement the java.io .Serializable interface in order to be serializable. Remember that the whole purpose of serialization is to save the state of an object so that it can be re-created later; for some types of objects, this does not make sense (such as database connections, open file handles, and so forth).
- Serialization will add a significant amount of overhead to the size of a request/ response packet. Serializing an object not only writes the properties but also generates versioning and class file information. This may not be a big concern for you, but this additional data may have an impact on performance.
- Serialization errors may occur if the version of the object that was serialized differs from the one present when the object is deserialized. An example of this is having a new copy of an object on the client and an older (or missing) version of the object on the server.
- Some browsers (especially older versions) may not fully support serialization. Remember that serialization is a JDK 1.1 feature; but even if a browser claims to support 1.1, it may not properly support serialization.

Using ObjectOutputStream and ObjectInputStream

To illustrate how to marshal data with version 1.1 (or later) of the JDK, let's take a look at a simple client application that uses java.io.ObjectOutputStream for writing the request data and java.io.ObjectInputStream for reading the response data. This application is basically the same as the TestDataStream application we saw earlier. To recap, the flow of our client application is as follows:

1. Open an HTTP connection.
2. Format the request data.
3. Send the request to the server.
4. Read the response data.
5. Close the HTTP connection.

The server will simply read the request data and echo it back to the client.

To invoke the application, you must supply the URL of the servlet that will echo the data:

```
java com.omh.tunnel.TestObjectStream
    http://localhost:8080/jsdg-tunnel/ObjectStreamEcho
```

Note that the command has been split over multiple lines to improve readability; it should be entered as a single line. We will be using the server on the localhost to invoke the ObjectStreamEcho servlet (as configured in web.xml). The following is the code for the test application:

```
package com.omh.tunnel;

import java.io.*;

/**
 * This application shows how to read data from and write data
 * to a servlet using object input/output streams.
 */
public class TestObjectStream
{
    /**
     * Application entry point. This application requires
     * one parameter, which is the servlet URL
     */
    public static void main(String args[])
    {
        // Make sure we have an argument for the servlet URL
        if (args.length == 0)
        {
            System.out.println("\nServlet URL must be specified");
            return;
        }

        try
        {

            System.out.println("Attempting to connect to " + args[0]);

            // Get the server URL
            java.net.URL url = new java.net.URL(args[0]);

            // Attempt to connect to the host
            java.net.URLConnection con = url.openConnection();

            // Initialize the connection
            con.setUseCaches(false);
            con.setDoOutput(true);
            con.setDoInput(true);

            // Data will always be written to a byte array buffer so
```

```
// that we can tell the server the length of the data
ByteArrayOutputStream byteOut = new ByteArrayOutputStream();

// Create the output stream to be used to write the
// data to our buffer
ObjectOutputStream out = new ObjectOutputStream(byteOut);

System.out.println("Writing test objects");

// Write the test data
out.writeObject(new Boolean(true));
out.writeObject(new Byte((byte) 1));
out.writeObject(new Character((char) 2));
out.writeObject(new Short((short) 3));
out.writeObject(new Integer(4));
out.writeObject(new Float(5));
out.writeObject(new Double(6));
out.writeObject("Hello, Karl");

// Flush the data to the buffer
out.flush();

// Get our buffer to be sent
byte buf[] = byteOut.toByteArray();

// Set the content that we are sending
con.setRequestProperty("Content-type",
        "application/octet-stream");

// Set the length of the data buffer we are sending
con.setRequestProperty("Content-length",
        "" + buf.length);

// Get the output stream to the server and send our
// data buffer
DataOutputStream dataOut =
    new DataOutputStream(con.getOutputStream());
//out.write(buf, 0, buf.length);
dataOut.write(buf);

// Flush the output stream and close it
dataOut.flush();
dataOut.close();

System.out.println("Reading response");

// Get the input stream we can use to read the response
ObjectInputStream in =
    new ObjectInputStream(con.getInputStream());

// Read the data from the server
Boolean booleanValue = (Boolean) in.readObject();
Byte byteValue = (Byte) in.readObject();
```

```
            Character charValue = (Character) in.readObject();
            Short shortValue = (Short) in.readObject();
            Integer intValue = (Integer) in.readObject();
            Float floatValue = (Float) in.readObject();
            Double doubleValue = (Double) in.readObject();
            String stringValue = (String) in.readObject();

            // Close the input stream
            in.close();

            System.out.println("Data read: " +
                    booleanValue + " " +
                    byteValue + " " +
                    ((int) charValue.charValue()) + " " +
                    shortValue + " " +
                    intValue + " " +
                    floatValue + " " +
                    doubleValue + " " +
                    stringValue);
        }
        catch (Exception ex)
        {
            ex.printStackTrace();
        }

    }
}
```

Just like the TestDataStream application, the data is being written to an in-memory buffer. Notice how we are using the generic writeObject() method found in the ObjectInputStream class. The following description is given in the JDK documentation for writeObject():

> Write the specified object to the ObjectOutputStream. The class of the object, the signature of the class, and the values of the non-transient and non-static fields of the class and all of its supertypes are written. Default serialization for a class can be overridden using the writeObject and the readObject methods. Objects referenced by this object are written transitively so that a complete equivalent graph of objects can be reconstructed by an ObjectInputStream.

What this means is that writeObject() causes the object to be serialized to the underlying output stream, which then must be deserialized using the readObject() method of the ObjectInputStream class. The objects should be read in the same order that they were written. However, serialization has one distinct advantage over the simple marshaling that we have seen earlier; you can read a generic object and reflect upon the object to determine what type it is (such as using the instance of comparison operator).

The servlet used to read the response and echo the data is very similar to what we have seen before. Instead of using data input and output streams, we'll be using object input and output streams:

```
package com.omh.tunnel;

import javax.servlet.*;
import javax.servlet.http.*;
import java.io.*;

/**
 * This servlet shows how to read data from and write data
 * to a client using object input/output streams.
 */
public class ObjectStreamEcho
        extends HttpServlet
{
    public void service(HttpServletRequest req,
                        HttpServletResponse resp)
        throws ServletException, IOException
    {
        // Get the input stream for reading data from the client
        ObjectInputStream in =
            new ObjectInputStream(req.getInputStream());

        // We'll be sending binary data back to the client so
        // set the content type appropriately
        resp.setContentType("application/octet-stream");

        // Data will always be written to a byte array buffer so
        // that we can tell the client the length of the data
        ByteArrayOutputStream byteOut = new ByteArrayOutputStream();

        // Create the output stream to be used to write the
        // data to our buffer
        ObjectOutputStream out = new ObjectOutputStream(byteOut);

        // Read the objects from the client.
        try
        {
            Boolean booleanValue = (Boolean) in.readObject();
            Byte byteValue = (Byte) in.readObject();
            Character charValue = (Character) in.readObject();
            Short shortValue = (Short) in.readObject();
            Integer intValue = (Integer) in.readObject();
            Float floatValue = (Float) in.readObject();
            Double doubleValue = (Double) in.readObject();
            String stringValue = (String) in.readObject();

            // Write the data to our internal buffer.
            out.writeObject(booleanValue);
            out.writeObject(byteValue);
```

```
            out.writeObject(charValue);
            out.writeObject(shortValue);
            out.writeObject(intValue);
            out.writeObject(floatValue);
            out.writeObject(doubleValue);
            out.writeObject(stringValue);
        }
        catch (ClassNotFoundException ex)
        {
            // Serialization can throw a ClassNotFoundException.
            ex.printStackTrace();
        }

        // Flush the contents of the output stream to the
        // byte array
        out.flush();

        // Get the buffer that is holding our response
        byte[] buf = byteOut.toByteArray();

        // Notify the client how much data is being sent
        resp.setContentLength(buf.length);

        // Send the buffer to the client
        ServletOutputStream servletOut = resp.getOutputStream();

        // Wrap up
        servletOut.write(buf);
        servletOut.close();
    }
}
```

A Tunnel Client Class for Serialization

Writing the client implementation for our tunnel client that uses serialization is also very straightforward. The only real difference between this tunnel client and our lite client that we developed earlier is the type of input and output streams that will be used. The base tunnel client does not need to change, because you had the foresight to separate the creation of the input and output streams from the base code (great job!).

```
package com.omh.tunnel.client;

import java.io.*;

/**
 * This class implements the necessary TunnelClientInterface
 * methods for a JDK 1.1 tunneled client. The marshaling of
 * data is done with serialization.
 */
```

```
public abstract class TunnelClient
        extends BaseTunnelClient
{
    /**
     * Gets an input stream to be used for reading data
     * from the connection. The lite version uses a standard
     * data input stream for reading data.
     *
     * @param in Input stream from the connection URL
     * @return Input stream to read data from the connection
     */
    public DataInput _getInputStream(InputStream in)
        throws IOException
    {
        // Create a new DataInputStream for reading data from
        // the connection.
        return new ObjectInputStream(in);
    }

    /**
     * Gets an output stream to be used for writing data to
     * an internal buffer. The buffer will be written to the
     * connection. The lite version uses a standard data
     * output stream for writing data.
     *
     * @param buffer Buffer to hold the output data
     * @return Output stream to write data to the buffer
     */
    public DataOutput _getOutputStream(ByteArrayOutputStream buffer)
        throws IOException
    {
        // Create a new DataOutputStream for writing data to
        // the buffer.
        return new ObjectOutputStream(buffer);
    }

    /**
     * Flushes any buffered data to the output stream
     *
     * @param out Output stream to flush
     */
    public void _flush(DataOutput out) throws IOException
    {
        // Flush the data to the buffer
        ((ObjectOutputStream) out).flush();
    }
```

```
    /**
     * Closes the input stream
     *
     * @param in Input stream to close
     */
    public void _close(DataInput in) throws IOException
    {
        ((ObjectInputStream) in).close();
    }
}
```

A Tunnel Server Class for Serialization

As you might expect, the implementation for the tunnel server that uses serialization is the same as the lite version except that object input and output streams are used:

```
package com.omh.tunnel.server;

import javax.servlet.*;
import javax.servlet.http.*;
import java.io.*;

/**
 * This is the base class to be extended by server objects
 * that are using HTTP tunneling.
 */
public abstract class TunnelServer
        extends BaseTunnelServlet
{
    /**
     * Creates an input stream to be used to read data
     * sent from the client.
     *
     * @param servletInput Servlet input stream from the servlet
     * request header
     * @return Input stream to read data from the client
     */
    public DataInput _getInputStream(ServletInputStream servletInput)
        throws IOException
    {
        // Create a new DataInputStream for reading data from
        // the client.
        return new ObjectInputStream(servletInput);
    }

    /**
```

```
     * Closes the input stream
     *
     * @param in Input stream to close
     */
    public void _close(DataInput in) throws IOException
    {
        ((ObjectInputStream) in).close();
    }

    /**
     * Gets an output stream to be used for writing data to
     * an internal buffer. The buffer will be written to the
     * client
     *
     * @param buffer Buffer to hold the output data
     * @return Output stream to write data to the buffer
     */
    public DataOutput _getOutputStream(ByteArrayOutputStream buffer)
        throws IOException
    {
        // Create a new DataOutputStream for writing data to
        // the buffer.
        return new ObjectOutputStream(buffer);
    }

    /**
     * Flushes any buffered data to the output stream
     *
     * @param out Output stream to flush
     */
    public void _flush(DataOutput out) throws IOException
    {
        // Flush the data to the buffer
        ((ObjectOutputStream) out).flush();
    }
}
```

Tunneling Example: RemoteIndy

To further illustrate the use of Java serialization, let's develop a simple applet that will use HTTP tunneling to make method calls to a server-side object that will retrieve data from a database. The database contains a row for each year that the Indianapolis 500 was run; each row contains the year, the name of the winning driver, and the average speed of the winning car.

Writing the Server Interface

Let's start by writing an interface that describes the services available for our server-side object. By "services" I mean the methods, parameter types, and return types of the server object. Our server object will provide the following services:

- **Initialize** Calling the initialize() method will cause a database connection to be established and ready the object for use.
- **Query** The query() method will accept a single parameter, which will be used to form a SQL WHERE clause to select data out of the database. An object containing the selected data will be returned to the caller.
- **Close** Calling the close() method will close the database connection and perform any necessary cleanup in the server object.

The code listing for the Indy interface follows:

```
package com.omh.tunnel;

/**
 * This interface defines the methods available for
 * performing queries on the Indianapolis 500 database
 */
public interface IndyInterface
{
    /**
     * Connects to the database.
     *
     * @return True if the database connection was established
     */
    boolean connect();

    /**
     * Closes the database connection
     */
    void close();

    /**
     * Given the year return the corresponding Indianapolis
     * 500 record
     *
     * @param year Year of the race
```

```
     * @return Indy 500 record or null if not found
     */
    IndyRecord query(int year);
}
```

Notice that the query() method returns an IndyRecord object. This object contains a public attribute for each column in the database. Notice also that the IndyRecord class implements java.io.Serializable; by doing so, Java can properly serialize and deserialize the object.

```
package com.omh.tunnel;

import java.io.Serializable;

/**
 * This object encapsulates a single Indianapolis 500 record
 */
public class IndyRecord
        implements Serializable
{
    public int year;
    public String driver;
    public double speed;
}
```

Note that to be Java Beans–compliant, the IndyRecord class should really contain getter and setter methods for each of the properties; I have chosen to just make the properties public so that you can get the values directly.

Writing the Server Object

The beauty of writing the server object is that you do not need to know (or care) that the object will be used by HTTP tunneling; all we need to be concerned about is implementing the interface:

```
package com.omh.tunnel;

import java.sql.*;

/**
 * Implements the IndyInterface to provide query capabilities
 * into the Indianapolis 500 database.
 */
```

```
public class Indy implements IndyInterface
{
    // The JDBC Connection
    Connection connection = null;

    // A prepared statement to use to query the database
    PreparedStatement prepStmt = null;

    public boolean connect()
    {
        boolean rc = false;

        try
        {
            // Load the Bridge
            Class.forName("sun.jdbc.odbc.JdbcOdbcDriver").newInstance();

            // Connect to the Access database
            connection = DriverManager.getConnection("jdbc:odbc:MyAccessDataSource");

            // Go ahead and create a prepared statement
            prepStmt = connection.prepareStatement(
                "SELECT Year, Driver, AvgSpeed from IndyWinners " +
                "WHERE Year = ?");

            rc = true;
        }
        catch (Exception ex)
        {
            ex.printStackTrace();
        }

        return rc;
    }

    public void close()
    {
        // Close the connection if it was opened
        if (connection != null)
        {
            try
            {
                connection.close();
```

```
            }
            catch (SQLException ex)
            {
                ex.printStackTrace();
            }
            connection = null;
        }
    }

    public IndyRecord query(int year)
    {
        IndyRecord record = null;

        try
        {
            // Set the year parameter
            prepStmt.setInt(1, year);

            // Execute the query
            ResultSet rs = prepStmt.executeQuery();

            // Make sure a record exists
            if (rs.next())
            {
                // Create a new IndyRecord object
                record = new IndyRecord();

                // Set the values
                record.year = rs.getInt(1);
                record.driver = rs.getString(2);
                record.speed = rs.getDouble(3);
            }
            rs.close();
        }
        catch (SQLException ex)
        {
            ex.printStackTrace();
            record = null;
        }

        return record;
    }
}
```

Notice that the initialize() method is creating a database connection using the JDBC-ODBC Bridge and an Access database. Also, a JDBC PreparedStatement object is being created as well. Preparing a SQL statement is a great way to boost performance for queries that you will be using multiple times. In our case, we'll be re-executing the same query over and over with a different year value (this is done in the query() method).

Note also how the data is being gathered from the result of the select statement in the query() method. You should always retrieve column data in order, and each column should only be retrieved once; some JDBC drivers are rather strict in enforcing this requirement, especially the Bridge (due to the way ODBC functions).

The close() method simply ensures that the database connection is properly terminated. Make sure that you always close the database so that you don't have any unwanted memory leaks or wasted resources on the server.

Writing the Client Proxy

The client proxy is responsible for marshaling method and parameter data to the server and reading the return value from the response stream. Remember that we've already done a lot of work in the base client object, so the client proxy is quite simple:

```
package com.omh.tunnel;

import com.omh.tunnel.client.TunnelClient;
import com.omh.tunnel.client.TunnelException;

import java.io.*;

/**
 * This class implements the client for tunneling
 * calls to the Indy object.
 */
public class RemoteIndyClient
    extends TunnelClient
    implements IndyInterface
{

    /**
     * Constructs a new RemoteMathLiteClient for the
     * given URL. The URL should contain the root location of
```

```
 * the servlet (i.e. http://larryboy:8080/).
 */
public RemoteIndyClient(String url)
    throws TunnelException, IOException
{
    // Append the remote server name
    url += "RemoteIndyServer";

    // Set the URL
    _setURL(new java.net.URL(url));

    // Initialize the client and server
    _initialize();
}

public IndyRecord query(int year)
{
    IndyRecord record = null;
    try
    {
        // Create an internal buffer
        ByteArrayOutputStream baos = new ByteArrayOutputStream();

        // Create an object stream to write the request
        ObjectOutputStream out =
            (ObjectOutputStream) _createHeader(baos, 2);

        // Write the parameters
        out.writeObject(new Integer(year));

        // Invoke the method and read the response
        ObjectInputStream in =
            (ObjectInputStream)_invokeMethod(baos.toByteArray());

        // Read the return value
        record = (IndyRecord) in.readObject();

        // Wrap up
        out.close();
        in.close();
    }
```

```
        catch (Exception ex)
        {
            ex.printStackTrace();
        }

        return record;
    }
}
```

The constructor takes the base servlet URL (such as http://localhost:8080/) and causes a new server-side object to be instantiated. The rest of the client proxy implementation is very repetitive; because of this, I've only included the query() method.

Note that the method ordinal is unique within the method and is used to create the method header. Also notice how the object input and output streams are used to marshal data back and forth to the server.

Writing the Server Stub

The server stub (which is also the servlet that will be invoked) implements the _getNewInstance() and _invokeMethod() routines. The _getNewInstance() method will return an instance of the Indy object that will be persisted with the HTTP session object in the Web server.

The _invokeMethod() method will be given an instance of the server object (retrieved from the HTTP session), the method ordinal of the method to invoke on the server object, an input stream to read parameters from, and an output stream, which will be used to write return values. The RemoteIndyServer code follows:

```
package com.omh.tunnel;

import com.omh.tunnel.server.TunnelServer;
import javax.servlet.*;
import javax.servlet.http.*;
import java.io.*;

/**
 * This class implements the server for tunneling
 * remote Indy method calls
 */
public class RemoteIndyServer
    extends TunnelServer
{
    /**
```

```
     * Creates a new instance of the server object.
     *
     * @return Instance of the server object
     */
    public Object _getNewInstance()
        throws ServletException
    {
        return new Indy();
    }

    /**
     * Invokes the method for the ordinal given. If the method
     * throws an exception it will be sent to the client.
     *
     * @param Object Server object
     * @param ordinal Method ordinal
     * @param in Input stream to read additional parameters
     * @param out Output stream to write return values
     */
    public void _invokeMethod(Object serverObject, int ordinal,
                              DataInput in, DataOutput out)
        throws Exception
    {
        // Cast the server object
        Indy indy = (Indy) serverObject;

        // Cast the input/output streams
        ObjectInputStream objectIn = (ObjectInputStream) in;
        ObjectOutputStream objectOut = (ObjectOutputStream) out;

        // Evaluate the ordinal
        switch (ordinal)
        {

        case 0: // connect
            boolean b0 = indy.connect();
            objectOut.writeObject(new Boolean(b0));
            break;

        case 1: // close
            indy.close();
            break;
```

```
            case 2: // query
                Integer i2 = (Integer) objectIn.readObject();
                IndyRecord record = indy.query(i2.intValue());
                objectOut.writeObject(record);
                break;

            default:
                throw new Exception("Invalid ordinal: " + ordinal);
            }
        }
}
```

Writing the Applet

Now it's time to put our remote object to use by writing a simple applet that uses the client proxy. Most of the work involved is in formatting the display; calling methods on the remote object is nothing more than instantiating a new client proxy and making Java method calls on the Indy interface:

```
package com.omh.tunnel;

import java.applet.*;
import java.awt.*;
import java.awt.event.*;

/**
 * This applet demonstrates how to use the tunnel clients
 * to perform remote method calls using serialization
 */
public class IndyApplet
    extends Applet
    implements ActionListener
{
    // Define our global components
    TextField year = new TextField(10);
    TextField driver = new TextField(20);
    TextField speed = new TextField(10);
    Button query = new Button("Query");
    IndyInterface indy;

    /**
     * Initialize the applet
     */
```

```
public void init()
{
    // Don't allow the results to be edited
    driver.setEditable(false);
    speed.setEditable(false);

    // Use a grid bag layout
    GridBagLayout gridbag = new GridBagLayout();
    GridBagConstraints gbcon = new GridBagConstraints();
    setLayout(gridbag);

    // Set up the reusable constraint
    gbcon.weightx = 1.0;
    gbcon.weighty = 0.0;
    gbcon.anchor = gbcon.CENTER;
    gbcon.fill = gbcon.NONE;
    gbcon.gridwidth = gbcon.REMAINDER;

    // Add listeners
    query.addActionListener(this);

    // Add the components
    add(new Label("Enter the year:"));
    gridbag.setConstraints(year, gbcon);
    add(year);

    add(new Label("Press to query:"));
    gridbag.setConstraints(query, gbcon);
    add(query);

    add(new Label("Driver(s):"));
    gridbag.setConstraints(driver, gbcon);
    add(driver);

    add(new Label("Average Speed:"));
    gridbag.setConstraints(speed, gbcon);
    add(speed);

    // Create an instance of our remote object
    try
    {
        indy = new RemoteIndyClient(getCodeBase() + "/");
```

```
            // Open the database connection
            boolean rc = indy.connect();
            if (!rc)
            {
                System.out.println("Connection not initialized");
                indy = null;
            }
        }
        catch (Exception ex)
        {
            ex.printStackTrace();
        }
    }

    /**
     * Called when the applet is being destroyed
     */
    public void destroy()
    {
        // If the remote object was created close the connection
        if (indy != null)
        {
            indy.close();
            indy = null;
        }
    }

    /**
     * Process an action
     */
    public void actionPerformed(ActionEvent event)
    {
        Object o = event.getSource();

        // Figure out which component caused the event
        if (o == query)
        {
            // If the indy object was not created, get out
```

```
            if (indy == null)
            {
                return;
            }

            // Clear the display fields
            driver.setText("");
            speed.setText("");

            // Get the year entered by the user
            int n = 0;
            try
            {
                n = Integer.parseInt(year.getText());
            }
            catch (Exception ex)
            {
            }

            // Get the indy record
            IndyRecord r = indy.query(n);

            // Populate
            if (r != null)
            {
                driver.setText(r.driver);
                speed.setText("" + r.speed);
            }
        }
    }
}
```

Note that the applet implements the ActionListener interface; doing so forces us to implement the actionPerformed() method. After registering the applet as an action listener for the button (addActionListener), the actionPerformed() method will be called whenever the button is clicked. We can then perform our query, which will return the results from the database.

See It in Action

After adding the RemoteIndyServer servlet to web.xml and writing a simple HTML page to load our applet, it's time to give it a test drive. Once again, I've placed all of the supporting client classes in a JAR file, named Indy.jar, and specified the location of the JAR file in the archive attribute of the <APPLET> tag.

```
<html>
<head>
<title>Indianapolis 500 Winners</title>
</head>
<body>
<h2>Simple applet that uses applet to servlet
communication to query an Indianapolis 500
database
<center>
<hr>
<applet width=300
        height=200
        name="IndyApplet"
        code="com.omh.tunnel.IndyApplet"
        archive="client/Indy.jar">
</applet>
</center>
</body>
</html>
```

After entering the year, clicking the Query button will tunnel a method call to the servlet and display the results, as shown next.

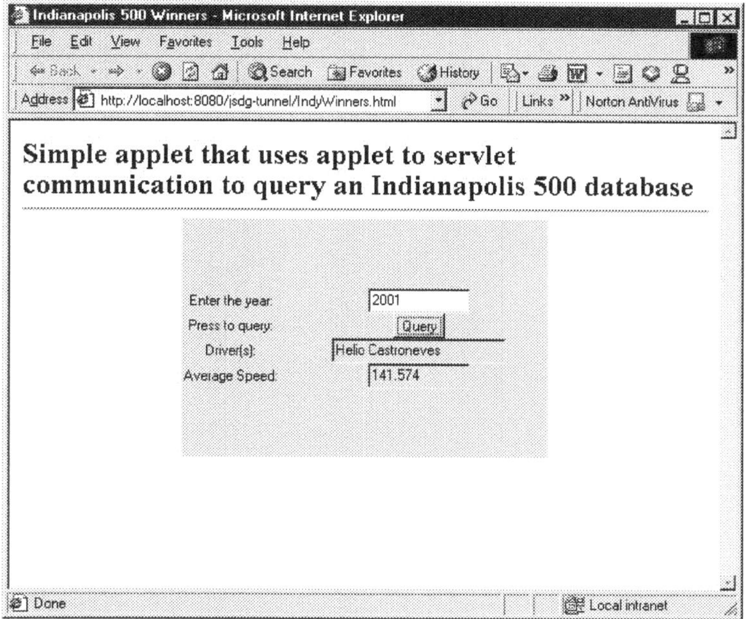

Summary

In this chapter, we've covered how to make remote method calls using HTTP tunneling, also referred to as applet to servlet communication. We've seen how to marshal data generically for all versions of the JDK (which we called the "lite" version) as well as how to marshal data specifically for JDK 1.1 and higher. Along the way, a base class was developed for both the client and server, which made writing client proxies and server stubs much easier. We also wrote applets to exercise the remote objects that were developed; these applets can be deployed over the Internet very easily.

In Chapter 11, we'll make developing remote objects painless by automating the process. You may have noticed that writing client proxies and server stubs was somewhat repetitive; we'll be developing an application that will automatically generate the source code for these classes by using Java reflection to discover the methods, parameters, and return types of the server object.

CHAPTER

11

Automating Applet-to-Servlet Programming

IN THIS CHAPTER:

Writing the Client Is Always the Same

Writing the Server Is Always the Same

Letting Java Write the Client and Server for You

Summary

In the last chapter, we took a look at how to tunnel method calls using HTTP and Java servlets. In this chapter, we'll take this one step further and use your computer to automatically generate the client and server source code necessary to make remote method calls. This is what I call real "power programming"—programming your computer to generate programs for you.

Writing the Client Is Always the Same

You may have noticed from the last chapter that writing the client proxy was very repetitive. To recap, the following are the basic steps for each method call:

1. Create a new in-memory buffer to hold the contents of the data stream.
2. Invoke a helper method to create the packet header.
3. Invoke a helper method to send the request packet to the server. This method will return an input stream that we can then use to read any return values from the server.

These steps are consistent for both the "lite" and regular versions of HTTP tunneling. Remember that the lite version uses basic data input and output streams and can be used with all JDK versions (including 1.0.2). The following code listing shows a single method call using lite tunneling:

```
public double add(double p0, double p1)
    {
        double retValue = 0;
        try {
            // Create an internal buffer
            ByteArrayOutputStream baos = new ByteArrayOutputStream();

            // Create a data stream to write the request
            DataOutputStream out =
                (DataOutputStream) _createHeader(baos, 0);
            out.writeDouble(p0);
            out.writeDouble(p1);

            // Invoke the method
            DataInputStream in =
                (DataInputStream) _invokeMethod(baos.toByteArray());

            // Get the return value
            retValue = in.readDouble();
            out.close();
```

```
            in.close();
        }
        catch (java.io.IOException ex) {
            ex.printStackTrace();
        }
        catch (TunnelException ex) {
            ex.printStackTrace();
        }
        return retValue;
    }
```

The next code listing shows a single method call using regular tunneling:

```
public com.omh.tunnel.IndyRecord query(int p0)
    {
        com.omh.tunnel.IndyRecord retValue = null;
        try {
            // Create an internal buffer
            ByteArrayOutputStream baos = new ByteArrayOutputStream();

            // Create an object stream to write the request
            ObjectOutputStream out =
                (ObjectOutputStream) _createHeader(baos, 1);
            out.writeObject(new Integer(p0));

            // Invoke the method
            ObjectInputStream in =
                (ObjectInputStream)_invokeMethod(baos.toByteArray());

            // Get the return value
            Object retObject = in.readObject();
            retValue = (com.omh.tunnel.IndyRecord) retObject;
            out.close();
            in.close();
        }
        catch (java.io.IOException ex) {
            ex.printStackTrace();
        }
        catch (ClassNotFoundException ex) {
            ex.printStackTrace();
        }
        catch (TunnelException ex) {
            ex.printStackTrace();
        }
        return retValue;
    }
```

The actual method calls that are being made are not important. What is important is that you understand the process flow for each type of client. The helper methods were developed in Chapter 10; we'll be reusing them here.

Writing the Server Is Always the Same

Just like the client proxy, writing the server-side stub is tedious and repetitive. To refresh your memory, the following are the basic server-side steps:

1. Create an input stream to read the request from the client.
2. Get the instance of the server-side object from the session.
3. Set up the response header.
4. Create an in-memory buffer to hold the raw data of the response.
5. Read the method ordinal indicating which method to invoke on the server object.
6. Invoke the method. The server implementation will evaluate the method ordinal, read any parameters, and invoke the proper method. Once the method has been invoked, the server implementation will write any return value to the output stream so that it can be forwarded to the client.
7. Send the response buffer to the client.

Most of this work is being done by the base classes that we developed in the last chapter, so all we need to be concerned with is the server implementation. The following code shows an example server implementation for lite tunneling:

```
/**
 * Invokes the method for the ordinal given. If the method
 * throws an exception it will be sent to the client.
 *
 * @param Object Server object
 * @param ordinal Method ordinal
 * @param in Input stream to read additional parameters
 * @param out Output stream to write return values
 */
public void _invokeMethod(Object serverObject, int ordinal,
        DataInput in, DataOutput out)
        throws Exception
{
    // Cast the server object
    com.omh.codeGen.math.Math o =
       (com.omh.codeGen.math.Math) serverObject;

    // Evaluate the ordinal
    switch (ordinal) {
    case 0: //add
        double p0_0 =
            ((DataInputStream) in).readDouble();
        double p0_1 =
```

```
                ((DataInputStream) in).readDouble();
            double r0 = o.add(p0_0, p0_1);
            ((DataOutputStream) out).writeDouble(r0);
            break;
        case 1: //subtract
            double p1_0 =
                ((DataInputStream) in).readDouble();
            double p1_1 =
                ((DataInputStream) in).readDouble();
            double r1 = o.subtract(p1_0, p1_1);
            ((DataOutputStream) out).writeDouble(r1);
            break;
        case 2: //multiply
            double p2_0 =
                ((DataInputStream) in).readDouble();
            double p2_1 =
                ((DataInputStream) in).readDouble();
            double r2 = o.multiply(p2_0, p2_1);
            ((DataOutputStream) out).writeDouble(r2);
            break;
        default:
            throw new Exception("Invalid ordinal: " + ordinal);
        }
    }
}
```

The following code shows an implementation for regular tunneling:

```
/**
 * Invokes the method for the ordinal given. If the method
 * throws an exception it will be sent to the client.
 *
 * @param Object Server object
 * @param ordinal Method ordinal
 * @param in Input stream to read additional parameters
 * @param out Output stream to write return values
 */
public void _invokeMethod(Object serverObject, int ordinal,
        DataInput in, DataOutput out)
        throws Exception
{
    // Cast the server object
    com.omh.codeGen.indy.Indy o =
       (com.omh.codeGen.indy.Indy) serverObject;

    // Evaluate the ordinal
    switch (ordinal) {
    case 0: //close
        o.close();
        break;
    case 1: //query
        int p1_0 =
            ((Integer) read(in)).intValue();
```

```
            com.omh.tunnel.IndyRecord r1 = o.query(p1_0);
            ((ObjectOutputStream) out).writeObject(r1);
            break;
        case 2: //connect
            boolean r2 = o.connect();
            ((ObjectOutputStream) out).writeObject(new Boolean(r2));
            break;
        default:
            throw new Exception("Invalid ordinal: " + ordinal);
        }
}
```

Again, the actual method calls that are being made are not important. Note that the main differences between the two types of server implementation are the different types of input and output streams being used, which dictate how data is marshaled between the client and server. As with the client, we will be reusing the base classes we developed in Chapter 10.

Letting Java Write the Client and Server for You

Since there is a lot of repetitive programming going on with writing the client and server tunneling code, wouldn't it be nice to put someone else to work writing this code for you? Instead of someone else, how about something else, such as your computer? Let's outline the steps that need to take place and see if we can come up with a solution for each problem:

1. The server-side object to which method calls are being tunneled must be defined.
2. A new process must be defined that will interpret the server-side object and enumerate all of the methods to be called.
3. For each method to be called, the appropriate tunneling code must be generated.

The first step is easy. In Chapter 10, we discussed how to use Java interfaces to describe the services available for a particular object. The interface describes the signatures (name, parameter[s], and return type) for each method available to outside consumers (such as an applet). By using an interface on the client side, we do not need to know (or care) about the actual implementation—whether it be the actual object or some type of client proxy.

The second step may seem like an impossible task, but by the end of this chapter, you will consider it quite trivial. Starting with version 1.1, Sun has included something called the Reflection API in the JDK. The Reflection API, which is in the java.lang.reflect package, allows applications to inspect the internal makeup of other classes (as well as themselves). Using reflection, you can get a list of all the constructors, methods, and fields of any class, as well as invoke methods on-the-fly. The Reflection API is dynamic, as opposed to static, insofar as you discover things about classes at run time rather than at compile time. I consider the Reflection API to be one of the most powerful aspects of the Java language, giving you abilities not found in other high-level languages (such as C). Stay tuned; we'll start using the Reflection API in the next section.

The third step involves generating Java source code and saving it to a disk file. While this is not a difficult task, we'll take a look at making things easier by creating a template file that will serve as the starting point for the generated source. As you will see later, we'll actually be creating several different source code generators to handle both the lite and regular versions of HTTP tunneling for the client and server.

Using the Reflection API: ShowClass

As mentioned previously, the Reflection API included with the JDK (starting with version 1.1) enables Java applications to gather information about any other Java classes. You may not realize it, but the Reflection API is built into every class; its starting point is java.lang.Class, which is the base for all Java classes. The following table shows a partial listing of the methods found in java.lang.Class that are part of the Reflection API.

Method	Description
getConstructors	Returns an array of Constructor objects representing the public constructors found in the current class.
getDeclaredConstructors	Returns an array of Constructor objects representing the declared constructors found in the current class.
getDeclaredFields	Returns an array of Field objects representing the declared fields found in the current class.
getDeclaredMethods	Returns an array of Method objects representing the declared methods found in the current class.
getFields	Returns an array of Field objects representing the public fields found in the current class. This includes all declared and inherited fields.
getInterfaces	Returns an array of Class objects representing all the interfaces directly implemented or extended by the current class.

Method	Description
getMethods	Returns an array of Method objects representing the methods found in the current class. This includes all declared and inherited methods.
getModifiers	Returns an encoded integer describing the Java language modifiers (such as abstract, public, interface, and so on).
getName	Returns the fully qualified name of the current class.
getPackage	Returns the package of the current class, or null if part of the default package.
getSuperclass	Returns a Class object representing the superclass of the current class, or null for java.lang.Object.

As you can see, once you have a reference to a Class object, you can discover just about everything you would ever want to know. Note that using the Reflection API is considered a security violation by most browsers, so you will be restricted in its use from applets.

To further illustrate the use of the Reflection API, let's develop a simple application, ShowClass, that will take the place of the Java utility javap. The javap utility shows the superclass, interface, and method information for a given class. Gathering this information using the Reflection API is a breeze. Let's take a look at the basic flow of the ShowClass application:

1. Get the class name supplied as a command-line argument.
2. Use the class name to get a Class object.
3. Get the list of all the superclasses for the class.
4. Get the list of all the interfaces implemented or extended by the class.
5. Get the list of all the declared fields in the class.
6. Get the list of all the declared methods in the class.
7. Display all the information.

The following is the main routine that will gather and display all the class information. Remember that the complete source code for the ShowClass application can be found on the Web site www.servletguru.com.

```
/**
 * Given a class name, display the classes extended,
 * interfaces implemented, and declared methods
 *
 * @param className Name of the class to process
 */
```

```
public void go(String className)
{
    try
    {
        // Attempt to load the given class

        Class c = Class.forName(className);

        // Get the list of classes that it extends
        Collection extendList = getSuperClasses(c);

        // Get the list of interfaces that this class implements
        Collection interfaceList = getInterfaces(c);

        // Get the list of declared fields for this class
        Collection fields = getFields(c);

        // Get the list of declared constructors for this class
        Collection ctors = getConstructors(c);

        // Get the list of declared methods for this class
        Collection methods = getMethods(c);

        // Display the class information
        System.out.println("\n" +
                getModifierString(c.getModifiers()) +
                " " + c.getName());

        // Display the extend list
        print(extendList, "extends");

        // Display the implements list
        print(interfaceList, "implements");

        // Display the fields
        print(fields, "Fields");

        // Display the constructors
        print(ctors, "Constructors");

        // Display the methods
        print(methods, "Methods");
    }
    catch (ClassNotFoundException ex)
    {
        System.out.println("Class '" + className + "' not found.");
    }
    catch (Exception ex)
    {
        ex.printStackTrace();
    }
}
```

Note how a Class object is created using the Class.forName() method, which will attempt to locate the given class name on the current CLASSPATH. A ClassNotFoundException will be thrown if the given class name cannot be located. Once the Class object has been created, the Reflection API can be used to gather the class information. This is the routine that gets all the superclasses for the class:

```
/**
 * Return a list of all of the superclasses for the given
 * class
 *
 * @param c Class to check
 * @return List of superclasses
 */
public Collection getSuperClasses(Class c)
{
    List list = new ArrayList();

    // Get the first superclass
    c = c.getSuperclass();

    // Loop while a class exists
    while (c != null)
    {
        // Add the superclass name to the list
        list.add(c.getName());

        // Get the next superclass
        c = c.getSuperclass();
    }
    return list;
}
```

Note how we continue to call getSuperclass() until a null value is returned, meaning we have reached the base Object. We'll be using this same loop to get all the implemented or extended interfaces. The code used to get all of the interfaces follows:

```
/**
 * Returns a list containing all of the interface names
 * implemented by the given class. This includes not only
 * the interfaces implemented by the class, but all interfaces
 * implemented by any super classes as well
 *
 * @param c Class to check
 * @return List of implemented interfaces
 */
public Collection getInterfaces(Class c)
{
    // Keep a list of all of the implemented interfaces
    Set list = new TreeSet();
```

```
    // Loop while a class exists
    while (c != null)
    {
        // Get the interfaces for this class
        getInterfaces(c, list);

        // Get the next super class
        c = c.getSuperclass();
    }

    return list;
}

/**
 * Get the interfaces implemented for the given
 * class. This routine will be called recursively
 *
 * @param c Class to check
 * @param set Collection containing the list of all of the
 * implemented interfaces. Do not allow duplicates.
 */
public void getInterfaces(Class c, Set list)
{
    // If the class given is an interface add it to the list
    if (c.isInterface())
    {
        list.add(c.getName());
    }

    // Get the interfaces implemented for the class
    Class interfaces[] = c.getInterfaces();

    // Loop for each interface
    for (int i = 0; i < interfaces.length; i++)
    {
        // Get the interfaces extended for this interface
        getInterfaces(interfaces[i], list);
    }
}
```

For each class in the hierarchy, all the implemented or extended interfaces are gathered. This is complicated by the fact that each interface may extend other interfaces as well; for this reason, the getInterfaces() method is called recursively.

Next, we need to get the list of all the declared fields for the class:

```
/**
 * Returns a sorted list of declared fields for the
 * given class
 *
 * @param c Class to check
 * @return List of declared fields
 */
```

```
public Collection getFields(Class c)
{
    Map map = new TreeMap();
    List list = new ArrayList();

    // Get the list of declared fields
    Field f[] = c.getDeclaredFields();

    // Loop for each field
    for (int i = 0; i < f.length; i++)
    {
        // Get the name, type, and modifiers
        String name = f[i].getName();
        String type = f[i].getType().getName();
        String modifiers = getModifierString(f[i].getModifiers());

        // Save in sorted map. Key is field name
        map.put(name, modifiers + " " + decodeType(type)
                + " " + name);
    }

    // Move the map sorted by name into our list. We need
    // to return the modifier + type + name for display
    Iterator iterator = map.values().iterator();
    while (iterator.hasNext())
    {
        list.add(iterator.next());
    }
    return list;
}
```

Of note here is how the Java language modifier is retrieved from the Field object and converted into a String. The getModifierString() method simply uses the static Modifier.toString() method to convert the integer value returned by getModifiers() into the Java language representation.

The following shows the code necessary for gathering all the declared methods for the class:

```
/**
 * Returns the list of declared methods for the class
 *
 * @param c Class to check
 * @return List of declared methods
 */
public Collection getMethods(Class c)
{
    Map map = new TreeMap();
    List list = new ArrayList();
```

```
    // Get the list of declared methods
    Method methods[] = c.getDeclaredMethods();

    // Loop for each method
    for (int i = 0; i < methods.length; i++)
    {
        // Get the name, type, modifiers, and parameter types
        String name = methods[i].getName();
        String type = methods[i].getReturnType().getName();
        String modifiers =
        getModifierString(methods[i].getModifiers());
        String params =
            getParameterString(methods[i].getParameterTypes());

        // Save in the map; the key is the method name and
        // parameter list
        map.put(name + " " + params, modifiers + " " +
            decodeType(type) + " " + name + "(" + params + ")");
    }

    // Move the map sorted by name into our list. We need
    // to return the modifier + type + name + params
    Iterator iterator = map.values().iterator();
    while (iterator.hasNext())
    {
        list.add(iterator.next());
    }
    return list;
}
```

Nothing too difficult here; this code simply gets the declared methods using the Reflection API and walks through the list picking out the information we are interested in. The following shows our application in action, displaying the contents of the java.io.DataOutputStream class:

```
public java.io.DataOutputStream
 extends:
  java.io.FilterOutputStream
  java.io.OutputStream
  java.lang.Object
 implements:
  java.io.DataOutput
 Fields:
  protected int written
 Constructors:
  public java.io.DataOutputStream(java.io.OutputStream)
 Methods:
  public void flush()
```

```
private void incCount(int)
public final int size()
public synchronized void write(byte[], int, int)
public synchronized void write(int)
public final void writeBoolean(boolean)
public final void writeByte(int)
public final void writeBytes(java.lang.String)
public final void writeChar(int)
public final void writeChars(java.lang.String)
public final void writeDouble(double)
public final void writeFloat(float)
public final void writeInt(int)
public final void writeLong(long)
public final void writeShort(int)
public final void writeUTF(java.lang.String)
static int writeUTF(java.lang.String, java.io.DataOutput)
```

Writing ServletGen

Now that you are an expert in using the Reflection API, it's time to put it to real use, to help you automatically generate the client and server code necessary for HTTP tunneling. We have already taken an in-depth look at the client and server code and how it is very repetitive; we'll be using the Reflection API on the server object's interface to determine the methods that need to be tunneled and then to generate the appropriate Java source code.

Starting with a Template

I have found that when generating source code, it is quite nice to start with some type of template. This template is a regular text file that can be edited as necessary and contains special tags that direct the code generator to insert certain code snippets in specific locations. This not only reduces the amount of hard-coded information in the code generator, but also greatly improves maintainability and readability.

The client proxy template that we'll be using follows. We'll actually be using four different templates (client and server for lite and regular tunneling), but since they are all almost identical, I'll focus on just one.

```
/*
 * %CLIENT_NAME%
 *
 * Generated by %GENERATOR_NAME%
 *  on %TIMESTAMP%
 *
 * Copyright (c) 1998-2002 Karl Moss. All Rights Reserved.
 *
 * Developed in conjunction with the book "Java Servlets Developer's
```

```
 * Guide" published by McGraw-Hill/Osborne Media Group
 *
 * You may study, use, modify, and distribute this software for any
 * purpose.
 *
 * This software is provided WITHOUT WARRANTY either expressed or
 * implied.
 */

%PACKAGE_STATEMENT%

import java.io.*;
import com.omh.tunnel.client.*;

/**
 * This class implements the client for tunneling
 * calls to the %OBJECT_NAME% object.
 */
public class %CLIENT_NAME%
#extends %SUPER_CLASS%
#implements %INTERFACE_NAME%
{

#/**
# * Constructs a new %CLIENT_NAME% for the
# * given URL. This will create a new %OBJECT_NAME%
# * object on the server as well.
# * @param url The server root URL for servlets
# */
#public %CLIENT_NAME%(String url)
##throws TunnelException, IOException
#{
##this(url, false);
#}

#/**
# * Constructs a new %CLIENT_NAME% for the
# * given URL. This will create a new %OBJECT_NAME%
# * object on the server as well.
# * @param url The server root URL for servlets
# * @param usePackage Indicates whether to use the package name
# * in the servlet URL
# */
#public %CLIENT_NAME%(String url, boolean usePackage)
##throws TunnelException, IOException
#{
##// Append the package name if necessary
##if (usePackage) {
###url += "%PACKAGE_NAME%";
##}
##
```

```
##// Append the remote server name
##url += "%SERVER_NAME%";

##// Set the URL
##_setURL(new java.net.URL(url));

##// Initialize the client and server
##_initialize();
#}

#%METHODS%

}
```

Notice the # characters that start many of the lines. The code generator will replace each of these with the appropriate tab character. Some people prefer a "real" tab (\t) while others prefer to use some number of spaces. You can customize the code generator to use what you prefer; the default in this example is spaces, since that's what I prefer.

You will also notice a number of special tags (starting and ending with %). These tags are code generator directives that control what type of code gets inserted into the source file. The following table lists each of the valid tags and what type of code will be inserted in its place.

Tag	Description
CLIENT_NAME	The name of the client proxy.
GENERATOR_NAME	The name of the code generator used to create the source code.
INTERFACE_NAME	The name of the interface to be implemented.
METHODS	The insertion point for the code generated for each method.
OBJECT_NAME	The name of the server object that is receiving the tunneled method calls.
PACKAGE_STATEMENT	The package statement, if the generated class is part of a package. If the generated class is not in a package, then nothing is generated.
SERVER_NAME	The name of the server-side stub.
SUPER_CLASS	The name of the superclass that this class extends.
TIMESTAMP	The date and time that the code generation took place.

Writing the Base Code Generator

Let's take a look at the basic flow of our new code generator:

1. Open the template file.
2. Create a temporary buffer to hold the generated source code.
3. Read each line from the template file and search for tags.
4. If a tag is found, generate the appropriate code.
5. When the end-of-file is reached for the template file, the temporary buffer containing the source code will be written to disk.

As usual, I prefer to start with a base class to provide common functionality, especially since we'll be creating four generators. This base class, com.omh.codeGen.BaseCodeGen, will open and read the template file, process tags, and write the final source file to disk; the following shows the main processing routine that contains these steps:

```
/**
 * Generates the source file.
 */
public void generate()
    throws IOException
{
    // Attempt to open the template file
    BufferedReader in = openTemplate();

    // The target output file
    PrintWriter outFile = null;

    // Create a new in-memory output stream that will hold
    // the contents of the generated file. We will not create
    // the output file until all processing has completed.
    ByteArrayOutputStream baos = new ByteArrayOutputStream();
    PrintWriter out = new PrintWriter(baos);

    try
    {
        // Process the template file. Read each line until
        // the end of file
        String line;

        while (true)
        {
            // Read the next line
            line = in.readLine();

            // readLine returns null if EOF
            if (line == null)
            {
                break;
            }
```

```
                // Strip off any indentation characters
                int numIndent = 0;
                while ((line.length() > 0) &&
                    line.startsWith(indentPattern))
                {
                    numIndent++;
                    line = line.substring(indentPattern.length());
                }

                // Process any embedded tags
                process(line, numIndent, out);
            }

            // Flush the output stream
            out.flush();

            // Processing is complete. Write the generated source
            // code.
            String fileName = stripPackage(getObjectName());
            fileName = getTargetName(fileName) + ".java";
            System.out.println("Writing " + fileName);
            FileOutputStream fos = new FileOutputStream(fileName);
            outFile = new PrintWriter(fos);

            // Turn our buffered output stream into an input stream
            ByteArrayInputStream bais =
                new ByteArrayInputStream(baos.toByteArray());
            InputStreamReader isr = new InputStreamReader(bais);
            BufferedReader br = new BufferedReader(isr);

            // Read the contents of our buffer and dump it to the
            // output file
            while (true)
            {
                // Read the next line
                line = br.readLine();

                // readLine returns null when EOF is reached
                if (line == null)
                {
                    break;
                }

                // Output the line
                outFile.println(line);
            }
        }
        finally
        {
            // Always close properly
            if (in != null)
            {
                in.close();
```

```
        }
        if (outFile != null)
        {
            outFile.close();
        }
    }
}
```

Each line read out of the template file is provided to the process() method that will search for tags, process any tags that are found, and output the line to the in-memory buffer. The process() and processTag() methods follow:

```
/**
 * Processes the given line. This involves scanning the line
 * for any embedded tags. If no tags exist the line will be
 * printed to the output stream.
 *
 * @param line Line from the template file
 * @param numIndent Number of indentations (tabs)
 * @param out Print writer
 */
protected void process(String line, int numIndent, PrintWriter out)
    throws IOException
{
    // Look for tags until all have been processed
    while (line != null)
    {
        // Search for the tag pattern
        int begPos = line.indexOf(tagPattern);

        // If no tag pattern exists, exit
        if (begPos < 0)
        {
            break;
        }

        // We have a starting tag pattern; look for an ending
        // tag pattern
        int endPos = line.indexOf(tagPattern, begPos + 1);

        // No ending tag pattern, exit
        if (endPos < 0)
        {
            break;
        }

        // Get the tag name
        String tag = line.substring(begPos + 1, endPos);

        // Process the tag
        line = processTag(line, tag, begPos, numIndent, out);
    }
```

```
        // If the line is not null it must be written to the
        // output stream
        if (line != null)
        {
            out.println(indent(numIndent) + line);
        }
    }

    /**
     * Process the tag for the given line. This method may be
     * overridden; just be sure to call super.processTag().
     *
     * @param line Line from the template file
     * @param tag Tag name
     * @param pos Starting position of the tag in the line
     * @param numIndent Number of indentations (tabs)
     * @param out Print writer
     * @return Line after tag replacement or null if the replacement
     * was written directly to the output stream
     */
    protected String processTag(String line, String tag, int pos,
                                int numIndent, PrintWriter out)
        throws IOException
    {
        // Replacement code for the tag
        String code = null;

        if (tag.equals("GENERATOR_NAME"))
        {
            code = getClass().getName();
        }
        else if (tag.equals("TIMESTAMP"))
        {
            code = new java.util.Date().toString();
        }
        else if (tag.equals("CLIENT_NAME"))
        {
            String objectName = getObjectName();

            // Strip off the package name
            objectName = stripPackage(objectName);

            // Get the name of the client
            code = getClientName(objectName);
        }
        else if (tag.equals("SERVER_NAME"))
        {
            String objectName = getObjectName();

            // Strip off the package name
            objectName = stripPackage(objectName);

            // Get the name of the server
```

```
    code = getServerName(objectName);
}
else if (tag.equals("PACKAGE_NAME"))
{
    code  = getPackageName(getInterfaceName());
    if (code == null)
    {
        code = "";
    }
    else if (code.length() > 0)
    {
        code += ".";
    }
}
else if (tag.equals("PACKAGE_STATEMENT"))
{
    // Assume that the code is going in the same package
    // as the interface
    String p = getPackageName(getInterfaceName());

    // No package. Do not output a line
    if (p.length() == 0)
    {
        line = null;
    }
    else
    {
        code = "package " + p + ";";
    }
}
else if (tag.equals("OBJECT_NAME"))
{
    code = getObjectName();
}
else if (tag.equals("SUPER_CLASS"))
{
    code = getSuperclass();
}
else if (tag.equals("INTERFACE_NAME"))
{
    code = getInterfaceName();
}
else if (tag.equals("METHODS"))
{

    // Process the interface methods
    processMethods(numIndent, out);

    // All code was written directly to the output stream
    line = null;
}
else
{
```

```
            // Unknown tag
            System.out.println("WARNING: Unknown tag '" + tag + "'");
            code = "<UNKNOWN TAG " + tag + ">";
        }

        // If a code replacement was created, replace it in the
        // line
        if (code != null)
        {
            line = line.substring(0, pos) + code +
            line.substring(pos + tag.length() + 2);
        }
        return line;
    }
```

Note how the tags are processed; most are handled by making abstract method calls to gather additional information. These abstract method calls must be implemented by the final code generator (which we will look at later). The one exception is the METHODS tag, which uses the Reflection API to get all the methods for the server object's interface:

```
/**
 * Process the METHODS tag. This involves reflecting upon
 * the interface and generating proxy code for each method
 *
 * @param numIndent Number of indentations (tabs)
 * @param out Print writer
 */
protected void processMethods(int numIndent, PrintWriter out)
    throws IOException
{
    // Get the interface class
    Class c = getInterfaceClass();

    // Get all of the methods for the interface
    java.lang.reflect.Method methods[] = c.getMethods();

    // Loop for each method in the interface
    for (int i = 0; i < methods.length; i++)
    {
        // Only generate code for public methods
        int modifiers = methods[i].getModifiers();
        if (!java.lang.reflect.Modifier.isPublic(modifiers))
        {
            continue;
        }

        // Generate the code for the method
        codeMethod(methods[i], numIndent, out);
    }
}
```

Note that the code generator requires an interface that defines the server object. All the methods in the interface are discovered using the Reflection API, and each method is then used to generate the appropriate code.

Writing the Code Generator

Now that the base code generator class is complete, we can focus on writing the final implementation for each of the client proxy and server stub code generators. There are a number of abstract methods that must be implemented, the most interesting of which is the codeMethod() routine. The codeMethod() routine is the heart of the code generator, generating the repetitive code necessary for each method call. The following shows the codeMethod() routine for the HTTP tunneling client:

```
/**
 * Generates the code for the given method
 *
 * @param m Method to generate
 * @param numIndent Number of indentations (tabs)
 * @param out Print writer
 */
public void codeMethod(Method m, int numIndent, PrintWriter out)
    throws IOException
{
    String line;
    String tab = indent(numIndent);

    // Get the method return type
    Class ret = m.getReturnType();
    String retName = decodeType(ret.getName());

    // Validate the return type to ensure we can marshal it
    if (!ServletGenLiteServer.validateType(ret))
    {
        throw new IOException("Invalid return data type " +
                retName);
    }

    // Get the method parameters
    Class params[] = m.getParameterTypes();

    // Get the exceptions thrown by the method
    Class exceptions[] = m.getExceptionTypes();

    // Generate the method signature
    line = "public " + retName + " " +
            m.getName() + "(";

    // Loop for each parameter
    for (int i = 0; i < params.length; i++)
    {
```

```
        // Validate the parameter type to ensure we can marshal it
        if (!ServletGenLiteServer.validateType(params[i]))
        {
            throw new IOException("Invalid parameter " +
                    "data type " + retName);
        }

        // Insert a comma if necessary
        if (i > 0)
        {
            line += ", ";
        }

        // Call the parameters p0, p1, etc.
        line += decodeType(params[i].getName()) + " p" + i;
    }

    // Add the ending paren
    line += ")";

    // Write out the method signature
    out.println(tab + line);

    // Take care of any exceptions thrown by the method
    if (exceptions.length > 0)
    {
        line = "throws ";
        for (int i = 0; i < exceptions.length; i++)
        {
            // Insert a comma if necessary
            if (i > 0)
            {
                line += ", ";
            }
            line += exceptions[i].getName();
        }
        out.println(tab + indent(1) + line);
    }

    // Start the method body
    numIndent++;
    tab = indent(numIndent);
    out.println(tab + "{");
    numIndent++;
    tab = indent(numIndent);

    // Generate the default return value
    if (!retName.equals("void"))
    {
        line = retName + " retValue = ";

        // Determine the default value
```

```
        if (retName.equals("boolean"))
        {
            line += "false;";
        }
        else if (retName.equals("char") ||
                 retName.equals("byte") ||
                 retName.equals("short") ||
                 retName.equals("int") ||
                 retName.equals("long") ||
                 retName.equals("float") ||
                 retName.equals("double"))
        {
            line += "0;";
        }
        else
        {
            line += "null;";
        }
        out.println(tab + line);
    }

    out.println(tab + "try {");
    numIndent++;
    tab = indent(numIndent);

    out.println(tab + "// Create an internal buffer");
    out.println(tab + "ByteArrayOutputStream baos = " +
            "new ByteArrayOutputStream();");
    out.println("");
    out.println(tab + "// Create a data stream to write " +
            "the request");
    out.println(tab + "DataOutputStream out =");
    out.println(tab + indent(1) + "(DataOutputStream) "+
            "_createHeader(baos, " + methodNum + ");");

    // Write the parameters
    for (int i = 0; i < params.length; i++)
    {
        String write = "bad_type";
        String param = "p" + i;
        String paramType = decodeType(params[i].getName());
        boolean checkParamForNull = false;

        // Convert scalars to the proper object
        if (paramType.equals("boolean"))
        {
            write = "writeBoolean";
        }
        else if (paramType.equals("byte"))
        {
            write = "writeByte";
        }
        else if (paramType.equals("char"))
```

```
{
    write = "writeChar";
}
else if (paramType.equals("short"))
{
    write = "writeShort";
}
else if (paramType.equals("int"))
{
    write = "writeInt";
}
else if (paramType.equals("long"))
{
    write = "writeLong";
}
else if (paramType.equals("float"))
{
    write = "writeFloat";
}
else if (paramType.equals("double"))
{
    write = "writeDouble";
}
else if (paramType.equals("java.lang.String"))
{
    write = "writeUTF";
    checkParamForNull = true;
}
else if (paramType.equals("byte[]"))
{
    write = "write";
    checkParamForNull = true;
}
int indents = 0;
if (checkParamForNull)
{
    // Write a flag that indicates whether the value is
    // null or not
    out.println(tab + "out.writeBoolean((" + param +
            " == null));");
    out.println(tab + "if (" + param + " != null)");
    indents = 1;
}

if (paramType.equals("byte[]"))
{
    // Write the length if necessary
    out.println(tab + indent(1) +
            "out.writeInt(" + param + ".length);");
    out.println(tab + "if (" + param + " != null)");
}

out.println(tab + indent(indents) + "out." + write + "(" +
```

```
            param + ");");
    }

        // Invoke the method
        out.println("");
        out.println(tab + "// Invoke the method");
        out.println(tab + "DataInputStream in = ");
        out.println(tab + indent(1) + "(DataInputStream) " +
        "_invokeMethod(baos.toByteArray());");

        // Get the return value if necessary
        if (!retName.equals("void"))
        {
            boolean checkReturnForNull = false;
            out.println("");
            out.println(tab + "// Get the return value");
            String reader = "bad_type";
            if (retName.equals("boolean"))
            {
                reader = "readBoolean";
            }
            else if (retName.equals("byte"))
            {
                reader = "readByte";
            }
            else if (retName.equals("char"))
            {
                reader = "readChar";
            }
            else if (retName.equals("short"))
            {
                reader = "readShort";
            }
            else if (retName.equals("int"))
            {
                reader = "readInt";
            }
            else if (retName.equals("long"))
            {
                reader = "readLong";
            }
            else if (retName.equals("float"))
            {
                reader = "readFloat";
            }
            else if (retName.equals("double"))
            {
                reader = "readDouble";
            }
            else if (retName.equals("java.lang.String"))
            {
                reader = "readUTF";
                checkReturnForNull = true;
```

```
        }
        else if (retName.equals("byte[]"))
        {
            reader = "read";
            checkReturnForNull = true;
        }

        int indents = 0;
        String inParam = "";
        String inReturn = "retValue = ";

        // Check for null values
        if (checkReturnForNull)
        {
            out.println(tab + "boolean isNull = in.readBoolean();");

            // Allocate the byte array if necessary
            if (retName.equals("byte[]"))
            {
                out.println(tab + "if (!isNull)");
                out.println(tab + indent(1) +
                        "retValue = new byte[in.readInt()];");
                inParam = "retValue";
                inReturn = "";
            }
            out.println(tab + "if (!isNull)");
            indents = 1;
        }

        out.println(tab + indent(indents) + inReturn + "in." +
                reader + "(" + inParam + ");");
    }

    // Wrap up
    out.println(tab + "out.close();");
    out.println(tab + "in.close();");

    // End the try block
    numIndent--;
    out.println(indent(numIndent) + "}");
    out.println(indent(numIndent) +
            "catch (java.io.IOException ex) {");
    out.println(indent(numIndent + 1) + "ex.printStackTrace();");
    out.println(indent(numIndent) + "}");

    out.println(indent(numIndent) +
            "catch (TunnelException ex) {");
    out.println(indent(numIndent + 1) + "ex.printStackTrace();");
    out.println(indent(numIndent) + "}");

    // Write the return value
    if (!retName.equals("void"))
    {
```

```
            out.println(indent(numIndent) + "return retValue;");
        }

        // End the method body
        numIndent--;
        out.println(indent(numIndent) + "}");
        out.println("");

        // Increment the method number
        methodNum++;
    }
```

Let's break down what's going on in this method:

1. The return type is validated to ensure that it can be marshaled properly.
2. The method signature is created. This includes any language modifiers, return type, method name, parameter types, and exceptions. Each parameter type is validated to ensure that it can be marshaled properly.
3. The method body is created.

Validating the data types to ensure they can be marshaled properly is different depending upon which type of HTTP tunneling is being used. "Lite" tunneling, which can be used with JDK 1.0.2, uses DataInputStream and DataOutputStream to marshal data; thus, only the scalars and the String object can be used (and arrays of any of these types). Regular tunneling uses ObjectInputStream and ObjectOutputStream to marshal data and requires that the object being used implements java.io.Serializable.

The last thing to do after each of the code generators has been implemented is to create an application that ties them all together. This application, ServletGen, accepts command-line arguments and invokes the proper code generators:

```
package com.omh.codeGen;

/**
 * This application will invoke the proper code generator
 * depending upon the command-line options given:
 *
 *   -i  Interface name
 *   -c  Class name
 *   -l  (option) Lite version
 *
 * All generated source will be created in the current directory.
 */
public class ServletGen
{
    public static void main(String args[])
    {
        // Get the interface name
        String interfaceName = getArg(args, "-i");
```

```
        // Get the class name
        String className = getArg(args, "-c");

        // Get the optional 'lite' arg
        boolean lite = argExists(args, "-l");

        // Make sure the required parameters were given
        if ((interfaceName == null) ||
            (className == null))
        {
            System.out.println("\nServletGen usage:\n");
            System.out.println("ServletGen -i<interface> -c<class> " +
                    "[-l]");
            return;
        }

        try
        {
            BaseCodeGen client;
            BaseCodeGen server;

            // Get the appropriate code generators
            if (lite)
            {
                client = new ServletGenLiteClient();
                server = new ServletGenLiteServer();
            }
            else
            {
                client = new ServletGenClient();
                server = new ServletGenServer();
            }

            // Generate the client
            client.setInterfaceName(interfaceName);
            client.setObjectName(className);
            System.out.println("Generating servlet client proxy");
            client.generate();

            // Generate the server
            server.setInterfaceName(interfaceName);
            server.setObjectName(className);
            System.out.println("Generating servlet server stub");
            server.generate();
        }
        catch (Exception ex)
        {
            ex.printStackTrace();
        }
    }

    /**
```

```
 * Find the given argument switch.
 *
 * @param args Array of command-line arguments
 * @param s Switch to find
 * @return Value of the argument or null if not found
 */
public static String getArg(String args[], String s)
{
    String arg = null;

    if (args != null)
    {
        // Find the switch in the array
        for (int i = 0; i < args.length; i++)
        {
            // Does the switch match?
            if (args[i].startsWith(s))
            {
                if (args[i].length() > s.length())
                {
                    // Get the value
                    arg = args[i].substring(s.length());
                    break;
                }
            }
        }
    }

    return arg;
}

/**
 * Determines if the given argument switch exists.
 *
 * @param args Array of command-line arguments
 * @param s Switch to find
 * @return true if the switch exists
 */
public static boolean argExists(String args[], String s)
{
    boolean rc = false;

    if (args != null)
    {
        // Find the switch in the array
        for (int i = 0; i < args.length; i++)
        {
            // Does the switch match?
            if (args[i].startsWith(s))
            {
                rc = true;
                break;
            }
```

```
            }
        }

        return rc;
    }
}
```

Tunneling Example Revisited: RemoteMathLite

In Chapter 10, we developed a very basic Math object. We started by defining the interface for the object, as follows:

```
package com.omh.codeGen.math;

/**
 * This interface defines the methods available for
 * performing math
 */
public interface MathInterface
{
    /**
     * Adds two numbers
     */
    double add(double a, double b);

    /**
     * Subtracts two numbers
     */
    double subtract(double a, double b);

    /**
     * Multiplies two numbers
     */
    double multiply(double a, double b);

}
```

We must also implement the interface:

```
package com.omh.codeGen.math;

import com.omh.tunnel.MathInterface;
```

```
/**
 * This class performs simple math functions in order to
 * illustrate remote method tunneling.
 */
public class Math implements MathInterface
{
    public double add(double a, double b)
    {
        return (a + b);
    }

    public double subtract(double a, double b)
    {
        return (a - b);
    }

    public double multiply(double a, double b)
    {
        return (a * b);
    }

}
```

Once complete, a client proxy and server-side stub were handwritten to enable lite HTTP-tunneled method calls to the Math object residing on the server.

Now comes the exciting part. Instead of writing the client proxy and server stub by hand, let's use our new code generator to do all of the work for us (the java command has been split into two lines to improve readability):

```
java com.omh.codeGen.ServletGen
    -icom.omh.codeGen.math.MathInterface
    -ccom.omh.codeGen.math.Math -l
Generating servlet client proxy
Writing RemoteMathLiteClient.java
Generating servlet server stub
Writing RemoteMathLiteServer.java
```

In a matter of seconds, ServletGen has used the Reflection API to discover all the methods in the specified interface (com.omh.codeGen.math.MathInterface) and generated both the client proxy and server stub for lite HTTP tunneling (specified by the -l switch). The following shows the RemoteMathLiteClient and RemoteMathLiteServer code. Remember, both of these source files were completely machine generated starting with our template files.

```
/*
 * RemoteMathLiteClient
 *
 * Generated by com.omh.codeGen.ServletGenLiteClient
```

```
 *  on Fri Nov 30 22:55:26 EST 2001
 *
 * Copyright (c) 1998-2002 Karl Moss. All Rights Reserved.
 *
 * Developed in conjunction with the book "Java Servlets Developer's
 * Guide" published by McGraw-Hill/Osborne Media Group
 *
 * You may study, use, modify, and distribute this software for any
 * purpose.
 *
 * This software is provided WITHOUT WARRANTY either expressed or
 * implied.
 */
package com.omh.codeGen.math;

import java.io.*;
import com.omh.tunnel.client.*;

/**
 * This class implements the lite client for tunneling
 * calls to the com.omh.codeGen.math.Math object. 'Lite' clients use
 * simple data input and output streams and can be used
 * with JDK 1.0.2
 */
public class RemoteMathLiteClient
    extends com.omh.tunnel.client.TunnelLiteClient
    implements com.omh.codeGen.math.MathInterface
{

    /**
     * Constructs a new RemoteMathLiteClient for the
     * given URL. This will create a new com.omh.codeGen.math.Math
     * object on the server as well.
     */
    public RemoteMathLiteClient(String url)
        throws TunnelException, IOException
    {
        // Append the remote server name
        url += "RemoteMathLiteServer";

        // Set the URL
        _setURL(new java.net.URL(url));

        // Initialize the client and server
        _initialize();
    }

    public double add(double p0, double p1)
        {
            double retValue = 0;
            try {
                // Create an internal buffer
```

```
            ByteArrayOutputStream baos = new ByteArrayOutputStream();

            // Create a data stream to write the request
            DataOutputStream out =
                (DataOutputStream) _createHeader(baos, 0);
            out.writeDouble(p0);
            out.writeDouble(p1);

            // Invoke the method
            DataInputStream in =
                (DataInputStream) _invokeMethod(baos.toByteArray());

            // Get the return value
            retValue = in.readDouble();
            out.close();
            in.close();
        }
        catch (java.io.IOException ex) {
            ex.printStackTrace();
        }
        catch (TunnelException ex) {
            ex.printStackTrace();
        }
        return retValue;
    }

}
```

The code for RemoteMathLiteServer follows:

```
/*
 * RemoteMathLiteServer
 *
 * Generated by com.omh.codeGen.ServletGenLiteServer
 *  on Fri Nov 30 22:55:26 EST 2001
 *
 * Copyright (c) 1998-2002 Karl Moss. All Rights Reserved.
 *
 * Developed in conjunction with the book "Java Servlets Developer's
 * Guide" published by McGraw-Hill/Osborne Media Group
 *
 * You may study, use, modify, and distribute this software for any
 * purpose.
 *
 * This software is provided WITHOUT WARRANTY either expressed or
 * implied.
 */

package com.omh.codeGen.math;

import javax.servlet.*;
import javax.servlet.http.*;
import java.io.*;
import com.omh.tunnel.server.*;
```

```
/**
 * This class implements the lite server for tunneling
 * calls to the com.omh.codeGen.math.Math object. 'Lite' servers use
 * simple data input and output streams and can be used
 * with JDK 1.0.2
 */
public class RemoteMathLiteServer
    extends com.omh.tunnel.server.TunnelLiteServer
{
    /**
     * Creates a new instance of the server object.
     *
     * @return Instance of the server object
     */
    public Object _getNewInstance()
        throws ServletException
    {
        return new com.omh.codeGen.math.Math();
    }

    /**
     * Invokes the method for the ordinal given. If the method
     * throws an exception it will be sent to the client.
     *
     * @param Object Server object
     * @param ordinal Method ordinal
     * @param in Input stream to read additional parameters
     * @param out Output stream to write return values
     */
    public void _invokeMethod(Object serverObject, int ordinal,
            DataInput in, DataOutput out)
            throws Exception
    {
        // Cast the server object
        com.omh.codeGen.math.Math o =

        (com.omh.codeGen.math.Math) ServerObject;

        // Evaluate the ordinal
        switch (ordinal) {
        case 0: //add
            double p0_0 =
                ((DataInputStream) in).readDouble();
            double p0_1 =
                ((DataInputStream) in).readDouble();
            double r0 = o.add(p0_0, p0_1);
            ((DataOutputStream) out).writeDouble(r0);
            break;
        case 1: //subtract
            double p1_0 =
                ((DataInputStream) in).readDouble();
       double p1_1 =
           ((DataInputStream) in).readDouble();
```

```
                double r1 = o.subtract(p1_0, p1_1);
                ((DataOutputStream) out).writeDouble(r1);
                break;
            case 2: //multiply
                double p2_0 =
                    ((DataInputStream) in).readDouble();
                double p2_1 =
                    ((DataInputStream) in).readDouble();
                double r2 = o.multiply(p2_0, p2_1);
                ((DataOutputStream) out).writeDouble(r2);
                break;
            default:
                throw new Exception("Invalid ordinal: " + ordinal);
            }
        }
}
```

Tunneling Example Revisited: RemoteIndy

In Chapter 10, we also developed a simple object that uses JDBC, called Indy. This object gathers information about the Indianapolis 500 winner for a given year and returns it to the client. The interface was defined and the implementation was written as follows:

```
package com.omh.codeGen.indy;

import com.omh.tunnel.IndyRecord;

/**
 * This interface defines the methods available for
 * performing queries on the Indianapolis 500 database
 */
public interface IndyInterface
{
    /**
     * Connects to the database.
     *
     * @return True if the database connection was established
     */
    boolean connect();

    /**
     * Closes the database connection
     */
    void close();

    /**
     * Given the year return the corresponding Indianapolis
     * 500 record
     *
     * @param year Year of the race
```

```
     * @return Indy 500 record or null if not found
     */
    IndyRecord query(int year);
}
package com.omh.codeGen.indy;

import com.omh.tunnel.IndyInterface;
import com.omh.tunnel.IndyRecord;

import java.sql.*;

/**
 * Implements the IndyInterface to provide query capabilities
 * into the Indianapolis 500 database.
 */
public class Indy implements IndyInterface
{
    // The JDBC Connection
    Connection connection = null;

    // A prepared statement to use to query the database
    PreparedStatement prepStmt = null;

    public boolean connect()
    {
        boolean rc = false;

        try
        {
            // Load the Bridge
            Class.forName("sun.jdbc.odbc.JdbcOdbcDriver").newInstance();

            // Connect to the Access database
            connection =

                DriverManager.getConnection("jdbc:odbc:MyAccessDataSource");

            // Go ahead and create a prepared statement
            prepStmt = connection.prepareStatement(
                "SELECT Year, Driver, AvgSpeed from IndyWinners " +
                "WHERE Year = ?");

            rc = true;
        }
        catch (Exception ex)
        {
            ex.printStackTrace();
        }

        return rc;
    }

    public void close()
```

```
    {
        // Close the connection if it was opened
        if (connection != null)
        {
            try
            {
                connection.close();
            }
            catch (SQLException ex)
            {
                ex.printStackTrace();
            }
            connection = null;
        }
    }

    public IndyRecord query(int year)
    {
        IndyRecord record = null;

        try
        {
            // Set the year parameter
            prepStmt.setInt(1, year);

            // Execute the query
            ResultSet rs = prepStmt.executeQuery();

            // Make sure a record exists
            if (rs.next())
            {
                // Create a new IndyRecord object
                record = new IndyRecord();

                // Set the values
                record.year = rs.getInt(1);
                record.driver = rs.getString(2);
                record.speed = rs.getDouble(3);
            }
            rs.close();
        }
        catch (SQLException ex)
        {
            ex.printStackTrace();
            record = null;
        }

        return record;
    }
}
```

In Chapter 10, we then wrote a client proxy and server stub for HTTP tunneling by hand; now it's time to sit back, relax, and let your computer do the work for you:

```
java com.omh.codeGen.ServletGen
    -icom.omh.codeGen.indy.IndyInterface
    -ccom.omh.codeGen.indy.Indy
Generating servlet client proxy
Writing RemoteIndyClient.java
Generating servlet server stub
Writing RemoteIndyServer.java
```

This time ServletGen has created the client proxy and server stub for regular HTTP-tunneled method calls (using ObjectInputStream and ObjectOutputStream to marshal data). The generated RemoteIndyClient and RemoteIndyServer code follows:

```
/*
 * RemoteIndyClient
 *
 * Generated by com.omh.codeGen.ServletGenClient
 *  on Fri Nov 30 23:03:36 EST 2001
 *
 * Copyright (c) 1998-2002 Karl Moss. All Rights Reserved.
 *
 * Developed in conjunction with the book "Java Servlets Developer's
 * Guide" published by McGraw-Hill/Osborne Media Group
 *
 * You may study, use, modify, and distribute this software for any
 * purpose.
 *
 * This software is provided WITHOUT WARRANTY either expressed or
 * implied.
 */

package com.omh.codeGen.indy;

import java.io.*;
import com.omh.tunnel.client.*;

/**
 * This class implements the client for tunneling
 * calls to the com.omh.codeGen.indy.Indy object.
 */
public class RemoteIndyClient
    extends com.omh.tunnel.client.TunnelClient
    implements com.omh.codeGen.indy.IndyInterface
{

    /**
     * Constructs a new RemoteIndyClient for the
     * given URL. This will create a new com.omh.codeGen.indy.Indy
     * object on the server as well.
     * @param url The server root URL for servlets
     */
    public RemoteIndyClient(String url)
```

```
    throws TunnelException, IOException
{
    this(url, false);
}

/**
 * Constructs a new RemoteIndyClient for the
 * given URL. This will create a new com.omh.codeGen.indy.Indy
 * object on the server as well.
 * @param url The server root URL for servlets
 * @param usePackage Indicates whether to use the package name
 * in the servlet URL
 */
public RemoteIndyClient(String url, boolean usePackage)
    throws TunnelException, IOException
{
    // Append the package name if necessary
    if (usePackage) {
        url += "com.omh.codeGen.indy.";
    }

    // Append the remote server name
    url += "RemoteIndyServer";

    // Set the URL
    _setURL(new java.net.URL(url));

    // Initialize the client and server
    _initialize();
}

public void close()
    {
        try {
            // Create an internal buffer
            ByteArrayOutputStream baos = new ByteArrayOutputStream();

            // Create an object stream to write the request
            ObjectOutputStream out =
                (ObjectOutputStream) _createHeader(baos, 0);

            // Invoke the method
            ObjectInputStream in =
                (ObjectInputStream) _invokeMethod(baos.toByteArray());
            out.close();
            in.close();
        }
        catch (java.io.IOException ex) {
            ex.printStackTrace();
        }
        catch (TunnelException ex) {
            ex.printStackTrace();
```

```
            }
        }

}
/*
 * RemoteIndyServer
 *
 * Generated by com.omh.codeGen.ServletGenServer
 *  on Fri Nov 30 23:03:36 EST 2001
 *
 * Copyright (c) 1998-2002 Karl Moss. All Rights Reserved.
 *
 * Developed in conjunction with the book "Java Servlets Developer's
 * Guide" published by McGraw-Hill/Osborne Media Group
 *
 * You may study, use, modify, and distribute this software for any
 * purpose.
 *
 * This software is provided WITHOUT WARRANTY either expressed or
 * implied.
 */

package com.omh.codeGen.indy;

import javax.servlet.*;
import javax.servlet.http.*;
import java.io.*;
import com.omh.tunnel.server.*;

/**
 * This class implements the server for tunneling
 * calls to the com.omh.codeGen.indy.Indy object.
 */
public class RemoteIndyServer
    extends com.omh.tunnel.server.TunnelServer
{
    /**
     * Creates a new instance of the server object.
     *
     * @return Instance of the server object
     */
    public Object _getNewInstance()
        throws ServletException
    {
        return new com.omh.codeGen.indy.Indy();
    }

    /**
     * Invokes the method for the ordinal given. If the method
     * throws an exception it will be sent to the client.
     *
     * @param Object Server object
     * @param ordinal Method ordinal
```

```
     * @param in Input stream to read additional parameters
     * @param out Output stream to write return values
     */
    public void _invokeMethod(Object serverObject, int ordinal,
            DataInput in, DataOutput out)
            throws Exception
    {
        // Cast the server object
        com.omh.codeGen.indy.Indy o =
           (com.omh.codeGen.indy.Indy) ServerObject;

        // Evaluate the ordinal
        switch (ordinal) {
        case 0: //close
            o.close();
            break;
        case 1: //query
            int p1_0 =
                ((Integer) read(in)).intValue();
            com.omh.tunnel.IndyRecord r1 = o.query(p1_0);
            ((ObjectOutputStream) out).writeObject(r1);
            break;
        case 2: //connect
            boolean r2 = o.connect();
            ((ObjectOutputStream) out).writeObject(new Boolean(r2));
            break;
        default:
            throw new Exception("Invalid ordinal: " + ordinal);
        }
    }

    /**
     * Helper method to read an object from the input stream
     *
     * @param in Input stream
     * @return The next object read from the input stream
     */
    protected Object read(DataInput in)
            throws Exception
    {
        return ((ObjectInputStream) in).readObject();
    }
}
```

Summary

In this chapter, we have moved to the next level of Java programming: using the built-in features of Java to automatically create other Java classes. The foundation that enables this to happen is the Reflection API, a series of methods and classes that provides information about the internal structure of classes. We used this powerful API to develop a code generator that creates the client proxy and server-side stub necessary for tunneling method calls over HTTP.

In Chapter 12, we'll take a look at how to use servlets from another type of client: micro devices.

CHAPTER

12

J2ME-to-Servlet Communication

IN THIS CHAPTER:

In Chapter 10, we discussed how to communicate between an applet and a servlet. In this chapter, we'll take much of the work that we have already done and adapt it to the Java 2 Micro Edition (J2ME) environment, allowing us to communicate between a wireless micro device and a servlet.

J2ME Overview

A funny thing happened on the way to the enterprise—Java got big! Java was originally designed for consumer devices, specifically interactive TV. Java (code named "Oak" in the early days) quickly progressed from the realm of these consumer devices into the world of corporate computing. Corporate applications require significantly more functionality than your kitchen toaster and thus the system libraries swelled (and continue to do so) to a size that is prohibitive to devices without large computing power and storage.

In January 1998, a project code named "Spotless" was started by Sun to research how Java could be leveraged on small devices that had very limited resources (cell phones, for example). The goal was to build a Java run-time environment that would operate using just a fraction of the current Java 2 Standard Edition (J2SE) environment. Out of the Spotless project came a working Java Virtual Machine (JVM) known today as the K Virtual Machine (KVM); the *K* is for kilobytes (instead of using the typical megabytes required with J2SE).

Two direct results of the Spotless project were important standardizations driven by multiple vendors who would be using this new KVM. These standardizations were needed to guarantee interoperability between the myriad different small devices that would now be using Java. In October 1999, the Connected Limited Device Configuration (CLDC) standard was started to define the lowest common denominator necessary to run Java on small, connected, resource-limited devices. The CLDC specification (see http://java.sun.com/products/cldc) defines the Java programming language, virtual machine features, core libraries, networking, I/O, and security that will be available to consumer devices utilizing the KVM. Note that the CLDC does not name a specific target device. Rather, it is the base platform on which profiles for specific devices (or groups of devices) will be defined.

The Mobile Information Device Profile (MIDP) standard, which was started in November 1999, built upon the CLDC to add additional APIs and features specifically for two-way wireless devices (such as cell phones). For further reading, see http://java.sun.com/products/midp. We will build an application that uses the MIDP architecture to perform HTTP tunneling to communicate with a servlet.

The Basic Flow

The general flow of making a remote method call using HTTP is the same as in Chapter 10 when we worked with applets:

1. Open the HTTP connection. Always remember that HTTP is a stateless protocol; because of this, you will have to open a new connection for each request.
2. Format the method request. This will include some type of method indicator that describes which method to invoke and any parameters that are required by the method.
3. Set the HTTP request headers. This includes the type of data being sent (binary) and the total length of the data.
4. Send the request. Write the binary stream to the server.
5. Read the request. The target servlet will be invoked and given the HTTP request data. The servlet can then extract the method to invoke and any necessary parameters. Note that if this is the first request for a given client, a new instance of the server object will be created.
6. Invoke the method. The method will be called on the server object.
7. Format the method response. If the method that was invoked throws an exception, the error message will be sent to the client; otherwise, the return type (if any) will be sent.
8. Set the HTTP response headers. Just like the request headers, the type and length of the data being sent must be set.
9. Send the response. The binary data stream will be sent to the web server, which, in turn, will be returned back to the client.
10. Close the connection.

Due to the nature of the devices that use the KVM, it is even more compelling to offload some of the processing to the server. Also keep in mind that many of the enterprise service APIs have been purposely removed from the KVM, so the only alternative is to access these services remotely.

Marshaling Parameters and Return Values

Part of the diet that the VM was put on to slim down to the KVM size included cutting out serialization. Remember that serialization allowed us to pass objects and their state between two different Virtual Machines. Since the KVM does not include serialization, we'll have to fall back to using standard DataInput and DataOutput streams, writing just the scalar data types (excluding floating-point numbers, which are not supported by the KVM either). Because of this limitation, we'll be utilizing our "lite" method of communication used with JDK 1.0.2. What is interesting about the KVM is that it looks a lot like the VM of old (before all that enterprise functionality bloated it so badly).

The Base Micro Tunnel Client

Just as in Chapter 10 when working with applets, we'll use a base class for all MIDP applications (called MIDlets). This base class is responsible for opening the HTTP connection, formatting the request, and returning the response:

```
package com.omh.micro.client;

import javax.microedition.io.HttpConnection;
import javax.microedition.io.Connector;
import java.io.*;

public class MicroTunnelClient
{
    // The connection url
    String _url;

    // The server object handle
    private int objectHandle;

    // The session cookie
    private String sessionCookie;

    // The user agent. This consists of the CLDC version
    // and the MIDP version
    private static String userAgent;

    public MicroTunnelClient()
    {
        if (userAgent == null)
```

```
    {
        userAgent = "Profile:" +
                System.getProperty("microedition.profiles") +
                " Configuration:" +
                System.getProperty("microedition.configuration");
    }
}

/**
 * Sets the URL of the connection
 *
 * @param url Connection URL
 */
public void _setURL(String url)
{
    _url = url;
}

/**
 * Gets the URL of the connection
 *
 * @return The connection URL
 */
public String _getURL()
{
    return _url;
}

/**
 * Initializes the client. Also makes a server request
 * to initialize the server as well.
 */
public void _initialize() throws TunnelException
{
    try
    {
        // Create a new buffer that will hold our data
        ByteArrayOutputStream buffer = new ByteArrayOutputStream();

        // Create a method header. An ordinal value of -1 is
        // reserved for initializing the server
        _createHeader(buffer, -1);

        // Invoke the method. This will send the initialization
```

```
            // header to the server
            DataInputStream in = _invokeMethod(buffer.toByteArray());

            // Get the handle to the object that was just
            // created
            objectHandle = in.readInt();

            // Close properly
            in.close();
        }
        catch (IOException ex)
        {
            // Re-throw as a tunnel exception
            ex.printStackTrace();
            throw new TunnelException(ex.getMessage());
        }
    }

    /**
     * Starts a method by creating the method header.
     * The header consists of the method ordinal to invoke.
     *
     * @param buffer Buffer to hold the header data
     * @param ordinal Method ordinal to invoke on the server
     * @return Output stream to be used to send parameters
     */
    public DataOutputStream _createHeader(ByteArrayOutputStream buffer,
             int ordinal)
        throws TunnelException
    {
        try
        {
            // Get an output stream to use to write data to the buffer

            DataOutputStream out = new DataOutputStream(buffer);

            // Write the method ordinal
            out.writeInt(ordinal);

            // If we are not initializing the object, we need to send
            // the object handle along with the header
            if (ordinal != -1)
            {
                out.writeInt(objectHandle);
```

```
        }

        out.flush();
        return out;
    }
    catch (IOException ex)
    {
        // Re-throw as a tunnel exception
        ex.printStackTrace();
        throw new TunnelException(ex.getMessage());
    }
}

/**
 * Sends the given buffer that will cause a remote
 * method to be invoked.
 *
 * @param buffer Buffer containing data to send to the server
 * @return Input stream to be used to read the response from
 * the server
 */
public DataInputStream _invokeMethod(byte buf[])
    throws TunnelException
{
    DataInputStream in = null;

    try
    {
        // Get the server URL
        String url = _getURL();
        if (url == null)
        {
            throw new IOException("Server URL has not been set");
        }

        // Attempt to connect to the host
        HttpConnection con = (HttpConnection) Connector.open(url);

        // Set the request method
        con.setRequestMethod(HttpConnection.POST);

        // Set the user agent
        con.setRequestProperty("User-Agent", userAgent);
```

```
// Set the session cookie if we have one
if (sessionCookie != null)
{
    con.setRequestProperty("cookie", sessionCookie);
}

// Set the content that we are sending
con.setRequestProperty("Content-type",
                       "application/octet-stream");

// Set the length of the data buffer we are sending
con.setRequestProperty("Content-length",
                       "" + buf.length);

// Get the output stream to the server and send our
// data buffer
DataOutputStream out =
        new DataOutputStream(con.openOutputStream());
out.write(buf);

// Flush the output stream and close it
out.flush();
out.close();

// Get the response status
int status = con.getResponseCode();
if (status != HttpConnection.HTTP_OK)
{
    throw new TunnelException("Invalid response: " + status);
}

// Get the input stream we can use to read the response
in = new DataInputStream(con.openInputStream());

// The server will always respond with an int value
// that will either be the method ordinal that was
// invoked, or a -2 indicating an exception was thrown
// from the server
int ordinal = in.readInt();

// Check for an exception on the server.
if (ordinal == -2)
{
    // Read the exception message and throw it
    String msg = in.readUTF();
```

```
                throw new TunnelException(msg);
            }

            // Get the session cookie if we don't have one yet
            if (sessionCookie == null)
            {
                String cookie = con.getHeaderField("set-cookie");
                if (cookie != null)
                {
                    sessionCookie = parseCookie(cookie);
                }
            }
        }
        catch (IOException ex)
        {
            // Re-throw as a tunnel exception
            ex.printStackTrace();
            throw new TunnelException(ex.getMessage());
        }

        // Return the input stream to be used to read the rest
        // of the response from the server
        return in;
    }

    /**
     * Gets the cookie name and value from a cookie field
     */
    public static String parseCookie(String raw)
    {
        String c = raw;
        if (raw != null)
        {
            // Find the first ';'
            int endPos = raw.indexOf(';');

            if (endPos >= 0)
            {
                c = raw.substring(0, endPos);
            }
        }
        return c;
    }
}
```

You may be wondering why we didn't extend the base class developed in Chapter 10, overriding methods for the new MIDP style of communication. The main reason we can't do this is that the base class may be using classes and methods not available to the KVM. Also, since we are dealing with a limited resource device, it's best to keep the necessary code to a minimum; we could override methods, but the base class would still need to be loaded and resolved by the VM, chewing up precious resources.

The Base Tunnel Server

Amazingly enough, we can reuse the TunnelLiteServer we developed in Chapter 10 without modification! That's what I call code reuse. To recap, the TunnelLiteServer is actually a servlet that helps read the request sent by the client, instantiate the remote object, invoke the appropriate method, and return the results.

MIDlet Example: IndyMIDlet

To illustrate how to use these base classes, let's take a look at a very simple MIDlet. Note that this is not a book on MIDlet programming (there are many of those now available), so I'll just be focusing on the communication aspects of the application. Before starting, you will need to download and install the J2ME development environment (http://java.sun.com/j2me), also referred to as the J2ME Wireless Toolkit.

Before we can start on the MIDlet, we need to first implement the client proxy that will extend MicroTunnelClient:

```
package com.omh.micro;

import com.omh.micro.client.MicroTunnelClient;
import com.omh.micro.client.TunnelException;
import java.io.*;

public class RemoteIndyMicroClient
        extends MicroTunnelClient
        implements IndyInterface
{
    /**
     * Constructs a new RemoteMathLiteClient for the
     * given URL. The URL should contain the location of
     * servlet scripts (i.e. http://larryboy/servlet/).
     */
    public RemoteIndyMicroClient(String url)
```

```
    throws TunnelException, IOException
{
    // Append the remote server name
    if (!url.endsWith("/"))
    {
        url += "/";
    }
    url += "RemoteIndyMicroServer";

    // Set the URL
    _setURL(url);

    // Initialize the client and server
    _initialize();
}

public boolean connect()
{
    boolean rc = false;
    try
    {
        // Create an internal buffer
        ByteArrayOutputStream baos = new ByteArrayOutputStream();

        // Create an object stream to write the request
        DataOutputStream out = _createHeader(baos, 0);

        // Invoke the method and read the response
        DataInputStream in = _invokeMethod(baos.toByteArray());

        // Read the return value
        rc = in.readBoolean();

        // Wrap up
        out.close();
        in.close();
    }
    catch (Exception ex)
    {
        ex.printStackTrace();
    }

    return rc;
}
```

```
public void close()
{
    try
    {
        // Create an internal buffer
        ByteArrayOutputStream baos = new ByteArrayOutputStream();

        // Create an object stream to write the request
        DataOutputStream out = _createHeader(baos, 1);

        // Invoke the method
        _invokeMethod(baos.toByteArray());

        // Wrap up
        out.close();
    }
    catch (Exception ex)
    {
        ex.printStackTrace();
    }
}

public IndyRecord query(int year)
{
    IndyRecord record = null;
    try
    {
        // Create an internal buffer
        ByteArrayOutputStream baos = new ByteArrayOutputStream();

        // Create an object stream to write the request
        DataOutputStream out = _createHeader(baos, 2);

        // Write the parameters
        out.writeInt(year);

        // Invoke the method and read the response
        DataInputStream in = _invokeMethod(baos.toByteArray());

        // Read the return value
        record = new IndyRecord();
        record.year = in.readInt();
        record.driver = in.readUTF();
```

```
            record.speed = in.readUTF();

            // Wrap up
            out.close();
            in.close();
        }
        catch (Exception ex)
        {
            ex.printStackTrace();
        }

        return record;
    }
}
```

Just as in Chapter 10, this client proxy implements a simple interface. The IndyInterface defines the methods that will be available on the remote object:

```
package com.omh.micro;

public interface IndyInterface
{
    /**
     * Connects to the database.
     *
     * @return True if the database connection was established
     */
    boolean connect();

    /**
     * Closes the database connection
     */
    void close();

    /**
     * Given the year return the corresponding Indianapolis
     * 500 record
     *
     * @param year Year of the race
     * @return Indy 500 record or null if not found
     */
    IndyRecord query(int year);
}
```

Note that since we cannot use serialization within the KVM, the IndyRecord being returned will have to be sent using scalar data types (int, String, and so on). The client will need to read the individual pieces of data in the same order in which the server wrote them.

Now all that is left to do is plug the remote client proxy into the MIDlet:

```
package com.omh.micro;

import javax.microedition.midlet.MIDlet;
import javax.microedition.lcdui.*;
import javax.microedition.io.HttpConnection;

public class IndyMIDlet
        extends MIDlet
        implements CommandListener
{
    // User interface command to exit the current application
    private Command exitCommand  = new Command("Exit", Command.EXIT, 2);

    // User interface command to confirm current operation
    private Command okCommand = new Command("OK", Command.OK, 1);

    // The year to fetch
    int year = 2001;

    // The text box used to query the winner
    private TextBox getWinner;

    // Our remote indy object
    private IndyInterface remoteIndy;

    /**
     * Start creates the thread to do the timing.
     * It should return immediately to keep the dispatcher
     * from hanging.
     */
    public void startApp()
    {
        mainScreen();
    }
```

```
/**
 * Destroy must cleanup everything.  The thread is signaled
 * to stop and no result is produced.
 * @param unconditional Flag to indicate that forced shutdown
 * is requested
 */
public void destroyApp(boolean unconditional)
{
    if (remoteIndy != null)
    {
        try
        {
            remoteIndy.close();
        }
        catch (Exception ex)
        {
            displayMessage("Error", ex.getMessage());
        }
    }
}

/**
 * Pause signals the thread to stop by clearing the thread field.
 * If stopped before done with the iterations it will
 * be restarted from scratch later.
 */
public void pauseApp()
{
}

/**
 * Display the main screen.
 */
void mainScreen()
{
    String s = "Press OK to fetch the winner of the " +
               year + " Indianapolis 500";

    getWinner = new TextBox("Indy Winners", s, s.length(), 0);

    getWinner.addCommand(okCommand);
```

```
        getWinner.addCommand(exitCommand);
        getWinner.setCommandListener(this);
        Display.getDisplay(this).setCurrent(getWinner);
    }

    /**
     * Display an error
     */
    protected void displayMessage(String title, String msg)
    {
        TextBox tb = new TextBox(title, msg, msg.length(), 0);

        tb.addCommand(okCommand);
        tb.setCommandListener(this);
        Display.getDisplay(this).setCurrent(tb);
    }

    /**
     * Request the winner through our remote object
     */
    protected void requestWinner()
    {
        if (remoteIndy == null)
        {
            // Instantiate a new remote object
            String url = "http://localhost:8080/jsdg-micro";
            try
            {
                remoteIndy = new RemoteIndyMicroClient(url);

                // Connect to the database
                remoteIndy.connect();
            }
            catch (Exception ex)
            {
                displayMessage("Error", ex.getMessage());
            }
        }

        if (remoteIndy != null)
        {
            try
```

```
            {
                IndyRecord record = remoteIndy.query(year);
                String msg = "The winner in " + record.year +
                             " was " + record.driver +
                             " at " + record.speed + "mph";
                displayMessage("Results", msg);
            }
            catch (Exception ex)
            {
                displayMessage("Error", ex.getMessage());
            }
        }
    }

    /**
     * Respond to commands, including exit
     * @param c command to perform
     * @param s Screen displayable object
     */
    public void commandAction(Command c, Displayable s)
    {
        if (c == exitCommand)
        {
            destroyApp(false);
            notifyDestroyed();
        }
        else if (c == okCommand)
        {
            if (s == getWinner)
            {
                requestWinner();
            }
            else
            {
                // User pressed 'ok' from results page. Go
                // back to the main screen
                mainScreen();
            }
        }
    }
}
```

There are a lot of development and configuration issues when dealing with MIDlets that may be new to you (they certainly were to me). I would suggest reading the documentation and trying the sample applications, which are part of the J2ME toolkit. Not only do you need to compile the MIDlet with the class libraries supplied with the J2ME, but you must also run a preverifier, which validates the class files and rearranges them for easier loading by the KVM. You must also create a manifest before generating a JAR file for the MIDlet, and then describe the application via a Java Application Descriptor (JAD) file. Again, I'll leave the specifics to the J2ME documentation.

The initial display of the IndyMIDlet in the device emulator (included in the J2ME toolkit) is shown next. Note that the Indy.jad file is used to display the initial list of applications.

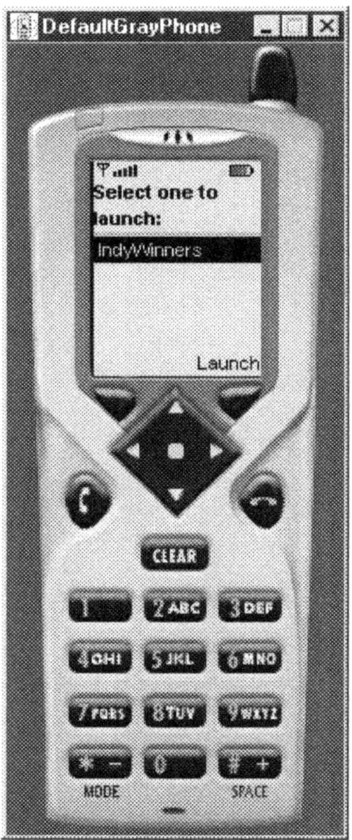

Launching the IndyWinners application will cause the IndyMIDlet to be started. This results in the application calling the IndyInterface.connect() method, which ends up opening a JDBC connection on the server (through the magic of HTTP tunneling). The user will then be prompted to click OK to get the winner information of a particular race year.

The following shows the application running in a simulated phone provided with the Wireless Toolkit:

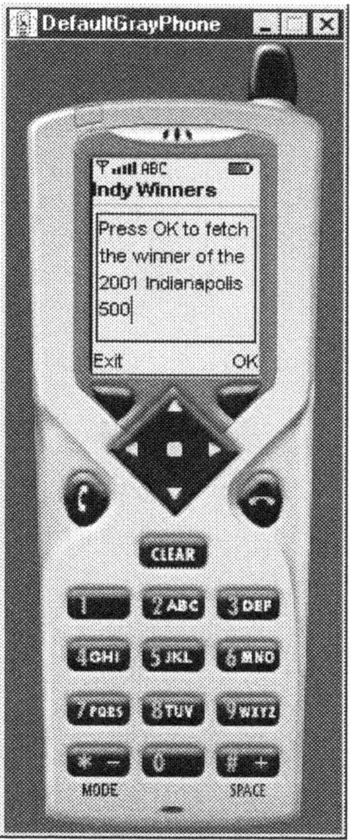

Clicking OK will cause the IndyInterface.query() method to be invoked. This causes the year to be written to the output stream so that the server can read it and format the appropriate JDBC query. Once the query is complete, the results are written back to the client where they are read (in the same order that the results were written) and used to create a new IndyRecord object. The data in this object is used to format the results page displayed to the user.

The following shows the results being displayed on a simulated phone:

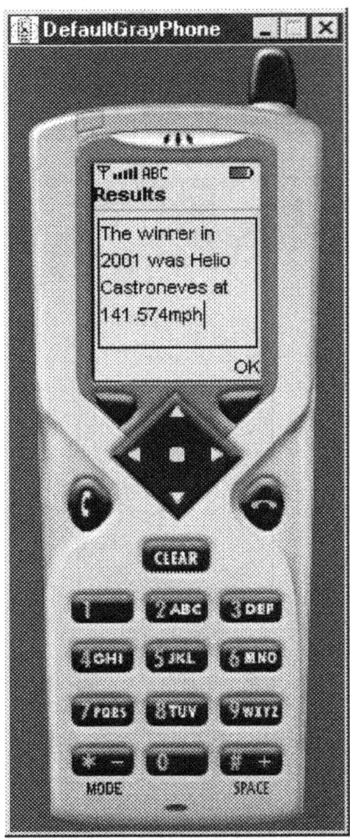

The Remote Server

Now that you've seen what happens on the client, let's take a peek at the server. Just like the tunnel lite server presented in Chapter 10, the micro server code uses DataInput and DataOutput streams to read and write raw scalar data:

```
package com.omh.micro;

import com.omh.tunnel.server.TunnelLiteServer;
import com.omh.tunnel.Indy;
import com.omh.tunnel.IndyRecord;
import javax.servlet.ServletException;
import java.io.*;
```

```
public class RemoteIndyMicroServer
        extends TunnelLiteServer
{
    /**
     * Creates a new instance of the server object.
     *
     * @return Instance of the server object
     */
    public Object _getNewInstance()
        throws ServletException
    {
        return new Indy();
    }

    /**
     * Invokes the method for the ordinal given. If the method
     * throws an exception it will be sent to the client.
     *
     * @param Object Server object
     * @param ordinal Method ordinal
     * @param in Input stream to read additional parameters
     * @param out Output stream to write return values
     */
    public void _invokeMethod(Object serverObject, int ordinal,
                              DataInput in, DataOutput out)
        throws Exception
    {
        // Cast the server object
        Indy indy = (Indy) serverObject;

        // Cast the input/output streams
        DataInputStream dataIn = (DataInputStream) in;
        DataOutputStream dataOut = (DataOutputStream) out;

        // Evaluate the ordinal
        switch (ordinal)
        {

        case 0: // connect
```

```
                boolean b0 = indy.connect();
                dataOut.writeBoolean(b0);
                break;

            case 1: // close
                indy.close();
                break;

            case 2: // query
                int i2 = dataIn.readInt();
                IndyRecord record = indy.query(i2);
                dataOut.writeInt(record.year);
                dataOut.writeUTF(record.driver);
                dataOut.writeUTF("" + record.speed);
                break;

            default:
                throw new Exception("Invalid ordinal: " + ordinal);
            }
        }
    }
```

As in Chapter 10, you must configure the RemoteIndyMicroServer as a servlet within web.xml:

```
<servlet>
  <servlet-name>RemoteIndyMicroServer</servlet-name>
  <servlet-class>com.omh.micro.RemoteIndyMicroServer</servlet-class>
</servlet>

<servlet-mapping>
  <servlet-name>RemoteIndyMicroServer</servlet-name>
  <url-pattern>/RemoteIndyMicroServer</url-pattern>
</servlet-mapping>
```

A Challenge

If you want to take J2ME programming to the next level, feel free to use the concepts covered in Chapter 11 to automate the generation of J2ME components as well. You should be able to easily use the same base program generator code and create a new template for both the client and server proxies.

Summary

In this chapter, we discovered how to tunnel method calls from a J2ME client to a servlet. The concepts explored here were an extension to what was covered in Chapter 10 and allowed us to reuse much of the code that we had already developed. A very simple MIDlet was developed that made multiple requests to a client proxy, which marshaled data, invoked a remote object, and then read the response of the remote method call.

CHAPTER

13

Generating WML for Wireless Devices

IN THIS CHAPTER:

WAP Background

WML Example: HelloPhone

Using XSLT to Transform Stock Quote Data (Revisited)

Summary

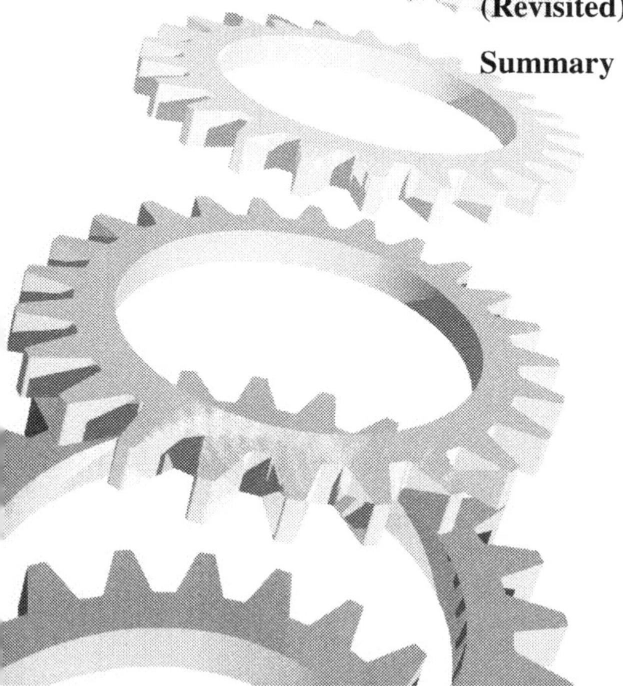

In the last chapter, we developed Java classes that run inside a KVM residing on a Java-enabled wireless device. In this chapter, we'll focus on another category of wireless devices, which more closely resemble a browser in that they render a markup language as opposed to executing a Java application. This language, Wireless Markup Language (WML), is very similar to HTML and can very easily be generated by servlets.

WAP Background

In 1997, the Wireless Application Protocol (WAP) was in the spotlight. This new protocol, targeted for mobile devices, specified not only a new communication protocol, but also an entire application environment providing, among other things, Internet access. WAP was born out of a consortium of vendors that formed the WAP Forum (www.wapforum.org). These vendors, including Ericsson, Nokia, and Motorola, worked together to share knowledge and ideas to help shape the WAP specification.

To better understand some of the basics of WAP, let's take a look at the general flow of a request generated by a mobile device, and how it is serviced by a server (see Figure 13-1):

1. The WAP-enabled mobile device (a phone or PDA) makes a WAP request. The request may contain encoded headers along with the URL of a WML page to display.
2. The WAP Gateway receives the message. The message is decoded and, if it contains a request for a WML page or WBMP (Wireless Bitmap) image, an HTTP request is created to retrieve the content from a web server.
3. An HTTP request is made for content.
4. A web server processes the HTTP request and services the requested document or image.
5. The HTTP response is sent back to the WAP Gateway.
6. The WAP Gateway receives the HTTP response. If the content is WML, the Gateway compiles the page into binary form, known as WMLC (Compiled), in an effort to reduce the size of the transmission.
7. The WAP response is sent back to the wireless device.

Many nuances surrounding application development for WAP devices are well outside the scope of this book; however, there are many WAP-specific books on the

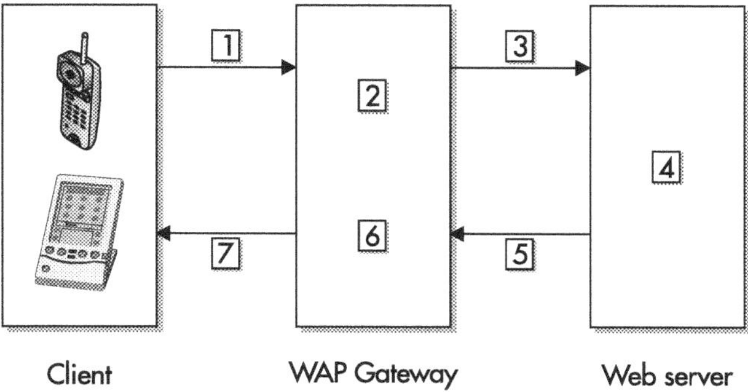

Figure 13-1 *General flow of a WAP application*

market today that address these issues. The remainder of this chapter will focus on how to generate proper WML from a servlet.

WML Example: HelloPhone

Let's start by looking at a very simple servlet that generates a WML document:

```
package com.omh.wap;

import javax.servlet.*;
import javax.servlet.http.*;
import java.io.*;
import java.util.*;

/**
 * Simple servlet that generates a basic WML page for a WAP
 * device
 */
public class HelloPhone
        extends HttpServlet
{
    public void service(HttpServletRequest req,
                        HttpServletResponse resp)
        throws ServletException, IOException
    {
        // Set the content type of the response
        resp.setContentType("text/vnd.wap.wml");
```

```
        // Create a PrintWriter to write the response
        PrintWriter out =
            new PrintWriter(resp.getOutputStream());

        // Print a standard header
        out.println("<?xml version=\"1.0\"?>");
        out.println("<!DOCTYPE wml " +

                    "PUBLIC \"-//WAPFORUM//DTD WML 1.1//EN\"");
        out.println(" \"http://www.wapforum.org/DTD/wml_1.1.xml\">");
        out.println("<wml>");
        out.println(" <card id=\"main\">");
        out.println("  <p>");
        out.println("   Hello Phone!");
        out.println("  </p>");
        out.println(" </card>");

        // Wrap up
        out.println("</wml>");
        out.flush();
    }
}
```

The most important new aspect of generating WML is setting the content type to let the WAP Gateway know what type of document has been served. In our case, we need to call response.setContentType() with "text/vnd.wap.wml" (when serving WBMP images, the content type is "image/vnd.wap.wbmp").

Before continuing, let's take a look at what is actually generated by this servlet:

```
<?xml version="1.0"?>
<!DOCTYPE wml PUBLIC "-//WAPFORUM//DTD WML 1.1//EN"
 "http://www.wapforum.org/DTD/wml_1.1.xml">
<wml>
 <card id="main">
  <p>
   Hello Phone!
  </p>
 </card>
</wml>
```

Remember that WML is very similar to HTML (many of the tags are the same), and can be thought of as a very small subset. For more information about WML, as well as examples and explanations of each tag, go to www.wapforum.org.

Now that you have a servlet generating WML, you can't just make a request from your standard browser; you need to test it with a WAP-enabled device (or emulator) to see it in action. The best way to do this is to grab the Nokia Mobile Internet Toolkit (available at www.forum.nokia.com). This toolkit includes WAP phone emulators that allow you to easily test the HelloPhone servlet. The following illustration shows the results of requesting http://localhost:8080/HelloPhone within the Nokia Mobile Internet Toolkit:

Remember that you need to set up the servlet definition and servlet mapping in the web application descriptor (web.xml):

```
<servlet>
  <servlet-name>HelloPhone</servlet-name>
  <servlet-class>com.omh.wap.HelloPhone</servlet-class>
</servlet>

<servlet-mapping>
  <servlet-name>HelloPhone</servlet-name>
  <url-pattern>/HelloPhone</url-pattern>
</servlet-mapping>
```

Using XSLT to Transform Stock Quote Data (Revisited)

In Chapter 6, we developed a general-purpose servlet filter that transformed the XML output of a stock quote servlet into HTML using an XSL template. As promised, we'll reuse this technique to transform the XML output into WML. As a reminder, the following illustration shows the XML output of the stock quote servlet:

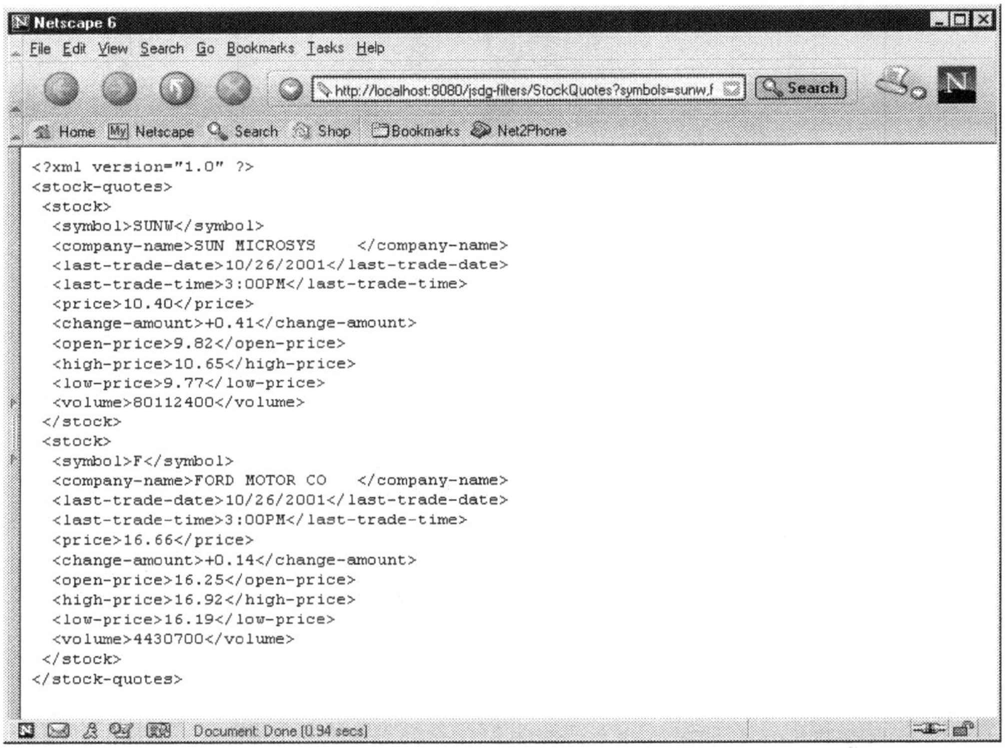

```
<?xml version="1.0" ?>
<stock-quotes>
 <stock>
  <symbol>SUNW</symbol>
  <company-name>SUN MICROSYS     </company-name>
  <last-trade-date>10/26/2001</last-trade-date>
  <last-trade-time>3:00PM</last-trade-time>
  <price>10.40</price>
  <change-amount>+0.41</change-amount>
  <open-price>9.82</open-price>
  <high-price>10.65</high-price>
  <low-price>9.77</low-price>
  <volume>80112400</volume>
 </stock>
 <stock>
  <symbol>F</symbol>
  <company-name>FORD MOTOR CO    </company-name>
  <last-trade-date>10/26/2001</last-trade-date>
  <last-trade-time>3:00PM</last-trade-time>
  <price>16.66</price>
  <change-amount>+0.14</change-amount>
  <open-price>16.25</open-price>
  <high-price>16.92</high-price>
  <low-price>16.19</low-price>
  <volume>4430700</volume>
 </stock>
</stock-quotes>
```

The first step is to create a new XSL template that will generate the appropriate WML:

```
<?xml version="1.0"?>
<xsl:stylesheet xmlns:xsl="http://www.w3.org/1999/XSL/Transform"
version="1.0">
```

```
<xsl:output method="xml"
            media-type="text/vnd.wap.wml"
            doctype-public="-//WAPFORUM//DTD WML 1.1//EN"
            doctype-system="http://www.wapforum.org/DTD/wml_1.1.xml"
            encoding="ISO-8859-1"/>
<xsl:template match="/">
 <wml>
  <card id="main" title="Stock Quotes">
   <p>
   <table align="right" columns="3">
   <xsl:for-each select="stock-quotes/stock">
    <tr>
     <td><xsl:value-of select="symbol" /></td>
     <td><xsl:value-of select="price" /></td>
     <td><xsl:value-of select="change-amount" /></td>
    </tr>
   </xsl:for-each>
   </table>
   </p>
  </card>
 </wml>
</xsl:template>
</xsl:stylesheet>
```

This template will create a WML page containing a table with the requested stock quotes. Note that using a table in WML may not be the best solution; not all mobile devices will support tables, not to mention that you may have a very limited display area.

Take special notice of the xsl:output tag. This tag defines special properties to be used when translating the input XML document. The doctype-public and doctype-system attributes are used to assemble the DOCTYPE element, while the media-type attribute defines the content type of the resulting document. We'll need to update the TransformationFilter applyTemplate() method to get the media-type output property and set the content type accordingly:

```
protected void applyTemplate(String content,
                             String name,
                             HttpServletResponse response)
    throws ServletException, IOException
{
```

```
        InputStream in = null;

        try
        {
            in = config.getServletContext().getResourceAsStream(name);
            if (in == null)
            {
                // The resource was not found. Raise an exception
                throw new ServletException(name + " not found");
            }

            // Create a transformer to work with the given style
            // sheet
            StreamSource source = new StreamSource(in);
            Transformer transformer =
                    factory.newTransformer(source);

            // Transform it!
            StringReader reader = new StringReader(content);
            source = new StreamSource(reader);

            // Buffer the results. We can't set any headers
            // (such as the content type) if output has been
            // committed to the response stream.
            StringWriter writer = new StringWriter();
            StreamResult result = new StreamResult(writer);
            transformer.transform(source, result);

            // Set the content type to the media-type output
            // property if one was specified in the XSL template
            String mediaType = transformer.getOutputProperty("media-type");
            if (mediaType != null)
            {
                response.setContentType(mediaType);
            }

            // Now stream the results to the "real" output
            // writer
            PrintWriter out = response.getWriter();
            out.print(writer.toString());
```

```
            out.close();
        }
        catch (Exception ex)
        {
            throw new ServletException(ex.getMessage(), ex);
        }
        finally
        {
            // Make sure the input stream gets closed
            if (in != null)
            {
                try
                {
                    in.close();
                }
                catch (Exception ex)
                {
                    // Ignore exceptions on close
                }
            }
        }
    }
```

One other change that was made to the applyTemplate() method was to cache the results of the transformation in a StringWriter object instead of sending it directly to the response writer. This is necessary since we may need to set the content type of the response, which cannot be done after output has been committed to the response buffer.

As a refresher, the following shows the filter definition in web.xml as well as the StockQuotes servlet elements:

```
<filter>
  <filter-name>StockServlet XSL Transformation Filter</filter-name>
  <filter-class>com.omh.filters.TransformationFilter</filter-class>
    <init-param>
      <param-name>agentMappings</param-name>
      <param-value>/stocks/agentMappings.properties</param-value>
    </init-param>
</filter>
```

```
<filter-mapping>
  <filter-name>StockServlet XSL Transformation Filter</filter-name>
  <servlet-name>StockQuotes</servlet-name>
</filter-mapping>

<servlet>
  <servlet-name>StockQuotes</servlet-name>
  <servlet-class>com.omh.stocks.StockServlet</servlet-class>
</servlet>

<servlet-mapping>
  <servlet-name>StockQuotes</servlet-name>
  <url-pattern>/StockQuotes</url-pattern>
</servlet-mapping>
```

Don't forget to update the agent mappings file (defined in the agentMappings initialization parameter for the TransformationFilter). The XSL template for WML output can be found in stocks/wml_nokia.xsl (within the web application root directory) and will be applied to any response to a user agent that begins with "Nokia":

```
# agentMappings.properties
#
# Provides a mapping between an agent type and an XSL
# stylesheet that should be used in transforming a
# document that has the com.omg.filter.TransformationFilter
# filter applied
#
# User agents will be matched if the agent starts with the
# string given
#
# A special agent name of "*" is reserved to indicate that
# all agents should default to using the given xsl template
#
# The xsl template can be an absolute path, or relative
# path that will use the document base of this properties
# file.
#

Mozilla/4.0\ (compatible;\ MSIE=html_ie.xsl
Nokia=wml_nokia.xsl
```

Just to make sure all is still well, let's request the stock quotes from within our web browser first, as shown in the following illustration:

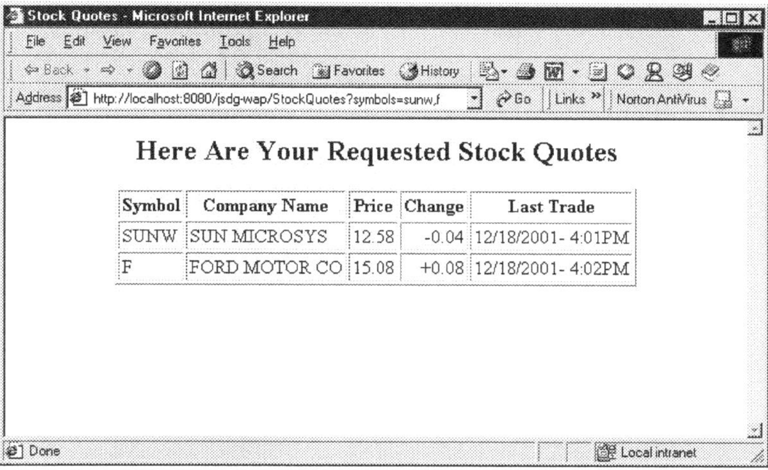

Now let's try the same exact URL from within the Nokia Mobile Internet Toolkit WAP emulator, shown next:

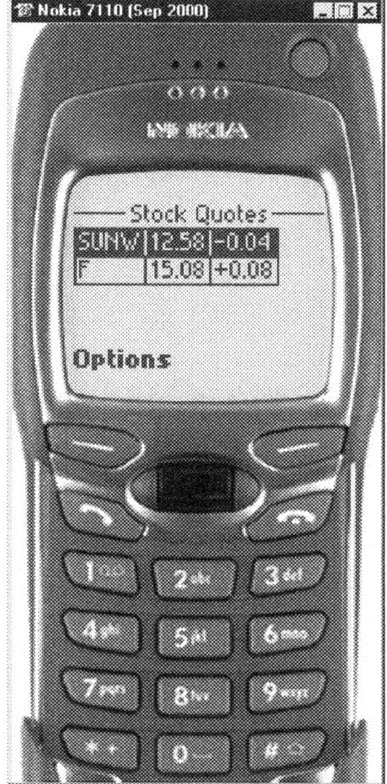

Wow! A single servlet has generated stock data in XML, which has been transformed to the appropriate markup language depending upon the type of client (via the user-agent header). I certainly hope you see the power in using this methodology.

Summary

In this chapter, we've taken a quick look at how to properly generate WML for WAP-enabled mobile devices. We also revisited the XSL translation filter developed in Chapter 6 and adapted it to translate XML stock quote information given into WML. Other than a few modifications to set the response content type properly, all we needed to do was create a new XSL template, which handled all of the translation details.

CHAPTER

14

Sending E-Mail from Servlets

IN THIS CHAPTER:

In this chapter, we'll cover how to send e-mail messages from a servlet (or any type of Java application for that matter). You may want to send an e-mail message if someone registers at your site for the first time, or send a message with the statistics of a running servlet (imagine a servlet that charges the user for every time the servlet is used—you might want to get an e-mail message each day summarizing the activity so you can count your royalties!). Maybe you want a notification if your servlet throws an exception, or encounters a severe error. You may even want to create a custom online e-mail system with which you can read and write e-mail messages over the Internet. The possibilities are almost endless.

What Are the Options?

Almost all problems can be solved in many different ways. The same is true for sending an e-mail message from an application written in Java:

- You can open a socket connection to a mail server and communicate using a low-level protocol, such as the Simple Mail Transport Protocol (SMTP, defined in RFC 821). All of the intricacies and quirks of the protocol have to be handled by you.
- You can use one of the many freely available mail classes that sit on top of a low-level protocol. The use of these types of classes abstract the details of the transport. Many of these classes support only the sending (not reading) of e-mail messages.
- You can use the JavaMail API from Sun Microsystems, which was designed to make adding e-mail capability to Java applications easy.

Which is best for you? It depends. If you really want to get down and dirty and have a burning desire to understand how a transport protocol works, you may want to just use a raw socket to a mail server. Others may prefer using a convenience class (provided by someone else) for the simplicity. Of course, by doing so, you are limited to the functionality provided by the class, but it may serve your needs quite well. If you want to drive the Cadillac of mail systems for Java, you'll definitely want to explore using JavaMail. The JavaMail API is very robust and encompasses all of the e-mail functionality that you will ever need.

Having used all three options, I can tell you that programming at the transport protocol level is way too detailed and error prone. Why waste your time dealing with the low-level details when many others have already endured this pain for you? Using a convenience class, which we'll cover next, makes much more sense and keeps life simple.

Sending Mail Using SmtpClient

Sun has provided a convenience class with its version of the JDK named sun.net.smtp.SmtpClient. Because this class resides in the "sun" tree (as opposed to the "java" tree), it should be considered unsupported (not to mention the fact that it is undocumented). For companies that require only the use of officially released and supported software, using this class may not be an option. Also keep in mind that vendors who port the Java Virtual Machine to other platforms are not required to port any classes contained in the sun tree. This means that all JVM implementations may not provide the SmtpClient class (although most do).

The SmtpClient class implements SMTP. To send an e-mail, you follow these steps:

1. Instantiate a new SmtpClient.
2. Call the to() method to specify the recipients.
3. Call the from() method to name the sender.
4. Call the startMessage() method, which returns an output stream that you use to write the message headers and text.
5. Close the SmtpClient to send the message on its way.

The following code listing shows the SendMailServlet that creates an HTML form to gather the sender, subject, and message text. Once the form has been submitted (the form submits itself back to the SendMailServlet), the sun.net.smtp.SmtpClient class is used to send the message.

```
package com.omh.mail;

import sun.net.smtp.SmtpClient;

import javax.servlet.http.HttpServletRequest;
import javax.servlet.http.HttpServletResponse;
import javax.servlet.http.HttpServlet;
import javax.servlet.ServletException;
import java.io.IOException;
import java.io.PrintWriter;

/**
 * <p>This servlet will format an e-mail form in HTML and, when
 * the user submits the form, will e-mail the message using
 * SMTP
 */
public class SendMailServlet
```

```
        extends HttpServlet
{
    public static String MAIL_FROM = "from";
    public static String MAIL_SUBJECT = "subject";
    public static String MAIL_BODY = "body";

    // Multiple 'to' addresses can be separated by commas
    public static String MAIL_TO = "karl@servletguru.com";

    // The SMTP server
    public static String MAIL_HOST = "larry-boy";

    public void doGet(HttpServletRequest req,
                      HttpServletResponse resp)
        throws ServletException, IOException
    {
        // Set the content type of the response
        resp.setContentType("text/html");

        // Get the PrintWriter to write the response
        PrintWriter out = resp.getWriter();

        // Create the HTML form
        out.println("<html>");
        out.println("<head>");
        out.println("<title>Send E-Mail</title>");
        out.println("<center><h2>Send E-Mail to Karl Moss</h2>");
        out.println("<br><form method=POST action=\"" +
                    req.getRequestURI() + "\">");
        out.println("<table>");
        out.println("<tr><td>From:</td>");
        out.println("<td><input type=text name=" +
                    MAIL_FROM + " size=30></td></tr>");
        out.println("<tr><td>Subject:</td>");
        out.println("<td><input type=text name=" +
                    MAIL_SUBJECT + " size=30></td></tr>");
        out.println("<tr><td>Text:</td>");
        out.println("<td><textarea name=" + MAIL_BODY +
                    " cols=40 rows=6></textarea></td></tr>");
        out.println("</table><br>");
        out.println("<input type=submit value=\"Send\">");
        out.println("<input type=reset value=\"Reset\">");
        out.println("</form></center></body></html>");

        // Wrap up
```

```
        out.println("</body>");
        out.println("</html>");
        out.flush();
    }

    public void doPost(HttpServletRequest req,
                       HttpServletResponse resp)
            throws ServletException, IOException
    {
        // Set the content type of the response
        resp.setContentType("text/html");

        // Create a PrintWriter to write the response
        PrintWriter out = new PrintWriter(resp.getOutputStream());

        // Get the data from the form
        String from = req.getParameter(MAIL_FROM);
        String subject = req.getParameter(MAIL_SUBJECT);
        String body = req.getParameter(MAIL_BODY);

        try
        {
            // Create a new SMTP client
            SmtpClient mailer = new SmtpClient(MAIL_HOST);

            // Set the 'from' and 'to' addresses
            mailer.from(from);
            mailer.to(MAIL_TO);

            // Get the PrintStream for writing the rest of the message
            java.io.PrintStream ps = mailer.startMessage();

            // Write out any mail headers
            ps.println("From: " + from);
            ps.println("To: " + MAIL_TO);
            ps.println("Subject: " + subject);

            // Write out the message body
            ps.print("\r\n");
            ps.println(body);

            ps.flush();
            ps.close();

            // Send the message
```

```
            mailer.closeServer();

            // Let the user know that the mail was sent
            out.println("<html>");
            out.println("<head>");
            out.println("<title>Send E-Mail</title>");
            out.println("<body><center>");
            out.println("<h2>Your e-mail has been sent!</h2>");
            out.println("</center></body></html>");
        }
        catch (Exception ex)
        {
            // Got an error sending the e-mail; notify the client
            out.println("<html>");
            out.println("<head>");
            out.println("<title>Send E-Mail Error</title>");
            out.println("<body><center>");
            out.println("<h2>There was an error sending your e-mail</h2>");
            out.println("<br>Message=" + ex.getMessage());
            out.println("</center>");
            out.println("</body></html>");
        }

        // Wrap up
        out.flush();
    }
}
```

Note that you will want to customize the MAIL_HOST and MAIL_TO fields to specify the SMTP server name and your e-mail address. If you do not have an SMTP server available (either on your network or through an ISP), you might want to check out one of the free SMTP servers available. I've used the PostCast Server from Gate Comm Software (www.postcast.com).

The initial HTML form, which follows, is created in the doGet() method, while the message is sent in the doPost() method. The recipient is hard-coded, but you could very easily add an input field to the form to get this as well. You should also be able to recognize how you can use the SmtpClient to send messages automatically (such as sending an e-mail to yourself if your servlet encounters an exception).

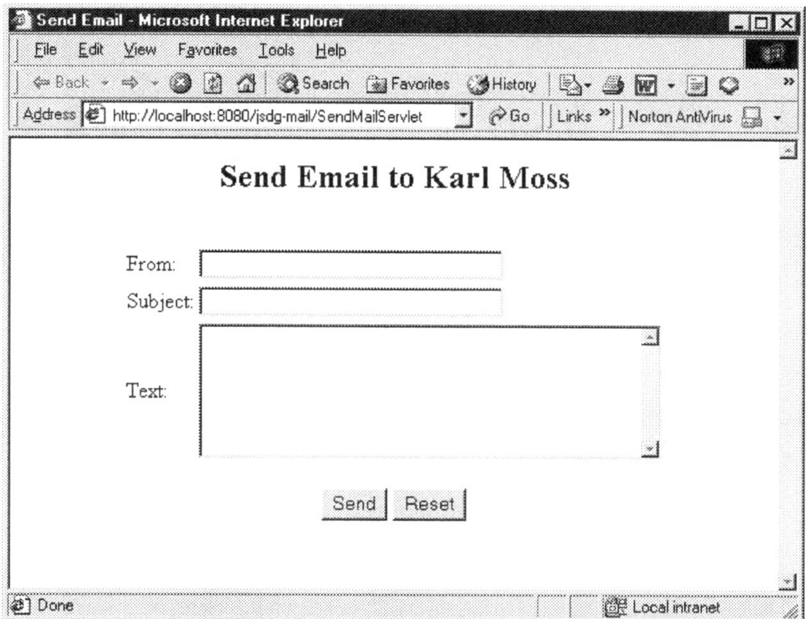

The only tricky part about using the SmtpClient class is writing the mail headers. This isn't the fault of the class; rather, it is a necessary evil that results from using SMTP to send the message. The mail headers must conform to RFC (Request For Comments) 822. RFC 822 replaces RFC 733, "Standard for the Format of ARPA Network Text Messages." The new title of the RFC is "Standard for the Format of ARPA Internet Text Messages" (note the progression from "Network Text Messages" to "Internet Text Messages"). All of the message headers are defined in the Syntax section of RFC 822, but most are rarely used. Some of the more important message headers are the following:

```
From: <Name of sender>

Date: <Date and time>

To: <One or more recipients>

cc: <Zero or more recipients>

Subject: <Subject text>
```

While the message headers are not required to be in any certain order, it's probably best to add them in the order given. All message headers are in the format "name: value," such as "To: karl@servletguru.com." For more concrete examples of how to use message headers, see Appendix A of RFC 822 (if you don't have it, just search for RFC 822 on the Internet—you'll find myriad sites containing the RFC).

What is missing from the SmtpClient is the ability to read messages. In many cases, this will pose no problem because you may just need to send a message. But what if you want to check your personal e-mail account? SMTP does not address this, so you will need to use a more robust set of classes, such as those defined by the JavaMail API, discussed next.

The JavaMail API

JavaMail was designed from the beginning to make adding e-mail capabilities to Java applications as easy as possible. This does not mean that the API is limiting in its functionality (as is the SmtpClient class). JavaMail is very robust, drawing from a number of existing messaging systems (such as MAPI and IMAP). The JavaMail API defines a common interface that can be used for managing mail, while third-party vendors supply the implementation for specific messaging systems. JavaMail allows you to write your application with the interfaces defined in the API and then request a certain type of implementation to be used at run time.

The four major components defined within the JavaMail API are the Message, Folder, and Store classes and the Session object. The Message class defines a set of attributes, such as addressing information, and the content type(s) for an e-mail message. All messages are stored within a folder, such as the familiar INBOX folder. Folders can contain subfolders, to create a tree-like hierarchy. The Folder class defines methods that fetch, copy, append, and delete messages. The Store class defines a database that holds the folder hierarchy (including the messages contained within the folders). The Store class also defines the type of access protocol being used to access folders and messages. The Session object is responsible for authenticating users and controlling access to the message store and transport.

The basic flow for reading e-mail within a JavaMail application is as follows:

1. Create a new Session object and define what type of store (IMAP or POP3, for example) and transport (such as SMTP) will be used.
2. Using the Session object, create a new Store object. Before the message store can be accessed, the current user must be authenticated.

3. Get a folder from the Store class, such as the INBOX.
4. Retrieve the messages from the folder.

The basic flow for writing e-mail within a JavaMail application is as follows:

1. Create a new Session object and define what type of store (IMAP or POP3, for example) and transport (such as SMTP) will be used.
2. Using the Session object, create a new Message object and set the header attributes, such as the "from" name and recipients.
3. Invoke the Transport.send() method with the message. This will send the message using the appropriate transport based on the recipients given in the message header.

Before you get started with JavaMail, you will need to download and install the latest release (from http://java.sun.com/products/javamail). The release includes the API (found in mail.jar) as well as a store provider for IMAP and a transport provider for SMTP. Some servlet containers may include mail.jar in their default classpaths, but it's probably best to add it to your web application WEB-INF/lib directory. Make sure you read the installation instructions carefully; you will also need an additional component called the JavaBeans Activation Framework (JAF), available from the JavaMail download site.

If you need to use some other type of service (such as a POP3 store, for example), you will need to locate a vendor that provides that particular service provider. There is a POP3 store provider available that was implemented by Sun (also available at http://java.sun.com/products/javamail). Just follow the instructions and be sure to add the JAR file to WEB-INF/lib.

Instead of getting into the gory details of the JavaMail API specification, let's take a look at an example. The rest of the chapter will be devoted to a servlet, named SimpleMailReader, which will open and read a mailbox, display messages (including multipart messages), and allow messages to be sent. Since the servlet is somewhat long, I'll just be showing you the critical methods. As always, the complete source code can be found at www.servletguru.com.

Logging In to the Store

Before you can read your e-mail, you must first log in. The SimpleMailReader will use session management (covered in Chapter 3) to determine if the user must log into the store. If so, an HTML form will be created to gather the login information, as shown next.

In addition to gathering the mail host, username, and password, the login form presents the user with a choice of supported transport and store protocols. How did the servlet find out what protocols are supported? The JavaMail API provides a method to retrieve the transport and store protocols that are currently installed. You may recall that you needed to place the JAR file of the service provider in the web application WEB-INF/lib directory. Not only do the implementation classes reside inside this JAR file, but a description of the contents is also contained in the meta-inf/javamail.providers file. This file contains information about the name of the service, the protocol type (store or transport), the name of the implementing class, as well as the name of the vendor. The following is the javamail.providers file for the POP3 store provider (there doesn't seem to be any good reason for the extra space in the vendor name "Microsy stems"):

```
# JavaMail POP3 provider Sun Microsystems, Inc
protocol=pop3; type=store; class=com.sun.mail.pop3.POP3Store;
vendor=Sun Microsy stems, Inc;
```

After the user fills in the appropriate information and clicks the Login button, SimpleMailServlet attempts to log into the mail store on the given host using the selected store protocol. The following shows the code necessary to log in:

```
/**
 * Attempt to log into to the Store host
 *
 * @param req The request from the client
 * @param resp The response from the servlet
 * @param mailUser The current SimpleMailUser
 */
public void login(HttpServletRequest req,
                  HttpServletResponse resp,
                  SimpleMailUser mailUser)
    throws ServletException, IOException
{
    String transport = req.getParameter(FORM_TRANSPORT);
    String transportHost = req.getParameter(FORM_TRANSPORTHOST);
    String store = req.getParameter(FORM_STORE);
    String storeHost = req.getParameter(FORM_STOREHOST);
    String user = req.getParameter(FORM_USER);
    String password = req.getParameter(FORM_PASSWORD);

    // Attempt to log on
    try
    {
        mailUser.login(store, storeHost,
        transport, transportHost,
        user, password);
    }
    catch (MessagingException ex)
    {
        createErrorPage(req, resp, "Unable to login", ex);
        return;
    }

    showInbox(req, resp, mailUser);
}
```

If the login is successful, a new page will be created containing all the messages in the user's INBOX; otherwise, an error is returned to the user and the login must be attempted again. Since session management is being used, you could very easily limit the number of login attempts by keeping a counter for each user in the session data.

Reading Mail Using JavaMail

During the login procedure, we connected to the mail store and then opened a folder named INBOX. Now that the folder is open, we can very easily retrieve all the messages and display the inbox for the user. The code used to accomplish this is shown here:

```
/**
 * Shows all of the messages in the current user's inbox
 *
 * @param req The request from the client
 * @param resp The response from the servlet
 * @param mailUser The current SimpleMailUser
 */
public void showInbox(HttpServletRequest req,
                      HttpServletResponse resp,
                      SimpleMailUser mailUser)
    throws ServletException, IOException
{
    // Set the content type of the response
    resp.setContentType("text/html");

    // Get the PrintWriter to write the response
    PrintWriter out = resp.getWriter();

    // Set the response header to force the browser to
    // load the HTML page from the server instead of
    // from a cache
    resp.setHeader("Expires", "Tues, 01 Jan 1980 00:00:00 GMT");

    // Get the URI of this request
    String uri = req.getRequestURI();

    // Print a standard header
    out.println("<html>");
    out.println("<head>");
    out.println("<title>" + FORM_TITLE + "</title>");
    out.println("<body><center><h2>");
    out.println("INBOX for " + mailUser.getUser() +
                " using " + mailUser.getStoreProtocol() +
                " on host " + mailUser.getStoreHost());
    out.println("</h2>");

    try
    {
        // Get the inbox
```

```
Folder inbox = mailUser.getInbox();

// Get the number of messages in the inbox
int n = inbox.getMessageCount();

// Get the messages from the inbox
Message[] msgs = inbox.getMessages();

out.println("Total number of messages: " + n + "<br>");

out.println("<form action=\"" + uri + "\" METHOD=\"POST\">");
out.println("<input type=submit name=" +
            FORM_ACTION + " value=\"" +
            ACTION_LOGOFF + "\">");
out.println("<input type=submit name=" +
            FORM_ACTION + " value=\"" +
            ACTION_WRITE + "\">");
            out.println("</form>");

out.println("<table border>");
out.println("<tr><th></th>");
out.println("<th>From</th>");
out.println("<th>Sent</th>");
out.println("<th>Subject</th></tr>");

// Loop through the inbox
for (int i = 0; i < n; i++)
{
    Message m = msgs[i];

    // Skip deleted messages
    if (m.isSet(Flags.Flag.DELETED))
    {
        continue;
    }

    out.println("<tr>");

    // Give the user somewhere to click to view the
    // message
    out.println("<td><a href=\"" +
                uri + "?" + FORM_ACTION + "=" +
                ACTION_VIEW + "&" + FORM_MSG + "=" + i +
                "\">" + ACTION_VIEW + "</a>");
```

```
            // Show the from address
            Address from[] = m.getFrom();
            Address addr = null;
            if ((from != null) && (from.length > 0))
            {
                addr = from[0];
            }

            out.println("<td>" + getAddress(addr) + "</td>");

            // Show the sent date
            Date date = m.getSentDate();
            String s = "";
            if (date != null)
            {
                s = "" + date;
            }
            out.println("<td>" + s + "</td>");

            // Show the subject
            s = m.getSubject();
            if (s == null)
            {
                s = "";
            }
            out.println("<td>" + s + "</td>");

            out.println("</tr>");
        }

        out.println("</table>");
    }
    catch (MessagingException ex)
    {
        out.println("<br>");
        out.println("ERROR: " + ex.getMessage());
    }

    // Wrap up
    out.println("</center>");
    out.println("</body>");
    out.println("</html>");
    out.flush();
}
```

An example INBOX page is shown here:

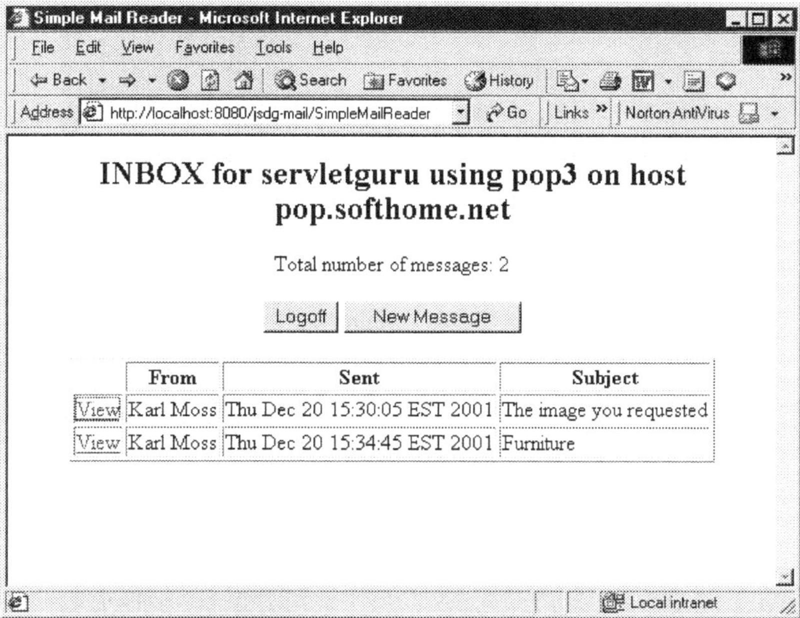

Notice that only the mail headers are being displayed, namely the from address, date, and subject. In addition to these headers, a link was created for each message that, if selected by the user, will display the contents of the individual message. If you looked at the code closely, you may be wondering what the mailUser object is. This is the object (of type SimpleMailUser) that is stored with the servlet session and contains the user information as well as the open connection to the mail store. The SimpleMailUser class implements the HttpSessionBindingListener interface so that it will receive notification when the session has been removed. This gives us an opportunity to ensure that the mail store is closed properly when the browser session has been terminated.

Displaying a message using JavaMail is also quite easy, even multipart messages (such as those with attachments). JavaMail provides methods to discover the content type of a message, and each message part, thus allowing us to control how it is displayed. Plain text messages are easy; we just dump the text to the HTML page. But what about multipart messages? We simply need to iterate through all the parts and figure out the content type of each part. If the part is text, dump it to the HTML page; if not, we'll create a link that the user can click that will open the part using its content type. So, for example, if there is an image (GIF) attachment, the user can click the name of the image and the SimpleMailReader will read the image, set the appropriate content type in the response, and send the contents of the image file back to the browser. The code for reading messages and parts follows:

```
/**
 * Shows the specified message
 *
 * @param req The request from the client
 * @param resp The response from the servlet
 * @param mailUser The current SimpleMailUser
 * @param msg The message number to display
 */
public void showMessage(HttpServletRequest req,
                        HttpServletResponse resp,
                        SimpleMailUser mailUser, int msg)
    throws ServletException, IOException
{
    // Set the content type of the response
    resp.setContentType("text/html");

    // Get the PrintWriter to write the response
    PrintWriter out = resp.getWriter();

    // Set the response header to force the browser to
    // load the HTML page from the server instead of
    // from a cache
    resp.setHeader("Expires", "Tues, 01 Jan 1980 00:00:00 GMT");

    // Get the URI of this request
    String uri = req.getRequestURI();

    // Print a standard header
    out.println("<html>");
    out.println("<head>");
    out.println("<title>" + FORM_TITLE + "</title>");
    out.println("<body>");

    try
    {
        // Get the inbox
        Folder inbox = mailUser.getInbox();

        // Get the messages from the inbox
        Message[] msgs = inbox.getMessages();

        // Get the requested message
```

```
Message m = msgs[msg];

// Show the date
out.println("Date: " + m.getSentDate() + "<br>");

// Show the from addresses.
Address a[] = m.getFrom();
out.println("From: " + formatAddresses(a) + "<br>");

// Show the to addresses
a = m.getRecipients(Message.RecipientType.TO);
out.println("To: " + formatAddresses(a) + "<br>");

// Show the copy addresses
a = m.getRecipients(Message.RecipientType.CC);
out.println("Cc: " + formatAddresses(a) + "<br>");

// Show the subject
String s = m.getSubject();
if (s == null)
{
    s = "";
}
out.println("Subject: <b>" + s + "</b><br><hr>");

// Display the message
Object o = m.getContent();

// Figure out what kind of message we have
if (m.isMimeType("text/plain"))
{
    // Plain text message
    out.println("<pre>" + o + "</pre>");
}
else if (m.isMimeType("multipart/*"))
{
    // Multi-part message
    Multipart mp = (Multipart) o;

    // Loop through the parts
    for (int j = 0; j < mp.getCount(); j++)
    {
        Part part = mp.getBodyPart(j);

        // Get the content type of this part
```

```
                String contentType = part.getContentType();
                if (contentType == null)
                {
                    out.println("Bad content type for part " + j);
                    continue;
                }
                ContentType ct = new ContentType(contentType);

                if (j != 0)
                {
                    out.println("<hr>");
                }

                // Plain text part
                if (ct.match("text/plain"))
                {
                    out.println("<pre>" + part.getContent() + "</pre>");
                }
                else
                {
                    String desc = "Attachment ";
                    s = part.getFileName();
                    if (s != null)
                    {
                        desc += s;
                    }

                    // Generate a URL for this part
                    out.println("<td><a href=\"" +
                                uri + "?" + FORM_ACTION + "=" +
                                ACTION_VIEW + "&" + FORM_MSG + "=" + msg

                                "&" + FORM_PART + "=" + j +
                                "\">" + desc + "</a>");
                }
            }
        }
        else
        {
            // Unknown MIME type
            out.println(m.getContentType());
        }
    }
    catch (MessagingException ex)
```

```
        {
            out.println("<br>");
            out.println("ERROR: " + ex.getMessage());
        }

        // Wrap up
        out.println("</body>");
        out.println("</html>");
        out.flush();
    }
```

An example multipart message is shown next:

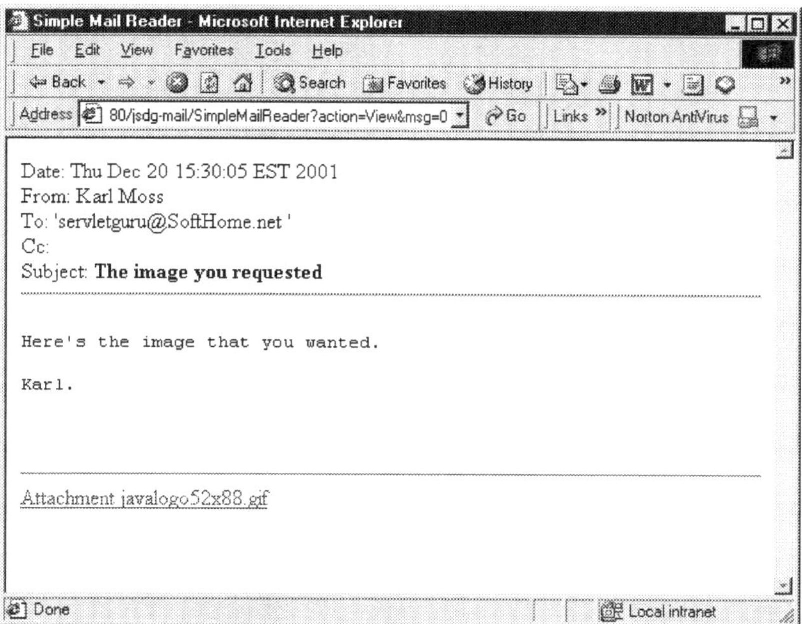

Sending Mail Using JavaMail

I think you will soon agree that sending messages using JavaMail is even easier than using the SmtpClient we explored earlier. You don't need to worry about setting message headers or be concerned about output streams. The following code is used to send a message with JavaMail. Once a new message object is created, it is a simple matter of setting who the message is from, all the recipients, the subject of the message, and the message body. Once this is complete, the transport protocol is used to send the message off into cyberspace.

```
/**
 * Sends the composed message. Note that the 'To' and 'Cc'
 * fields can contain multiple addresses separated by
 * either a comma or space.
 *
 * @param req The request from the client
 * @param resp The response from the servlet
 * @param mailUser The current SimpleMailUser
 */
public void sendMessage(HttpServletRequest req,
                        HttpServletResponse resp,
                        SimpleMailUser mailUser)
    throws ServletException, IOException
{
    // Set the content type of the response
    resp.setContentType("text/html");

    // Get the PrintWriter to write the response
    PrintWriter out = resp.getWriter();

    // Create the HTML form
    out.println("<html>");
    out.println("<head>");
    out.println("<title>" + FORM_TITLE + "</title>");
    out.println("<body>");

    // Get the form input fields
    String from = req.getParameter(FORM_FROM);
    String to = req.getParameter(FORM_TO);
    String cc = req.getParameter(FORM_CC);
    String subject = req.getParameter(FORM_SUBJECT);
    String msg = req.getParameter(FORM_MSG);

    // Validate
    if ((from == null) || (from.trim().length() == 0))
    {
        out.println("'From' name must be given");
    }
    else if ((to == null) || (to.trim().length() == 0))
    {
        out.println("'To' address(es) must be given");
    }
    else
    {
```

```
        try
        {
            // Create a new message
            Message m = new MimeMessage(mailUser.getSession());

            InternetAddress[] iAddr = null;

            // Set the 'from' address
            m.setFrom(new InternetAddress(from));

            // Save the 'from' address in the mail user object
            mailUser.setFromName(from);

            // Set the 'to' address(es)
            iAddr = InternetAddress.parse(to, false);
            m.setRecipients(Message.RecipientType.TO, iAddr);

            // Set the 'cc' address(es) if given
            if ((cc != null) && (cc.trim().length() > 0))
            {
                iAddr = InternetAddress.parse(cc, false);
                m.setRecipients(Message.RecipientType.CC, iAddr);
            }

            // Set the subject
            m.setSubject(subject);

            // Set the message
            m.setText(msg);

            // Send the message on its way!
            Transport.send(m);

            // Redirect to ourselves to re-display the inbox
            String me = req.getRequestURI();
            resp.sendRedirect(me);
        }
        catch (Exception ex)
        {
            out.println("Unable to send message: " + ex.getMessage());
        }
    }

    // Wrap up
```

```
        out.println("</body>");
        out.println("</html>");
        out.flush();
    }
```

The message entry form follows. This simple form only allows a simple text message to be sent, but JavaMail also provides an easy interface for sending multipart messages as well.

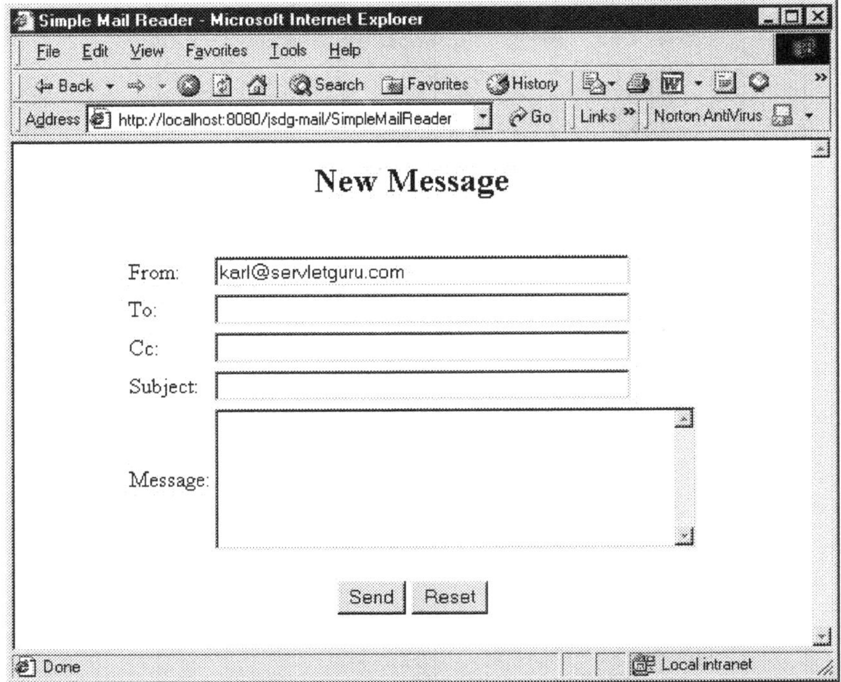

What's Missing?

The SimpleMailReader servlet isn't full-featured, nor does it even come close to exploiting all the features of the JavaMail API. I'll leave that as an exercise for you! Among other things, the JavaMail API can be used to do the following:

- Delete messages
- Forward messages
- Create multipart messages

Incorporating these features into a servlet-based mail system wouldn't be very difficult, especially since using the JavaMail API makes everything easy. One important reminder: not all service providers (such as the POP3 provider) can or will implement every feature defined in the JavaMail API. Some providers may not allow the deleting of messages, for example, so be prepared to handle any errors that may occur.

Summary

This chapter has been devoted to sending e-mail messages from Java applications, which, in our case, were servlets. We discussed different approaches for sending e-mail messages, such as opening a raw socket connection, using convenience classes, and using the powerful JavaMail API. That was followed by examples of how to use a convenience class provided by Sun named SmtpClient, and how to retrieve and send messages using the JavaMail API. What is the best way to send e-mail? I recommend using the approach that best suits your needs; in many cases, the SmtpClient class will provide all the functionality that you need, while more demanding requirements may necessitate the use of the robust JavaMail API.

CHAPTER

15

Using Servlets and Native Code

IN THIS CHAPTER:

JNI Overview

Obligatory Hello World

Invoking Java Methods from C

Listing ODBC Data Sources

Summary

In some situations, you may need to jump out of the Java environment and access some resources only available from native code (which is assumed to be C for the purposes of this chapter). Maybe you've got existing libraries that you would like to utilize, or perhaps you have a database product that can only be accessed via a C interface. Maybe you know that you will be running on a certain platform and want to take advantage of some features not available in Java, or want to implement some time-critical code in a lower-level language. In any case, Java allows you to do this by way of the Java Native Interface (JNI).

JNI Overview

The JNI is part of the core JDK and provides a framework for interfacing to native code. The native code that you use is, of course, not easily portable across different hardware platforms (and certainly doesn't happen automatically), so keep in mind that by using native code, you take away one of the major advantages of using Java.

The JNI framework allows your native code to utilize Java objects in much the same way that you are used to using them from within Java. Native methods not only can use Java objects passed as arguments, but can also create Java objects and return them back to the caller. Native methods even possess the ability to update Java objects as well.

But JNI isn't just a one-way street; native methods can also make Java method calls. Using JNI, you can take advantage of all the capabilities built into the Java programming language from native methods. Using the Invocation API, you can locate the methods available with a particular Java object, invoke methods, pass parameters, and retrieve return values. You can also catch exceptions thrown by Java methods and, perhaps more importantly, throw Java exceptions from native methods that will be handled by the Java application.

More information about JNI, as well as complete documentation, can be found at http://java.sun.com/j2se/1.3/docs/guide/jni/index.html.

Obligatory Hello World

No example using C would be complete without showing how to write a simple "Hello World" program. Our first example will use JNI to return a text string, containing the "Hello World" message, from a native program written in C to a simple Java servlet. Before getting started, let's take a look at the basic steps of developing native methods for Java:

1. Design the interface. Before you can get started using native methods, you need to design the methods, parameters, return values, and exception types that you will be using. This is easy for new applications since you can start with a clean slate. If you are using an existing library that you now want to utilize from Java, you will most likely need to create a "wrapper" native method that your Java application can invoke, which will then invoke the method from your library.
2. Create the Java class that defines the native methods. You declare native methods using the Java method modifier of "native."
3. Generate a header file for the native methods using the javah tool (with the -jni switch) that is provided with the JDK. Once the header file has been generated, you can use the method signatures that were created to implement the method.
4. Implement the native method in your language of choice, such as C, C++, or Assembler. If you are using an existing library, the implementation may be as simple as calling a library method directly. This is exactly how the JDBC-ODBC Bridge works, and we'll be taking a look at an example later in this chapter that uses other functionality of the ODBC API that illustrates this notion.
5. Compile the native code and create a shared library file (either a shared object for Unix, or a dynamic link library for Windows).
6. Run the Java application. The Java application is responsible for loading the shared library so that it is available for use.

Let's use these basic steps to create a Java servlet that retrieves a "Hello World" message from a native method.

Design the Interface

Before we get into the fun part of writing code, we need to figure out what the interface between Java and our native code will look like. For our simple "Hello World" example, all we need is a single method that returns a message string to the calling application:

```
String getMessage();
```

If you were creating a native interface for an existing library, especially for one that requires many different types of objects as parameters, designing the interface would be more of a challenge. The JNI documentation has further information about passing parameters, as well as how data types map between Java and C.

Create the Java Class

Now that we know what the native interface looks like, it's time to write the Java code that will declare the native methods:

```
package com.omh.nativeCode;

import javax.servlet.*;
import javax.servlet.http.*;
import java.io.IOException;
import java.io.PrintWriter;

/**
 * This servlet uses native code to get a "Hello World" message
 */
public class HelloWorld
        extends HttpServlet
{
    /**
     * Use a static initializer to load the native code that
     * is contained within a library. This initializer is
     * called when the class loader first loads this class.
     */
    static
    {
        System.out.println("Loading HelloWorld Library");
        System.loadLibrary("HelloWorld");
    }

    public void doGet(HttpServletRequest req,
                      HttpServletResponse resp)
        throws ServletException, IOException
    {
        // Set the content type of the response
        resp.setContentType("text/html");

        // Get the PrintWriter to write the response
        PrintWriter out = resp.getWriter();
```

```
        // Create the header
        out.println("<html>");
        out.println("<head>");
        out.println("<title>Hello World Using Native Code</title>");
        out.println("</head>");
        out.println("<body><center>");
        out.println("Native code returning: " + getMessage());

        // Wrap up
        out.println("</body>");
        out.println("</html>");
        out.flush();
    }

    /**
     * Gets a message from a native library
     * @return A message
     */
    public native String getMessage();

}
```

Notice the use of the “native” keyword. This method modifier tells the Java compiler that the implementation for the method can be found within a shared library file. The great thing about using native methods in Java is that the caller doesn’t know (or care) that the method isn’t written in Java. In fact, many standard Java methods are actually written in native code (many of the methods in the java.io package are native, for example).

You may also notice the use of a static initializer, which gets invoked (only once) when the class is loaded for the first time (this differs from a constructor that gets invoked whenever an instance of the class is created). This is a great time to load the shared library using the System.loadLibrary method. Loading the library into the HelloWorld class maps the implementation of the native method to its implementation.

Generate the Header File

Now that we have defined the native method in Java, it’s time to generate a header file that contains the C function signatures for the corresponding native methods. The JDK comes with a utility named javah, which investigates the class given and generates the method signatures for each native method. The general format of the command is as follows (refer to the JDK documentation for more information about the javah command):

```
javah -jni <class name>
```

By default, javah creates a new header file in the same directory as the class file. The name of the header file is the full package name with all periods replaced with underscores:

```
javah -jni com.omh.nativeCode.HelloWorld
```

This generates the following file:

```
com_omh_nativeCode_HelloWorld.h
```

The contents of the generated header file follow:

```
/* DO NOT EDIT THIS FILE - it is machine generated */
#include <jni.h>
/* Header for class com_omh_nativeCode_HelloWorld */

#ifndef _Included_com_omh_nativeCode_HelloWorld
#define _Included_com_omh_nativeCode_HelloWorld
#ifdef __cplusplus
extern "C" {
#endif
/* Inaccessible static: lStrings */
/*
 * Class:     com_omh_nativeCode_HelloWorld
 * Method:    getMessage
 * Signature: ()Ljava/lang/String;
 */
JNIEXPORT jstring JNICALL Java_com_omh_nativeCode_HelloWorld_getMessage
  (JNIEnv *, jobject);

#ifdef __cplusplus
}
#endif
#endif
```

If the HelloWorld class defined any other native methods, they would appear in the same header file. You may be wondering why the native method declaration contains two arguments, even though our original getMessage method had none. JNI dictates that every native method contain the same first two parameters, which are the Java environment handle and a reference to the current object. The environment handle, JNIEnv, is an interface pointer that gives your native code access to a wide variety of methods to help you bridge between your native code and Java (such as creating objects, invoking methods, and so forth). The current object pointer is a handle back to the object that invoked the native method; in essence, the "this" variable from Java.

Implement the Native Methods

Now you can get down to business and start writing native code. The methods that you write must be implemented using the same method signatures that were generated by javah. The following shows the simple implementation for our getMessage method:

```
#include <windows.h>
#include <jni.h>
#include "com_omh_nativeCode_HelloWorld.h"

#define HELLO "Hello World"

/*
 * Class:     com_omh_nativeCode_HelloWorld
 * Method:    getMessage
 * Signature: ()Ljava/lang/String;
 */
JNIEXPORT jstring JNICALL
  Java_com_omh_nativeCode_HelloWorld_getMessage
    (JNIEnv *env, jobject caller)
{
    return (*env)->NewStringUTF(env, HELLO);
}
```

Nothing too complicated here. The getMessage() method was implemented using the generated method signature, and the message text is returned by creating a new Java string using the JNIEnv interface (see the JDK documentation for a full listing of all the JNIEnv interface methods). Traditional HelloWorld examples use printf to display the "Hello World" message, but this serves little use from within a servlet.

The native code also includes the generated header file as well as jni.h, which contains definitions required to interact with the Java run-time system. The JNI headers are divided into two groups: common headers and platform-specific headers. The common headers can be found in the <java home>/include directory. The platform-specific headers are located underneath the include directory, such as <java home>/include/win32 or <java home>/include/solaris.

Compile the Native Code and Create the Shared Library

Now that you have implemented the native methods, it's time to compile the code and create a shared library. The way that you compile and create libraries is very machine-specific.

For Solaris, the following is the general command for creating the HelloWorld shared object:

```
cc -G -I<java home>/include -I<java home>/include/solaris
    HelloWorld.c -o HelloWorld
```

For Microsoft Visual C++, the following is the general command for creating the HelloWorld dynamic link library:

```
cl -I<java home>/include -I<java home>/include/win32 -LD
    HelloWorld.c -FeHelloWorld
```

Note that the commands may differ depending upon the compiler and operating system in use. Another way to create the library is to use an IDE (such as Microsoft Developer's Studio) to create the project. Just be sure to add the path to the JNI headers. You can name the shared library anything that you want; the name simply needs to match that of the library loaded in the static initializer of the Java class. Also, when loading the library via Java, it is not necessary to specify the library extension (such as .so or .dll) since the appropriate extension will be added by the run-time system.

Exercise the Native Code

Let's give our native code a try! But before we do, make sure that you move the shared library to a location where it will be found by the Java Virtual Machine. The VM is going to search all of the paths listed in the "java.library.path" system variable (for Windows, this will include the PATH entries). Note that the servlet specification does not address where native code should be placed within a web application, since loading native code is a function of the VM, not the servlet container. The following shows the result of our HelloWorld servlet. Not very exciting, but our native code is being executed.

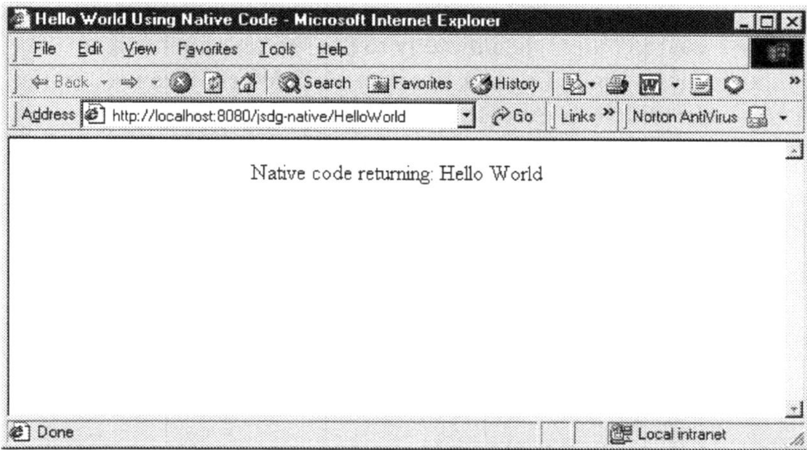

Invoking Java Methods from C

So now you've seen how to invoke a native method from Java. What if you want to turn the tables and call Java from a native method? JNI once again comes to the rescue. Using features provided by JNI, it is quite easy to call Java methods, pass arguments, get return values, and throw exceptions. To illustrate just how easy this is, let's expand on our simple HelloWorld example. Instead of returning a "Hello World" message back to the servlet, let's pass the servlet output stream to the native method and print the message directly to the output stream. This will require us to invoke the println() message directly through our native code. We'll first need to add a new native method declaration:

```
/**
 * Gets a message from a native library
 * @return A message
 */
public native String getMessage();

/**
 * Prints a message to the print stream
```

```
 * @param out The print stream
 */
public native void printMessage(PrintWriter out);
```

This new native method, called printMessage(), will be passed the PrintWriter that can then be used to output data directly to the servlet output stream. The following shows the generated header file after HelloWorld.java is compiled and javah (with the -jni switch) is executed:

```
/* DO NOT EDIT THIS FILE - it is machine generated */
#include <jni.h>
/* Header for class com_omh_nativeCode_HelloWorld */

#ifndef _Included_com_omh_nativeCode_HelloWorld
#define _Included_com_omh_nativeCode_HelloWorld
#ifdef __cplusplus
extern "C" {
#endif
/* Inaccessible static: lStrings */
/*
 * Class:     com_omh_nativeCode_HelloWorld
 * Method:    getMessage
 * Signature: ()Ljava/lang/String;
 */
JNIEXPORT jstring JNICALL Java_com_omh_nativeCode_HelloWorld_getMessage
  (JNIEnv *, jobject);

/*
 * Class:     com_omh_nativeCode_HelloWorld
 * Method:    printMessage
 * Signature: (Ljava/io/PrintWriter;)V
 */
JNIEXPORT void JNICALL Java_com_omh_nativeCode_HelloWorld_printMessage
  (JNIEnv *, jobject, jobject);

#ifdef __cplusplus
}
#endif
#endif
```

Note that the Java_com_omh_nativeCode_HelloWorld_printMessage method takes three arguments: the environment interface, the current object, and the PrintWriter (which is passed as a generic object type). Now that you have a handle to the object that was passed as a parameter, what do you do with it? The answer to that question is given next.

Calling a Java Method

Once you have a reference to a Java object, you can easily invoke an instance method by following these steps:

1. Call the GetObjectClass method, which is provided as part of the JNIEnv interface, with the object that contains the method(s) that you want to invoke. The GetObjectClass method will return a class object that is the type of the given object. This is synonymous with the Object.getClass method found in Java.
2. Once you have the class object, call the GetMethodID method (also part of the JNIEnv interface). GetMethodID will perform a lookup for the Java method in the given class object. As a convenience (and a nice one at that), if the method is not found (GetMethodID returns 0), an immediate return from the native method will cause a NoSuchMethodError to be thrown.
3. Invoke the method. This involves a method that is part of the JNIEnv interface, which, in our case, is called CallVoidMethod. The JNIEnv interface provides a set of Call<type>Method methods, which will invoke a method with the corresponding return type. Thus, CallVoidMethod will invoke a method that returns nothing, while CallObjectMethod will invoke a method that returns some type of object (like a String). Note that the Call<type>Method methods take a variable list of arguments, so you pass whatever parameters are necessary to invoke the method. (Refer to the JNI documentation for a complete list of methods provided with the JNIEnv interface.)

Each one of these steps is performed in the native implementation of printMessage(). The only tricky part here is forming the method signature to use when calling GetMethodID():

```
/*
 * Class:     com_omh_nativeCode_HelloWorld
 * Method:    printMessage
 * Signature: (Ljava/io/PrintWriter;)V
```

```
 */
JNIEXPORT void JNICALL
  Java_com_omh_nativeCode_HelloWorld_printMessage
    (JNIEnv *env, jobject caller, jobject out)
{
    jclass jcls;
    jmethodID jmid;

    // Get the PrintWriter class and find the println method
    jcls = (*env)->GetObjectClass(env, out);
    if (jcls) {
        jmid = (*env)->GetMethodID(env, jcls, "println",
                                   "(Ljava/lang/String;)V");
        if (jmid == 0) {
            return;
        }

        // Invoke the println method on the PrintStream object
        (*env)->CallVoidMethod(env, out, jmid,
                               (*env)->NewStringUTF(env, HELLO));
    }
}
```

Forming Method Signatures

If you look closely at the previous listing, you will notice that the println() method is found using GetMethodID(). The fourth parameter is the method signature, which, if you are not familiar with the JVM-type signatures, may look a little strange. The general format of the method signature is as follows:

```
"(argument-types)return-type"
```

The println() method takes a String parameter (Ljava/lang/String;) and has a void return type (V). There are several rules for creating the method signature as well as symbols for primitive types (such as *I* for int). Instead of bothering with these rules and symbols, I find it easier to use the built-in javap command to list all of the signatures for a given class.

javap, which is the Java class file disassembler, will create a listing of the method signatures that you can then cut and paste into your GetMethodID() call. The following shows the partial output that javap generated for java.io.PrintWriter. The -s switch outputs the method signatures, and the -p switch causes javap to include private members (methods and fields) as well.

```
javap -s -p java.io.PrintWriter
Compiled from PrintWriter.java
public class java.io.PrintWriter extends java.io.Writer {
    public void flush();
      /*    ()V    */
    public void close();
      /*    ()V    */
    public void write(char[], int, int);
      /*    ([CII)V    */
    public void write(char[]);
      /*    ([C)V    */
    public void print(java.lang.String);
      /*    (Ljava/lang/String;)V    */
    public void println(java.lang.String);
      /*    (Ljava/lang/String;)V    */
}
```

See It In Action

Just like the first incarnation of the HelloWorld servlet, there's not a whole lot to see. The following shows the HTML page generated by the servlet and native code:

The HelloWorld servlet loaded a native library and invoked a native method, and that method then called back into the JVM and invoked a Java method. Wow! This is so exciting that I think I'll say it again—backwards. Wow!

Listing ODBC Data Sources

Now that we've got the trivial "Hello World" application behind us, it's time to write some native code that we can really use. One frequently encountered problem when using the JDBC-ODBC Bridge on NT is determining which Data Source names are available to the servlet engine. When administering ODBC, most people add "user" Data Source names (mostly because this is the default). What happens, though, is that most servlet containers can run as an NT service; applications running as an NT service only have access to "system" Data Source names. Thus, the "user" Data Source names that work properly for Java applications cannot be found when attempting to perform a JDBC connection from a servlet.

The solution? Let's develop some native code to query the ODBC Driver Manager for a list of the Data Source names that are currently available. Executing this code from within a servlet and giving the user a list of valid Data Source names should eliminate all questions as to what ODBC Data Sources can be found by servlets using the JDBC-ODBC Bridge. So, why can't we just use JDBC to query the Data Source names? The simple answer is that it is not supported in the API. Data Source names are a very ODBC-specific notion, one that doesn't fit well into the generic JDBC API.

Let's get started. The first thing we need to do is design the native interface. Since all we need to do is call a few ODBC API functions, we can just adopt the same method names and similar function arguments. In the HelloWorld servlet, I chose to embed the native method definitions in the servlet class. A much cleaner way to do this, in my opinion, is to create a separate utility class that contains all of the native method calls:

```
package com.omh.nativeCode;

/**
 * This class defines all of the native methods used to bridge
 * from Java to ODBC.
 */
public class JavaToODBC
{
    /**
     * Use a static initializer to load the native code that
     * is contained within a library. This initializer is
```

```
     * called when the class loader first loads this class.
     */
    static
    {
        System.out.println("Loading JavaToODBC Library");
        System.loadLibrary("JavaToODBC");
    }

    /**
     * Creates an environment handle and initializes the ODBC
     * call level interface. SQLAllocEnv must be called
     * prior to calling any other ODBC functions.
     * @return The environment handle
     */
    public static native int SQLAllocEnv() throws Exception;

    /**
     * Frees the environment handle and releases all memory
     * associated with the environment handle
     * @param The environment handle
     */
    public static native void SQLFreeEnv(int henv) throws Exception;

    /**
     * Returns information about the next data source. The first
     * time this method is called the first data source will
     * be used; any subsequent calls will return the next data
     * source.
     * @param henv The environment handle
     * @param dataSource The DataSource object which will hold
     * the information for the data source
     * @return true if the data source is valid; false if no more
     * data source names were found
     */
    public static native boolean SQLDataSources(int henv, DataSource ds)
        throws Exception;
}
```

A common design issue that you will encounter is that many C functions will return multiple values via address pointers. ODBC is especially fond of using this technique, so what I like to do is create a class that will contain all of the data that is returned by a single function call. An instance of this class can be passed to the native method, and the native method can call back into the JVM and set the data in the object as necessary. One such data holder class, DataSource, holds the Data Source name and description:

```
package com.omh.nativeCode;

/**
 * This class represents a single ODBC data source
 */
public class DataSource
{
    String name;
    String desc;

    /**
     * Sets the data source name
     * @param name The data source name
     */
    public void setName(String value)
    {
        name = value;
    }

    /**
     * Gets the data source name
     * @return The data source name
     */
    public String getName()
    {
        return name;
    }

    /**
     * Sets the data source description
     * @param desc The data source description
     */
    public void setDescription(String value)
    {
        desc = value;
    }
```

```
    /**
     * Gets the data source description
     * @return The data source description
     */
    public String getDescription()
    {
        return desc;
    }
}
```

After compiling JavaToODBC, we need to generate the native code header. Once again, we'll be using javah to generate the header file:

```
javah -jni com.omh.nativeCode.JavaToODBC
```

Now that the method signatures have been created, it's time to implement the native methods (the code follows). Of special interest may be the throwException() method, which shows how to throw a Java exception that will be handled by the caller.

```
#include <windows.h>
#include <jni.h>
#include "sql.h"
#include "sqlext.h"
#include "com_omh_nativeCode_JavaToODBC.h"

/**
  * Helper function to throw an exception.
  * @param env JNIEnv interface pointer
  * @param cls The exception class name
  * @param desc The exception description
  */
void throwException(JNIEnv *env, char* cls, char* desc)
{
    jclass c;

    // Clear any pending exceptions
    (*env)->ExceptionDescribe(env);
    (*env)->ExceptionClear(env);

    // Load the exception class
    c = (*env)->FindClass(env, cls);

    // Make sure the class was found
```

```
    if (c) {

        // Throw the exception
        (*env)->ThrowNew(env, c, desc);
    }
}

/*
 * Class:     com_omh_nativeCode_JavaToODBC
 * Method:    SQLAllocEnv
 * Signature: ()I
 */
JNIEXPORT jint JNICALL
  Java_com_omh_nativeCode_JavaToODBC_SQLAllocEnv
    (JNIEnv *env, jclass cls)
{
    // The environment handle
    HENV henv;

    // The return code
    RETCODE retcode;

    // Allocate an environment handle
    retcode = SQLAllocEnv(&henv);

    // Throw an exception if the environment cannot be allocated
    if (retcode == SQL_ERROR) {
        throwException(env, "java/lang/Exception",
                       "Environment handle cannot be allocated");
        return 0;
    }

    return (jint) henv;
}

/*
 * Class:     com_omh_nativeCode_JavaToODBC
 * Method:    SQLFreeEnv
 * Signature: ()I
 */
JNIEXPORT void JNICALL
  Java_com_omh_nativeCode_JavaToODBC_SQLFreeEnv
    (JNIEnv *env, jclass cls, jint henv)
```

```
{
    // The return code
    RETCODE retcode;

    // Free the handle
    retcode = SQLFreeEnv((HENV) henv);

    // Check for errors
    if (retcode == SQL_ERROR) {
        throwException(env, "java/lang/Exception",
                       "Unable to free environment handle");
        return;
    }
    else if (retcode == SQL_INVALID_HANDLE) {
        throwException(env, "java/lang/Exception",
                       "Invalid environment handle");
        return;
    }
    return;
}

/*
 * Class:     com_omh_nativeCode_JavaToODBC
 * Method:    SQLDataSources
 * Signature: (Lcom/omh/nativeCode/DataSource;)Z
 */
JNIEXPORT jboolean JNICALL
  Java_com_omh_nativeCode_JavaToODBC_SQLDataSources
    (JNIEnv *env, jclass cls, jint henv, jobject dataSource)
{
    // Return code
    RETCODE retcode;

    // Storage for the name and description
    UCHAR szDSN[SQL_MAX_DSN_LENGTH + 1];
    UCHAR szDesc[255];

    // Actual length of name and description
    SWORD cbDSN;
    SWORD cbDesc;

    // A java class
    jclass jcls;
```

```
// A java method ID
jmethodID jmid;

// Make sure we've got a DataSource object to work with
if (!dataSource) {
    throwException(env, "java/lang/Exception",
                   "DataSource object is null");
    return FALSE;
}

// Get the next data source entry
retcode = SQLDataSources((HENV) henv, SQL_FETCH_NEXT,
                         &szDSN[0], (SWORD) sizeof(szDSN),
                         &cbDSN, &szDesc[0],
                         (SWORD) sizeof(szDesc), &cbDesc);

// Check for errors
if (retcode == SQL_ERROR) {
    throwException(env, "java/lang/Exception",
                   "Unable to get data source information");
    return FALSE;
}
else if (retcode == SQL_INVALID_HANDLE) {
    throwException(env, "java/lang/Exception",
                   "Invalid environment handle");
    return FALSE;
}
else if (retcode == SQL_NO_DATA_FOUND) {

    // End of data sources
    return FALSE;
}

// Get the DataSource class and find the setName method
jcls = (*env)->GetObjectClass(env, dataSource);
if (!jcls) {
    throwException(env, "java/lang/Exception",
                   "Unable to find DataSource class");
    return FALSE;
}
jmid = (*env)->GetMethodID(env, jcls, "setName",
                           "(Ljava/lang/String;)V");
```

```
    if (!jmid) {
        throwException(env, "java/lang/Exception",
                       "Unable to find DataSource.setName");
        return FALSE;
    }

    // Invoke the setName method on the DataSource object
    (*env)->CallVoidMethod(env, dataSource, jmid,
                           (*env)->NewStringUTF(env, szDSN));

    // Find the setDescription method
    jmid = (*env)->GetMethodID(env, jcls, "setDescription",
                               "(Ljava/lang/String;)V");
    if (!jmid) {
        throwException(env, "java/lang/Exception",
                       "Unable to find DataSource.setDescription");
        return FALSE;
    }

    // Invoke the setDescription method on the DataSource object
    (*env)->CallVoidMethod(env, dataSource, jmid,
                           (*env)->NewStringUTF(env, szDesc));

    return TRUE;
}
```

There are two simple methods that just wrap an ODBC function: SQLAllocEnv(), which allocates an ODBC environment handle, and SQLFreeEnv(), which frees it when the application is finished (I've left off the com_omh_nativeCode_JavaToODBC prefix). Most of the real work is done in the SQLDataSources() method. The first call to SQLDataSources() will return information about the first ODBC Data Source from the ODBC Driver Manager; any subsequent calls will return the next Data Source in the list. The return code will be set to SQL_NO_DATA_FOUND when the end of the Data Source list is reached. After retrieving information about a Data Source, the native code calls back into the JVM to set the data elements of the DataSource object. Notice how a null-terminated string in C is converted into a Java String in order to be passed to the "set" methods.

After compiling JavaToODBC.c and creating a shared library (don't forget to link with odbc32.lib and odbccp32.lib), be sure to move the resulting library to the proper location so that it can be found by the servlet container.

The next step is to write the servlet that will make the native method calls. This servlet, named DataSourceList, follows:

```
package com.omh.nativeCode;

import javax.servlet.*;
import javax.servlet.http.*;
import java.io.IOException;
import java.io.PrintWriter;

/**
 * This servlet uses native code to gather a list of the
 * current ODBC data sources.
 */
public class DataSourceList
        extends HttpServlet
{
    public void doGet(HttpServletRequest req,
                      HttpServletResponse resp)
    throws ServletException, IOException
    {
        // Set the content type of the response
        resp.setContentType("text/html");

        // Get the PrintWriter to write the response
        PrintWriter out = resp.getWriter();

        // Create the header
        out.println("<html>");
        out.println("<head>");
        out.println("<title>ODBC Data Source List</title>");
        out.println("</head>");
        out.println("<body><center>");
        out.println("<h2>ODBC Data Sources Available To Servlets " +
                    "Running in the Current Servlet Container</h2>");
        out.println("<br>");
        out.println("<table border>");
        out.println("<tr><th>Data Source Name</th>");
        out.println("<th>Description</th></tr>");

        int henv = 0;

        try
        {
            // Allocate an environment handle
            henv = JavaToODBC.SQLAllocEnv();
```

```
}
catch (Exception ex)
{
    out.println("ERROR: Unable to allocate environment");
}

// Loop through the data sources until the end of file
// is reached
while (true)
{
    // Create a new DataSource object to hold the
    // data source attributes (name, description)
    DataSource ds = new DataSource();
    boolean b = false;

    try
    {
        // Make a native ODBC call to get the next data source
        // entry. The first call will return the first data source;
        // any subsequent calls will return the next data source
        b = JavaToODBC.SQLDataSources(henv, ds);
    }
    catch (Exception ex)
    {
        ex.printStackTrace();
        out.println("</table><br>ERROR: " + ex.getMessage());
        break;
    }

    // SQLDataSources returns false if there are no more
    // data sources
    if (!b)
    {
        break;
    }

    // Add this data source to the table
    out.println("<tr><td>" + ds.getName() +
                "</td><td>" + ds.getDescription() + "</td></tr>");
}

if (henv != 0)
{
    try
    {
        // Free the environment handle
        JavaToODBC.SQLFreeEnv(henv);
```

```
            }
            catch (Exception ex)
            {
                // Ignore any errors
            }
        }

        // Wrap up
        out.println("</table></center>");
        out.println("</body>");
        out.println("</html>");
        out.flush();
    }
}
```

Nothing complex here; just allocate the ODBC environment handle, call SQLDataSources() until the end of the file is reached, and then free the environment handle. Notice how an instance of the DataSource object is passed to the native method. When the method returns, the DataSource object will have been updated with the information for the next Data Source in the list. It is quite simple to get the data from the object and create an HTML table like the one that follows.

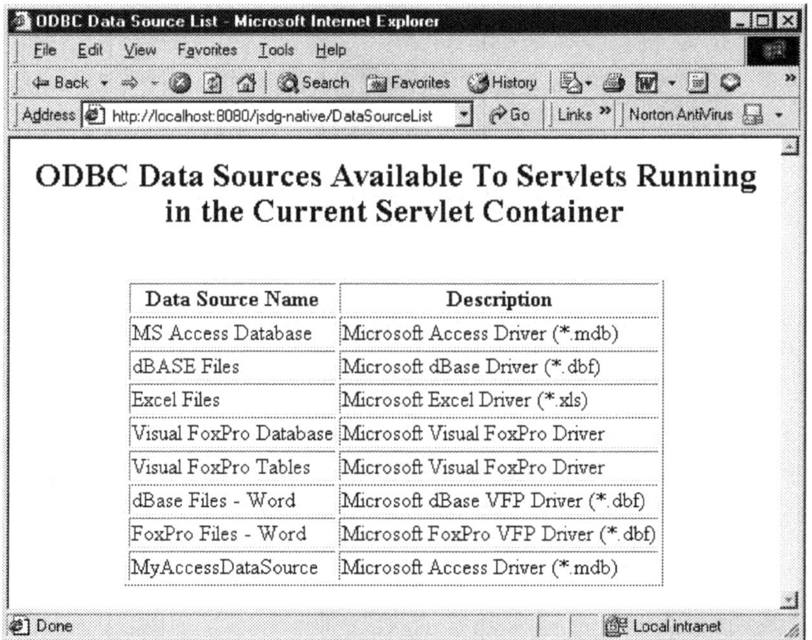

Using the DataSourceList servlet is a great way to discover which ODBC Data Sources your servlet container has access to. It would also be quite easy to use this information to provide the user with a choice of Data Sources to connect with via JDBC, similar to the ODBC SQLBrowseConnect() function.

Summary

In this chapter, we have focused on how to utilize native code from Java applications, specifically Java servlets. We developed a simple "Hello World" servlet, and demonstrated how to make Java method calls from within a native method. We then created a servlet that listed all of the current ODBC Data Source names available to servlets using the JDBC-ODBC Bridge. This servlet was used to show how to throw exceptions from native code, as well as other techniques for designing native interfaces.

CHAPTER

16

Performance Tips and Tricks

IN THIS CHAPTER:

Avoid String Concatenation

Avoid Debugging Statements

Avoid Use of StringTokenizer

Avoid Unnecessary Synchronization

Use a Connection Pool

Use a PreparedStatement

Cache Expensive Objects

Tune Your Servlet Container

Tune Your Virtual Machine

Summary

In this, the final chapter, we'll take a look at some general tips to maintain good performance when writing servlets. I will not attempt to quantify any of these suggestions; there are such a wide variety of processors and Virtual Machines that trying to compare performance timings can be very misleading. Keep in mind that as VMs continue to improve and processors continue to get faster, the overall relevance of the following tips may diminish. Even so, coding for performance will pay off in the long run, especially when creating servlets that will be used by hundreds, or even thousands, of concurrent users. Even small gains in performance can provide huge gains in scalability.

Avoid String Concatenation

Even though I've used String concatenation throughout this book, mostly to improve readability, you should try to avoid this habit and use a StringBuffer instead. For example, the following:

```
String a = "Hello ";
String b = "Karl";
String c = a + b;
```

should be replaced with this:

```
String a = "Hello";
String b = "Karl";
StringBuffer sb = new StringBuffer(a);
sb.append(b);
String c = sb.toString();
```

String concatenation results in a new String and StringBuffer instance to be created by the Virtual Machine and reassigned to the new String value; each old String is released for garbage collection, resulting in many short-lived objects. Note that this is not true for String literals; the compiler will optimize "Hello " + "Karl" as "Hello Karl" automatically.

Also, if you have a good idea of how large the final String may be, you can also preallocate the size of the StringBuffer by using a different constructor:

```
StringBuffer sb = new StringBuffer(256);
```

A very nice feature of the StringBuffer class is that the append() method returns the StringBuffer instance, so you can cascade the append() calls:

```
StringBuffer sb = new StringBuffer();
sb.append("Hello ").append("Karl");
```

Avoid Debugging Statements

Many developers like to use System.out.println() for debugging. Sometimes it's just a lot easier to use this crude debugging method instead of firing up an IDE. Some developers will move the actual printing of debug messages to a common method so that it can be turned on and off:

```
public void debug(String msg)
{
    if (debugEnabled)
    {
        System.out.println(msg);
    }
}
```

You can even add a timestamp to each message when you print it, or change the target of the message (to a file, for example). In your servlet, you could then simply call the debug routine:

```
debug("The value is " + someValue);
```

To get debug messages, you simply need to make sure that debugging is enabled in the debug() method. Sounds great, doesn't it?

Look out! This is a nonobvious performance drain. You will end up performing String concatenation of the message to be debugged before you realize whether the message will even be used. If debugging is not enabled, you will still end up creating unused String messages. I'm not suggesting that you throw away using a debug() method, but you should provide some way for the caller to check to see if debugging is enabled first before calling the debug() method:

```
if (isDebugEnabled())
{
    debug("The value is " + someValue);
}
```

Avoid Use of StringTokenizer

A common performance hotspot that I have run across when using profiling tools is the use of java.util.StringTokenizer. While there is convenience in using the StringTokenizer, there is a tradeoff in performance. If you are using a StringTokenizer simply to scan for a single delimiter, it is very easy to use simple String functions instead.

Consider the following example, which uses StringTokenizer to parse a String:

```
import java.util.StringTokenizer;

public class TestStringTokenizer
{
    public static void main(String[] args)
    {
        String s = "a,b,c,d";

        StringTokenizer st = new StringTokenizer(s, ",");
        while (st.hasMoreTokens())
        {
            String token = st.nextToken();
            System.out.println(token);
        }
    }
}
```

Executing this application will result in the following output:

```
a
b
c
d
```

The following code replaces the StringTokenizer with a loop that uses String.indexOf() to find the next delimiter:

```
public class TestIndexOf
{
    public static void main(String[] args)
    {
        String s = "a,b,c,d";
        int begin = 0;
```

```
        int end = s.indexOf(",");
        while (true)
        {
            String token = null;
            if (end == -1)
            {
                token = s.substring(begin);
            }
            else
            {
                token = s.substring(begin, end);
            }

            System.out.println(token);

            // End if there are no more delimiters
            if (end == -1) break;
            begin = end + 1;
            end = s.indexOf(",", begin);
        }
    }
}
```

Is it easier to read and understand? Definitely not, but it is much more efficient than using the StringTokenizer. Life is full of tradeoffs; you sometimes must choose between readability and performance.

Avoid Unnecessary Synchronization

You always need to remember that servlets operate in a multithreaded, multiuser environment, with the multiple threads working with a single instance of your servlet. When you decide to synchronize a block of code, it will result in only a single thread being able to operate on your servlet at any point in time.

There are certainly cases in which you need to synchronize access to a particular block of code, such as generating a unique ID or atomically updating a series of counters. Instead of synchronizing an entire method (or worse yet, an entire class), synchronize only the blocks of code that really need to be synchronized. It is easy to synchronize an entire method just to be safe; try to avoid this if at all possible.

Use a Connection Pool

Chapter 9 covered the benefits of using a JDBC connection pool, but it deserves another mention. I cannot stress enough how performance-critical it is to use a pool of JDBC connections to provide the response times that your users will demand.

You should find that using a connection pool will take your average connection times from seconds to milliseconds.

Use a PreparedStatement

When using JDBC it is tempting to always use a java.sql.Statement object to execute your queries. While this is easy, it may not be the most efficient way to query your database. If you are executing the same query multiple times, you may want to consider using a java.sql.PreparedStatement instead. By using a PreparedStatement the database engine will only have to evaluate the SQL statement you are using once. Evaluating a SQL statement can tend to be expensive. The use of a PreparedStatement is covered in Chapter 9.

Cache Expensive Objects

In the early days of Java, it was advantageous to cache just about every kind of object in an effort to eliminate object creation altogether. With today's Virtual Machines, object creation is not nearly as taxing on the system, and the additional overhead of maintaining a cache may outweigh the benefits of avoiding another object instantiation. There are some types of objects, however, that may prove to be expensive to instantiate. Certainly, a JDBC Connection object classifies as being expensive to create, but there are many other objects that you may want to consider caching. Which ones? This is where some time with a code profiler comes in handy. Most of the time, these objects will be ones that you have developed. I would suggest taking a hard look to see what is going on in the constructors of your objects; if lots of other objects are being created during construction, your single object may actually result in many smaller objects being created as well. If this is the case, you may be better off creating a cache (or pool) of these objects, much like we did in Chapter 9 for JDBC connections.

One simple technique that I like to use is to create a java.util.Stack to serve as a cache. When you need an object, pop() one off the Stack; if the Stack is empty, create a new instance of the object you need. When you are finished with the object, push() it back onto the Stack. The Stack will grow as the number of concurrent users increases. The technique is shown in the following servlet, which uses a Stack to cache SimpleDateFormat objects (which are expensive to instantiate and are not thread-safe):

```
import javax.servlet.*;
import javax.servlet.http.*;
import java.io.IOException;
import java.io.PrintWriter;
import java.util.Stack;
import java.util.Date;
import java.util.EmptyStackException;
import java.text.DateFormat;
import java.text.SimpleDateFormat;

/**
 * Simple servlet that gets the current date and time. Uses a simple
 * cache (a Stack) for the Date objects.
 */
public class GetDate
        extends HttpServlet
{
    // The cache of Date objects
    Stack dateCache = new Stack();

    public void doGet(HttpServletRequest req,
                      HttpServletResponse resp)
        throws ServletException, IOException
    {
        // Get an output stream that takes into account
        // the proper character encoding
        PrintWriter out = resp.getWriter();

        // Print the HTML header to the output stream
        out.println("<html>");
        out.println("<head>");
        out.println("<title>The Server Date</title>");
        out.println("</head>");
        out.println("<h2>");

        // Get a DateFormat from the cache
        DateFormat dateFormat = getDateFormat();
```

```
        String now = dateFormat.format(new Date());

        out.println("The date/time on the server is: " + now);
        out.println("<br>");

        // We're done with the DateFormat. Put it back
        putDateFormat(dateFormat);

        // Wrap up
        out.println("</html>");
        out.flush();
    }

    /**
     * Get a DateFormat object from the cache. If one does not
     * exist, create a new one
     */
    public DateFormat getDateFormat()
    {
        DateFormat dateFormat = null;
        try
        {
            dateFormat = (DateFormat) dateCache.pop();
        }
        catch (EmptyStackException ex)
        {
            // Create a new Date object if the stack is empty
            dateFormat = new SimpleDateFormat("yyyy.MM.dd hh:mm:ss z");
        }
        return dateFormat;
    }

    /**
     * Puts the DateFormat object back into the cache
     */
    public void putDateFormat(DateFormat dateFormat)
    {
        dateCache.push(dateFormat);
    }
}
```

Tune Your Servlet Container

The servlet container you are using may also provide you with opportunities for optimization. Since there are numerous servlet containers, and they are all quite different in the way they are managed and configured, I will simply provide you with some general suggestions of areas that you might be able to tune:

- **Thread usage** Many servlet containers allow you to tune the number of threads that the container will use to serve requests. Increasing the number of threads may improve overall performance when the container is under load. Beware, however, that simply setting the thread count higher may result in system resources being used unnecessarily.
- **File read cache size** Some servlet container may maintain an internal cache to hold the contents of static files. Increasing the size of the cache may result in more files being retained in memory at the expense of more system memory being used.
- **Disable logging** Once you have your applications up and running, you may want to turn off any verbose (or debug) logging in your servlet container.
- **Disable servlet reloading** Many servlet containers support automatic reloading of servlet class files, allowing you to simply recompile a servlet and have it automatically reload. This turns out to be an expensive trick, because the servlet container must check the last-modified date of the servlet class file with each request. In production systems, you will most likely want to disable this feature.

In addition to these general suggestions I would advise you to read the documentation for the servlet container you are using for other tuning parameters.

Tune Your Virtual Machine

Perhaps one of the easiest ways to boost the performance of your servlet container is to tune the Virtual Machine. In most cases, you can increase the initial size of the heap. But be careful: Using a larger heap size decreases the frequency of garbage collection by the VM, but increases the time that the garbage collector takes when it does run. The heap size is controlled by the –mx option, but you should check the documentation for the particular VM you are using before attempting to modify the size of the heap.

Summary

In this chapter, we have focused on ways to ensure that your servlet performance is at a level that keeps your users happy. There are lots of common performance pitfalls when using Java, such as String concatenation or synchronization, that can have a negative impact on your application. Simply being aware of these pitfalls, and how to work around them, can help you to write efficient servlets.

Once you have written your servlets, there are also ways to boost performance by tuning the servlet container you are using, as well as the underlying Virtual Machine.

APPENDIX

A

The Servlet API

This appendix describes each class in the two main Servlet API packages:

```
javax.servlet
javax.servlet.http
```

Note that deprecated classes and methods are not listed, because they should not be used.

Filter

Interface name:	javax.servlet.Filter
Implemented by:	(none)
Extends:	(none)

A filter is an object that performs filtering tasks on the request to a resource (a servlet or static content), on the response from a resource, or on both.

Filters perform filtering in the doFilter() method. Every filter has access to a FilterConfig object from which it can obtain its initialization parameters, and a reference to the ServletContext, which it can use, for example, to load resources needed for filtering tasks.

Filters are configured in the deployment descriptor of a web application (see Chapter 6 for extensive examples).

Interface Summary

```
public interface javax.servlet.Filter
{
    public void init(javax.servlet.FilterConfig)
        throws javax.servlet.ServletException;
    public void doFilter(javax.servlet.ServletRequest,
        javax.servlet.ServletResponse, javax.servlet.FilterChain)
        throws java.io.IOException, javax.servlet.ServletException;
    public void destroy();
}
```

Method Detail

The following section describes all of the methods that are defined in the Filter interface.

init

```
public void init(javax.servlet.FilterConfig)
    throws javax.servlet.ServletException;
```

Called by the web container to indicate to a filter that it is being placed into service. The servlet container calls the init() method exactly once after instantiating the filter. The init() method must complete successfully before the filter is asked to do any filtering work.

The web container cannot place the filter into service if the init() method either throws a ServletException or does not return within a time period defined by the web container.

doFilter

```
public void doFilter(javax.servlet.ServletRequest,
    javax.servlet.ServletResponse, javax.servlet.FilterChain)
    throws java.io.IOException, javax.servlet.ServletException;
```

The doFilter() method of the Filter class is called by the container each time a request/response pair is passed through the chain due to a client request for a resource at the end of the chain. The FilterChain passed in to this method allows the filter to pass on the request and response to the next entity in the chain, or skip the next filter if necessary.

A typical implementation of this method would follow the following pattern:

1. Examine the request.
2. Optionally wrap the request object with a custom implementation to filter content or headers for input filtering.
3. Optionally wrap the response object with a custom implementation to filter content or headers for output filtering.
4. Either invoke the next entity in the chain using the FilterChain object chain.doFilter() or do not invoke the next entity in the filter chain to block the request processing.
5. Directly set headers on the response after invocation of the next entity in the filter chain.

destroy

```
public void destroy();
```

Called by the web container to indicate to a filter that it is being taken out of service. This method is only called after all threads within the filter's doFilter() method have exited or after a timeout period has passed. After the web container calls this method, it will not call the doFilter() method again on this instance of the filter.

This method gives the filter an opportunity to clean up any resources that are being held (for example, memory, file handles, and threads) and make sure that any persistent state is synchronized with the filter's current state in memory.

FilterChain

Interface name:	javax.servlet.FilterChain
Implemented by:	(none)
Extends:	(none)

A FilterChain is an object provided by the servlet container to the developer that gives a view into the invocation chain of a filtered request for a resource. Filters use the FilterChain to invoke the next filter in the chain, or if the calling filter is the last filter in the chain, to invoke the resource at the end of the chain.

Interface Summary

```
public interface javax.servlet.FilterChain
{
    public void doFilter(javax.servlet.ServletRequest,
        javax.servlet.ServletResponse)
        throws java.io.IOException, javax.servlet.ServletException;
}
```

Method Detail

The following section describes all of the methods that are defined in the FilterChain interface.

doFilter

```
public void doFilter(javax.servlet.ServletRequest,
    javax.servlet.ServletResponse)
    throws java.io.IOException, javax.servlet.ServletException;
```

Causes the next filter in the chain to be invoked, or if the calling filter is the last filter in the chain, causes the resource at the end of the chain to be invoked.

FilterConfig

Interface name:	javax.servlet.FilterConfig
Implemented by:	(none)
Extends:	(none)

A filter configuration object created by a servlet container used to pass information to a filter during initialization during the filter init() method.

Interface Summary

```
public interface javax.servlet.FilterConfig
{
    public java.lang.String getFilterName();
    public javax.servlet.ServletContext getServletContext();
    public java.lang.String getInitParameter(java.lang.String);
    public java.util.Enumeration getInitParameterNames();
}
```

Method Detail

The following section describes all of the methods that are defined in the FilterConfig interface.

getFilterName

```
public java.lang.String getFilterName();
```

Returns the filter name of this filter as defined in the deployment descriptor (web.xml).

getServletContext

```
public javax.servlet.ServletContext getServletContext();
```

Returns a reference to the ServletContext in which the filter is executing.

getInitParameter

```
public java.lang.String getInitParameter(java.lang.String);
```

Returns a String containing the value of the named initialization parameter, or null if the parameter does not exist. Initialization parameters are supplied in the deployment descriptor (web.xml). See Chapter 6 for examples of how to configure initialization parameters.

getInitParameterNames

```
public java.util.Enumeration getInitParameterNames();
```

Returns the names of the filter's initialization parameters as an Enumeration of String objects, or an empty Enumeration if the filter has no initialization parameters.

GenericServlet

Class name:	javax.servlet.GenericServlet
Superclass:	java.lang.Object
Direct subclasses:	javax.servlet.http.HttpServlet
Implements:	javax.servlet.Servlet javax.servlet.ServletConfig java.io.Serializable

Defines a generic, protocol-independent servlet. To write an HTTP servlet for use on the Web, extend javax.servlet.http.HttpServlet instead. GenericServlet may be directly extended by a servlet, although it's more common to extend a protocol-specific subclass such as HttpServlet.

GenericServlet makes writing servlets easier. It provides simple versions of the lifecycle methods init() and destroy(), and the methods in the ServletConfig interface. GenericServlet also implements the log() method, declared in the ServletContext interface.

To write a generic servlet, you need only override the abstract service() method.

Class Summary

```
public abstract class javax.servlet.GenericServlet
    extends java.lang.Object
    implements javax.servlet.Servlet,
               javax.servlet.ServletConfig,
               java.io.Serializable
{
    public javax.servlet.GenericServlet();
    public void destroy();
    public java.lang.String getInitParameter(java.lang.String);
    public java.util.Enumeration getInitParameterNames();
    public javax.servlet.ServletConfig getServletConfig();
    public javax.servlet.ServletContext getServletContext();
    public java.lang.String getServletInfo();
    public void init(javax.servlet.ServletConfig)
        throws javax.servlet.ServletException;
    public void init()
        throws javax.servlet.ServletException;
    public void log(java.lang.String);
    public void log(java.lang.String, java.lang.Throwable);
    public abstract void service(javax.servlet.ServletRequest,
        javax.servlet.ServletResponse)
        throws javax.servlet.ServletException, java.io.IOException;
    public java.lang.String getServletName();
}
```

Constructor Detail

The following section describes all of the methods that are defined in the GenericServlet class.

GenericServlet

```
public javax.servlet.GenericServlet();
```

Does nothing. All of the servlet initialization is done by one of the init() methods.

Method Detail

The following section describes all of the methods that are defined in the GenericFilter class.

destroy

```
public void destroy();
```

Called by the servlet container to indicate to a servlet that the servlet is being taken out of service.

getInitParameter

```
public java.lang.String getInitParameter(java.lang.String);
```

Returns a String containing the value of the named initialization parameter, or null if the parameter does not exist. This method is supplied for convenience. It gets the value of the named parameter from the servlet's ServletConfig object.

getInitParameterNames

```
public java.util.Enumeration getInitParameterNames();
```

Returns the names of the servlet's initialization parameters as an Enumeration of String objects, or an empty Enumeration if the servlet has no initialization parameters. This method is supplied for convenience. It gets the parameter names from the servlet's ServletConfig object.

getServletConfig

```
public javax.servlet.ServletConfig getServletConfig();
```

Returns this servlet's ServletConfig object, which was supplied in the init() method.

getServletContext

```
public javax.servlet.ServletContext getServletContext();
```

Returns a reference to the ServletContext in which this servlet is running. This method is supplied for convenience. It gets the context from the servlet's ServletConfig object.

getServletInfo

```
public java.lang.String getServletInfo();
```

Returns information about the servlet, such as author, version, and copyright. By default, this method returns an empty string. Override this method to have it return a meaningful value. Note that there is no standard that specifies the format of the value.

init

```
public void init(javax.servlet.ServletConfig)
    throws javax.servlet.ServletException;
```

Called by the servlet container to indicate to a servlet that the servlet is being placed into service. This implementation stores the ServletConfig object it receives from the servlet container for later use. When overriding this form of the method, call super.init(config).

init

```
public void init()
```

A convenience method that can be overridden so that there's no need to call super.init(config). Instead of overriding init(ServletConfig), simply override this method and it will be called by GenericServlet.init(ServletConfig config). The ServletConfig object can still be retrieved via getServletConfig().

log

```
public void log(java.lang.String);
```

Writes the specified message to a servlet log file in a servlet container-specific manner.

log

```
public void log(java.lang.String, java.lang.Throwable);
```

Writes an explanatory message and a stack trace for a given Throwable exception to the servlet container log file.

service

```
public abstract void service(javax.servlet.ServletRequest,
    javax.servlet.ServletResponse)
    throws javax.servlet.ServletException, java.io.IOException;
```

Called by the servlet container to allow the servlet to respond to a request. This method is declared abstract so subclasses, such as javax.servlet.http.HttpServlet, must override it.

getServletName

```
public java.lang.String getServletName();
```

Returns the name of this servlet instance.

RequestDispatcher

Interface name:	javax.servlet.RequestDispatcher
Implemented by:	(none)
Extends:	(none)

Defines an object that receives requests from the client and sends them to any resource (such as a servlet, HTML file, or JSP file) on the server. The servlet container creates the RequestDispatcher object, which is used as a wrapper around a server resource located at a particular path or given by a particular name.

This interface is intended to wrap servlets, but a servlet container can create RequestDispatcher objects to wrap any type of resource.

Interface Summary

```
public interface javax.servlet.RequestDispatcher
{
    public void forward(javax.servlet.ServletRequest,
        javax.servlet.ServletResponse)
        throws javax.servlet.ServletException, java.io.IOException;
    public void include(javax.servlet.ServletRequest,
        javax.servlet.ServletResponse)
        throws javax.servlet.ServletException, java.io.IOException;
}
```

Method Detail

The following section describes all of the methods that are defined in the RequestDispatcher interface.

forward

```
public void forward(javax.servlet.ServletRequest,
    javax.servlet.ServletResponse)
    throws javax.servlet.ServletException, java.io.IOException;
```

Forwards a request from a servlet to another resource (a servlet, JSP file, or HTML file) on the server. This method allows one servlet to do preliminary processing of a request and another resource to generate the response.

The forward() method should be called before the response has been committed to the client (before response body output has been flushed). If the response already has been committed, this method throws an IllegalStateException.

Uncommitted output in the response buffer is automatically cleared before the forward.

The request and response parameters must be either the same objects as were passed to the calling servlet's service() method or subclasses of the ServletRequestWrapper or ServletResponseWrapper classes that wrap them.

include

```
public void include(javax.servlet.ServletRequest,
    javax.servlet.ServletResponse)
    throws javax.servlet.ServletException, java.io.IOException;
```

Includes the content of a resource (a servlet, JSP page, or HTML file) in the response. In essence, this method enables programmatic server-side includes.

The ServletResponse object has its path elements and parameters remain unchanged from the caller's. The included servlet cannot change the response status code or set headers; any attempt to make a change is ignored.

The request and response parameters must be either the same objects as were passed to the calling servlet's service() method or subclasses of the ServletRequestWrapper or ServletResponseWrapper classes that wrap them.

Servlet

Interface name:	javax.servlet.Servlet
Implemented by:	javax.servlet.GenericServlet
Extends:	(none)

Defines methods that all servlets must implement. To implement this interface, you can write a generic servlet that extends javax.servlet.GenericServlet or write an HTTP servlet that extends javax.servlet.http.HttpServlet.

In addition to the life-cycle methods, this interface provides the getServletConfig() method, which the servlet can use to get any startup information.

Interface Summary

```
public interface javax.servlet.Servlet
{
    public void init(javax.servlet.ServletConfig)
        throws javax.servlet.ServletException;
    public javax.servlet.ServletConfig getServletConfig();
    public void service(javax.servlet.ServletRequest,
        javax.servlet.ServletResponse)
        throws javax.servlet.ServletException, java.io.IOException;
    public java.lang.String getServletInfo();
    public void destroy();
}
```

Method Detail

The following section describes all of the methods that are defined in the Servlet interface.

init

```
public void init(javax.servlet.ServletConfig)
    throws javax.servlet.ServletException;
```

Called by the servlet container to indicate to a servlet that the servlet is being placed into service. The servlet container calls the init() method exactly once after instantiating the servlet. The init() method must complete successfully before the servlet can receive any requests. The servlet container cannot place the servlet into service if the init() method throws a ServletException or does not return within a time period defined by the web container.

getServletConfig

```
public javax.servlet.ServletConfig getServletConfig();
```

Returns a ServletConfig object, which contains initialization and startup parameters for this servlet. The ServletConfig object returned is the one passed to the init() method.

service

```
public void service(javax.servlet.ServletRequest,
    javax.servlet.ServletResponse)
    throws javax.servlet.ServletException, java.io.IOException;
```

Called by the servlet container to allow the servlet to respond to a request. This method is only called after the servlet's init() method has completed successfully.

getServletInfo

```
public java.lang.String getServletInfo();
```

Returns information about the servlet, such as author, version, and copyright. The string that this method returns should be plain text and not markup of any kind (such as HTML, XML, and so forth).

destroy

```
public void destroy();
```

Called by the servlet container to indicate to a servlet that the servlet is being taken out of service. This method is only called once all threads within the servlet's service() method have exited or after a timeout period has passed. After the servlet container calls this method, it will not call the service() method again on this servlet.

This method gives the servlet an opportunity to clean up any resources that are being held (for example, memory, file handles, and threads).

ServletConfig

Interface name:	javax.servlet.ServletConfig
Implemented by:	(none)
Extends:	(none)

A servlet configuration object created by a servlet container used to pass information to a servlet during initialization.

Interface Summary

```
public interface javax.servlet.ServletConfig
{
    public java.lang.String getServletName();
    public javax.servlet.ServletContext getServletContext();
    public java.lang.String getInitParameter(java.lang.String);
    public java.util.Enumeration getInitParameterNames();
}
```

Method Detail

The following section describes all of the methods that are defined in the ServletConfig interface.

getServletName

```
public java.lang.String getServletName();
```

Returns the name of this servlet instance as defined in the web application deployment descriptor (web.xml).

getServletContext

```
public javax.servlet.ServletContext getServletContext();
```

Returns a reference to the ServletContext in which the servlet is executing.

getInitParameter

```
public java.lang.String getInitParameter(java.lang.String);
```

Returns a String containing the value of the named initialization parameter, or null if the parameter does not exist.

getInitParameterNames

```
public java.util.Enumeration getInitParameterNames();
```

Returns the names of the servlet's initialization parameters as an Enumeration of String objects, or an empty Enumeration if the servlet has no initialization parameters defined.

ServletContext

Interface name:	javax.servlet.ServletContext
Implemented by:	(none)
Extends:	(none)

Defines a set of methods that a servlet uses to communicate with its servlet container; for example, to get the MIME type of a file, dispatch requests, pass attributes, or write to a log file.

The ServletContext object is contained within the ServletConfig object, which the web server provides the servlet when the servlet is initialized.

Interface Summary

```
public interface javax.servlet.ServletContext
{
    public javax.servlet.ServletContext getContext(java.lang.String);
    public int getMajorVersion();
    public int getMinorVersion();
    public java.lang.String getMimeType(java.lang.String);
    public java.util.Set getResourcePaths(java.lang.String);
    public java.net.URL getResource(java.lang.String)
        throws java.net.MalformedURLException;
    public java.io.InputStream getResourceAsStream(java.lang.String);
    public javax.servlet.RequestDispatcher
        getRequestDispatcher(java.lang.String);
    public javax.servlet.RequestDispatcher
        getNamedDispatcher(java.lang.String);
```

```
    public void log(java.lang.String);
    public void log(java.lang.String, java.lang.Throwable);
    public java.lang.String getRealPath(java.lang.String);
    public java.lang.String getServerInfo();
    public java.lang.String getInitParameter(java.lang.String);
    public java.util.Enumeration getInitParameterNames();
    public java.lang.Object getAttribute(java.lang.String);
    public java.util.Enumeration getAttributeNames();
    public void setAttribute(java.lang.String, java.lang.Object);
    public void removeAttribute(java.lang.String);
    public java.lang.String getServletContextName();
}
```

Method Detail

The following section describes all of the methods that are defined in the ServletContext interface.

getContext

```
public javax.servlet.ServletContext getContext(java.lang.String);
```

Returns a ServletContext object that corresponds to a specified URL on the server. This method allows servlets to gain access to the context for various parts of the server and, as needed, obtain RequestDispatcher objects from the context.

The given path must be begin with /, is interpreted relative to the server's document root, and is matched against the context roots of other web applications hosted on this container.

In a security-conscious environment, the servlet container may return null for a given URL.

getMajorVersion

```
public int getMajorVersion();
```

Returns the major version of the Java Servlet API that this servlet container supports. All implementations that comply with version 2.3 must have this method return the integer 2.

getMinorVersion

```
public int getMinorVersion();
```

Returns the minor version of the Servlet API that this servlet container supports. All implementations that comply with version 2.3 must have this method return the integer 3.

getMimeType

```
public java.lang.String getMimeType(java.lang.String);
```

Returns the MIME type of the specified file, or null if the MIME type is not known. The MIME type is determined by the configuration of the servlet container, and may be specified in a web application deployment descriptor (web.xml).

getResourcePaths

```
public java.util.Set getResourcePaths(java.lang.String);
```

Returns a directory-like listing of all the paths to resources within the web application whose longest subpath matches the supplied path argument. Paths indicating subdirectory paths end with a /. The returned paths are all relative to the root of the web application and have a leading /. For example, a web application containing:

```
/welcome.html
/catalog/index.html
/catalog/products.html
/catalog/offers/books.html
/catalog/offers/music.html
/customer/login.jsp
/WEB-INF/web.xml
/WEB-INF/classes/com.acme.OrderServlet.class
```

would cause the following to be returned by getResourcePaths("/"):

```
"/welcome.html"
"/catalog/"
"/customer/"
"/WEB-INF/"
```

getResource

```
public java.net.URL getResource(java.lang.String)
        throws java.net.MalformedURLException;
```

Returns a URL to the resource that is mapped to a specified path. The path must begin with a / and is interpreted as relative to the current context root. This method returns null if no resource is mapped to the pathname.

getResourceAsStream

```
public java.io.InputStream getResourceAsStream(java.lang.String);
```

Returns the resource located at the named path as an InputStream object. The data in the InputStream can be of any type or length. The path must be specified according to the rules given in getResource() method. This method returns null if no resource exists at the specified path.

getRequestDispatcher

```
public javax.servlet.RequestDispatcher
    getRequestDispatcher(java.lang.String);
```

Returns a RequestDispatcher object that acts as a wrapper for the resource located at the given path. A RequestDispatcher object can be used to forward a request to the resource or to include the resource in a response. The pathname must begin with a / and is interpreted as relative to the current context root.

getNamedDispatcher

```
public javax.servlet.RequestDispatcher
    getNamedDispatcher(java.lang.String);
```

Returns a RequestDispatcher object that acts as a wrapper for the named servlet. Servlets may be given names via the web application deployment descriptor (web.xml).

log

```
public void log(java.lang.String);
```

Writes the specified message to a servlet log file, usually an event log. The name and type of the servlet log file are specific to the servlet container.

log

```
public void log(java.lang.String, java.lang.Throwable);
```

Writes the specified message and a stack trace for a given Throwable exception to the servlet log file. The name and type of the servlet log file is specific to the servlet container, usually an event log.

getRealPath

```
public java.lang.String getRealPath(java.lang.String);
```

Returns a String containing the real path for a given virtual path. For example, the path "/index.html" returns the absolute file path on the server's file system.

getServerInfo

```
public java.lang.String getServerInfo();
```

Returns the name and version of the servlet container on which the servlet is running. The form of the returned string is servername/versionnumber.

getInitParameter

```
public java.lang.String getInitParameter(java.lang.String);
```

Returns a String containing the value of the named context-wide initialization parameter, or null if the parameter does not exist. Initialization parameters are specified in the web application deployment descriptor (web.xml).

getInitParameterNames

```
public java.util.Enumeration getInitParameterNames();
```

Returns the names of the context's initialization parameters as an Enumeration of String objects, or an empty Enumeration if the context has no initialization parameters.

getAttribute

```
public java.lang.Object getAttribute(java.lang.String);
```

Returns the servlet container attribute with the given name, or null if there is no attribute by that name. Attribute names should follow the same convention as package names. The Java Servlet API specification reserves names matching java.*, javax.*, and sun.*.

getAttributeNames

```
public java.util.Enumeration getAttributeNames();
```

Returns an Enumeration containing the attribute names available within this servlet context. Use the getAttribute() method with an attribute name to get the value of an attribute.

setAttribute

```
public void setAttribute(java.lang.String, java.lang.Object);
```

Binds an object to a given attribute name in this servlet context. If the name specified is already used for an attribute, this method will replace the attribute with the new attribute. If a null value is passed, the effect is the same as calling removeAttribute().

Attribute names should follow the same convention as package names. The Java Servlet API specification reserves names matching java.*, javax.*, and sun.*.

removeAttribute

```
public void removeAttribute(java.lang.String);
```

Removes the attribute with the given name from the servlet context.

getServletContextName

```
public java.lang.String getServletContextName();
```

Returns the name of the web application corresponding to the current ServletContext as specified in the deployment descriptor display-name element.

ServletContextAttributeEvent

Class name:	javax.servlet.ServletContextAttributeEvent
Superclass:	javax.servlet.ServletContextEvent
Direct subclasses:	(none)
Implements:	(none)

This is the event class for notifications about changes to the attributes of the servlet context of a web application.

Class Summary

```
public class javax.servlet.ServletContextAttributeEvent
    extends javax.servlet.ServletContextEvent
{
    public javax.servlet.ServletContextAttributeEvent(
        javax.servlet.ServletContext,
        java.lang.String,java.lang.Object);
    public java.lang.String getName();
    public java.lang.Object getValue();
}
```

Constructor Detail

The following section describes all of the methods that are defined in the ServletContextAttributeEvent class.

ServletContextAttributeEvent

```
public javax.servlet.ServletContextAttributeEvent(
    javax.servlet.ServletContext,
    java.lang.String,java.lang.Object);
```

Constructs a ServletContextAttributeEvent from the given context for the given attribute name and attribute value.

Method Detail

The following section describes all of the methods that are defined in the ServletContextAttributeEvent class.

getName

```
public java.lang.String getName();
```

Returns the name of the attribute that changed on the ServletContext.

getValue

```
public java.lang.Object getValue();
```

Returns the value of the attribute that has been added, removed, or replaced. If the attribute was added, this is the value of the attribute. If the attribute was removed, this is the value of the removed attribute. If the attribute was replaced, this is the old value of the attribute.

ServletContextAttributeListener

Interface name:	javax.servlet.ServletContextAttributeListener
Implemented by:	java.util.EventListener
Extends:	(none)

Implementations of this interface receive notifications of changes to the attribute list on the servlet context of a web application. To receive notification events, the implementation class must be configured in the deployment descriptor for the web application.

Interface Summary

```
public interface javax.servlet.ServletContextAttributeListener
    extends java.util.EventListener
{
    public void
attributeAdded(
    javax.servlet.ServletContextAttributeEvent);
    public void attributeRemoved(
```

```
        javax.servlet.ServletContextAttributeEvent);
    public void attributeReplaced(
        javax.servlet.ServletContextAttributeEvent);
}
```

Method Detail

The following section describes all of the methods that are defined in the ServletContextAttributeListener interface.

attributeAdded

```
public void attributeAdded(javax.servlet.ServletContextAttributeEvent);
```

Notification that a new attribute was added to the servlet context. Called after the attribute is added.

attributeRemoved

```
public void attributeRemoved(
    javax.servlet.ServletContextAttributeEvent);
```

Notification that an existing attribute has been removed from the servlet context. Called after the attribute is removed.

attributeReplaced

```
public void attributeReplaced(
    javax.servlet.ServletContextAttributeEvent);
```

Notification that an attribute on the servlet context has been replaced. Called after the attribute is replaced.

ServletContextEvent

Class name:	javax.servlet.ServletContextEvent
Superclass:	java.util.EventObject
Direct subclasses:	javax.servlet.ServletContextAttributeEvent
Implements:	(none)

This is the event class for notifications about changes to the servlet context of a web application.

Class Summary

```
public class javax.servlet.ServletContextEvent
    extends java.util.EventObject
{
    public javax.servlet.ServletContextEvent(
javax.servlet.ServletContext);
    public javax.servlet.ServletContext getServletContext();
}
```

Constructor Detail

The following section describes all of the methods that are defined in the ServletContextEvent class.

ServletContextEvent

```
public javax.servlet.ServletContextEvent(javax.servlet.ServletContext);
```

Constructs a ServletContextEvent from the given context.

Method Detail

The following section describes all of the methods that are defined in the ServletContextEvent class.

getServletContext

```
public javax.servlet.ServletContext getServletContext();
```

Returns the ServletContext that changed.

ServletContextListener

Interface name:	javax.servlet.ServletContextListener
Implemented by:	(none)
Extends:	(none)

Implementations of this interface receive notifications about changes to the servlet context of the web application they are part of. To receive notification events, the implementation class must be configured in the deployment descriptor for the web application.

Interface Summary

```
public interface javax.servlet.ServletContextListener
    extends java.util.EventListener
{
    public void contextInitialized(javax.servlet.ServletContextEvent);
    public void contextDestroyed(javax.servlet.ServletContextEvent);
}
```

Method Detail

The following section describes all of the methods that are defined in the ServletContextListener interface.

contextInitialized

```
public void contextInitialized(javax.servlet.ServletContextEvent);
```

Notification that the web application is ready to process requests.

contextDestroyed

```
public void contextDestroyed(javax.servlet.ServletContextEvent);
```

Notification that the servlet context is about to be shut down.

ServletException

Class name:	javax.servlet.ServletException
Superclass:	java.lang.Exception
Direct subclasses:	javax.servlet.UnavailableException
Implements:	(none)

Defines a general exception a servlet can throw when it encounters difficulty.

Class Summary

```
public class javax.servlet.ServletException
    extends java.lang.Exception
{
    public javax.servlet.ServletException();
    public javax.servlet.ServletException(java.lang.String);
    public javax.servlet.ServletException(
        java.lang.String, java.lang.Throwable);
    public javax.servlet.ServletException(java.lang.Throwable);
    public java.lang.Throwable getRootCause();
}
```

Constructor Detail

The following section describes all of the methods that are defined in the ServletException class.

ServletException

```
public javax.servlet.ServletException();
```

Constructs a new servlet exception.

ServletException

```
public javax.servlet.ServletException(java.lang.String);
```

Constructs a new servlet exception with the specified message. The message can be written to the server log and/or displayed for the user.

ServletException

```
public javax.servlet.ServletException(
    java.lang.String, java.lang.Throwable);
```

Constructs a new servlet exception when the servlet needs to throw an exception and include a message about the "root cause" exception that interfered with its normal operation, including a description message.

ServletException

```
public javax.servlet.ServletException(java.lang.Throwable);
```

Constructs a new servlet exception when the servlet needs to throw an exception and include a message about the "root cause" exception that interfered with its normal operation. The exception's message is based on the localized message of the underlying exception.

Method Detail

The following section describes all of the methods that are defined in the ServletException class.

getRootCause

```
public java.lang.Throwable getRootCause();
```

Returns the exception that caused this servlet exception.

ServletInputStream

Class name:	javax.servlet.ServletInputStream
Superclass:	java.io.InputStream
Direct subclasses:	(none)
Implements:	(none)

Provides an input stream for reading binary data from a client request, including an efficient readLine() method for reading data one line at a time. With some protocols, such as HTTP POST and PUT, a ServletInputStream object can be used to read data sent from the client.

Class Summary

```
public abstract class javax.servlet.ServletInputStream
    extends java.io.InputStream
{
    protected javax.servlet.ServletInputStream();
    public int readLine(byte[], int, int)
        throws java.io.IOException;
}
```

Constructor Detail

The following section describes all of the methods that are defined in the ServletInputStream class.

ServletInputStream

```
protected javax.servlet.ServletInputStream();
```

Does nothing, because this is an abstract class.

Method Detail

The following section describes all of the methods that are defined in the ServletInputStream class.

readLine

```
public int readLine(byte[], int, int)
    throws java.io.IOException;
```

Reads the input stream, one line at a time. Starting at an offset, it reads bytes into an array, until it reads a certain number of bytes or reaches a newline character, which it reads into the array as well. This method returns –1 if it reaches the end of the input stream before reading the maximum number of bytes.

ServletOutputStream

Class name:	javax.servlet.ServletOutputStream
Superclass:	java.io.OutputStream
Direct subclasses:	(none)
Implements:	(none)

Provides an output stream for sending binary data to the client.

Class Summary

```
public abstract class javax.servlet.ServletOutputStream
    extends java.io.OutputStream
{
    protected javax.servlet.ServletOutputStream();
    public void print(java.lang.String) throws java.io.IOException;
    public void print(boolean) throws java.io.IOException;
    public void print(char) throws java.io.IOException;
    public void print(int) throws java.io.IOException;
    public void print(long) throws java.io.IOException;
    public void print(float) throws java.io.IOException;
    public void print(double) throws java.io.IOException;
    public void println() throws java.io.IOException;
    public void println(java.lang.String) throws java.io.IOException;
    public void println(boolean) throws java.io.IOException;
    public void println(char) throws java.io.IOException;
    public void println(int) throws java.io.IOException;
    public void println(long) throws java.io.IOException;
    public void println(float) throws java.io.IOException;
    public void println(double) throws java.io.IOException;
}
```

Constructor Detail

The following section describes all of the methods that are defined in the ServletOutputStream class.

ServletOutputStream

```
protected javax.servlet.ServletOutputStream();
```

Does nothing, because this is an abstract class.

Method Detail

The following section describes all of the methods that are defined in the ServletOutputStream class.

print

```
public void print(java.lang.String) throws java.io.IOException;
```

Writes a String to the client, without a carriage return, line feed (CRLF) character at the end.

print

```
public void print(boolean) throws java.io.IOException;
```

Writes a boolean value to the client, with no carriage return, line feed (CRLF) character at the end.

print

```
public void print(char) throws java.io.IOException;
```

Writes a character to the client, with no carriage return, line feed (CRLF) at the end.

print

```
public void print(int) throws java.io.IOException;
```

Writes an int to the client, with no carriage return, line feed (CRLF) at the end.

print

```
public void print(long) throws java.io.IOException;
```

Writes a long value to the client, with no carriage return, line feed (CRLF) at the end.

print

```
public void print(float) throws java.io.IOException;
```

Writes a float value to the client, with no carriage return, line feed (CRLF) at the end.

print

```
public void print(double) throws java.io.IOException;
```

Writes a double value to the client, with no carriage return, line feed (CRLF) at the end.

println

```
public void println() throws java.io.IOException;
```

Writes a carriage return, line feed (CRLF) to the client.

println

```
public void println(java.lang.String) throws java.io.IOException;
```

Writes a String to the client, followed by a carriage return, line feed (CRLF).

println

```
public void println(boolean) throws java.io.IOException;
```

Writes a boolean value to the client, followed by a carriage return, line feed (CRLF).

println

```
public void println(char) throws java.io.IOException;
```

Writes a character to the client, followed by a carriage return, line feed (CRLF).

println

```
public void println(int) throws java.io.IOException;
```

Writes an int to the client, followed by a carriage return, line feed (CRLF) character.

println

```
public void println(long) throws java.io.IOException;
```

Writes a long value to the client, followed by a carriage return, line feed (CRLF).

println

```
public void println(float) throws java.io.IOException;
```

Writes a float value to the client, followed by a carriage return, line feed (CRLF).

println

```
public void println(double) throws java.io.IOException;
```

Writes a double value to the client, followed by a carriage return, line feed (CRLF).

ServletRequest

Interface name:	javax.servlet.ServletRequest
Implemented by:	javax.servlet.ServletRequestWrapper
Extends:	(none)
Extended by:	javax.servlet.http.HttpServletRequest

Defines an object to provide client request information to a servlet. The servlet container creates a ServletRequest object and passes it as an argument to the servlet's service() method.

Interface Summary

```
public interface javax.servlet.ServletRequest
{
    public java.lang.Object getAttribute(java.lang.String);
    public java.util.Enumeration getAttributeNames();
    public java.lang.String getCharacterEncoding();
    public void setCharacterEncoding(java.lang.String)
        throws java.io.UnsupportedEncodingException;
    public int getContentLength();
    public java.lang.String getContentType();
    public javax.servlet.ServletInputStream getInputStream()
        throws java.io.IOException;
    public java.lang.String getParameter(java.lang.String);
    public java.util.Enumeration getParameterNames();
```

```
    public java.lang.String getParameterValues(java.lang.String)[];
    public java.util.Map getParameterMap();
    public java.lang.String getProtocol();
    public java.lang.String getScheme();
    public java.lang.String getServerName();
    public int getServerPort();
    public java.io.BufferedReader getReader() throws java.io.IOException;
    public java.lang.String getRemoteAddr();
    public java.lang.String getRemoteHost();
    public void setAttribute(java.lang.String, java.lang.Object);
    public void removeAttribute(java.lang.String);
    public java.util.Locale getLocale();
    public java.util.Enumeration getLocales();
    public boolean isSecure();
    public javax.servlet.RequestDispatcher
      getRequestDispatcher(java.lang.String);
}
```

Method Detail

The following section describes all of the methods that are defined in the ServletRequest interface.

getAttribute

```
public java.lang.Object getAttribute(java.lang.String);
```

Returns the value of the named attribute as an Object, or null if no attribute of the given name exists. Attributes can be set in two ways. The servlet container may set attributes to make available custom information about a request. Attributes can also be set programmatically using ServletRequest.setAttribute(). This allows information to be embedded into a request before a RequestDispatcher call.

Attribute names should follow the same conventions as package names. The servlet specification reserves names matching java.*, javax.*, and sun.*.

getAttributeNames

```
public java.util.Enumeration getAttributeNames();
```

Returns an Enumeration containing the names of the attributes available to this request. This method returns an empty Enumeration if the request has no attributes available to it.

getCharacterEncoding

```
public java.lang.String getCharacterEncoding();
```

Returns the name of the character encoding used in the body of this request. This method returns null if the request does not specify a character encoding.

setCharacterEncoding

```
public void setCharacterEncoding(java.lang.String)
    throws java.io.UnsupportedEncodingException;
```

Overrides the name of the character encoding used in the body of this request. This method must be called prior to reading request parameters or reading input using getReader().

getContentLength

```
public int getContentLength();
```

Returns the length, in bytes, of the request body made available by the input stream, or –1 if the length is not known. For HTTP servlets, this is the same as the value of the CGI variable CONTENT_LENGTH.

getContentType

```
public java.lang.String getContentType();
```

Returns the MIME type of the body of the request, or null if the type is not known. For HTTP servlets, this is the same as the value of the CGI variable CONTENT_TYPE.

getInputStream

```
public javax.servlet.ServletInputStream getInputStream()
    throws java.io.IOException;
```

Retrieves the body of the request as binary data using a ServletInputStream. Either this method or getReader() may be called to read the body, but not both.

getParameter

```
public java.lang.String getParameter(java.lang.String);
```

Returns the value of a request parameter as a String, or null if the parameter does not exist. Request parameters are extra information sent with the request. For HTTP servlets, parameters are contained in the query string or posted form data.

You should only use this method when you are sure the parameter has only one value. If the parameter might have more than one value, use getParameterValues().

getParameterNames

```
public java.util.Enumeration getParameterNames();
```

Returns an Enumeration of String objects containing the names of the parameters contained in this request. If the request has no parameters, the method returns an empty Enumeration.

getParameterValues

```
public java.lang.String getParameterValues(java.lang.String)[];
```

Returns an array of String objects containing all of the values the given request parameter has, or null if the parameter does not exist. If the parameter has a single value, the array has a length of 1.

getParameterMap

```
public java.util.Map getParameterMap();
```

Returns a java.util.Map of the parameters of this request.

getProtocol

```
public java.lang.String getProtocol();
```

Returns the name and version of the protocol the request uses in the form protocol/majorVersion.minorVersion; for example, HTTP/1.1. For HTTP servlets, the value returned is the same as the value of the CGI variable SERVER_PROTOCOL.

getScheme

```
public java.lang.String getScheme();
```

Returns the name of the scheme used to make this request; for example, http, https, or ftp. Different schemes have different rules for constructing URLs, as noted in RFC 1738.

getServerName

```
public java.lang.String getServerName();
```

Returns the hostname of the server that received the request. For HTTP servlets, this is the same as the value of the CGI variable SERVER_NAME.

getServerPort

```
public int getServerPort();
```

Returns the port number on which this request was received. For HTTP servlets, this is the same as the value of the CGI variable SERVER_PORT.

getReader

```
public java.io.BufferedReader getReader() throws java.io.IOException;
```

Retrieves the body of the request as character data using a BufferedReader. The reader translates the character data according to the character encoding used on the body.

getRemoteAddr

```
public java.lang.String getRemoteAddr();
```

Returns the Internet Protocol (IP) address of the client that sent the request. For HTTP servlets, this is the same as the value of the CGI variable REMOTE_ADDR.

getRemoteHost

```
public java.lang.String getRemoteHost();
```

Returns the fully qualified name of the client that sent the request. If the engine cannot or chooses not to resolve the hostname (to improve performance), this method returns the dotted-string form of the IP address. For HTTP servlets, this is the same as the value of the CGI variable REMOTE_HOST.

setAttribute

```
public void setAttribute(java.lang.String, java.lang.Object);
```

Stores an attribute in this request. Attributes are reset between requests. This method is most often used in conjunction with using a RequestDispatcher to pass attributes between servlets.

removeAttribute

```
public void removeAttribute(java.lang.String);
```

Removes an attribute from this request. This method is not generally needed, because attributes only persist as long as the request is being handled.

getLocale

```
public java.util.Locale getLocale();
```

Returns the preferred locale that the client will accept content in, based on the Accept-Language header. If the client request doesn't provide an Accept-Language header, this method returns the default locale for the server.

getLocales

```
public java.util.Enumeration getLocales();
```

Returns an Enumeration of locale objects indicating, in decreasing order starting with the preferred locale, the locales that are acceptable to the client based on the Accept-Language header.

If the client request doesn't provide an Accept-Language header, this method returns an Enumeration containing one locale, the default locale for the server.

isSecure

```
public boolean isSecure();
```

Returns a boolean indicating whether this request was made using a secure channel, such as HTTPS.

getRequestDispatcher

```
public javax.servlet.RequestDispatcher
   getRequestDispatcher(java.lang.String);
```

Returns a RequestDispatcher object that acts as a wrapper for the resource located at the given path. A RequestDispatcher object can be used to forward a request to the resource or to include the resource in a response.

The pathname specified may be relative, although it cannot extend outside the current servlet context. If the path begins with a /, it is interpreted as relative to the current context root. This method returns null if the servlet container cannot return a RequestDispatcher.

ServletRequestWrapper

Class name:	javax.servlet.ServletRequestWrapper
Superclass:	java.lang.Object
Direct subclasses:	javax.servlet.http.HttpServletRequestWrapper
Implements:	javax.servlet.ServletRequest

Provides a convenient implementation of the ServletRequest interface that can be subclassed by developers wishing to adapt the request to a Servlet. This class implements the Wrapper or Decorator pattern. Methods default to calling through to the wrapped request object. See the javax.servlet.ServletRequest interface for the methods available when using this class.

Constructor Detail

The following section describes all of the methods that are defined in the ServletRequestWrapper class.

ServletRequestWrapper

```
public javax.servlet.ServletRequestWrapper(
    javax.servlet.ServletRequest);
```

Creates a ServletRequest adaptor wrapping the given request object.

ServletResponse

Interface name:	javax.servlet.ServletResponse
Implemented by:	javax.servlet.ServletResponseWrapper
Extends:	(none)
Extended by:	javax.servlet.http.HttpServletResponse

Defines an object to assist a servlet in sending a response to the client. The servlet container creates a ServletResponse object and passes it as an argument to the servlet's service method.

Interface Summary

```
public interface javax.servlet.ServletResponse
{
    public java.lang.String getCharacterEncoding();
    public javax.servlet.ServletOutputStream getOutputStream()
        throws java.io.IOException;
    public java.io.PrintWriter getWriter() throws java.io.IOException;
    public void setContentLength(int);
    public void setContentType(java.lang.String);
    public void setBufferSize(int);
    public int getBufferSize();
    public void flushBuffer() throws java.io.IOException;
    public void resetBuffer();
    public boolean isCommitted();
    public void reset();
    public void setLocale(java.util.Locale);
    public java.util.Locale getLocale();
}
```

Method Detail

The following section describes all of the methods that are defined in the ServletResponse interface.

getCharacterEncoding

```
public java.lang.String getCharacterEncoding();
```

Returns the name of the charset used for the MIME body sent in this response. If no charset has been assigned, it is implicitly set to ISO-8859-1 (Latin-1). See RFC 2047 (http://ds.internic.net/rfc/rfc2045.txt) for more information about character encoding and MIME.

getOutputStream

```
public javax.servlet.ServletOutputStream getOutputStream()
    throws java.io.IOException;
```

Returns a ServletOutputStream suitable for writing binary data in the response. The servlet container does not encode the binary data. Either this method or getWriter() may be called to write the body, but not both.

getWriter

```
public java.io.PrintWriter getWriter() throws java.io.IOException;
```

Returns a PrintWriter object that can send character text to the client. The character encoding used is the one specified in the "charset=" property of the setContentType() method, which must be called before calling this method. Either this method or getOutputStream() may be called to write the body, but not both.

setContentLength

```
public void setContentLength(int);
```

Sets the length of the content body in the response. In HTTP servlets, this method sets the HTTP Content-Length header.

setContentType

```
public void setContentType(java.lang.String);
```

Sets the content type of the response being sent to the client. The content type may include the type of character encoding used; for example, "text/html; charset=ISO-8859-4".

If obtaining a PrintWriter, this method should be called first.

setBufferSize

```
public void setBufferSize(int);
```

Sets the preferred buffer size for the body of the response. The servlet container will use a buffer at least as large as the size requested. The actual buffer size used can be found using getBufferSize().

A larger buffer allows more content to be written before anything is actually sent, thus providing the servlet with more time to set appropriate status codes and headers. A smaller buffer decreases server memory load and allows the client to start receiving data more quickly.

This method must be called before any response body content is written; if content has been written, this method throws an IllegalStateException.

getBufferSize

```
public int getBufferSize();
```

Returns the actual buffer size used for the response. If no buffering is used, this method returns 0.

flushBuffer

```
public void flushBuffer() throws java.io.IOException;
```

Forces any content in the buffer to be written to the client. A call to this method automatically commits the response, meaning the status code and headers will be written.

resetBuffer

```
public void resetBuffer();
```

Clears the content of the underlying buffer in the response without clearing headers or status code. If the response has been committed, this method throws an IllegalStateException.

isCommitted

```
public boolean isCommitted();
```

Returns a boolean indicating if the response has been committed. A committed response has already had its status code and headers written.

reset

```
public void reset();
```

Clears any data that exists in the buffer as well as the status code and headers. If the response has been committed, this method throws an IllegalStateException.

setLocale

```
public void setLocale(java.util.Locale);
```

Sets the locale of the response, setting the headers (including the Content-Type's charset) as appropriate. This method should be called before a call to getWriter(). By default, the response locale is the default locale for the server.

getLocale

```
public java.util.Locale getLocale();
```

Returns the locale assigned to the response.

ServletResponseWrapper

Class name:	javax.servlet.ServletResponseWrapper
Superclass:	java.lang.Object
Direct subclasses:	javax.servlet.http.HttpServletResponseWrapper
Implements:	javax.servlet.ServletResponse

Provides a convenient implementation of the ServletResponse interface that can be subclassed by developers wishing to adapt the response from a Servlet. This class implements the Wrapper or Decorator pattern. Methods default to calling through to the wrapped response object. See the javax.servlet.ServletResponse interface for the methods available when using this class.

Constructor Detail

The following section describes all of the methods that are defined in the ServletResponseWrapper class.

ServletResponseWrapper

```
public javax.servlet.ServletResponseWrapper(
    javax.servlet.ServletResponse);
```

Creates a ServletResponse adaptor wrapping the given response object.

SingleThreadModel

Interface name:	javax.servlet.SingleThreadModel
Implemented by:	(none)
Extends:	(none)

Ensures that servlets handle only one request at a time. This interface has no methods.

If a servlet implements this interface, you are guaranteed that no two threads will execute concurrently in the servlet's service() method. The servlet container can make this guarantee by synchronizing access to a single instance of the servlet, or by maintaining a pool of servlet instances and dispatching each new request to a free servlet.

This interface does not prevent synchronization problems that result from servlets accessing shared resources, such as static class variables or classes outside the scope of the servlet.

Use of the SingleThreadModel is generally discouraged.

UnavailableException

Class name:	javax.servlet.UnavailableException
Superclass:	javax.servlet.ServletException
Direct subclasses:	(none)
Implements:	(none)

Defines an exception that a servlet or filter throws to indicate that it is permanently or temporarily unavailable. When a servlet or filter is permanently unavailable, something is wrong with it, and it cannot handle requests until some action is taken. For example, a servlet might be configured incorrectly, or a filter's state may be corrupted. The component should log both the error and the corrective action that is needed.

A servlet or filter is temporarily unavailable if it cannot handle requests momentarily due to some system-wide problem. For example, a third-tier server might not be accessible, or there may be insufficient memory or disk storage to handle requests. A system administrator may need to take corrective action.

Servlet containers can safely treat both types of unavailable exceptions in the same way. However, treating temporary unavailability effectively makes the servlet container more robust. Specifically, the servlet container might block requests to the servlet or filter for a period of time suggested by the exception, rather than rejecting them until the servlet container restarts.

Class Summary

```
public class javax.servlet.UnavailableException
    extends javax.servlet.ServletException
{
    public javax.servlet.UnavailableException(java.lang.String);
    public javax.servlet.UnavailableException(java.lang.String, int);
    public boolean isPermanent();
    public int getUnavailableSeconds();
}
```

Constructor Detail

The following section describes all of the methods that are defined in the UnavailableException class.

UnavailableException

```
public javax.servlet.UnavailableException(java.lang.String);
```

Constructs a new exception with a descriptive message indicating that the servlet is permanently unavailable.

UnavailableException

```
public javax.servlet.UnavailableException(java.lang.String, int);
```

Constructs a new exception with a descriptive message indicating that the servlet is temporarily unavailable and giving an estimate of how long it will be unavailable.

In some cases, the servlet cannot make an estimate. For example, the servlet might know that a server it needs is not running, but not be able to report how long it will take to be restored to functionality. This can be indicated with a negative or zero value for the seconds argument.

Method Detail

The following section describes all of the methods that are defined in the UnavailableException class.

isPermanent

```
public boolean isPermanent();
```

Returns a boolean indicating whether the servlet is permanently unavailable. If so, something is wrong with the servlet, and the system administrator must take some corrective action.

getUnavailableSeconds

```
public int getUnavailableSeconds();
```

Returns the number of seconds the servlet expects to be temporarily unavailable. If this method returns a negative number, the servlet is permanently unavailable or cannot provide an estimate of how long it will be unavailable. No effort is made to correct for the time elapsed since the exception was first reported.

Cookie

Class name:	javax.servlet.http.Cookie
Superclass:	java.lang.Object
Direct subclasses:	(none)
Implements:	java.lang.Cloneable

Creates a *cookie,* a small amount of information sent by a servlet to a client (such as a web browser), saved by the client, and later sent back to the server. A cookie's value can uniquely identify a client, so cookies are commonly used for session management.

A cookie has a name, a single value, and optional attributes such as a comment, path and domain qualifiers, a maximum age, and a version number. Some web browsers have bugs in how they handle the optional attributes, so use them sparingly to improve the interoperability of your servlets.

The servlet sends cookies to the browser by using the HttpServletResponse addCookie() method, which adds fields to HTTP response headers to send cookies to the browser, one at a time. The browser is expected to support 20 cookies for each web server, 300 cookies total, and may limit cookie size to 4KB each.

This class supports both the version 0 (by Netscape) and version 1 (by RFC 2109) cookie specifications. By default, cookies are created using version 0 to ensure the best interoperability.

Class Summary

```
public class javax.servlet.http.Cookie
    extends java.lang.Object
    implements java.lang.Cloneable
{
    public javax.servlet.http.Cookie(java.lang.String,java.lang.String);
    public void setComment(java.lang.String);
    public java.lang.String getComment();
    public void setDomain(java.lang.String);
    public java.lang.String getDomain();
    public void setMaxAge(int);
    public int getMaxAge();
    public void setPath(java.lang.String);
    public java.lang.String getPath();
    public void setSecure(boolean);
    public boolean getSecure();
    public java.lang.String getName();
    public void setValue(java.lang.String);
    public java.lang.String getValue();
    public int getVersion();
    public void setVersion(int);
    public java.lang.Object clone();
}
```

Constructor Detail

The following section describes all of the methods that are defined in the Cookie class.

Cookie

```
public javax.servlet.http.Cookie(java.lang.String,java.lang.String);
```

Constructs a cookie with a specified name and value. The name must conform to RFC 2109. That means it can contain only ASCII alphanumeric characters, cannot contain commas, semicolons, or white space, and cannot begin with a $ character. The cookie's name cannot be changed after creation.

The value can be anything the server chooses to send. Its value is probably of interest only to the server. The cookie's value can be changed after creation with the setValue() method.

By default, cookies are created according to the Netscape cookie specification. The version can be changed with the setVersion() method.

Method Detail

The following section describes all of the methods that are defined in the Cookie class.

setComment

```
public void setComment(java.lang.String);
```

Specifies a comment that describes a cookie's purpose. The comment is useful if the browser presents the cookie to the user. Comments are not supported by Netscape version 0 cookies. Comments will not be sent back to the servlet by the browser.

getComment

```
public java.lang.String getComment();
```

Returns the comment describing the purpose of this cookie, or null if the cookie has no comment.

setDomain

```
public void setDomain(java.lang.String);
```

Specifies the domain within which this cookie should be presented. The form of the domain name is specified by RFC 2109. A domain name begins with a dot (such as .foo.com) and means that the cookie is utilized by servers in a specified Domain Name System (DNS) zone (for example, www.foo.com, but not a.b.foo.com). By default, cookies are only returned to the server that sent them.

getDomain

```
public java.lang.String getDomain();
```

Returns the domain name set for this cookie. The form of the domain name is set by RFC 2109.

setMaxAge

```
public void setMaxAge(int);
```

Sets the maximum age of the cookie, in seconds. A positive value indicates that the cookie will expire after that many seconds have passed. Note that the value is the maximum age when the cookie will expire, not the cookie's current age. A negative value means that the cookie is not stored persistently and will be deleted when the web browser exits. A zero value causes the cookie to be deleted.

getMaxAge

```
public int getMaxAge();
```

Returns the maximum age of the cookie, specified in seconds, By default, –1 indicates the cookie will persist until the browser session has ended.

setPath

```
public void setPath(java.lang.String);
```

Specifies a path for the cookie to which the client should return the cookie. The cookie is visible to all the pages in the directory you specify, and all the pages in that directory's subdirectories. A cookie's path must include the servlet that set the cookie: for example, /catalog, which makes the cookie visible to all directories on the server under /catalog.

Consult RFC 2109 for more information on setting pathnames for cookies.

getPath

```
public java.lang.String getPath();
```

Returns the path on the server to which the browser returns this cookie. The cookie is visible to all subpaths on the server.

setSecure

```
public void setSecure(boolean);
```

Indicates to the browser whether the cookie should only be sent using a secure protocol, such as HTTPS or SSL. The default value is false.

getSecure

```
public boolean getSecure();
```

Returns true if the browser is sending cookies only over a secure protocol, or false if the browser can send cookies using any protocol.

getName

```
public java.lang.String getName();
```

Returns the name of the cookie. The name cannot be changed after creation.

setValue

```
public void setValue(java.lang.String);
```

Assigns a new value to a cookie after the cookie is created. If you use a binary value, you may want to use Base64 encoding. With version 0 cookies, values should not contain white space, brackets, parentheses, equal signs, commas, double quotes, slashes, question marks, at signs, colons, or semicolons. Empty values may not behave the same way on all browsers.

getValue

```
public java.lang.String getValue();
```

Returns the value of the cookie.

getVersion

```
public int getVersion();
```

Returns the version of the protocol this cookie complies with. Version 1 complies with RFC 2109, and version 0 complies with the original cookie specification drafted by Netscape. Cookies provided by a browser use and identify the browser's cookie version.

setVersion

```
public void setVersion(int);
```

Sets the version of the cookie protocol this cookie complies with. Version 0 complies with the original Netscape cookie specification. Version 1 complies with RFC 2109.

Version 1 cookies are still considered experimental since not all browsers support RFC 2109.

clone

```
public java.lang.Object clone();
```

Overrides the standard java.lang.Object clone() method to return a copy of this cookie.

HttpServlet

Class name:	javax.servlet.http.HttpServlet
Superclass:	javax.servlet.GenericServlet
Direct subclasses:	(none)
Implements:	java.lang.Serializable

Provides an abstract class to be subclassed to create an HTTP servlet suitable for a web site. A subclass of HttpServlet must override at least one method, usually one of these:

- doGet() if the servlet supports HTTP GET requests
- doPost() for HTTP POST requests
- doPut() for HTTP PUT requests
- doDelete() for HTTP DELETE requests
- init() and/or destroy() to manage resources that are held for the life of the servlet
- getServletInfo(), which the servlet uses to provide information about itself

There is almost no reason to ever override the service() method. The service() method handles standard HTTP requests by dispatching them to the handler methods for each HTTP request type (the do*XXX* methods). Likewise, there's almost no reason to override the doOptions(), doHead(), and doTrace() methods.

Class Summary

```
public abstract class javax.servlet.http.HttpServlet
    extends javax.servlet.GenericServlet
    implements java.io.Serializable
{
    public javax.servlet.http.HttpServlet();
    protected void doGet(javax.servlet.http.HttpServletRequest,
        javax.servlet.http.HttpServletResponse)
        throws javax.servlet.ServletException, java.io.IOException;
    protected long getLastModified(javax.servlet.http.HttpServletRequest);
    protected void doHead(javax.servlet.http.HttpServletRequest,
        javax.servlet.http.HttpServletResponse)
        throws javax.servlet.ServletException, java.io.IOException;
    protected void doPost(javax.servlet.http.HttpServletRequest,
        javax.servlet.http.HttpServletResponse)
        throws javax.servlet.ServletException, java.io.IOException;
    protected void doPut(javax.servlet.http.HttpServletRequest,
        javax.servlet.http.HttpServletResponse)
        throws javax.servlet.ServletException, java.io.IOException;
    protected void doDelete(javax.servlet.http.HttpServletRequest,
        javax.servlet.http.HttpServletResponse)
        throws javax.servlet.ServletException, java.io.IOException;
    protected void doOptions(javax.servlet.http.HttpServletRequest,
        javax.servlet.http.HttpServletResponse)
        throws javax.servlet.ServletException, java.io.IOException;
    protected void doTrace(javax.servlet.http.HttpServletRequest,
        javax.servlet.http.HttpServletResponse)
        throws javax.servlet.ServletException, java.io.IOException;
    protected void service(javax.servlet.http.HttpServletRequest,
        javax.servlet.http.HttpServletResponse)
        throws javax.servlet.ServletException, java.io.IOException;
    public void service(javax.servlet.ServletRequest,
        javax.servlet.ServletResponse)
        throws javax.servlet.ServletException, java.io.IOException;
}
```

Constructor Detail

The following section describes all of the methods that are defined in the HttpServlet class.

HttpServlet

```
public javax.servlet.http.HttpServlet();
```

Does nothing, because this is an abstract class.

Method Detail

The following section describes all of the methods that are defined in the HttpServlet class.

doGet

```
protected void doGet(javax.servlet.http.HttpServletRequest,
    javax.servlet.http.HttpServletResponse)
    throws javax.servlet.ServletException, java.io.IOException;
```

Called by the server (via the service() method) to allow a servlet to handle an HTTP GET request. Overriding this method to support a GET request also automatically supports an HTTP HEAD request. A HEAD request is a GET request that returns no body in the response, only the request header fields.

Where possible, set the Content-Length header (with the javax.servlet. ServletResponse setContentLength() method), to allow the servlet container to use a persistent connection to return its response to the client, improving performance. The content length is automatically set if the entire response fits inside the response buffer.

The GET method should be safe; that is, it should not cause any side effects for which users are held responsible. For example, most form queries have no side effects. If a client request is intended to change stored data, the request should use some other HTTP method (such as POST).

The GET method should also be idempotent, meaning that it can be safely repeated. Sometimes making a method safe also makes it idempotent. For example, repeating queries is both safe and idempotent, but buying a product online or modifying data is neither safe nor idempotent.

getLastModified

```
protected long getLastModified(javax.servlet.http.HttpServletRequest);
```

Returns the time the HttpServletRequest object was last modified, in milliseconds since midnight January 1, 1970 GMT. If the time is unknown, this method returns a negative number (the default).

Servlets that support HTTP GET requests and that can quickly determine their last modification time should override this method. This makes browser and proxy caches work more effectively, reducing the load on server and network resources.

doHead

```
protected void doHead(javax.servlet.http.HttpServletRequest,
    javax.servlet.http.HttpServletResponse)
    throws javax.servlet.ServletException, java.io.IOException;
```

Receives an HTTP HEAD request from the protected service() method and handles the request. The client sends a HEAD request when it wants to see only the headers of a response, such as Content-Type or Content-Length. The HTTP HEAD method counts the output bytes in the response to set the Content-Length header accurately.

doPost

```
protected void doPost(javax.servlet.http.HttpServletRequest,
    javax.servlet.http.HttpServletResponse)
    throws javax.servlet.ServletException, java.io.IOException;
```

Called by the server (via the service() method) to allow a servlet to handle a POST request. The HTTP POST method allows the client to send data of unlimited length to the web server a single time and is useful when posting information such as credit card numbers.

Where possible, set the Content-Length header (with the javax.servlet. ServletResponse setContentLength() method), to allow the servlet container to use a persistent connection to return its response to the client, improving performance. The content length is automatically set if the entire response fits inside the response buffer.

When using HTTP 1.1 chunked encoding (which means that the response has a Transfer-Encoding header), do not set the Content-Length header.

This method does not need to be either safe or idempotent. Operations requested through POST can have side effects for which the user can be held accountable, such as updating stored data or buying items online.

doPut

```
protected void doPut(javax.servlet.http.HttpServletRequest,
    javax.servlet.http.HttpServletResponse)
    throws javax.servlet.ServletException, java.io.IOException;
```

Called by the server (via the service() method) to allow a servlet to handle a PUT request. The PUT operation allows a client to place a file on the server and is similar to sending a file by FTP.

When overriding this method, leave intact any content headers sent with the request (including Content-Length, Content-Type, Content-Transfer-Encoding, Content-Encoding, Content-Base, Content-Language, Content-Location, Content-MD5, and Content-Range). If your method cannot handle a content header, it must issue an error message (HTTP 501 – Not Implemented) and discard the request. For more information on HTTP 1.1, see RFC 2068.

This method does not need to be either safe or idempotent. Operations that doPut() performs can have side effects for which the user can be held accountable. When using this method, it may be useful to save a copy of the affected URL in temporary storage.

doDelete

```
protected void doDelete(javax.servlet.http.HttpServletRequest,
    javax.servlet.http.HttpServletResponse)
    throws javax.servlet.ServletException, java.io.IOException;
```

Called by the server (via the service() method) to allow a servlet to handle a DELETE request. The DELETE operation allows a client to remove a document or web page from the server.

This method does not need to be either safe or idempotent. Operations requested through DELETE can have side effects for which users can be held accountable. When using this method, it may be useful to save a copy of the affected URL in temporary storage.

doOptions

```
protected void doOptions(javax.servlet.http.HttpServletRequest,
    javax.servlet.http.HttpServletResponse)
    throws javax.servlet.ServletException, java.io.IOException;
```

Called by the server (via the service() method) to allow a servlet to handle an OPTIONS request. The OPTIONS request determines which HTTP methods the server supports and returns an appropriate header. For example, if a servlet overrides doGet(), this method returns the following header:

```
Allow: GET, HEAD, TRACE, OPTIONS
```

There's no need to override this method unless the servlet implements new HTTP methods, beyond those implemented by HTTP 1.1.

doTrace

```
protected void doTrace(javax.servlet.http.HttpServletRequest,
    javax.servlet.http.HttpServletResponse)
    throws javax.servlet.ServletException, java.io.IOException;
```

Called by the server (via the service() method) to allow a servlet to handle a TRACE request. A TRACE returns the headers sent with the TRACE request to the client, so that they can be used in debugging. There is no need to override this method.

service

```
protected void service(javax.servlet.http.HttpServletRequest,
    javax.servlet.http.HttpServletResponse)
    throws javax.servlet.ServletException, java.io.IOException;
```

Receives standard HTTP requests from the public service() method and dispatches them to the do*XXX* methods defined in this class. This method is an HTTP-specific version of the javax.servlet.Servlet service() method. There is no need to override this method.

service

```
public void service(javax.servlet.ServletRequest,
    javax.servlet.ServletResponse)
    throws javax.servlet.ServletException, java.io.IOException;
```

Dispatches client requests to the protected service() method. There is no need to override this method.

HttpServletRequest

Interface name:	javax.servlet.http.HttpServletRequest
Extended by:	javax.servlet.http.HttpServletRequestWrapper
Extends:	javax.servlet.ServletRequest

Extends the javax.servlet.ServletRequest interface to provide request information for HTTP servlets. The servlet container creates an HttpServletRequest object and passes it as an argument to the servlet's service() methods (doGet(), doPost(), and so forth).

Interface Summary

```
public interface javax.servlet.http.HttpServletRequest
    extends javax.servlet.ServletRequest
{
    public static final java.lang.String BASIC_AUTH;
    public static final java.lang.String FORM_AUTH;
    public static final java.lang.String CLIENT_CERT_AUTH;
    public static final java.lang.String DIGEST_AUTH;
    public java.lang.String getAuthType();
    public javax.servlet.http.Cookie getCookies()[];
    public long getDateHeader(java.lang.String);
    public java.lang.String getHeader(java.lang.String);
    public java.util.Enumeration getHeaders(java.lang.String);
    public java.util.Enumeration getHeaderNames();
    public int getIntHeader(java.lang.String);
    public java.lang.String getMethod();
    public java.lang.String getPathInfo();
    public java.lang.String getPathTranslated();
    public java.lang.String getContextPath();
    public java.lang.String getQueryString();
    public java.lang.String getRemoteUser();
    public boolean isUserInRole(java.lang.String);
    public java.security.Principal getUserPrincipal();
    public java.lang.String getRequestedSessionId();
    public java.lang.String getRequestURI();
    public java.lang.StringBuffer getRequestURL();
    public java.lang.String getServletPath();
    public javax.servlet.http.HttpSession getSession(boolean);
    public javax.servlet.http.HttpSession getSession();
```

```
    public boolean isRequestedSessionIdValid();
    public boolean isRequestedSessionIdFromCookie();
    public boolean isRequestedSessionIdFromURL();
}
```

Field Detail

The following section describes all of the fields that are defined in the HttpServletRequest class.

BASIC_AUTH

String identifier for basic authentication. Value "BASIC".

FORM_AUTH

String identifier for form authentication. Value "FORM".

CLIENT_CERT_AUTH

String identifier for client certificate authentication. Value "CLIENT_CERT".

DIGEST_AUTH

String identifier for digest authentication. Value "DIGEST".

Method Detail

The following section describes all of the methods that are defined in the HttpServletRequest class.

getAuthType

```
public java.lang.String getAuthType();
```

Returns the name of the authentication scheme used to protect the servlet. All servlet containers support basic, form, and client certificate authentication, and may additionally support digest authentication. If the servlet is not authenticated, null is returned.

The return value from getAuthType() is the same as the value of the CGI variable AUTH_TYPE.

getCookies

```
public javax.servlet.http.Cookie getCookies()[];
```

Returns an array containing all of the Cookie objects the client sent with this request. This method returns null if no cookies were sent.

getDateHeader

```
public long getDateHeader(java.lang.String);
```

Returns the value of the specified request header as a long value that represents a java.util.Date object. Use this method with headers that contain dates, such as If-Modified-Since. The date is returned as the number of milliseconds since January 1, 1970 GMT. The header name is case insensitive.

If the request did not have a header of the specified name, this method returns –1. If the header can't be converted to a date, the method throws an IllegalArgumentException.

getHeader

```
public java.lang.String getHeader(java.lang.String);
```

Returns the value of the specified request header as a String. If the request did not include a header of the specified name, this method returns null. The header name is case insensitive. You can use this method with any request header.

getHeaders

```
public java.util.Enumeration getHeaders(java.lang.String);
```

Returns all the values of the specified request header as an Enumeration of String objects. Some headers, such as Accept-Language, can be sent by clients as several headers, each with a different value, rather than sending the header as a comma-separated list. If the request did not include any headers of the specified name, this method returns an empty Enumeration. The header name is case insensitive. You can use this method with any request header.

getHeaderNames

```
public java.util.Enumeration getHeaderNames();
```

Returns an enumeration of all the header names this request contains. If the request has no headers, this method returns an empty enumeration. Some servlet containers do not allow servlets to access headers using this method, in which case this method returns null.

getIntHeader

```
public int getIntHeader(java.lang.String);
```

Returns the value of the specified request header as an int. If the request does not have a header of the specified name, this method returns –1. If the header cannot be converted to an integer, this method throws a NumberFormatException. The header name is case insensitive.

getMethod

```
public java.lang.String getMethod();
```

Returns the name of the HTTP method with which this request was made, such as GET, POST, or PUT. The return value from getMethod() is the same as the value of the CGI variable REQUEST_METHOD.

getPathInfo

```
public java.lang.String getPathInfo();
```

Returns any extra path information associated with the URL the client sent when it made this request. The extra path information follows the servlet path but precedes the query string. This method returns null if there was no extra path information. The return value from getPathInfo() is the same as the value of the CGI variable PATH_INFO.

getPathTranslated

```
public java.lang.String getPathTranslated();
```

Returns any extra path information after the servlet name but before the query string, and translates it to a real path. The return value from getPathTranslated() is the same as the value of the CGI variable PATH_TRANSLATED. If the URL does not have any extra path information, this method returns null.

getContextPath

```
public java.lang.String getContextPath();
```

Returns the portion of the request URI that indicates the context of the request. The context path always comes first in a request URI. The path starts with a /

character but does not end with a / character. For servlets in the default (root) context, this method returns "".

getQueryString

```
public java.lang.String getQueryString();
```

Returns the query string that is contained in the request URL after the path. This method returns null if the URL does not have a query string. The return value from getQueryString() is the same as the value of the CGI variable QUERY_STRING.

getRemoteUser

```
public java.lang.String getRemoteUser();
```

Returns the login name of the user making this request if the user has been authenticated, or null if the user has not been authenticated. Whether the username is sent with each subsequent request depends on the browser and type of authentication. The return value from getRemoteUser() is the same as the value of the CGI variable REMOTE_USER.

isUserInRole

```
public boolean isUserInRole(java.lang.String);
```

Returns a boolean indicating whether the authenticated user is included in the specified logical role. Roles and role membership can be defined using deployment descriptors. If the user has not been authenticated, the method returns false. See Chapter 4 for more information about using this method.

getUserPrincipal

```
public java.security.Principal getUserPrincipal();
```

Returns a java.security.Principal object containing the name of the current authenticated user. If the user has not been authenticated, the method returns null.

getRequestedSessionId

```
public java.lang.String getRequestedSessionId();
```

Returns the session ID specified by the client. This may not be the same as the ID of the actual session in use. For example, if the request specified an old (expired) session ID and the server has started a new session, this method gets a new session with a new ID. If the request did not specify a session ID, this method returns null.

getRequestURI

```
public java.lang.String getRequestURI();
```

Returns the part of this request's URL from the protocol name up to the query string in the first line of the HTTP request.

For example:

HTTP Request	Return Value from getRequestURI()
POST /some/path.html	/some/path.html
GET http://foo.bar/a.html	/a.html

getRequestURL

```
public java.lang.StringBuffer getRequestURL();
```

Reconstructs the URL the client used to make the request. The returned URL contains a protocol, server name, port number, and server path, but it does not include query string parameters.

Because this method returns a StringBuffer, not a string, you can modify the URL easily, for example, to append query parameters.

This method is useful for creating redirect messages and for reporting errors.

getServletPath

```
public java.lang.String getServletPath();
```

Returns the part of this request's URL that calls the servlet. This includes either the servlet name or a path to the servlet, but does not include any extra path information or a query string. The return value from getServletPath() is the same as the value of the CGI variable SCRIPT_NAME.

getSession

```
public javax.servlet.http.HttpSession getSession(boolean);
```

Returns the current HttpSession associated with this request or, if there is no current session and create is true, returns a new session. If create is false and the request has no valid HttpSession, this method returns null.

To make sure the session is properly maintained, you must call this method before the response is committed. If the container is using cookies to maintain session integrity and is asked to create a new session when the response is committed, an IllegalStateException is thrown.

getSession

```
public javax.servlet.http.HttpSession getSession();
```

Returns the current session associated with this request or, if the request does not have a session, creates one.

isRequestedSessionIdValid

```
public boolean isRequestedSessionIdValid();
```

Checks whether the requested session ID is still valid.

isRequestedSessionIdFromCookie

```
public boolean isRequestedSessionIdFromCookie();
```

Checks whether the requested session ID came in as a cookie.

isRequestedSessionIdFromURL

```
public boolean isRequestedSessionIdFromURL();
```

Checks whether the requested session ID came in as part of the request URL.

HttpServletRequestWrapper

Class name:	javax.servlet.http.HttpServletRequestWrapper
Superclass:	javax.servlet.ServletRequestWrapper
Direct subclasses:	(none)
Implements:	javax.servlet.http.HttpServletRequest

Provides a convenient implementation of the HttpServletRequest interface that can be subclassed by developers wishing to adapt the request to a servlet. This class implements the Wrapper or Decorator pattern. Methods default to calling through to the wrapped request object. See the javax.servlet.http.HttpServletRequest interface for the methods available when using this class.

Constructor Detail

The following section describes all of the methods that are defined in the HttpServletRequestWrapper class.

HttpServletRequestWrapper

```
public javax.servlet.http.HttpServletRequestWrapper(
javax.servlet.http.HttpServletRequest);
```

Constructs a request object wrapping the given request.

HttpServletResponse

Interface name:	javax.servlet.http.HttpServletResponse
Implemented by:	javax.servlet.http.HttpServletResponseWrapper
Extends:	javax.servlet.ServletResponse

Extends the ServletResponse interface to provide HTTP-specific functionality in sending a response. For example, it has methods to access HTTP headers and cookies.

Interface Summary

```
public interface javax.servlet.http.HttpServletResponse
    extends javax.servlet.ServletResponse
{
    public static final int SC_CONTINUE;
    public static final int SC_SWITCHING_PROTOCOLS;
    public static final int SC_OK;
    public static final int SC_CREATED;
    public static final int SC_ACCEPTED;
    public static final int SC_NON_AUTHORITATIVE_INFORMATION;
```

```
public static final int SC_NO_CONTENT;
public static final int SC_RESET_CONTENT;
public static final int SC_PARTIAL_CONTENT;
public static final int SC_MULTIPLE_CHOICES;
public static final int SC_MOVED_PERMANENTLY;
public static final int SC_MOVED_TEMPORARILY;
public static final int SC_SEE_OTHER;
public static final int SC_NOT_MODIFIED;
public static final int SC_USE_PROXY;
public static final int SC_TEMPORARY_DIRECT;
public static final int SC_BAD_REQUEST;
public static final int SC_UNAUTHORIZED;
public static final int SC_PAYMENT_REQUIRED;
public static final int SC_FORBIDDEN;
public static final int SC_NOT_FOUND;
public static final int SC_METHOD_NOT_ALLOWED;
public static final int SC_NOT_ACCEPTABLE;
public static final int SC_PROXY_AUTHENTICATION_REQUIRED;
public static final int SC_REQUEST_TIMEOUT;
public static final int SC_CONFLICT;
public static final int SC_GONE;
public static final int SC_LENGTH_REQUIRED;
public static final int SC_PRECONDITION_FAILED;
public static final int SC_REQUEST_ENTITY_TOO_LARGE;
public static final int SC_REQUEST_URI_TOO_LONG;
public static final int SC_UNSUPPORTED_MEDIA_TYPE;
public static final int SC_REQUESTED_RANGE_NOT_SATISFIABLE;
public static final int SC_EXPECTATION_FAILED;
public static final int SC_INTERNAL_SERVER_ERROR;
public static final int SC_NOT_IMPLEMENTED;
public static final int SC_BAD_GATEWAY;
public static final int SC_SERVICE_UNAVAILABLE;
public static final int SC_GATEWAY_TIMEOUT;
public static final int SC_HTTP_VERSION_NOT_SUPPORTED;
public void addCookie(javax.servlet.http.Cookie);
public boolean containsHeader(java.lang.String);
public java.lang.String encodeURL(java.lang.String);
public java.lang.String encodeRedirectURL(java.lang.String);
public void sendError(int, java.lang.String)
    throws java.io.IOException;
public void sendError(int) throws java.io.IOException;
public void sendRedirect(java.lang.String)
    throws java.io.IOException;
```

```
    public void setDateHeader(java.lang.String, long);
    public void addDateHeader(java.lang.String, long);
    public void setHeader(java.lang.String, java.lang.String);
    public void addHeader(java.lang.String, java.lang.String);
    public void setIntHeader(java.lang.String, int);
    public void addIntHeader(java.lang.String, int);
    public void setStatus(int);
}
```

Field Detail

The following section describes all of the fields that are defined in the HttpServletResponse class.

SC_CONTINUE

Status code (100) indicating the client can continue.

SC_SWITCHING_PROTOCOLS

Status code (101) indicating the server is switching protocols according to the Upgrade header.

SC_OK

Status code (200) indicating the request succeeded normally.

SC_CREATED

Status code (201) indicating the request succeeded and created a new resource on the server.

SC_ACCEPTED

Status code (202) indicating that a request was accepted for processing, but was not completed.

SC_NON_AUTHORITATIVE_INFORMATION

Status code (203) indicating that the meta information presented by the client did not originate from the server.

SC_NO_CONTENT

Status code (204) indicating that the request succeeded but that there was no new information to return.

SC_RESET_CONTENT

Status code (205) indicating that the agent should reset the document view that caused the request to be sent.

SC_PARTIAL_CONTENT

Status code (206) indicating that the server has fulfilled the partial GET request for the resource.

SC_MULTIPLE_CHOICES

Status code (300) indicating that the requested resource corresponds to any one of a set of representations, each with its own specific location.

SC_MOVED_PERMANENTLY

Status code (301) indicating that the resource has permanently moved to a new location, and that future references should use a new URI with their requests.

SC_MOVED_TEMPORARILY

Status code (302) indicating that the resource has temporarily moved to another location, but that future references should still use the original URI to access the resource.

SC_SEE_OTHER

Status code (303) indicating that the response to the request can be found under a different URI.

SC_NOT_MODIFIED

Status code (304) indicating that a conditional GET operation found that the resource was available and not modified.

SC_USE_PROXY

Status code (305) indicating that the requested resource must be accessed through the proxy given by the Location field.

SC_TEMPORARY_REDIRECT

Status code (307) indicating that the requested resource resides temporarily under a different URI. The temporary URI should be given by the Location field in the response.

SC_BAD_REQUEST

Status code (400) indicating the request sent by the client was syntactically incorrect.

SC_UNAUTHORIZED

Status code (401) indicating that the request requires HTTP authentication.

SC_PAYMENT_REQUIRED

Status code (402) reserved for future use.

SC_FORBIDDEN

Status code (403) indicating the server understood the request but refused to fulfill it.

SC_NOT_FOUND

Status code (404) indicating that the requested resource is not available.

SC_METHOD_NOT_ALLOWED

Status code (405) indicating that the method specified in the Request-Line is not allowed for the resource identified by the Request-URI.

SC_NOT_ACCEPTABLE

Status code (406) indicating that the resource identified by the request is only capable of generating response entities that have content characteristics not acceptable according to the accept headers sent in the request.

SC_PROXY_AUTHENTICATION_REQUIRED

Status code (407) indicating that the client must first authenticate itself with the proxy.

SC_REQUEST_TIMEOUT

Status code (408) indicating that the client did not produce a request within the time that the server was prepared to wait.

SC_CONFLICT

Status code (409) indicating that the request could not be completed due to a conflict with the current state of the resource.

SC_GONE

Status code (410) indicating that the resource is no longer available at the server and no forwarding address is known. This condition should be considered permanent.

SC_LENGTH_REQUIRED

Status code (411) indicating that the request cannot be handled without a defined Content-Length.

SC_PRECONDITION_FAILED

Status code (412) indicating that the precondition given in one or more of the request header fields evaluated to false when it was tested on the server.

SC_REQUEST_ENTITY_TOO_LARGE

Status code (413) indicating that the server is refusing to process the request because the request entity is larger than the server is willing or able to process.

SC_REQUEST_URI_TOO_LONG

Status code (414) indicating that the server is refusing to service the request because the Request-URI is longer than the server is willing to interpret.

SC_UNSUPPORTED_MEDIA_TYPE

Status code (415) indicating that the server is refusing to service the request because the entity of the request is in a format not supported by the requested resource for the requested method.

SC_REQUESTED_RANGE_NOT_SATISFIABLE

Status code (416) indicating that the server cannot serve the requested byte range.

SC_EXPECTATION_FAILED

Status code (417) indicating that the server could not meet the expectation given in the Expect request header.

SC_INTERNAL_SERVER_ERROR

Status code (500) indicating an error inside the HTTP server that prevented it from fulfilling the request.

SC_NOT_IMPLEMENTED

Status code (501) indicating the HTTP server does not support the functionality needed to fulfill the request.

SC_BAD_GATEWAY

Status code (502) indicating that the HTTP server received an invalid response from a server it consulted when acting as a proxy or gateway.

SC_SERVICE_UNAVAILABLE

Status code (503) indicating that the HTTP server is temporarily overloaded, and unable to handle the request.

SC_GATEWAY_TIMEOUT

Status code (504) indicating that the server did not receive a timely response from the upstream server while acting as a gateway or proxy.

SC_HTTP_VERSION_NOT_SUPPORTED

Status code (505) indicating that the server does not support or refuses to support the HTTP protocol version that was used in the request message.

Method Detail

The following section describes all of the methods that are defined in the HttpServletResponse class.

addCookie

```
public void addCookie(javax.servlet.http.Cookie);
```

Adds the specified cookie to the response. This method can be called multiple times to set more than one cookie.

containsHeader

```
public boolean containsHeader(java.lang.String);
```

Returns a boolean indicating whether the named response header has already been set.

encodeURL

```
public java.lang.String encodeURL(java.lang.String);
```

Encodes the specified URL by including the session ID in it, or, if encoding is not needed, returns the URL unchanged. The implementation of this method includes the logic to determine whether the session ID needs to be encoded in the URL. For example, if the browser supports cookies, or session tracking is turned off, URL encoding is unnecessary.

For robust session tracking, all URLs emitted by a servlet should be run through this method. Otherwise, URL rewriting cannot be used with browsers that do not support cookies.

encodeRedirectURL

```
public java.lang.String encodeRedirectUrl(java.lang.String);
```

Encodes the specified URL for use in the sendRedirect() method or, if encoding is not needed, returns the URL unchanged. The implementation of this method includes the logic to determine whether the session ID needs to be encoded in the URL. Because the rules for making this determination can differ from those used to decide whether to encode a normal link, this method is separate from the encodeURL() method.

All URLs sent to the HttpServletResponse sendRedirect() method should be run through this method. Otherwise, URL rewriting cannot be used with browsers that do not support cookies.

sendError

```
public void sendError(int, java.lang.String)
    throws java.io.IOException;
```

Sends an error response to the client using the specified status and clears the buffer. The server defaults to creating the response to look like an HTML-formatted server error page containing the specified message, setting the content type to text/html, leaving cookies and other headers unmodified.

If an error-page declaration has been made for the web application corresponding to the status code passed in, it will be served back in preference to the suggested msg parameter.

If the response has already been committed, this method throws an IllegalStateException. After using this method, the response should be considered to be committed and should not be written to.

sendError

```
public void sendError(int) throws java.io.IOException;
```

Sends an error response to the client using the specified status code and clearing the buffer. If the response has already been committed, this method throws an IllegalStateException. After using this method, the response should be considered to be committed and should not be written to.

sendRedirect

```
public void sendRedirect(java.lang.String)
    throws java.io.IOException;
```

Sends a temporary redirect response to the client using the specified redirect location URL. This method can accept relative URLs; the servlet container must convert the relative URL to an absolute URL before sending the response to the client. If the location is relative *without* a leading /, the container interprets it as relative to the current request URI. If the location is relative *with* a leading /, the container interprets it as relative to the servlet container root.

If the response has already been committed, this method throws an IllegalStateException. After using this method, the response should be considered to be committed and should not be written to.

setDateHeader

```
public void setDateHeader(java.lang.String, long);
```

Sets a response header with the given name and date-value. The date is specified in terms of milliseconds since the epoch, which is January 1, 1970 GMT. If the header has already been set, the new value overwrites the previous one. The containsHeader() method can be used to test for the presence of a header before setting its value.

addDateHeader

```
public void addDateHeader(java.lang.String, long);
```

Adds a response header with the given name and date-value. The date is specified in terms of milliseconds since the epoch. This method allows response headers to have multiple values.

setHeader

```
public void setHeader(java.lang.String, java.lang.String);
```

Sets a response header with the given name and value. If the header has already been set, the new value overwrites the previous one. The containsHeader() method can be used to test for the presence of a header before setting its value.

addHeader

```
public void addHeader(java.lang.String, java.lang.String);
```

Adds a response header with the given name and value. This method allows response headers to have multiple values.

setIntHeader

```
public void setIntHeader(java.lang.String, int);
```

Sets a response header with the given name and integer value. If the header has already been set, the new value overwrites the previous one. The containsHeader() method can be used to test for the presence of a header before setting its value.

addIntHeader

```
public void addIntHeader(java.lang.String, int);
```

Adds a response header with the given name and integer value. This method allows response headers to have multiple values.

setStatus

```
public void setStatus(int);
```

Sets the status code for this response. This method is used to set the return status code when there is no error (for example, for the status codes SC_OK or SC_MOVED_TEMPORARILY). If there is an error, and the caller wishes to invoke an <error-page> defined in the web application, the sendError() method should be used instead.

The container clears the buffer and sets the Location header, preserving cookies and other headers.

HttpServletResponseWrapper

Class name:	javax.servlet.http.HttpServletResponseWrapper
Superclass:	javax.servlet.ServletResponseWrapper
Direct subclasses:	(none)
Implements:	javax.servlet.http.HttpServletResponse

Provides a convenient implementation of the HttpServletResponse interface that can be subclassed by developers wishing to adapt the response from a Servlet. This class implements the Wrapper or Decorator pattern. Methods default to calling through to the wrapped response object. See the javax.servlet.http.HttpServletResponse interface for the methods available when using this class.

Constructor Detail

The following section describes all of the methods that are defined in the HttpServletResponseWrapper class.

HttpServletResponseWrapper

```
public javax.servlet.http.HttpServletResponseWrapper(
javax.servlet.http.HttpServletResponse);
```

Constructs a response object wrapping the given response.

HttpSession

Interface name:	javax.servlet.http.HttpSession
Implemented by:	(none)
Extends:	(none)

Provides both a way to identify a user across more than one page request or visit to a web site and a way to store information about that user.

The servlet container uses this interface to create a session between an HTTP client and an HTTP server. The session persists for a specified time period, across more than one connection or page request from the user. A session usually corresponds to one user, who may visit a site many times. The server can maintain a session in many ways, such as using cookies or rewriting URLs.

This interface allows servlets to do the following:

- View and manipulate information about a session, such as the session identifier, creation time, and last accessed time
- Bind objects to sessions, allowing user information to persist across multiple user connections

When an application stores an object in or removes an object from a session, the session checks whether the object implements HttpSessionBindingListener. If it does, the servlet notifies the object that it has been bound to or unbound from the session. Notifications are sent after the binding methods complete. For sessions that are invalidated or expire, notifications are sent after the session has been invalidated or expired.

When a container migrates a session between VMs in a distributed container setting, all session attributes implementing the HttpSessionActivationListener interface are notified.

A servlet should be able to handle cases in which the client does not choose to join a session, such as when cookies are intentionally turned off. Until the client joins the session, isNew() returns true. If the client chooses not to join the session, getSession() will return a different session on each request, and isNew() will always return true.

Session information is scoped only to the current web application (ServletContext), so information stored in one context will not be directly visible in another.

Interface Summary

```
public interface javax.servlet.http.HttpSession
{
    public long getCreationTime();
    public java.lang.String getId();
    public long getLastAccessedTime();
    public javax.servlet.ServletContext getServletContext();
    public void setMaxInactiveInterval(int);
    public int getMaxInactiveInterval();
    public java.lang.Object getAttribute(java.lang.String);
```

```
    public java.util.Enumeration getAttributeNames();
    public void setAttribute(java.lang.String, java.lang.Object);
    public void removeAttribute(java.lang.String);
    public void invalidate();
    public boolean isNew();
}
```

Method Detail

The following section describes all of the methods that are defined in the HttpSession interface.

getCreationTime

```
public long getCreationTime();
```

Returns the time when this session was created, measured in milliseconds since midnight January 1, 1970 GMT.

getId

```
public java.lang.String getId();
```

Returns a string containing the unique identifier assigned to this session. The identifier is assigned by the servlet container and is implementation dependent.

getLastAccessedTime

```
public long getLastAccessedTime();
```

Returns the last time the client sent a request associated with this session, as the number of milliseconds since midnight January 1, 1970 GMT, and marked by the time the container received the request.

Actions that your application takes, such as getting or setting an attribute associated with the session, do not affect the access time.

getServletContext

```
public javax.servlet.ServletContext getServletContext();
```

Returns the ServletContext to which this session belongs.

setMaxInactiveInterval

```
public void setMaxInactiveInterval(int);
```

Specifies the time, in seconds, between client requests before the servlet container will invalidate this session. A negative time indicates the session should never timeout.

getMaxInactiveInterval

```
public int getMaxInactiveInterval();
```

Returns the maximum time interval, in seconds, that the servlet container will keep this session open between client accesses. After this interval, the servlet container will invalidate the session. The maximum time interval can be set with the setMaxInactiveInterval() method. A negative time indicates the session should never timeout.

getAttribute

```
public java.lang.Object getAttribute(java.lang.String);
```

Returns the object bound with the specified name in this session, or null if no object is bound under the name.

getAttributeNames

```
public java.util.Enumeration getAttributeNames();
```

Returns an Enumeration of String objects containing the names of all the objects bound to this session.

setAttribute

```
public void setAttribute(java.lang.String, java.lang.Object);
```

Binds an object to this session, using the name specified. If an object of the same name is already bound to the session, the object is replaced. After this method executes, and if the new object implements HttpSessionBindingListener, the container calls HttpSessionBindingListener valueBound(). The container then notifies any HttpSessionAttributeListeners in the web application.

If an object was already bound to the session with the same name which implements HttpSessionBindingListener, its HttpSessionBindingListener valueUnbound() method is called. If the value passed in is null, this has the same effect as calling removeAttribute().

removeAttribute

```
public void removeAttribute(java.lang.String);
```

Removes the object bound with the specified name from this session. If the session does not have an object bound with the specified name, this method does nothing.

After this method executes, and if the object implements HttpSessionBindingListener, the container calls HttpSessionBindingListener valueUnbound(). The container then notifies any HttpSessionAttributeListeners in the web application.

invalidate

```
public void invalidate();
```

Invalidates this session and then removes any attributes bound to it.

isNew

```
public boolean isNew();
```

Returns true if the client does not yet know about the session or if the client chooses not to join the session. For example, if the server used only cookie-based sessions, and the client had disabled the use of cookies, then a session would be new on each request.

HttpSessionActivationListener

Interface name:	javax.servlet.http.HttpSessionActivationListener
Implemented by:	(none)
Extends:	java.util.EventListener

Objects that are bound to a session may listen to container events notifying them that sessions will be passivated and that sessions will be activated. A container that migrates sessions between VMs or persists sessions is required to notify all attributes bound to sessions implementing HttpSessionActivationListener.

Interface Summary

```
public interface javax.servlet.http.HttpSessionActivationListener
    extends java.util.EventListener
{
    public void sessionWillPassivate(javax.servlet.http.HttpSessionEvent);
    public void sessionDidActivate(javax.servlet.http.HttpSessionEvent);
}
```

Method Detail

The following section describes all of the methods that are defined in the HttpSessionActivationListener interface.

sessionWillPassivate

```
public void
sessionWillPassivate(javax.servlet.http.HttpSessionEvent);
```

Provies notification that the session is about to be passivated.

sessionDidActivate

```
public void sessionDidActivate(javax.servlet.http.HttpSessionEvent);
```

Notification that the session has just been activated.

HttpSessionAttributeListener

Interface name:	javax.servlet.http.HttpSessionAttributeListener
Implemented by:	(none)
Extends:	java.util.EventListener

This listener interface can be implemented in order to get notifications of changes to the attribute lists of sessions within this web application.

Interface Summary

```
public interface javax.servlet.http.HttpSessionAttributeListener
    extends java.util.EventListener
{
    public void attributeAdded(javax.servlet.http.HttpSessionBindingEvent);
    public void attributeRemoved(
        javax.servlet.http.HttpSessionBindingEvent);
    public void attributeReplaced(
        javax.servlet.http.HttpSessionBindingEvent);
}
```

Method Detail

The following section describes all of the methods that are defined in the HttpSessionAttributeListener interface.

attributeAdded

```
public void attributeAdded(javax.servlet.http.HttpSessionBindingEvent);
```

Notification that an attribute has been added to a session. Called after the attribute is added.

attributeRemoved

```
public void attributeRemoved(
    javax.servlet.http.HttpSessionBindingEvent);
```

Notification that an attribute has been removed from a session. Called after the attribute is removed.

attributeReplaced

```
public void attributeReplaced(
    javax.servlet.http.HttpSessionBindingEvent);
```

Notification that an attribute has been replaced in a session. Called after the attribute is replaced.

HttpSessionBindingEvent

Class name:	javax.servlet.http.HttpSessionBindingEvent
Superclass:	javax.servlet.http.HttpSessionEvent
Direct subclasses:	(none)
Implements:	(none)

Events of this type are sent either to an object that implements HttpSessionBindingListener when it is bound or unbound from a session, or to a HttpSessionAttributeListener that has been configured in the deployment descriptor when any attribute is bound, unbound, or replaced in a session.

The session binds the object by a call to HttpSession setAttribute() and unbinds the object by a call to HttpSession removeAttribute().

Class Summary

```
public class javax.servlet.http.HttpSessionBindingEvent
    extends javax.servlet.http.HttpSessionEvent
{
    public javax.servlet.http.HttpSessionBindingEvent(
        javax.servlet.http.HttpSession, java.lang.String);
    public javax.servlet.http.HttpSessionBindingEvent(
        javax.servlet.http.HttpSession, java.lang.String, java.lang.Object);
    public javax.servlet.http.HttpSession getSession();
    public java.lang.String getName();
    public java.lang.Object getValue();
}
```

Constructor Detail

The following section describes all of the methods that are defined in the HttpSessionBindingEvent class.

HttpSessionBindingEvent

```
public javax.servlet.http.HttpSessionBindingEvent(
    javax.servlet.http.HttpSession, java.lang.String);
```

Constructs an event that notifies an object that it has been bound to or unbound from a session. To receive the event, the object must implement HttpSessionBindingListener.

HttpSessionBindingEvent

```
public javax.servlet.http.HttpSessionBindingEvent(
    javax.servlet.http.HttpSession, java.lang.String, java.lang.Object);
```

Constructs an event that notifies an object that it has been bound to or unbound from a session. To receive the event, the object must implement HttpSessionBindingListener.

Method Detail

The following section describes all of the methods that are defined in the HttpSessionBindingEvent class.

getSession

```
public javax.servlet.http.HttpSession getSession();
```

Returns the session that changed.

getName

```
public java.lang.String getName();
```

Returns the name with which the attribute is bound to or unbound from the session.

getValue

```
public java.lang.Object getValue();
```

Returns the value of the attribute that has been added, removed, or replaced. If the attribute was added (or bound), this is the value of the attribute. If the attribute was removed (or unbound), this is the value of the removed attribute. If the attribute was replaced, this is the old value of the attribute.

HttpSessionBindingListener

Interface name:	javax.servlet.http.HttpSessionBindingListener
Implemented by:	(none)
Extends:	java.util.EventListener

Causes an object to be notified when it is bound to or unbound from a session. The object is notified by an HttpSessionBindingEvent object. This may be as a result of a servlet programmer explicitly unbinding an attribute from a session, a session being invalidated, or a session timing out.

Interface Summary

```
public interface javax.servlet.http.HttpSessionBindingListener
    extends java.util.EventListener
{
    public void valueBound(javax.servlet.http.HttpSessionBindingEvent);
    public void valueUnbound(javax.servlet.http.HttpSessionBindingEvent);
}
```

Method Detail

The following section describes all of the methods that are defined in the HttpSessionBindingListener interface.

valueBound

```
public void valueBound(javax.servlet.http.HttpSessionBindingEvent);
```

Notifies the object that it is being bound to a session and identifies the session.

valueUnbound

```
public void valueUnbound(javax.servlet.http.HttpSessionBindingEvent);
```

Notifies the object that it is being unbound from a session and identifies the session.

HttpSessionEvent

Class name:	javax.servlet.http.HttpSessionEvent
Superclass:	java.util.EventObject
Direct subclasses:	javax.servlet.http.HttpSessionBindingEvent
Implements:	(none)

This is the class representing event notifications for changes to sessions within a web application.

Class Summary

```
public class javax.servlet.http.HttpSessionEvent
    extends java.util.EventObject
{
    public javax.servlet.http.HttpSessionEvent(
        javax.servlet.http.HttpSession);
    public javax.servlet.http.HttpSession getSession();
}
```

Constructor Detail

The following section describes all of the methods that are defined in the HttpSessionEvent class.

HttpSessionEvent

```
public javax.servlet.http.HttpSessionEvent(
    javax.servlet.http.HttpSession);
```

Constructs a session event from the given source.

Method Detail

The following section describes all of the methods that are defined in the HttpSessionEvent class.

getSession

```
public javax.servlet.http.HttpSession getSession();
```

Returns the session that changed.

HttpSessionListener

Interface name:	javax.servlet.http.HttpSessionListener
Implemented by:	(none)
Extends:	java.util.EventListener

Implementations of this interface are notified of changes to the list of active sessions in a web application. To receive notification events, the implementation class must be configured in the deployment descriptor for the web application.

Interface Summary

```
public interface javax.servlet.http.HttpSessionListener
    extends java.util.EventListener
{
    public void sessionCreated(javax.servlet.http.HttpSessionEvent);
    public void sessionDestroyed(javax.servlet.http.HttpSessionEvent);
}
```

Method Detail

The following section describes all of the methods that are defined in the HttpSessionListener interface.

sessionCreated

```
public void sessionCreated(javax.servlet.http.HttpSessionEvent);
```

Notification that a session was created.

sessionDestroyed

```
public void sessionDestroyed(javax.servlet.http.HttpSessionEvent);
```

Notification that a session was invalidated.

APPENDIX

B

The Web Application Deployment Descriptor

This appendix shows the valid elements of the web application deployment descriptor (web.xml). Examples of each of these elements are covered in Chapter 5.

web-app

The web-app element is the root of the deployment descriptor for a web application. Note that the order of elements within the web-app element is important; most servlet containers will use a validating parser that requires elements to be given in the same order as they appear in the deployment descriptor (DTD). For maximum portability, always format your web.xml elements in the same order as shown in the following section.

Note that several of the EJB-specific elements have been omitted.

Contents

Element	Occurrences	Description
icon	Zero or one	Contains small-icon and large-icon elements that specify the filenames for small and large GIF or JPEG icon images used to represent the parent element in a GUI tool.
display-name	Zero or one	Contains a short name that is intended to be displayed by tools. The display name need not be unique.
description	Zero or one	The description of the web application.
distributable	Zero or one	Indicates, by its presence in a web application deployment descriptor, that this web application is programmed appropriately to be deployed into a distributed servlet container.
context-param	Zero or more	Contains the declaration of a web application's servlet context initialization parameters.
filter	Zero or more	Declares a filter for the web application. Filters are covered in Chapter 6.
filter-mapping	Zero or more	Declaration of the filter mappings in this web application. The container uses the filter-mapping declarations to decide which filters to apply to a request, and in what order.
listener	Zero or more	Defines a web application listener. Listeners are covered in Chapter 7.

Element	Occurrences	Description
servlet	Zero or more	Contains the declarative data of a servlet.
servlet-mapping	Zero or more	Defines a mapping between a servlet and a URL pattern.
session-config	Zero or one	Defines the session parameters for this web application.
mime-mapping	Zero or more	Defines a mapping between an extension and a mime type.
welcome-file-list	Zero or one	Contains an ordered list of welcome-file elements.
error-page	Zero or more	Contains a mapping between an error code or exception type to the path of a resource in the web application.
security-constraint	Zero or more	Used to associate security constraints with one or more web resource collections.
login-config	Zero or one	Used to configure the authentication method that should be used, the realm name that should be used for this application, and the attributes that are needed by the form login mechanism.
security-role	Zero or more	Contains the definition of a security role. The definition consists of an optional description of the security role, and the security role name.

auth-constraint

The auth-constraint element indicates the user roles that should be permitted access to this resource collection. The role-name used here must either correspond to the role-name of one of the security-role elements defined for this web application, or be the specially reserved role-name "*" that is a compact syntax for indicating all roles in the web application. If both "*" and role-names appear, the container interprets this as all roles. If no roles are defined, no user is allowed access to the portion of the web application described by the containing security-constraint. The container matches role names case-sensitively when determining access.

Used in: security-constraint

Contents

Element	Occurrences	Description
description	Zero or one	The description of the authorization constraint.
role-name	Zero or more	The name of the security role.

context-param

The context-param element contains the declaration of a web application's servlet context initialization parameters.

Used in: web-app

Contents

Element	Occurrences	Description
param-name	One (required)	The name of the context initialization parameter.
param-value	One (required)	The value of the context initialization parameter.
description	Zero or one	The optional description of the context initialization parameter.

error-page

The error-page element contains a mapping between an error code or exception type and the path of a resource in the web application.

Used in: web-app

Contents

Element	Occurrences	Description
error-code or exception-type	One (required)	Either the numeric error code or fully qualified exception class name that will trigger a custom error page to be returned to the client.
location	One (required)	Contains the location of the resource in the web application relative to the root of the web application. The value of the location must have a leading /.

filter

Declares a filter that will be loaded by the web application. The filter is mapped to either a servlet or a URL pattern in the filter-mapping element. Filters can access the initialization parameters declared in the deployment descriptor at run time via the FilterConfig interface. Filters are covered in Chapter 6.

Used in: web-app

Contents

Element	Occurrences	Description
icon	Zero or one	Contains small-icon and large-icon elements that specify the filenames for small and large GIF or JPEG icon images used to represent the parent element in a GUI tool.
filter-name	One (required)	The logical name of the filter. This name is used to map the filter. Each filter name is unique within the web application.
display-name	Zero or one	Contains a short name that is intended to be displayed by tools. The display name need not be unique.
description	Zero or one	The description of the filter.
filter-class	One (required)	The fully qualified class name of the filter.
init-param	Zero or more	Filter initialization parameters.

filter-mapping

Declares a filter mapping for this web application. The container uses the filter-mapping declarations to decide which filters to apply to a request, and in what order. The container matches the request URI to a servlet in the normal way. To determine which filters to apply, it matches filter-mapping declarations either on servlet-name or on url-pattern for each filter-mapping element, depending on which style is used. The order in which filters are invoked is the order in which filter-mapping declarations that match a request URI for a servlet appear in the list of filter-mapping elements. The filter-name value must be the value of the <filter-name> subelements of one of the <filter> declarations in the deployment descriptor.

Used in: web-app

Contents

Element	Occurrences	Description
filter-name	One (required)	The logical name of the filter. This name is used to map the filter. Each filter name is unique within the web application.
url-pattern or servlet-name	One (required)	Either the url-pattern or servlet-name must be provided. When the servlet container receives a request for a matching url-pattern or servlet-name, this filter will be placed in the invocation chain.

form-login-config

The form-login-config element specifies the login and error pages that should be used in form-based login. If form-based authentication is not used, these elements are ignored.

Used in: login-config

Contents

Element	Occurrences	Description
form-login-page	One (required)	Defines the location in the web application where the page that can be used for login can be found. The path begins with a leading / and is interpreted relative to the root of the web application.
form-error-page	One (required)	Defines the location in the web app where the error page that is displayed when login is not successful can be found. The path begins with a leading / and is interpreted relative to the root of the web application.

icon

The icon element contains small-icon and large-icon elements that specify the filenames for small and large GIF or JPEG icon images used to represent the parent element in a GUI tool.

Used in: filter, servlet, web-app

Contents

Element	Occurrences	Description
small-icon	Zero or one	Contains the name of a file containing a small (16×16 pixels) icon image. The filename is a relative path within the web application's WAR file. The image may be either in the JPEG or GIF format.
large-icon	Zero or one	Contains the name of a file containing a large (32×32 pixels) icon image. The filename is a relative path within the web application's WAR file. The image may be either in the JPEG or GIF format.

init-param

The init-param element contains a name/value pair as an initialization parameter of the servlet or filter.

Used in: filter, servlet

Contents

Element	Occurrences	Description
param-name	One (required)	The initialization parameter name.
param-value	One (required)	The initialization parameter value.
description	Zero or one	The optional description of the initialization parameter.

listener

The listener element indicates the deployment properties for a web application listener bean. Listeners are covered in Chapter 7.

Used in: web-app

Contents

Element	Occurrences	Description
listener-class	One (required)	Declares a class in the application must be registered as a web application listener bean. The value is the fully qualified class name of the listener class.

login-config

The login-config element is used to configure the authentication method that should be used, the realm name that should be used for this application, and the attributes that are needed by the form login mechanism.

Used in: web-app

Contents

Element	Occurrences	Description
auth-method	Zero or one	Used to configure the authentication mechanism for the web application. As a prerequisite to gaining access to any web resources, which are protected by an authorization constraint, a user must have authenticated using the configured mechanism. Legal values for this element are "BASIC", "DIGEST", "FORM", or "CLIENT-CERT".
realm-name	Zero or one	Specifies the realm name to use in HTTP Basic authorization.
form-login-config	Zero or one	Specifies the login and error pages that should be used in form-based login.

mime-mapping

The mime-mapping element defines a mapping between an extension and a mime type.

Used in: web-app

Contents

Element	Occurrences	Description
extension	One (required)	Contains a string describing an extension, such as “txt”.
mime-type	One (required)	Contains a defined mime type, such as “text/plain”.

security-constraint

The security-constraint element is used to associate security constraints with one or more web resource collections.

Used in: web-app

Contents

Element	Occurrences	Description
display-name	Zero or one	Contains a short name that is intended to be displayed by tools. The display name need not be unique.
web-resource-collection	One or more	Used to identify a subset of the resources and HTTP methods on those resources within a web application to which a security constraint applies.
auth-constraint	Zero or one	Indicates the user roles that should be permitted access to this resource collection.
user-data-constraint	Zero or one	Used to indicate how data communicated between the client and container should be protected.

security-role

The security-role element contains the definition of a security role. The definition consists of an optional description of the security role, and the security role name.

Used in: web-app

Contents

Element	Occurrences	Description
description	Zero or one	The security role description.
role-name	One (required)	The name of a security role.

security-role-ref

The security-role-ref element contains the declaration of a security role reference in the web application's code. The declaration consists of an optional description, the security role name used in the code, and an optional link to a security role.

The value of the role-name element must be the String used as the parameter to the HttpServletRequest isUserInRole() method.

Used in: servlet

Contents

Element	Occurrences	Description
description	Zero or one	The security role reference description.
role-name	One (required)	The name of a security role.
role-link	Zero or one	A reference to a defined security role. The role-link element must contain the name of one of the security roles defined in the security-role elements.

servlet

The servlet element contains the declarative data of a servlet. If the jsp-file element is specified and the load-on-startup element is present, then the JSP should be precompiled and loaded.

Used in: web-app

Contents

Element	Occurrences	Description
icon	Zero or one	Contains small-icon and large-icon elements that specify the filenames for small and large GIF or JPEG icon images used to represent the parent element in a GUI tool.
servlet-name	One (required)	Contains the canonical name of the servlet. Each servlet name is unique within the web application.
display-name	Zero or one	Contains a short name that is intended to be displayed by tools. The display name need not be unique.
description	Zero or one	The description of the servlet.
servlet-class or jsp-file	One (required)	Either the fully qualified servlet class name or the name of a JSP file.
init-param	Zero or more	Servlet initialization parameters.
load-on-startup	Zero or one	Indicates that this servlet should be loaded (instantiated and have its init() method called) on the startup of the web application. The optional content of these elements must be an integer indicating the order in which the servlet should be loaded. If the value is a negative integer, or the element is not present, the container is free to load the servlet whenever it chooses. If the value is a positive integer or 0, the container must load and initialize the servlet as the application is deployed. The container must guarantee that servlets marked with lower integers are loaded before servlets marked with higher integers. The container may choose the order of loading of servlets with the same load-on-start-up value.
security-role-ref	Zero or more	Contains the declaration of a security role reference in the web application's code.

servlet-mapping

The servlet-mapping element defines a mapping between a servlet and a URL pattern.

Used in: web-app

Contents

Element	Occurrences	Description
servlet-name	One (required)	The servlet name as defined in a servlet-mapping element.
url-pattern	One (required)	Contains the URL pattern of the mapping, which must follow the rules specified in Section 11.2 of the Servlet API Specification.

session-config

The session-config element defines the session parameters for this web application.

Used in: web-app

Contents

Element	Occurrences	Description
session-timeout	Zero or one	Defines the default session timeout interval for all sessions created in this web application. The specified timeout must be expressed in a whole number of minutes. If the timeout is 0 or less, the container ensures the default behavior of sessions is never to time out.

user-data-constraint

The user-data-constraint element is used to indicate how data communicated between the client and container should be protected.

Used in: security-constraint

Contents

Element	Occurrences	Description
description	Zero or one	The description of the constraint.
transport-guarantee	One (required)	Specifies that the communication between client and server should be NONE, INTEGRAL, or CONFIDENTIAL. NONE means that the application does not require any transport guarantees. INTEGRAL means that the application requires that the data sent between the client and server be sent in such a way that it can't be changed in transit. CONFIDENTIAL means that the application requires that the data be transmitted in a fashion that prevents other entities from observing the contents of the transmission. In most cases, the presence of the INTEGRAL or CONFIDENTIAL flag will indicate that the use of SSL is required.

web-resource-collection

The web-resource-collection element is used to identify a subset of the resources and HTTP methods on those resources within a web application to which a security constraint applies. If no HTTP methods are specified, then the security constraint applies to all HTTP methods.

Used in: security-constraint

Contents

Element	Occurrences	Description
web-resource-name	One (required)	Contains the name of this web resource collection.
description	Zero or one	The description of this web resource collection.
url-pattern	Zero or more	Contains the URL pattern of the mapping, which must follow the rules specified in Section 11.2 of the Servlet API Specification.
http-method	Zero or more	The http-method, such as GET or POST.

welcome-file-list

The welcome-file-list contains an ordered list of welcome-file elements.

Used in: web-app

Contents

Element	Occurrences	Description
welcome-file	One or more	Contains the filename to use as a default welcome file, such as index.html.

APPENDIX

C

Online Servlet Resources

Fortunately for servlet developers, there are many great sites on the Web devoted to servlets (and more being added every day). This appendix contains a list of some very useful sites, which will serve as a great starting point. This is by no means an exhaustive list, but should get you started in the right direction.

- **http://java.sun.com/products/servlet/** The official home site for servlets. Always check here for the latest specification, documentation, tutorials, news, and other helpful links.
- **http://jakarta.apache.org/tomcat/** The servlet reference implementation. Check here for the latest builds (including source code). There are also several servlet-related mailing lists here that you may want to search for commonly asked questions.
- **www.servletguru.com/** The official home site for the *Java Servlets Developer's Guide*. Running examples, downloads of all source code for the book, and links to other servlet sites can be found here. This site is hosted by SERVLETS.NET. SERVLETS.NET provides web site and application hosting for developers utilizing servlets.
- **www.theserverside.com/** Contains articles, news items, and other resources for server-side developers (servlets, JSP, and J2EE).
- **www.servlets.com/** OK, it's a site for a competing book from another publisher, but it also contains documentation, downloads, and links that will be of interest to all servlet developers (no matter whose book they are reading).
- **www.javashareware.com/** JavaShareware promotes Java through sharing resources, namely documentation and source code. This site contains a section dedicated to servlets.
- **www.gamelan.com** Contains many Java-related resources, including documentation, free downloads, and vendor software.
- **www.jguru.com/faq/Servlets** Provides answers to common questions about servlet technologies and techniques.

Index

A

D

E

F

G

H

I

J

K

L

M

N

O

P

Q

R

S

T

U

V

W

INTERNATIONAL CONTACT INFORMATION

AUSTRALIA
McGraw-Hill Book Company Australia Pty. Ltd.
TEL +61-2-9417-9899
FAX +61-2-9417-5687
http://www.mcgraw-hill.com.au
books-it_sydney@mcgraw-hill.com

CANADA
McGraw-Hill Ryerson Ltd.
TEL +905-430-5000
FAX +905-430-5020
http://www.mcgrawhill.ca

GREECE, MIDDLE EAST, NORTHERN AFRICA
McGraw-Hill Hellas
TEL +30-1-656-0990-3-4
FAX +30-1-654-5525

MEXICO (Also serving Latin America)
McGraw-Hill Interamericana Editores S.A. de C.V.
TEL +525-117-1583
FAX +525-117-1589
http://www.mcgraw-hill.com.mx
fernando_castellanos@mcgraw-hill.com

SINGAPORE (Serving Asia)
McGraw-Hill Book Company
TEL +65-863-1580
FAX +65-862-3354
http://www.mcgraw-hill.com.sg
mghasia@mcgraw-hill.com

SOUTH AFRICA
McGraw-Hill South Africa
TEL +27-11-622-7512
FAX +27-11-622-9045
robyn_swanepoel@mcgraw-hill.com

UNITED KINGDOM & EUROPE (Excluding Southern Europe)
McGraw-Hill Education Europe
TEL +44-1-628-502500
FAX +44-1-628-770224
http://www.mcgraw-hill.co.uk
computing_neurope@mcgraw-hill.com

ALL OTHER INQUIRIES Contact:
Osborne/McGraw-Hill
TEL +1-510-549-6600
FAX +1-510-883-7600
http://www.osborne.com
omg_international@mcgraw-hill.com

www.ingramcontent.com/pod-product-compliance
Lightning Source LLC
Chambersburg PA
CBHW080130060326
40689CB00018B/3738
9780072222623